THAILAND

KING BHUMIBOL ADULYADEJ
THE GOLDEN JUBILEE

1946 - 1996

Amway (Thailand) Ltd.

Jim Thompson Thai Silk Co.

The Regent Bangkok

Bangkok Bank Public Co. Ltd.

Loxley Public Co. Ltd.

Siam Commercial Bank Public Co. Ltd.

Boon Rawd Brewery Co. Ltd.

Ministry of Foreign Affairs

Thai Airways International Public Co. Ltd.

Citibank, N.A.

Mitsubishi Motors

Thai Charoen Commercial Group of Companies

Diethelm & Co. Ltd.

IBM (Thailand) Co. Ltd.

Petroleum Authority of Thailand

Thai Oil Co. Ltd.

The publishers gratefully acknowledge the support of:
Tourism Authority of Thailand, The Nation and **Bangkok PR**

Published and distributed by
ASIA BOOKS CO. LTD
5 Sukhumvit Road, Soi 61 P.O. Box 40 Bangkok 10110, Thailand
Tel: (662) 714-0741-2 ext: 225-259 Fax: (662) 391-2277, 381-1621
© Editions Didier Millet Pte. Ltd. 1996

Color separation by Colourscan
Printed in Singapore by Star Standard Printing (Pte) Ltd

THAILAND

KING BHUMIBOL ADULYADEJ
THE GOLDEN JUBILEE

1946 - 1996

ASIA BOOKS

Contents

FOREWORD

This book was conceived over a year and a half ago, as a way to celebrate the occasion of His Majesty King Bhumibol Adulyadej's Golden Jubilee on the Throne of Thailand. In its preparation, dozens of people contributed their knowledge, expertise and experience to tell two interwoven stories—the story of Thailand itself over the past half century and, most important, the story of the role played by His Majesty the King during those eventful times.

Vast changes have taken place in almost every aspect of Thai life in the last fifty years. An economy that was almost solely based on agriculture has been transformed by industry, so that the country is now a leading exporter of a wide variety of goods and services to markets throughout the world. Society has been altered as well, bringing new job opportunities, new mobility, and greatly heightened interaction with the world beyond. Thanks to roads and modern communications, even the most remote areas are accessible, their people exposed to innovative concepts and ways of life scarcely imaginable a mere generation ago. At the same time, Thai politics has steadily evolved, leaving behind old concepts that seemed solidly entrenched and stirring new hopes and aspirations at all levels of our society. These changes are examined by the various writers who have contributed to this book, drawing on their own broad experience in such areas as agriculture, economics, social development, tourism, environmental protection and management and international affairs.

Running like a thread through all those changes, directly and indirectly, has been the influence of Thailand's monarchy, an institution unlike any other in the world today and largely devised, in its present form, by a single individual—His Majesty King Bhumibol Adulyadej. Since coming to the throne half a century ago, His Majesty has concentrated on three areas: the well-being of His people, particularly those in rural areas; the promotion of national harmony and development; and the strengthening of security and stability throughout the Kingdom.

The Thai monarchy is deeply traditional, fulfilling needs for ritual and continuity that go far back into history, and His Majesty has carefully retained that aspect of His role. At the same time, however, He has been creatively modern in fashioning a new concept of monarchy suited to our contemporary world. Always remaining within the constitutional limits of His position, He has nevertheless managed to use His rights to be consulted, to warn, and to encourage—in a word, to guide—in ways that have profoundly affected the course of events during His long reign.

King Ramkhamhaeng the Great of Sukhothai established a dramatic concept of open monarchy, symbolized by a bell outside the palace which could be rung by any citizen seeking an audience to voice a grievance. While this ideal of accessibility was sometimes obscured in the centuries that followed, especially during much of the Ayutthaya period, it has never been entirely lost. It has, indeed, been carried to new heights in the present reign. His Majesty the King displays a unique ability to establish rapport with His people on a wide variety of levels. He is always open and honest with them and listens carefully to what they have to say. Despite the hierarchic structure of Thai society, with its traditional awe of the monarchy, He intuitively achieves a blend of formality and informality that produces trust and encourages those who meet Him to speak what is within their hearts.

Perhaps the most dramatic example of His Majesty's activities, examined in detail by several writers in this book, is His work to alleviate rural problems. These have taken Him to every part of the country, no matter how remote, and have brought Him into closer personal contact with His subjects than any ruler in Thai history. His regular use of the Internet as one source of information on technical subjects facilitates His planning for and analysis of development projects. These activities have resulted in major changes, ranging from new methods of agriculture to improved primary health care and education, as well as a greater sense of national unity.

The thread of His Majesty's influence has extended into other areas as well. Firmly committed to the development of democratic processes, He has discouraged coups as a means of resolving power struggles between competing factions and, acting within His right to warn and encourage, has offered effective counsel during times of traumatic national crisis. The underlying political stability that has played such an essential role in Thailand's remarkable economic growth over the past two decades has been due in large part to His leadership and the respect He commands from the leaders of all factions.

As will become clear to our readers, the Thai monarchy as developed by His Majesty the King is far more than an ancient institution linking past and present. It is a vital force that strengthens the very fabric of our nation, in rice fields and city streets, in home and work place, forming the core of what it means to be Thai. That is why this Jubilee Celebration is an event of such unusual historic significance. It is also why this book has been produced, as a record of the event, of the years which led to it, and of His Majesty Himself, without whose guiding hand Thailand would not be where it is today.

ANAND PANYARACHUN
Chairman of the Editorial Advisory Board

ROYAL ADDRESS OF HIS MAJESTY
KING BHUMIBOL ADULYADEJ

**on the occasion of granting a grand audience to officials of the realm and members
of the general public during the auspicious occasion of the
fiftieth anniversary (Golden Jubilee) celebrations of
His Majesty's accession to the throne**

Sanam Luang
Sunday, June 9, 1996

"*I* am very pleased and happy to be in this impressive gathering of people from every institution in the country. I wish to thank you for the kind words and the grand celebrations that have been especially organized for me by everyone, as well as for the amity and goodwill which you have all extended to me by giving me your support in various endeavors for the past fifty years.

It is everyone's wish that his country is endowed with security and happiness and that the majority of the people enjoy a high standard of living in accordance with their disposition. Such a wish, however, could not become a reality of its own accord; everyone and every party, particularly those with the responsibility of administering the country, must see to it that this wish is realized. It can be achieved by each and every one of you performing your duties expeditiously in a supportive and concerted manner, so as to realize the goal which you have set out. On this special occasion, I ask all of you together with the Thai people everywhere to set your minds firmly to carrying out your tasks with honesty, diligence and perseverance. The correct and esteemed kinds of diligence and perseverance which one should strive for are, firstly, the diligence and perseverance that will eliminate the deterioration and degeneration within society while at the same time prevent such deterioration and degeneration from recurring; and, secondly, the diligence and perseverance that will bring about goodness and progress to society while at the same time protect and prevent such goodness and progress from declining. These two kinds of diligence and perseverance are important factors in the conduct of oneself and in one's work. If everyone in the nation sets his mind and heart to striving for these two kinds of diligence and perseverance, then greater benefits and happiness will accrue to everyone as well as to the society as a whole. Thus, our country will be able to maintain the normal state of affairs and our security while, at the same time, be able to develop and advance further as desired.

I now wish to invoke the power of the Triple Gems and other sacred objects in the world to watch over and protect Thailand from all kinds of distress, misfortunes and dangers, as well as bring ever increasing success and happiness to all the Thai people. "

Golden Jubilee Celebrations

Clockwise from top left: King Bhumibol presiding over the Jubilee celebrations on June 9, 1996, and (inset) the King and Queen at the oblatory pavilion; Lighting of candles by the King and Queen; The King presenting gifts to monks on June 8; The King with the Crown Prince and Crown Princess at Chakri Maha Prasat, the Grand Palace, on June 12.

Top left: Lighted portrait of the King; Above, left to right: Arches at Rajadamnern Avenue; Left: Lights around the statue of Rama VI; Left, below: Democracy Monument at night; Far left, second row from top: The former Parliament House lit up for the Golden Jubilee; Below: Decorated gate of Government House; Bottom: Jubilee decoration outside the Grand Palace.

*Right: Fireworks over the
Chao Phraya river; Far right:
Night view of the Grand
Palace; Centre row, left to
right: Royal barge procession;
Bottom: Crowd milling
around Golden Jubilee
celebrations at twilight.*

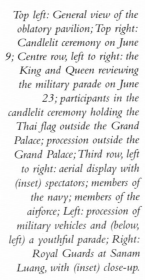

Top left: General view of the oblatory pavilion; Top right: Candlelit ceremony on June 9; Centre row, left to right: the King and Queen reviewing the military parade on June 23; participants in the candlelit ceremony holding the Thai flag outside the Grand Palace; procession outside the Grand Palace; Third row, left to right: aerial display with (inset) spectators; members of the navy; members of the airforce; Left: procession of military vehicles and (below, left) a youthful parade; Right: Royal Guards at Sanam Luang, with (inset) close-up.

Royal Diplomacy

Between 1959 and 1967, Their Majesties the King and Queen made a series of notable State Visits to foreign countries. Some were to neighboring states such as Malaysia, Burma and Indonesia, while others were to the United States and Europe. On all, Their Majesties not only brought international recognition to their Kingdom and its culture but also gained useful insights and became personally acquainted with world leaders of the time, ties that proved of incalculable value in Thailand's future relationships.

In addition to public events widely covered by the media, the State Visits also included more informal ones during which Their Majesties relaxed or made less publicized excursions to points of interest. On these pages we present a selection of both in photographs chosen primarily because they offer a glimpse of the Royal Party away from the splendid banquets and speeches that characterize such occasions. Some of the pictures were taken by His Majesty, himself an enthusiastic photographer; most are the work of Khun Khwankeo Vajarodaya, the Grand Chamberlain, who accompanied the Royal Party and compiled his own record of events during the tours.

We would like to express our gratitude to His Majesty for his gracious permission to reproduce the photographs in this album of memorable moments.

Royal Visits Abroad

ASIA

Vietnam
December 18–21, 1959
Hosted by President Ngô Dinh Diêm

Indonesia
February 8–16, 1960
Hosted by President Ahmed Sukarno

Burma
March 2–5, 1960
Hosted by President U Win Muang and Prime Minister General Ne Win

Pakistan
March 11–22, 1962
Hosted by President Mohammed Ayub Khan

The Federation of Malaya
June 20–27, 1962
Hosted by His Majesty the Yang di-Pertuan Agong Syed Putra Jamalullail and Prime Minister Tunku Abdul Rahman Al-Haj

Japan
May 27–June 5, 1963
Hosted by His Imperial Majesty Emperor Hirohito and Prime Minister Hayato Ikeda

The Republic of China
June 5–8, 1963
Hosted by President General Chiang Kai-shek

The Philippines
July 9–14, 1963
Hosted by President Diosdado Macapagal

EUROPE

The United Kingdom
July 19–23, 1960
Hosted by Her Majesty Queen Elizabeth II and Prime Minister Harold Macmillan

Germany
July 25–August 2, 1960
Hosted by President Heinrich Lübke and Federal Chancellor Dr Konrad Adenauer

Portugal
August 22–25, 1960
Hosted by President Rear Admiral Americo Rodriguez Tomaz and Prime Minister Dr Antonio de Oliveirira Salazar

Switzerland
August 29–31, 1960
Hosted by President Max Petitpierre

Denmark
September 6–9, 1960
Hosted by His Majesty King Frederik IX and Prime Minister Viggo Kampmann

Norway
September 19–21, 1960
Hosted by His Majesty King Olav V and Prime Minister Einar Gerhardsen

Sweden
September 23–25, 1960
Hosted by His Majesty King Gustaf VI Adolf and Prime Minister Tage Erlander

Italy
September 28–October 1, 1960
Hosted by President Giovanni Gronchi and Prime Minister Amintore Fanfani

The Vatican State
October 1, 1960
Hosted by His Holiness Pope John XXIII

Belgium
October 4–7, 1960
Hosted by His Majesty King Baudouin and Prime Minister Gaston Eyskens

France
October 11–14, 1960
Hosted by President General Charles De Gaulle and Prime Minister Michel Debré

Luxemburg
October 17–19, 1960
Hosted by Her Royal Highness Grand Duchess Charlotte and Prime Minister Pierre Werner

The Netherlands
October 24–27, 1960
Hosted by Her Majesty Queen Juliana and Prime Minister J de Quay

Spain
November 3–8, 1960
Hosted by General Francisco Franco

Austria
September 29–October 5, 1964
September 29–October 2, 1966
Hosted by President Adolf Schaerf and Prime Minister Josef Klaus

Germany
August 22–28, 1966
Hosted by President Heinrich Lübke and Federal Chancellor Ludwig Erhard

AUSTRALIA AND NEW ZEALAND

New Zealand
August 18–26, 1962
Hosted by the Governor-General Viscount Cobham and Prime Minister Keith Holyoake

Australia
August 26–September 12, 1962
Hosted by the Administrator of the Government of the Commonwealth of Australia, General Sir Dallas Brooks, representing Governor-General Viscount De L'Isle and Prime Minister Robert G Menzies

THE MIDDLE EAST

Iran
April 23–30, 1967
Hosted by His Imperial Majesty Mohammad Reza Pahlavi Aryamehr Shahanshah and Prime Minister Amir Abbas Hoveyda

NORTH AMERICA

United States of America
June 14–July 15, 1960
Hosted by President Dwight D Eisenhower

United States of America
June 6–20 and June 24–29, 1967
Hosted by President Lyndon B Johnson

Canada
June 21–24, 1967
Hosted by the Governor-General Roland Michener and Prime Minister Lester B Pearson

Vietnam 1959

Their Majesties were greeted at Saigon's airport by President Ngo Dinh Diem. The wife of the President's brother, Ngo Dinh Nhu, acted as official hostess during the visit.

Indonesia 1960

President Sukarno was on hand at Kemajoran Airport to welcome Their Majesties and introduce them to high government officials.

THAILAND King Bhumibol Adulyadej – The Golden Jubilee 1946-1996

Indonesia 1960

Visits to the famous temple of Borobudur and the island of Bali were part of the Indonesian tour.

Burma 1960

Welcomed at Mingaladon Airport by President and Madame U Win Maung and Prime Minister and Madame Ne Win, Their Majesties were later given a state banquet and a visit to the Shwedagon Pagoda.

United States of America 1960

In California, Their Majesties paid a visit to Vandenburg Air Force, a center of rocket research.

Two of the royal children, Prince Vajiralongkorn and Princess Ubol Ratana, were given a tour of Disneyland by its founder Walt Disney.

In Hollywood, Their Majesties visited the set of Elvis Presley's film "G.I. Blues" and also met Bob Hope.

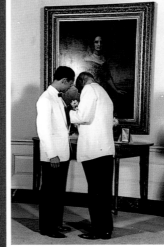

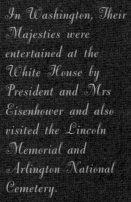

In Washington, Their Majesties were entertained at the White House by President and Mrs Eisenhower and also visited the Lincoln Memorial and Arlington National Cemetery.

United States of America 1960

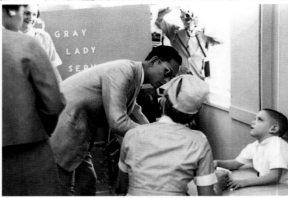

During the course of the American tour, Their Majesties visited Mount Vernon, the home of George Washington, and Mount Auburn Hospital in Cambridge, Mass., where

Among the hlight
of the New York
were a tickertape
from the Battery
City Hall, a sub
ride, a jazz sessio
Benny Goodman's
apartment, and vi
the Empire State
Building and the
skating rink at
Rockefeller Cente

United States of America 1960

The United Kingdom 1960

His Majesty rode with Queen
Elizabeth II in the royal carriage to
Buckingham Palace; the tour also
included a visit to the British Museum.

Germany 1960

The visit to Germany
began at Bonn
Station with a
welcome by President
Heinrich and Frau
Lübke. In Hamburg
they visited a
shipyard.

Germany 1960

In Sindelfingen, Their Majesties visited the Daimler-Benz AG Works.

Portugal 1960

President Tomaz and Prime Minister Salazar greeted Their Majesties in Lisbon, where they stayed at the Palais de Queluz.

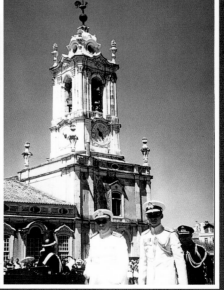

Switzerland 1960

On a private part of the visit, Their Majesties stayed at the Villa Fronzaley near Montreaux where they enjoyed winter sports.

Their Majesties traveled by train for part of their time during their visit to Switzerland.

In Bern, Their Majesties were welcomed by President Max Petitpierre; the tour included a visit to the Military School for Armor Corps Cadets as well as another to the Omega watch factory.

Switzerland 1960

Denmark 1960

In Copenhagen, Their Majesties were entertained at Christiansborg Palace by King Frederick IX and Queen Ingrid.

Norway 1960

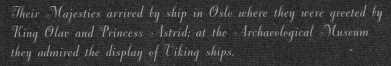

Their Majesties arrived by ship in Oslo where they were greeted by King Olav and Princess Astrid; at the Archaeological Museum they admired the display of Viking ships.

Sweden 1960

The Swedish tour included a visit to the Royal Swedish Fleet near Stockholm and a banquet given by the Swedish government. Top left photo shows King Gustaf VI and the Queen of Sweden, who were also at the banquet.

Italy & The Vatican State 1960

Their Majesties were given a reception at the Grand Hotel.

Italy & The Vatican State 1960

In Rome, His Majesty laid a wreath at the Tomb of the Unknown Warrior and toured the city in a motorcade. At the Apostolic Palace in the Vatican, Their Majesties met Pope John Paul XXIII.

Belgium 1960

In Brussels, King Baudouin of the Belgians entertained Their Majesties at various functions.

France 1960

Their Majesties were entertained in Paris at the Elysée Palace by President and Madame Charles de Gaulle. They also met André Malraux, Minister of Culture, visited Versailles and went cruising on the Seine.

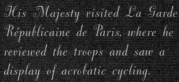

His Majesty visited La Garde Républicaine de Paris, where he reviewed the troops and saw a display of acrobatic cycling.

Luxemburg 1960

Their Majesties appeared on the balcony of Town Hall in Luxemburg and were also entertained by the Grand Duchess Charlotte.

The Netherlands 1960

Queen Juliana and Prince Bernhard entertained Their Majesties on their visit to the Netherlands.

Spain 1960

General Francisco Franco reviewed troops with His Majesty in Madrid; the royal party left Spain from Barcelona.

The Spanish visit also included a visit to Seville and a demonstration of flamenco dancing.

A Royal Welcome

Returning from their lengthy royal tour in January 1961, Their Majesties were given a festive welcome home by thousands who lined the streets of Bangkok.

Officials and family friends were on hand to greet them when they arrived at the Chitralada Palace.

Pakistan 1962

In Pakistan, Their Majesties visited Peshawar University and the famous Shalimar Gardens of Lahore.

The Federation of Malaya 1962

The Yang di-Pertuan Agong and the Raja Permaisuri greeted Their Majesties at Kuala Lumpur.

During the Malayan tour, Their Majesties visited Wat Chetawan at Petaling Jaya, where His Majesty presided at the temple's consecration ceremony.

Australia 1962

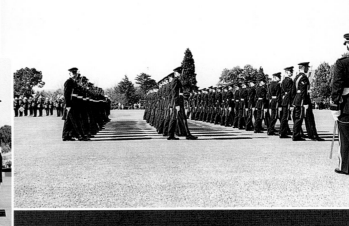

His Majesty reviewed a parade of cadets at the Royal Military College, Duntroon.

At Melbourne University during the Australian tour, an Honorary Degree of Doctor of Law was conferred on His Majesty.

Australia 1

New Zealand 1962

On arrival at Wellington Airport, Their Majesties were greeted by the Governor General, Viscount Cobham, and the Prime Minister, Keith Holyoake. The program included a visit to the Dental Nurse Training School.

At Rotorua the royal party was treated to a traditional Maori welcome ceremony.

Japan 1963

Their Majesties were given a banquet at the Imperial Palace by Emperor Hirohito and the Empress. Later in Kyoto they were greeted by Thais living in the area.

Both Nara and Kyoto were on the royal schedule; at the Sento Palace in Kyoto they saw a demonstration of the ancient Japanese tea ceremony.

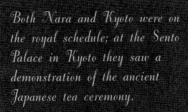

THAILAND King Bhumibol Adulyadej – The Golden Jubilee 1946-1996

The Republic of China 1963

In Taipei, a state banquet was given for Their Majesties by President and Madame Chiang Kai-shek at the Presidential Mansion.

His Majesty was given an air show at Kungkuan Airbase by a group called the Thunder Tigers.

THAILAND King Bhumibol Adulyadej – The Golden Jubilee 1946-1996

Philippines 1963

In Manila, President and Mrs Diosdado Macapagal gave a state banquet at Malacanang Palace. His Majesty laid wreaths at the Rizal Monument and at the Tomb of the Unknown Soldier.

Also part of the tour was a visit to the Philippines Military Academy near Baguio and a demonstration of Filipino folk dancing.

THAILAND King Bhumibol Adulyadej – The Golden Jubilee 1946-1996

Austria 1964

On arrival at Schwechat Airport, Their Majesties were greeted by President Adolf Schaerf; the Austrian tour included a visit to Mozart's house in Salzburg.

THAILAND King Bhumibol Adulyadej – The Golden Jubilee 1946-1996

Iran 1967

During the trip, they were entertained at Golestan Palace and taken on a tour of the ancient city of Isfahan.

United States of America 1967

On their brief visit to Honolulu, Their Majesties were greeted by hula dancers and dedicated a Thai pavilion at the East-West Center of the University of Hawaii.

The Queen with Mr James Linen III, President of Time Inc. Publishing, at a reception in New York.

Their Majesties also met Frank Sinatra at a dinner party in Los Angeles.

United States of America 1967

Their Majesties arrived at the White House by helicopter, where they were greeted by President Lyndon Johnson and Secretary of State Dean Rusk.

Among the guests at the banquet given in honor of the royal party at the White House were Lynda Bird Johnson, the President's daughter.

The visit to New York included a reception at the
Metropolitan Museum, while at Williams College in
Massachusetts, His Majesty was awarded an honorary degree.

Canada 1967

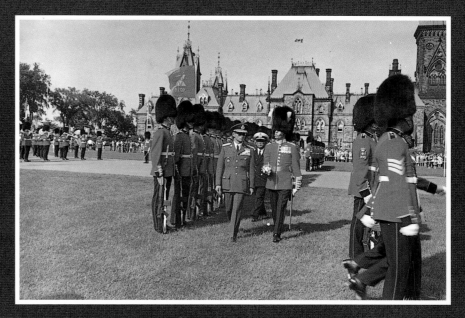

A fashion show was given at the Thai Pavilion at Expo '67 held at Montreal; the Thai model is Athasara Hongsakul, who was the first Thai selected as Miss Universe.

The Thai pavilion.

O*ver the years, Their Majesties the King and Queen have been hosts to numerous foreign rulers and heads of state from throughout the world, among them many notable figures. A high point of most such visits is a state banquet held in the splendid Chakri Throne Hall of the Grand Palace. Through these functions, as well as in less formal meetings during the visits, His Majesty has played a major role in promoting Thailand's harmonious relations with other countries.*

We feature selected excerpts from His Majesty's welcome addresses to some of these distinguished visitors.

Visitors to the Kingdom

King Norodom Sihanouk of Cambodia
December 15–21, 1954

President Ngô-Dinh Diêm of Vietnam
August 15–19, 1957

President Ahmed Sukarno of
Indonesia
April 16–20, 1961

President Arturo Frondizi and Madame
Frondizi of Argentina
December 8–11, 1961

Their Majesties King Frederik IX and
Queen Ingrid of Denmark
January 12–24, 1962

President Heinrich Lübke and Frau
Lübke of the Federal Republic of
Germany
November 21–26, 1962

General Ne Win of Burma
December 14–21, 1962

Their Majesties King Paul I and
Queen Frederika of the Hellenes
February 14–18, 1963

His Majesty King Sri Savang Vatthana
of Laos
March 22–25, 1963

Her Majesty Queen Juliana and HRH
Prince Bernhard of the Netherlands
October 15–22, 1963

Their Majesties King Baudouin and
Queen Fabiola of the Belgians
February 3–10, 1964

Their Majesties the Yang di-Pertuan
Agong and the Raja Permaisuri Agong
of Malaysia
February 24 –March 3, 1964

Their Imperial Highnesses Crown
Prince Akihito and Crown Princess
Michiko of Japan
December 14–21, 1964

His Majesty King Olav of Norway
January 15–23, 1965

HRH Prince Bertil of Sweden
February 2–10, 1965

President Park Chung Hee and
Madame Park of Korea
February 10–13, 1966

President Lyndon B Johnson and
Mrs Johnson of the United States of
America
October 28–30, 1966

President Franz Jonas of Austria
January 17–26, 1967

President Ferdinand E Marcos and
Madame Marcos of the Philippines
January 15–19, 1968

His Imperial Majesty Mohammad Reza
Pahlavi Aryamehr Shahanshah of Iran
and Her Imperial Majesty Farah
Pahlavi Shahbanou of Iran
January 22–29, 1968

His Imperial Majesty Haile Selassie I
of Ethiopia
May 1–4, 1968

President Richard M Nixon and
Mrs Nixon of the United States of
America
July 28–31, 1969

President General Suharto and
Madame Suharto of Indonesia
March 19–22, 1970

Her Majesty Queen Elizabeth II and
HRH Prince Philip, Duke of Edinburgh,
of the United Kingdom
February 9–15, 1972

President Shri Varahagiri Venkata Giri
and Shrimati Sarasvathi Giri of India
March 27–30, 1972

Their Majesties the Yang di-Pertuan
Agong and the Raja Permaisuri Agong
of Malaysia
February 1–8, 1973

President General Ne Win of Burma
March 4–6, 1979

President Ziaur Rahman and Begum
Ziaur Rahman of Bangladesh
April 8–10, 1979

President General Suharto of
Indonesia
March 25–26, 1981

President Chun Doo Hwan and
Madame Chun of Korea
July 3–6, 1981

Their Majesties King Hussein Bin
Talaland and Queen Noor Al-Hussein
of Jordan
September 25–27, 1983

President Karl Carstens and Frau
Carstens of the Federal Republic of
Germany
February 29–March 2, 1984

His Holiness Pope John Paul II of The
Vatican
May 10–11, 1984

Their Majesties King Birendra Bir
Bikram Shah Dev and Queen
Aishwarya Rajya Laxmi Devi Shah of
Nepal
December 12–15, 1984

President Li Xiannian and Madame
Lin Jiamei of China
March 11–15, 1985

Their Majesties the Yang di-Pertuan
Agong and the Raja Permaisuri
Agong and the Raja Permaisuri Agong
of Malaysia
December 17–21, 1985

Mrs Nancy Reagan, the wife of the
President of the United States of
America
May 3–5, 1986

Governor General Sir Ninian Stephen
and Lady Stephen of Australia
January 14–21, 1987

Governor General Jeanne Sauvé and
Maurice Sauvé of Canada
March 27–April 1, 1987

President General Mohammad Zia-ul-
Haq of Pakistan
October 21–24, 1987

Their Majesties King Juan Carlos I and
Queen Sofia of Spain
November 18–22, 1987

President Hussain Muhammad Ershad
and Begum Raushan Ershad of
Bangladesh
March 28–31, 1988

Their Majesties Sultan Haji Hassanal
Bolkiah and Raja Isteri Pengiran Anak
Saleha of Brunei Darussalam
November 1–4, 1988

Their Majesties the Yang di-Pertuan
Agong and the Raja Permaisuri Agong
of Malaysia
December 17–21, 1990

President Yang Shangkun of China
June 10–15, 1991

Their Majesties Emperor Akihito and
Empress Michiko of Japan
September 26–30, 1991

President Kaysone Phomvihane and
Madame Thongvin Phomvihane
of Laos
January 6–15, 1992

President Arpad Goncz and Madame
Zsuzsanna Maria Goncz of Hungary
February 15–18, 1993

President Vaclav Havel and Madame
Olga Havlova of the Czech Republic
February 11–14, 1994

President Nouhak Phoumsavanh and
Madame Bounma Phoumsavanh of
Laos
February 14–19, 1995

1954 ▼
HRH PRINCE NORODOM SIHANOUK OF CAMBODIA
December 15–21

1957
PRESIDENT NGÔ-DINH DIÊM OF VIETNAM
August 15–19

1961 ▼
PRESIDENT AHMED SUKARNO OF INDONESIA
April 16–20

1961
PRESIDENT ARTURO FRONDIZI AND MADAME FRONDIZI OF ARGENTINA
December 8–11

From HM's speech at the State Banquet on December 8: "It is indeed a privilege and a great pleasure for the Queen and myself to welcome Your Excellency, Madame Frondizi and members of your party tonight. Your presence among us certainly has a deep significance for it marks the first visit of a Chief of State from Latin America, and thus augurs well for the furtherance of Thailand's friendly relations not only with Argentina but with that important part of the world."

1962 ▼
THEIR MAJESTIES KING FREDERIK IX AND QUEEN INGRID OF DENMARK
January 12–24

From HM's speech at the State Banquet on January 13: "The Danish and the Thai people have much in common. To them liberty and independence are essential to human existence. Their outlook on life is tempered with justice and fair play. It is no wonder, therefore, that our countries have continually maintained very long and mutually satisfactory relations. Many Danish nationals have participated actively in our public service, such as in the organization of our naval defense and in the organization of our gendarmerie. Thai naval officers and students in various branches of study have found and still find in Denmark a very happy training ground for them....In short, our relations have always been based on the principle of mutual cooperation, and we may well be proud of this."

1962
PRESIDENT HEINRICH LÜBKE AND FRAU LÜBKE OF THE FEDERAL REPUBLIC OF GERMANY
November 21–26

From HM's speech at the State Banquet on November 21: "Thailand has cause to be grateful for ready cooperation rendered to it by Germany both in the past and at the present time. It is gratifying to see that since the conclusion of the Agreement on Economic and Technical Cooperation in October 1956 between our two countries, many of our economic and social projects have been realized. I am also glad to note that trade between our two countries is steadily increasing and, on the cultural side, the establishment in Bangkok of the German Cultural Institute and the Thai-German Cultural Society has greatly contributed to our cultural relations."

GENERAL NE WIN OF BURMA

December 14–21

THEIR MAJESTIES KING PAUL I AND QUEEN FREDERIKA OF THE HELLENES

February 14–18

From HM's speech at the State Banquet on February 15: "Greece is a country of ancient civilization and culture with a great past and with such a rich heritage in the sphere of art and science and in thought and philosophy that it is for us all to see and admire. Like Thailand, the Greek nation, imbued with patriotism and love of freedom and peace, has shown great determination in her struggle against domination and has succeeded so well in preserving the national independence."

HIS MAJESTY KING SRI SAVANG VATTHANA OF LAOS

March 22–25

HER MAJESTY QUEEN JULIANA AND HRH PRINCE BERNHARD OF THE NETHERLANDS

October 15–22

From HM's speech at the State Banquet on October 15: "That the relations between our two countries are old and longstanding is indeed well-known to us all. The Netherlands was the first European country with which Thailand had diplomatic relations, and since the beginning of the seventeenth century contacts between the two peoples have continued and remained unchanged to the present time. This is so because our two peoples in fact share similar ideals: we both cherish liberty and independence, and we both want to promote peaceful progress and welfare for our people. These similarities constitute a common ground on which our ties of friendship are based."

THEIR MAJESTIES KING BAUDOUIN AND QUEEN FABIOLA OF THE BELGIANS

February 3–10

From HM's speech at the State Banquet on February 4: "I still recall with deep gratification and gratitude the warm reception and friendly welcome which Your Majesty as well as the government and people of Belgium gave to us during our state visit to your magnificent country. Your visit to our land now, as well as that of your royal father three years ago, reflects the close relations and firm bonds of friendship which have been of long standing between our nations; and it does give, also, an opportunity to our government and people to show their deep feelings of respect and affection to Your Majesties in person.

"Historically our close ties of friendship have been marked, not only by the relations between the governments of both countries alone, but also by the contacts which our people have made with each other. Many Belgians have come to this country and rendered valuable services to us, the most illustrious example being that of Monsieur Rolin Jacquemyns in the reign of my grandfather, King Chulalongkorn. On our part, many of our students have been to study in Belgium; and there is, also, a continued mutual cooperation between our two peoples in various ways, socially, economically and commercially."

THEIR MAJESTIES THE YANG DI-PERTUAN AGONG AND THE RAJA PERMAISURI AGONG OF MALAYSIA

February 24–March 3

From HM's speech at the State Banquet on February 24: "We are greatly honored that Your Majesties should be visiting Thailand before any other country after your greater Federation had come into being. We are, at the same time, extremely delighted to be able to reciprocate the warm and cordial reception which you accorded us on our visit to your country last year. Malaysia and Thailand are good neighbors with a long history of happy relationship. We are closely linked not only by ties of friendship and culture, but also by our common membership in the Association of Southeast Asia and our respect for the ideals of peace, justice and freedom. Based on such foundations, the friendship between our two countries cannot but become more and more firmly established with the passing of time."

1964 ▲

THEIR IMPERIAL HIGHNESSES CROWN PRINCE AKIHITO AND CROWN PRINCESS MICHIKO OF JAPAN

December 14–21

From HM's speech at the State Banquet on December 15: "As you are aware, the relationship between our two countries has been very close and of long standing. The distinguished careers of your countrymen who served in the Thai court during the Ayutthaya period are well-known. Among them might be mentioned the celebrated Yamada of Japan. Since the establishment of the Japanese Legation in B.E. 2440, our relations have continued to grow. Trade and commerce steadily increased, and the cooperation between the two countries now covers many fields of activity. Many of our students have gone to Japan for further studies, thus enhancing the happy relations between Japan and this country."

1965

HIS MAJESTY KING OLAV OF NORWAY

January 15–23

From HM's speech at the State Banquet on January 15: "The history of the contact between our two peoples began in the latter half of the nineteenth century when the two countries had their first treaty of friendship and established diplomatic relations, and it was with the conclusion of the Treaty of Friendship, Commerce and Navigation in 1937 that our relations were formalized. The bonds of friendship were further strengthened when the governments of both countries agreed in 1960 to raise the status of their respective legations to that of embassies....Your Majesty's visit to our country at this moment is not only affording a unique opportunity to the Thai people to show their love and respect to you, but also ushers in a new epoch in the history of our friendly relations. I am sure that the people of this country will long cherish the memory of your visit."

1965

HRH PRINCE BERTIL OF SWEDEN

February 2–10

1966

PRESIDENT PARK CHUNG HEE AND MADAME PARK OF KOREA
February 10–13

From HM's speech at the State Banquet on February 10: "Your visit to us here is the first that a Chief of State from the Republic of Korea has ever made to Thailand, thereby marking the most significant milestone in the friendly relationship between the peoples of our two countries. We can therefore look forward to a period of still closer bonds of amity and friendship between our two countries and peoples.

"As you are aware, the Korean and Thai peoples share similar ideals and aspirations. For these reasons, the Thai people are proud to be numbered among other members of the United Nations to assist the Korean people in their struggle to uphold those ideals."

1966 ▼

PRESIDENT LYNDON B JOHNSON AND MRS JOHNSON OF THE UNITED STATES OF AMERICA
October 28–30

From HM's speech at the State Banquet on October 28: "Our two countries, Mr President, have had a long history of friendly relations dating back to the beginning of the nineteenth century;

the first Treaty of Amity and Commerce was signed in 1833, the first ever concluded by the United States with a nation of Asia. Since then there have developed mutual goodwill and closer cooperation. This year, another milestone was set by the signing of the Treaty of Amity and Economic Relations which, after ratification, will enable our two peoples to cooperate still further in the many fields of human endeavors. We are confident that your visit will serve to strengthen the bonds of friendship and mutual understanding between our two nations."

1967

PRESIDENT FRANZ JONAS OF AUSTRIA
January 17–26

1968 ▼

PRESIDENT FERDINAND E MARCOS AND MADAME MARCOS OF THE PHILIPPINES
January 15–19

From HM's speech at the State Banquet on January 15: "The Philippines and Thailand enjoy close and cordial relations with one another. Our close

ties are based on sincere friendship and understanding. The two peoples share many common aspirations. We both want to remain free and independent and to be able to secure to our peoples a better way of life and increased measures of prosperity. We both believe that the road to stable peace and prosperity is through active cooperation among each and all the free and friendly nations of this region. For this reason, we are not only fellow-members of the United Nations, but we are also co-signatories of the Southeast Asia Collective Defense Treaty and the Association of Southeast Asia. Recently, our concerted action for regional development has been crowned with success through joint participation in the Asian and Pacific Council and Association of South East Asian Nations."

HIS IMPERIAL MAJESTY MOHAMMAD REZA PAHLAVI ARYAMEHR SHAHANSHAH OF IRAN AND HER IMPERIAL MAJESTY FARAH PAHLAVI SHAHBANOU OF IRAN

January 22–29

From HM's speech at the State Banquet on January 23: "Iran and Thailand have cause to be proud of their freedom and independence throughout their history. Our peoples are peace-loving and share many common aspirations, and our two nations had established contacts with one another from the middle of the seventeenth century. For us, the visit of Your Majesties is an event of historic significance, for it is the first time that a reigning sovereign of Iran has made a state visit to Thailand."

1968

HIS IMPERIAL MAJESTY HAILE SELASSIE I OF ETHIOPIA

May 1–4

From HM's speech at the State Banquet on May 1: "We in this country are fully cognizant of Ethiopia's glorious past, as she has been an important center of civilization since ancient times. We are well aware, furthermore, of the outstanding qualities of leadership that Your Majesty has demonstrated to the world by manifesting personal courage and selflessness in defending the cause of peace and freedom in your country. Under your wise and benevolent leadership, Ethiopia has achieved considerable social progress and beneficial reform in various fields which have brought much happiness to your people."

1969 ▼

PRESIDENT RICHARD M NIXON AND MRS NIXON OF THE UNITED STATES OF AMERICA

July 28–31

From HM's speech at the State Banquet on July 28: "I consider it an auspicious omen that under your eminent leadership, Mr President, the unqualified success of man's first landing on the moon and the subsequent safe return of the astronauts have been achieved. For this momentous occasion, the Thai nation joins me in offering Your Excellency and the American people our heartfelt congratulations. Last week's breathtaking achievement of Apollo Eleven and its brave American crew cannot be measured solely in scientific terms, for it also indicates man's ability to look beyond his earthbound problems and to set his sights on new horizons in quest of wider knowledge and deeper understanding of himself and his environment."

PRESIDENT GENERAL SUHARTO AND MADAME SUHARTO OF INDONESIA

March 19–22

From HM's speech at the State Banquet on March 19: "The bonds of friendship between the Republic of Indonesia and Thailand are close and cordial and are based on mutual respect for each other and on the firm adherence to the ideas of peace, freedom and justice. In view of the present situation, our two countries are similarly placed by urgent needs for national development in order to preserve the dignity, independence and intrinsic values of our peoples from the critical dangers threatening us. That is why the Thai people are pleased with the important role assumed by Indonesia in the task of promoting regional unity and cooperation of our respective peoples."

HER MAJESTY QUEEN ELIZABETH II AND HRH PRINCE PHILIP, DUKE OF EDINBURGH, OF THE UNITED KINGDOM

February 9–15

From HM's speech at the State Banquet on February 10: "State visits are always moments of special importance, for it must be borne in mind that, in making them, the Heads of State are actually representing the desires of their peoples to strengthen their relations and become better acquainted with each other. For that reason, the actions and attitudes of Your Majesty and all members of your party during this visit will leave deep impressions on the minds of the Thai people as to the real British character and attitude toward our nation. Conversely, Your Majesty and the rest of your party will be able to gather from the manner of our welcome and what you see during this visit the measure of our attitude and goodwill toward the British people.

"This occasion is also an important milestone in the history of our relationship, being the first time that a British monarch is making a state visit to our country. Although begun over three centuries ago, the relationship between Thailand and Great Britain has been happily maintained and of mutual benefit. Many Thai people have gone to pursue their various studies or training in the United Kingdom and other countries of the Commonwealth and have come back to serve our country with efficiency in their various professions. For such benefits, we will always feel grateful to the lands and peoples of which Your Majesty is the worthy monarch."

PRESIDENT SHRI VARAHAGIRI VENKATA GIRI AND SHRIMATI SARASVATHI GIRI OF INDIA

March 27–30

From HM's speech at the State Banquet on March 27: "Your visit is made even more important for being the first time that an Indian President has paid a state visit to Thailand, even though the contacts and exchanges between our two

nations can be traced back many centuries. On the cultural side, in particular, there are many clear evidences of similarities and affinities in language, literature and other forms of art. Above all, the Buddhist faith, which originated in India, came to Thailand since its early days and has been upheld by the Thai people as one of the pillars of our society."

THEIR MAJESTIES THE YANG DI-PERTUAN AGONG AND THE RAJA PERMAISURI AGONG OF MALAYSIA

February 1–8

PRESIDENT GENERAL NE WIN OF BURMA

March 4–6

From HM's speech at the State Banquet on March 4: "It is indeed always pleasing to see that the Socialist Republic of the Union of Burma and Thailand have not only for a very long time enjoyed friendly relations as befitting close neighbors, but also possess several features which are similar in many important aspects. The populations of both countries, furthermore, follow similar kinds of customs, traditions, and cultures as well as conduct similar existences and methods of living."

PRESIDENT ZIAUR RAHMAN AND BEGUM ZIAUR RAHMAN OF BANGLADESH

April 8–10

PRESIDENT GENERAL SUHARTO OF INDONESIA

March 25–26

PRESIDENT CHUN DOO HWAN AND MADAME CHUN OF KOREA

July 3–6

1983
THEIR MAJESTIES KING HUSSEIN BIN TALALAND AND QUEEN NOOR AL-HUSSEIN OF JORDAN
September 25–27

1984 ▼
PRESIDENT KARL CARSTENS AND FRAU CARSTENS OF GERMANY
February 29–March 2

From HM's speech at the State Banquet on February 29: "The longstanding relations between Thailand and the Federal Republic of Germany have always been close and cordial. The relationship between our two countries began in 1861 when the German Diplomatic Mission under the leadership of Count zu Eulenberg, Minister Extraordinary and Plenipotentiary, arrived in Siam during the reign of King Mongkut. One year later on the seventh of February 1862, a Treaty of Amity, Commerce and Navigation was signed, thus establishing the relationship on a fully official basis. Soon after, the bonds of friendship and close association began to grow to cover all aspects, even though Germany and Thailand are situated far apart on different sides of the globe and communications were, in those days, still very arduous. Today, when one reflects on that achievement, it seems an altogether miraculous feat."

1984 ▲
HIS HOLINESS POPE JOHN PAUL II OF THE VATICAN
May 10–11

From HM's speech at the State Banquet on May 10: "Although full diplomatic relations have been established between the Vatican and Thailand only within recent times, a kind of deep attachment has always existed between us for a very long time as the Roman Catholic Church of the Christian religion has entered and operated in this country for centuries beginning in the period when our capital was still at Ayutthaya. Every group of priests and missionaries that had come in to propagate the Catholic faith had brought not only Christian teachings but also all kinds of science and technology which were flourishing in Europe at that time to introduce to the Thai people, thus giving Thai people the chance to learn about the Christian religion as well as all fields of advanced knowledge, together with the arts, cultures and traditions of Western people which we could incorporate and adapt for use in our national affairs with many benefits."

1984 ▼
THEIR MAJESTIES KING BIRENDRA BIR BIKRAM SHAH DEV AND QUEEN AISHWARYA RAJYA LAXMI DEVI SHAH OF NEPAL
December 12–15

From HM's speech at the State Banquet on December 12: "The Queen and I feel very pleased and gratified as well as highly proud and honored to have the opportunity of welcoming Your Majesty

and Her Majesty the Queen together with other distinguished guests from Nepal in your party in the Thai capital tonight. I cannot indeed refrain from mentioning that the relationship between our two royal families have always been extremely close and cordial. Thailand has had the honor of receiving the King and senior members of the Nepalese royal family many times, and five years ago Nepal extended a very cordial welcome to the Crown Prince of Thailand and his party."

1985 ▼
PRESIDENT LI XIANNIAN AND MADAME LIN JIAMEI OF CHINA
March 11–15

From HM's speech at the State Banquet on March 11: "China and Thailand have carried on a long relationship stretching back into ancient times. Such a relationship, be it between our two states or between members of our two races,

could be said to have been so close as to have become inseparable. This is because both sides have always been ready to be of support and assistance to each other as well as to allow the transfer of cultural heritage from one to another in numerous and profound ways throughout the ages. Thus those deep-rooted ties between our two nations have obviously provided strong and solid bases on which the new era of diplomatic relations, beginning in the year 1975, was founded and has been made to flourish in the best possible manner."

1985
THEIR MAJESTIES THE YANG DI-PERTUAN AGONG AND THE RAJA PERMAISURI AGONG OF MALAYSIA
December 17–21

1986

MRS NANCY REAGAN, THE WIFE OF THE PRESIDENT OF THE UNITED STATES OF AMERICA

May 3–5

1987

GOVERNOR GENERAL SIR NINIAN STEPHEN AND LADY STEPHEN OF AUSTRALIA

January 14–21

1987

GOVERNOR GENERAL JEANNE SAUVÉ AND MAURICE SAUVÉ OF CANADA

March 27–April 1

1987 ▲

PRESIDENT GENERAL MOHAMMAD ZIA-UL-HAQ OF PAKISTAN

October 21–24

From HM's speech at the State Banquet on October 21: "Although twenty-five years have passed since the Queen and I had the opportunity of visiting Pakistan, we can still recall very vividly those happy memories of the beautiful towns and countryside, together with the cordiality and friendliness of the people as well as the welcome that was full of amity and goodwill. Thus Pakistan has great attraction for us and we have always watched and followed her progress in the various fields, particularly during these recent years when there have been development and changes."

1987 ▼

THEIR MAJESTIES KING JUAN CARLOS I AND QUEEN SOFIA OF SPAIN

November 18–22

From HM's speech at the State Banquet on November 19: "The relationship between Spain and Thailand has existed for a long time, ever since the period in the sixteenth century of the Christian era when Spanish merchants came by boat to ply their trade and make cultural exchanges with Southeast Asian nations. In AD 1718, diplomatic relations were established between our two countries, thus reaffirming the already strong ties on both the national level and between the two peoples. Then the King of Thailand, His Majesty King Chulalongkorn, paid the first state visit to Spain in 1897, and on the latest occasion, which happened twenty-seven years ago, the Queen and myself had our own chance to go to Spain and we were received by the Spanish people with a great friendliness, the memory of which has lingered with us until these days."

1988 ▲

PRESIDENT HUSSAIN MUHAMMAD ERSHAD AND BEGUM RAUSHAN ERSHAD OF BANGLADESH

March 28–31

From HM's speech at the State Banquet on March 28: "Bangladesh and Thailand have enjoyed longstanding friendly relations, even before the establishment of diplomatic relations in the year 1972, and each side has received a great deal of advantages from the cooperation with one another in many fields of endeavor."

1988 ▼

THEIR MAJESTIES SULTAN HAJI HASSANAL BOLKIAH AND RAJA ISTERI PENGIRAN ANAK SALEHA OF BRUNEI DARUSSALAM

November 1–4

1990

THEIR MAJESTIES THE YANG DI-PERTUAN AGONG AND THE RAJA PERMAISURI AGONG OF MALAYSIA

December 17–21

1991 ▲

PRESIDENT YANG SHANGKUN OF CHINA

June 10–15

1991 ▼

THEIR MAJESTIES EMPEROR AKIHITO AND EMPRESS MICHIKO OF JAPAN

September 26–30

From HM's speech at the State Banquet on September 26: "The Thai people are forever conscious of the fact that they have been fortunate to have received Your Majesty once already, twenty-seven years ago, when Your Majesty was the Crown Prince and had been designated by His Majesty Emperor Showa to visit Thailand on His Majesty's behalf. But this time, they have the opportunity of

welcoming Their Majesties the Emperor and Empress of Japan themselves who have been so gracious as to be present here in Thailand. I am thus confident that during Your Majesty's stay in our country, Your Majesty will surely be aware of the profound respect and true admiration which everyone holds for Your Majesty. Those sentiments will be an important factor which will help to bring about more permanent and even more cordial ties of friendship and cooperation between Japan and Thailand."

1992 ▲

PRESIDENT KAYSONE PHOMVIHANE AND MADAME THONGVIN PHOMVIHANE OF LAOS

January 6–15

1993

PRESIDENT ARPAD GONCZ AND MADAME ZSUZSANNA MARIA GONCZ OF HUNGARY

February 15–18

1994 ▼

PRESIDENT VACLAV HAVEL AND MADAME OLGA HAVLOVA OF THE CZECH REPUBLIC

February 11–14

From HM's speech at the State Banquet on February 11: "Even though the Czech Republic was established not so long ago, it is a country with a lengthy history and a magnificent civilization since ancient times. The Thai people have watched and followed with great interest the continued progress achieved in various fields of endeavor, particularly during the period when great changes and reforms were taking place within your country. Thus, we are highly pleased and gratified to be able to welcome His Excellency President Vaclav Havel, who, apart from being a philosopher, an author, and a distinguished statesman, has been duly recognized by the community of nations as the person who has managed to revive and lead the Czech nation by peaceful means into an era of freedom."

1995

PRESIDENT NOUHAK PHOUMSAVANH AND MADAME BOUNMA PHOUMSAVANH OF LAOS

February 14–19

A Chronicle of Fifty Years
1946~96

A Chronicle of Fifty Years, 1946-96

AN END AND A BEGINNING

- **June 9.** HM King Ananda Mahidol (top left), His Royal Highness Prince Bhumibol's older brother, is found dead in bed, shot in the head with a pistol.

The First Pacific Overseas Airways Flight.

GENERAL PHIN CHUNHAVAN

1947

- **Nov 8.** General Phin Chunhavan mobilizes the military against the Thamrong government; the Prime Minister goes into exile along with former underground leader Pridi Banomyong.

1946

- **June 9.** The Ninth Reign of the Chakri Dynasty begins with the investiture ceremony for the accession to the throne of His Majesty King Bhumibol Adulyadej (Rama IX).
- **Aug 19.** His Majesty the King receives a rousing ovation from the crowd gathered at Wat Phra Keo prior to his departure for Europe to resume his studies. • **Aug 21.** Thamrong Narasawat becomes Prime Minister and Parliament opens for an historic ninety-day session.
- **Aug 24.** PM Thamrong names a new eighteen-member Cabinet.
- **Sept 13.** Thai and French troops exchange gunfire in a skirmish on the Thai-Cambodian border. • **Oct 11.** A bill outlawing Communism is passed by the House of Representatives.
- **Nov 1.** The official report on the inquiry into the death of His Majesty King Ananda Mahidol (Rama VIII) is submitted to the government.
- **Nov 21.** An attempted coup by Air Force noncommissioned officers is quashed.
- **Dec 16.** Siam becomes the fifty-fifth member of the United Nations as the country's representative, His Royal Highness Prince Wan Waithayakorn, signs the pledge to the UN Charter.

1947

- **May 26.** The first direct air links with the United States commence with a Pacific Overseas Airways flight to San Francisco via Hong Kong and Guam.
- **May 28.** The Thamrong government resigns; the following day Parliament selects Thamrong to again form a government.
- **June 11.** Police and the military launch a campaign to suppress Malay border bandits.
- **July 1.** PM Thamrong announces the formation of a Pan-Southeast Asian Union to be sponsored by France and Thailand.

Khuang Aphaiwong (left).

- **Nov 10.** Khuang Aphaiwong becomes Thailand's tenth Prime Minister.
- **Nov 15.** Suspects are held in the inquiry into the death of HM King Ananda.
- **Dec 22.** A phonograph recording of HM the King's New Year's message arrives in Bangkok.

1948

- **Jan 29.** A general election is held.
- **Apr 8.** Field Marshal Phibun Songkhram becomes Prime Minister.
- **May 12.** In a daring pre-dawn heist, robbers posing as police and military officials, steal 150 kg of gold from a well guarded security truck—the biggest theft in the country's history.
- **May 28.** Some 200,000

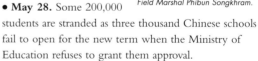

Field Marshal Phibun Songkhram.

students are stranded as three thousand Chinese schools fail to open for the new term when the Ministry of Education refuses to grant them approval.
- **May 30.** The government announces its plan for income tax reform. • **June 21.** The government cracks down on opium smoking. • **June 25.** PM Phibun says the government will actively counter Communism.
- **June 30.** Police formally charge five suspects in connection with the death of HM King Ananda.
- **July 20.** The Constituent Assembly discusses reverting the kingdom's name from Siam back to Thailand, as before the Second World War.
- **Aug 21.** PM Phibun receives two thousand letters urging him to use his office to curb rampant nationwide corruption.

1949

- **Jan 7.** A group of orchid growers forms the Siam Society of Plant Culture to promote the flower. • **Jan 10.** Thai and British officials agree on measures to suppress banditry along the Thai-Malay border.

- **Jan 14.** Parliament discusses the draft of a new constitution—the nation's fourth since 1932.
- **Jan 28.** Parliament passes the new Constitution.
- **Feb 1.** A new counter-corruption campaign is launched. • **Feb 8.** Strict enforcement of visa regulations leads to three hundred Chinese citizens being deported. • **Feb 16.** Following fourteen years in exile, Her Majesty Rambhai Barni—the widow of King Prajadhipok (Rama VII)—returns to Thailand. • **Feb 24.** The Cabinet declares a nationwide state of emergency in reaction to the cCommunist threat. • **Feb 26.** Having secretly returned to Thailand, former underground leader Pridi stages a coup against the government; defeated by the military, he returns to exile.

Her Majesty Queen Rambhai Barni.

- **June 4.** A general election is held.
- **July 19.** HM the King becomes engaged to Mom Rajawongse Sirikit Kitiyakorn, the seventeen-year-old daughter of the ambassador to France. • **Oct 27.** The House of Representatives passes the third and final reading of a bill to limit land ownership by foreigners.
- **Nov 23.** Bangkok is inundated with floodwaters, which rise to levels higher than those of the great floods of 1917. • **Nov 28.** Customs officials announce the seizure of a million baht worth of raw opium —the third largest haul to date.
- **Dec 16.** The country closes its northern and northeastern borders to Chinese immigrants.

1950

- **Mar 1.** Thailand officially announces its recognition of Laos, Cambodia and Burma. • **Mar 13.** The government extends its anti-communist program to schools and factories. • **Mar 24.** Thousands take to the streets to welcome HM the King home from his studies in Switzerland. • **Mar 31.** Foreigners are prohibited from owning land in Thailand.
- **Apr 11.** The US government announces its intention to contribute US$10 million in military aid to combat Communism. • **Apr 13.** HM the King signs a Royal Decree authorizing the use of military force to counter Communism. • **May 4.** HM the King begins his coronation ceremonies. • **June 1.** HM the King opens Parliament, only the third Thai monarch to perform such duties; in his speech, he warns of world conflict. • **June 5.** Thousands turn out in an emotional farewell as Their Majesties return to Europe.
- **Dec 9.** The government launches the kingdom's biggest public health campaign to date to combat tuberculosis and introduce pediatric programs.

1951

- **Feb 28.** In central Korea, Thai forces take action against Communist forces for the first time.
- **Mar 24.** HRH Prince Bira Bhanudej breaks the lap record at Goodwood Racetrack in Britain with a

HRH Prince Bira Bhanudej.

speed of 90.38 miles-per-hour. • **Mar 30.** Thai troops in Korea engage in a gun battle with Chinese forces.
- **Apr 5.** Their Majesties' first child, Princess Ubol Ratana, is born in Lausanne, Switzerland.
- **June 19.** The Thai gunboat Bangpakong participates in a battle off Wonsan Harbor in Korea.
- **June 29.** PM Phibun is kidnapped by officers during the ceremony to accept the gift of the American ship USS Manhattan on the Chao Phraya River. As the ship is being bombed, the Prime Minister swims to safety and the "Manhattan Coup" fails.

USS Manhattan under attack.

- **Sept 27.** A former Royal Palace attendant, Chit Singhaseni, is found guilty of conspiring to assassinate HM King Ananda and is sentenced to death.
- **Nov 5.** Having received his law degree, HM the King, accompanied by HM Queen Sirikit and Princess Ubol Ratana, embarks for Thailand.
- **Nov 29.** Police and military officials dissolve the National Assembly and announce over the radio their intention to abrogate the Constitution and replace it with the 1932 version; PM Phibun remains at his post.
- **Dec 2.** The Royal Family arrives back in the capital. • **Dec 7.** A Royal Proclamation restores the 1932 Constitution. • **Dec 27.** The Cabinet Council announces a plan to build a new official residence for HM the King in the Samsen district of Bangkok.

1950

A ROYAL WEDDING

- **Apr 28.** In the first Royal Wedding since that of King Rama VI, HM the King weds MR Sirikit Kitiyakorn in a simple yet dignified civil ceremony performed by the groom's paternal grandmother, Her Majesty Queen Savang Vadhana at her Srapathum Palace. After signing the marriage certificate, the Royal Couple present themselves to the Queen Grandmother, who pours lustral water over their hands, following which HM the King confers the Maha Chakri Order on his bride. Audiences are granted later at the Amarin Throne Hall.

THE CORONATION

1950

- **May 5.** In Thailand's first coronation in twenty-five years, HM the King receives the pure gold, diamond-studded Maha Mala Crown, weighing seven kilograms, and twenty-four other artifacts of Royal Regalia.

A ROYAL FUNERAL

1950

- **May 29.** Bangkok residents are overcome with both awe and grief today as they observe the pomp and ceremony of ancient Siamese tradition at the funeral of HM King Ananda. In the afternoon, HM the King performs the symbolic lighting of the funeral pyre, kneeling before the remains of his elder brother; later, at 10:00 pm, he performs the actual lighting of the pyre, and the flames cast a somber glow over the funeral ground. Thousands have waited all night for a glimpse of the procession.

1950 • **June 21.** The Broadway musical Peepshow opens in New York featuring the song "Blue Night" written by HM the King.

A ROYAL VISIT TO THE NORTHEAST

1955 • **Nov 2.** HM the King, accompanied by members of the Royal Family and entourage, leaves by Royal Train on a nineteen-day tour of the kingdom's northeast; this is the first time that a Thai monarch has made such an extensive official visit to the region.

1952

• **Feb 29.** Elections are held for the National Assembly. • **Mar 6.** Due to increasing conflict in Indochina, Thai military forces are dispatched to the Cambodian border for special exercises.
• **Mar 24.** The National Assembly endorses PM Phibun as the new Prime Minister.
• **May 1.** Korean War casualty figures are released: of the 419,456 official casualties of the twenty-two-month conflict, Thailand has lost forty-nine soldiers, with 365 wounded and four missing in action.
• **July 14.** Viewers watch Thai dancers in the kingdom's first television broadcast.
• **July 28.** HM the Queen gives birth to His Royal Highness Prince Vajiralongkorn at Amporn Villa in Dusit, Bangkok.

1953

• **Jan 2.** A Royal Decree is signed making identification papers compulsory for all Thai nationals between the ages of sixteen and seventy. • **Jan 6.** The Cabinet approves the new Nationality Bill.
• **Feb 2.** Bangkok police crack down on illegal parking on New Road. • **Feb 26.** PM Phibun condemns Chinese efforts to establish a rival "Thai" government in Yunnan province. • **Apr 13.** The Public Health Department launches an anti-mosquito campaign.
• **Apr 21.** PM Phibun orders border inspections as the Viet Minh invasion of Laos becomes serious.
• **Sept 1.** The Cabinet approves the establishment of an Organization for Provincial Electricity to bring power to every province in the kingdom.
• **Sept 23.** Representatives of twenty nations attend the First Asian Malaria Conference in Bangkok amid growing concern about the deadly disease.
• **Oct 1.** A new bus system is introduced in Bangkok paralyzing traffic and confusing commuters.
• **Oct 15.** Burmese planes in pursuit of Chinese Nationalist guerrillas bomb a village in Mae Hong Son. • **Nov 3.** Police issue fourteen rules for safe driving to curb rising traffic accidents.
• **Nov 6.** A massive rice trade racket is smashed by police.

1954

• **Mar 1.** Three WWII Japanese soldiers surrender on the Thai-Malay border after eight years in the jungle.
• **Apr 10.** The US announces Thailand had agreed to join a united front "against communist aggression in Southeast Asia". • **Apr 26.** HRH Prince Wan chairs the Geneva Conference on Peace in the Far East.
• The Thai film *Santivina* receives an award for explaining the East to the West at the First Asian Film Festival in Tokyo. • **July 9.** Thailand asks the UN to act on its request for a Southeast Asian "Peace Patrol".
• **Sept 9.** A huge fire razes the Central Market and more than a thousand houses in Ratchaburi province.
• **Sept 25.** The Cabinet pledges to step up its campaign against corruption. • **Oct 13.** The Supreme Court rules that HM King Ananda Mahidol was assassinated by three men—Chaliew Pathumros, Chit Singhaseni and Butr Pattamasirind—all are sentenced to death. • **Oct 29.** The government announces plans to reopen borders with Laos, Cambodia and Burma.
• **Dec 15.** His Royal Highness King Norodom Sihanouk of Cambodia arrives in Bangkok for a six-day visit.

1955

• **Jan 21.** The government launches a campaign to stop opium smuggling. • **Feb 17.** The three men convicted of complicity in the assassination of HM King Ananda are executed. • **Feb 27.** PM Phibun opens the First Conference of the Southeast Asian Collective Defense Treaty which is held at the National Assembly; HRH Prince Wan is elected chairman of and Bangkok is selected as the site for the organization's new secretariat. • **Mar 5.** Bangkok Lord Mayor General Mangkorn Promyothi promises a "long-term program to end mosquitoes".
• **Apr 2.** Her Majesty the Queen gives birth to Her Royal Highness Princess Sirindhorn, Their Majesties' second daughter. • **Apr 17.** Thailand joins twenty-eight other nations at the opening of the Asian-African Conference held in Bandung, Indonesia.

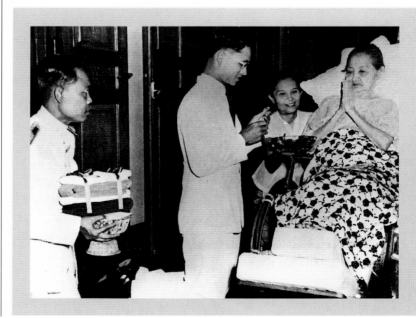

HM King Bhumibol's grandmother, Somdej Phra Sri Sawarin Paramarj-Thewi Phra Phan Wassa Ayika Chao.

- **Apr 18.** A government-sponsored Thai trade mission, seeking foreign investment, departs on a four-week tour of Europe, Japan and the US.
- **Apr 22.** The Thai-Cambodian train service begins.
- **May 26.** The lord mayor reports that there are now 1,064,243 people residing in the Bangkok.
- **July 6.** The Southeast Asian Treaty Organization (SEATO) Military Advisors' Conference opens in Bangkok. • **Aug 24.** The Cabinet approves a bill allowing the formation of political parties.
- **Nov 22.** Trade between Thailand and Japan is normalized for the first time since the Second World War.
- **Dec 10.** Demonstrators seeking the right to meet and parade clash with police following the arrest of their leaders. • **Dec 17.** Somdej Phra Sri Sawarin Paramarj-Thewi Phra Phan Wassa Ayika Chao, Dowager Consort of HM King Chulalongkorn and grandmother of HM the King, dies at the age of ninety-three.

1956
- **Jan 7.** The dramatic rise in traffic accidents prompts the Interior Ministry to launch a probe.
- **Jan 13.** PM Phibun announces that Thailand will only sell its rice, rubber, teak and tin to the "free world" and will not open its markets to China.
- **Nov 12.** Foreign Minister HRH Prince Wan is elected president of the General Assembly of the UN in New York.

1957
- **Jan 2.** A twelve-hour fire called "the biggest blaze in Thai history" razes five hundred buildings on a two-hundred-rai plot of the Phitsanuloke town market.
- **Feb 26.** A general election known as the "dirty elections" is held. PM Phibun's Seri Manangkhasila party gains a bare majority, causing PM Phibun to create a brief state of national emergency in the face of months of student protests. Field Marshal Sarit Thanarat is made responsible for public order.
- **July 4.** Her Royal Highness Princess Chulabhorn, Their Majesties' third daughter, is born in Bangkok.
- **Aug 15.** President Diêm of the Republic of Vietnam arrives in Bangkok for a four-day visit.
- **Sept 17.** The Lower Mekong Basin countries—Thailand, Laos, Cambodia and Vietnam—adopt a joint declaration expressing their wish to continue to pursue cooperative projects and studies.
- **Sept 17.** The army stages a bloodless coup at 4:00 am ousting PM Phibun, who soon leaves the country.
- **Sept 21.** Diplomat Pote Sarasin is elected Prime Minister by the Constituent Assembly in the new provisional government as Field Marshal Sarit prepares to

The Mekong River.

leave to the US and Britain for urgent medical treatment. • **Sept 23.** PM Pote announces that his government will oppose all subversive activities.
- **Dec 26.** PM Pote steps down disheartened after gaining a bare working majority in December's general election.

1958
- **Jan 1.** Sarit's deputy, General Thanom Kittikachorn, steps in as Prime Minister but will lose a majority of assembly seats to the Democrats in March, tying his hands. • **Jan 11.** Cambodia sends an informal note to the UN claiming sovereignty over the ruins of the ninth-century Khmer temple at Preah Vihear held by Thailand. • **Jan 27.** At the Southeast Asian Round Table Meeting, Thailand's new Prime Minister, Thanom Kittikachorn, argues for a canal linking the Andaman Sea and the Gulf of Thailand.
- **Feb 12.** The government announces that, under the new Constitution, the powers of the Prime Minister would be similar to those of the American president.
- **Mar 11.** It is announced that a new economic and social development board will be set up to create long-term plans for the development of the economy.
- **Mar 24.** The government says that it will establish an organization to promote foreign investment with assistance from the World Bank.
- **Aug 8.** The government declares a state of emergency along the Cambodian border as diplomatic relations with that country are broken.
- **Oct 20.** Returning from treatment and recuperation overseas, Field Marshal Sarit abrogates the Constitution, dissolves parliament and proclaims martial law, proclaiming that the events of September 1957 did not constitute a coup but a "revolution"; a Communist witch-hunt ensues and sympathizers are also arrested under the Anti-communist act.

1959
- **Jan 19.** The government bans the sale of all Chinese goods.
- **Feb 9.** Field Marshal Sarit becomes Thailand's fourteenth Prime Minister.
- **Apr 22.** PM Sarit establishes a committee to look into the formation of a national tourism organization.

Field Marshal Sarit.

- **June 24.** PM Sarit formally opens the Krungthep and Nontaburi bridges across the Chao Phraya River.
- **July 1.** Legal opium smoking comes to an end, a milestone burned into the night with a fire set with 8,935 confiscated opium pipes.
- **Aug 24.** Thai Airways and Scandinavian Airlines System (SAS) sign an agreement to form a new company – Thai Airways International – to operate international services from Thailand. The new company, due to begin operations by the end of 1959, will be owned mostly by Thais, with SAS taking a minority shareholding.
- **Dec 18.** Their Majesties the King and Queen embark on a state visit to the Republic of Vietnam.

HIS MAJESTY THE KING ENTERS THE MONKHOOD

1956

- **Oct 22.** In accordance with Thai tradition, HM the King takes the name Bhumibhalo and becomes a Buddhist monk for fifteen days, during which time HM the Queen assumes constitutional reign; a crowd of a hundred thousand gathers outside the Grand Palace while the Supreme Patriarch presides over the rites of the three denominations of Thai Buddhism—Phra Tamayud Nikai, Phra Maha Nikai and Phra Roman Nikai—at the Royal Chapel of the Temple of the Emerald Buddha.

ANCIENT PAINTING

1959

- **Jan 3.** The religious paintings and images of the Lord Buddha discovered under the stupa of Wat Rajburana in Ayutthaya are significant, says Professor Silpa Birasri of the Fine Arts Department. They reveal that Thai painting depicting the life of the Lord Buddha did not begin in the middle of the sixteenth century but 120 years earlier.

THE KINGDOM'S FIRST PRIZEFIGHTER

1960

● **Apr 16.** After the fight delay of several weeks, Pone Kingpetch wins the World Flyweight Championship from Argentina's Pasqual Perez by a majority decision at Lumpini Stadium, becoming Thailand's first world boxing champion.

THAI AIRWAYS FIRST FLIGHT

1960

● **May 1.** This Douglas DC-6B makes history as the start of a new international airline soon to become known around the world.

THE PREAH VIHEAR CASE

1962

● **June 15.** Following hearings that began on April 10, the International Court of Justice gives Cambodia sovereignty over the Khmer temple at Preah Vihear that has been occupied by Thai border police since 1957.

FIELD MARSHAL SARIT DIES

1963

● **Dec 8.** Field Marshal Sarit, Prime Minister since 1958, dies at the age of fifty-five. Entering Phra Chula Chom Klao Military Academy at the age of eleven, FM Sarit became Commander of the King's First Guards Regiment in 1946, emerging as a political figure the following year when he supported Phibun's coup to oust PM Pridi, subsequently sending PM Phibun into exile in the bloodless coup of 1957.

1960

● **Jan 20.** The Cabinet approves a bill to control prostitution.
● **Jan 25.** British author W Somerset Maugham celebrates his eighty-sixth birthday quietly at the Erawan Hotel before being honored by students at the Faculty of Arts of Chulalongkorn University.
● **Feb 1.** Implementing a cabinet decision to discourage rock and roll, the Interior Ministry orders Bangkok municipality to prohibit bands from playing it in Lumpini Park. ● **Feb 8.** Their Majesties the King and Queen embark on a state visit to Indonesia.
● **Mar 2.** Their Majesties the King and Queen embark on a tour of Burma. ● **Mar 3.** The government says that the new Tourist Organization of Thailand aims to ensure the fair treatment of tourists as well as to improve facilities. ● **June 14.** Their Majesties the King and Queen embark on a month-long tour of the US.
● **July 19.** Their Majesties the King and Queen arrive in Britain for a five-day state visit.

1961

● **Feb 13.** Following a two-day meeting in Kuala Lumpur, representatives of the governments of Thailand, Malaya and the Philippines sign an agreement for the formation of an association of Southeast Asian nations. ● **Apr 16.** President Ahmed Sukarno of Indonesia arrives for a five-day visit.
● **May 16.** US Vice President Lyndon B Johnson arrives in Thailand for talks with PM Sarit.
● **May 18.** The government announces that SEATO members will send troops to Thailand as a precaution against civil war in Laos, including some four thousand American soldiers. ● **July 31.** The governments of Thailand, Malaya and the Philippines announce the establishment of the Association of Southeast Asian States (ASA). "Asa", it is said, means "hope" in the languages of all three member countries.
● **Oct 3.** The Economic Committee for Asia and the Far East agrees to establish an Asian Institute for Economic Development in Bangkok.
● **Oct 23.** Cambodia breaks off its diplomatic relations with Thailand. ● **Oct 24.** The fiftieth anniversary of the death of HM King Chulalongkorn.
● **Dec 8.** The president of Argentina and Madame Frondizi arrive for a three-day visit.

1962

● **Jan 12.** Their Majesties King Frederik IX and Queen Ingrid of Denmark arrive for a twelve-day visit.
● **Aug 2.** PM Sarit opens the new premises of the National Economic Development Council on Krung Kasem Road, saying that, "the heart of the work of the Revolutionary Government is economic development". ● **Nov 21.** The president of the Federal Republic of Germany and Madame Heinrich Lübke arrive in Bangkok for a five-day visit.
● **Dec 14.** The chairman of the Revolutionary Council of the Union of Burma, General Ne Win, arrives for a week-long visit.

W Somerset Maugham with Chulalongkorn University students.

1963

● **Jan 4.** The nineteenth meeting of the Committee for the Coordination of Investigations of the Lower Mekong Basin is held in Vientiane, Laos; participants include the four riparian countries of Thailand, Laos, Cambodia and Vietnam, along with representatives of sixteen other countries and eleven UN agencies.
● **Jan 6.** The New York Couture Group's annual list of the World's Twelve Best Dressed Women includes HM the Queen, along with Jacqueline Kennedy and Britain's Princess Alexandra of Kent.
● **Feb 2.** HM the King opens the first Thai Industrial Fair at Saranrom Gardens.
● **Feb 14.** Their Majesties King Paul I and Queen Frederika of the Hellenes arrive for a two-week visit.
● **Mar 22.** His Majesty King Sri Savang Vatthana of Laos arrives for a three-day visit.
● **May 8.** The United States Southeast Asia Trade Center opens in Bangkok.
● **July 2.** In a televised address, PM Sarit explains that Thailand will comply with a World Court ruling and withdraw from the temple at Preah Vihear.
● **July 16.** The temple at Preah Vihear is officially returned to Cambodia. ● **Oct 15.** Her Majesty Queen Juliana and His Royal Highness Prince Bernhard of the Netherlands arrive for a week-long visit.
● **Dec 5.** HM the King celebrates his thirty-sixth birthday, thus entering his fourth twelve-year cycle of Buddhism. ● **Dec 9.** Following the death of PM Sarit, Thanom Kittikachorn returns as Prime Minister.
● **Dec 18.** The British government announces that, out of its commitment to SEATO, it will build an airfield near Mukdahan in northeastern Thailand.
● **Dec 30.** His Royal Highness Prince Chula Chakrabongse dies in Britain.

1964

● **Jan 10.** Cambodian Head of State Prince Norodom Sihanouk offers to sign a non-aggression pact with Thailand, the latter recognizes Cambodia's borders.
● **Jan 23.** Robert Kennedy arrives in Bangkok to discuss solutions to the conflict between Malaysia and Indonesia over the status of Sarawak and Sabah in Borneo. ● **Feb 3.** Their Majesties King Baudouin and Queen Fabiola of Belgium arrive in Bangkok for a week-long visit. ● **Feb 24.** Their Majesties the Yang di-Pertuan Agong and the Raja Permaisuri Agong of Malaysia arrive for a week-long visit.
● **Mar 17.** The late PM Sarit is cremated.

- **July 3.** Maritime laws are promulgated for the first time.
- **July 3.** HM the King holds an exhibition of his modern and abstract paintings at the National Museum.

- **Sept 7.** Thai and Malaysian officials hold "secret" talks on border security.
- **Sept 29.** Their Majesties the King and Queen attend the wedding of King Constantine of Greece and Princess Anne-Marie of Denmark.
- **Sept 29.** Their Majesties the King and Queen arrive in Austria for a week-long visit.
- **Oct 10.** Thailand sends a one hundred-member team to the Olympic Games in Tokyo.
- **Nov 18.** The Cabinet approves PM Thanom's use of Article XVII of the Interim Constitution to seize the estate of the late PM Sarit in order to retrieve 627 million baht he is alleged to have used for personal purposes. • **Dec 14.** Their Imperial Highnesses Crown Prince Akihito and Crown Princess Michiko of Japan arrive in Bangkok for a week-long visit.

1965

- **Jan 15.** His Majesty King Olav of Norway arrives in Bangkok for an eight-day visit.
- **Feb 2.** His Royal Highness Prince Bertil of Sweden arrives in Bangkok for an eight-day visit.
- **July 22.** PM Thanom and Deputy PM Prapass Charusathien cast doubt on the proposed new Constitution, concerned about communist subversion.
- **July 30.** The government announces a 100 million baht plan to ease traffic congestion.

1966

- **Feb 10.** The president of the Republic of Korea and Madame Park Chung Hee arrive in Bangkok for a three-day visit. • **Aug 22.** Their Majesties the King and Queen depart for state visits to Germany and Austria.
- **Oct 28.** US President Lyndon B Johnson visits Thailand as a guest of HM the King and receives an Honorary Doctor of Political Science degree from Chulalongkorn University. • **Dec 7.** The US government acknowledges that American helicopters are flying Thai troops to zones near anti-guerrilla operations in northeastern Thailand.

1967

- **Jan 3.** The government announces that a battalion of one thousand troops is to be sent to South Vietnam by March. • **Jan 17.** President Franz Jonas of the Republic of Austria arrives for a nine-day visit.
- **Jan 18.** The American ambassador confirms that the US has 35,000 troops in Thailand as part of its military

buildup. • **Feb 22.** American author John Steinbeck and his wife are granted an audience with HM the King. • **Mar 9.** Thai and American government officials confirm that American planes based in Thailand have been bombing targets in North Vietnam for the past two years. • **Mar 27.** Their Majesties the King and Queen open a three-day festival in celebration of the fiftieth anniversary of Chulalongkorn University.
- **Apr 23.** Their Majesties the King and Queen begin a week-long visit to Iran followed by a twenty-three-day visit to the US and Canada.
- **June 20.** Thai and Cambodian troops clash on the border; the government claims thirteen Cambodian casualties. • **Aug 10.** PM Thanom opens the biggest American-built airbase in Thailand at U-Tapao on the Eastern Seaboard. • **Sept 21.** 2,200 Thai infantry troops begin to arrive in Saigon, the first Thai combat forces in Vietnam. • **Oct 30.** PM Thanom announces that Thailand will send a division of twelve thousand troops to Vietnam. • **Dec 16.** HM the King shares a gold medal with Princess Ubol Ratana for yachting at the Southeast Asia Peninsular Games.

HM King Bhumibol out sailing.

1968

- **Jan 1.** HM the King tells the nation in his annual New Year's message that Thailand has sent troops to help South Vietnam, "because it benefits our country directly". • **Jan 12.** The new Constitution is passed in its second reading. • **Jan 15.** The president of the Philippines and Madame Ferdinand E Marcos arrive in Bangkok for a five-day visit.

FIELD MARSHAL PHIBUN DIES

1964

- **June 11.** Field Marshal Phibun Songkhram dies of an apparent heart attack in Tokyo at the age of sixty-seven. FM Phibun left Thailand in 1957 following a coup by Field Marshal Sarit and, after teaching at a college in California, went into quiet exile in Japan; he was Prime Minister from 1938 to 1944 and from 1948 to 1957.

THE FIRST MISS UNIVERSE

1965

- **July 12.** Standing in Miami Beach before an American television audience of some sixty million viewers, eighteen-year-old Apasara Hongsakula, nicknamed "Pook", beats fifty-six other international contestants and becomes the first Thai to be crowned Miss Universe.

A LEGEND VANISHES

1967

- **Mar 27.** James HW ("Jim") Thompson—a long-time resident of Thailand and the man credited with putting Thai silk on the world map—disappears mysteriously in Malaysia. The sixty-one-year-old silk magnate had "gone for a walk" in the jungles of the Cameron Highlands while on vacation; he never returned, but to this day the company he founded, which now employs some three thousand people, continues to sell silk around the world.

THE VIETNAM WAR HEATS UP

1968

● **Apr 11.** Thai troops join a hundred thousand allied soldiers from five countries in an offensive in eleven provinces around Saigon.

ASTRONAUTS TOUCH DOWN

1969

● **Oct 29.** Thousands of well-wishers turn out to greet Neil Armstrong and Edwin Aldrin; during their four-day visit, the "moon astronauts" receive the Key to Bangkok from the Lord Mayor and are granted an audience with HM the King.

DEATH OF A SUPERSTAR

1970

● **Oct 29.** The kingdom's most beloved movie star, Mitr Chaibancha, falls three hundred meters to his death from a rope dangling from a helicopter during a film shoot. Hugely popular among movie audiences nationwide, the star who preferred to do his own stunts was shooting the final scenes of *Inthree Thong*—"The Golden Eagle".

● **Jan 22.** Their Imperial Majesties Mohammad Reza Pahlavi Aryamehr Shahansha and Farah Pahlavi Shahbanou of Iran arrive for a week-long visit.
● **Jan 24.** The national Thai soccer team defeats Indonesia 1-0 to qualify for the Olympics for the first time. ● **Feb 14.** Spectacular fires rage through Chiang Mai and Khorat causing more than 100 million baht in damage. ● **Apr 17.** PM Thanom departs for a thirty-two-day trip to six countries.
● **May 1.** His Imperial Majesty Haile Selassie I of Ethiopia arrives in Bangkok for a four-day visit.
● **June 20.** HM the King presides over the promulgation of the new Constitution.
● **Dec 5.** Foreign Minister Thanat Khoman proposes special tariff arrangements between Thailand, the Philippines and Malaysia.
● **Dec 17.** HM the King opens a new power line across the Mekong River to Laos.

1969

● **Jan 1.** HM the King tells the nation in his New Year's radio address to remain united and alert to maintain prosperity and, "rid our nation of her enemies".
● **Jan 8.** The Cabinet approves in principle labor legislation that will allow workers to form associations.
● **Feb 10.** A general election is held—the tenth in the thirty seven years since absolute monarchy ended; Prime Minister Thanom Kittikachorn forms the government. ● **Apr 16.** The first Asian Highway Motor Rally begins, from Vientiane to Singapore via Thailand and Malaysia. ● **May 2.** The census shows that there are now 34 million Thais.

● **July 2.** Public health officials declare that the current cholera epidemic must be halted lest the economy suffers. ● **July 28.** The president of the United States and Madame Richard M Nixon arrive for a four-day visit.
● **Aug 19.** The Mekong River bursts its banks creating the worst floods in twenty-seven years.
● **Sept 26.** Armored units and troops are dispatched to the south to suppress bandits and Communists.
● **Oct 1.** The US government announces that it will withdraw six thousand military personnel from Thailand. ● **Dec 8.** Royal Thai Air Force planes strike at communist positions on the Malaysian border.
● **Dec 11.** The US government announces that it will cut thirty B52 bombers from its strike force in Thailand. ● **Dec 12.** The rail link between Thailand and Malaysia is cut by activists who blow up a bridge at Tok Mak village. ● **Dec 21.** The National Education Council grants permission to establish private colleges in Bangkok and Thonburi.

1970

● **Jan 3.** US Vice President Spiro Agnew arrives in Bangkok. ● **Jan 21.** WAR Wood—long-time resident consul general in Chiang Mai and author of *History of Siam* and *Consul in Paradise*—dies after forty years of retirement. ● **Feb 11.** Draft legislation is approved requiring foreigners to obtain permits to work or do business in Thailand. ● **Mar 19.** The president of the Republic of Indonesia and Madame Suharto arrive in Bangkok for a four-day visit.
● **Mar 20.** Chartchai Chionoi becomes the new world flyweight boxing champion after defeating Mexican Efren Torres in Bangkok. ● **Apr 7.** The second boxing champion in eighteen days is crowned in Bangkok as Berkerk Chartvanchai defeats Bernabe Villacampo.
● **Apr 28.** Their Majesties the King and Queen celebrate their twentieth wedding anniversary at the Summer Palace in Hua Hin.
● **July 2.** The government increases tariffs on two hundred imported items in an attempt to reduce the trade deficit. ● **Aug 27.** The worst floods in a decade leave nineteen provinces under water.
● **Sept 10.** Four thousand Chulalongkorn University students force their way into parliament for ninety minutes to obtain promises from the government to curb corruption. ● **Sept 21.** Communist insurgents murder Chiang Rai governor Prayad Samanmit.
● **Oct 10.** American playwright Tennessee Williams arrives in Bangkok to discuss an undisclosed illness with one of HM the King's physicians.
● **Dec 10.** In front of 25,000 spectators, HM the King declares the Sixth Asian Games officially open.
● **Dec 21.** As the Sixth Asian Games draws to a close, Thailand's medal tally of nine gold, seventeen silver and thirteen bronze puts the kingdom in third place behind Japan and South Korea.

1971

• **Jan 22.** Thousands turn out for the cremation of movie star Mitr Chaibancha at Wat Thepsirin in Bangkok. • **Feb 7.** HM the King tells Kasetsart University students to be doers and not talkers when they go out into the countryside to help the farming community. • **Feb 14.** Thai military forces are put on full alert after the Lao government announces a state of emergency. • **Apr 14.** PM Thanom signs a decree to lift martial law in thirty-four of the seventy-one provinces. • **May 1.** The government orders a complete overhaul of the nation's civil service.
• **May 16.** The kingdom's first "open" university—Ramkhamhaeng—accepts its first enrollments.
• **June 25.** The Cabinet appoints Dr Khunying Amphon Meesuk to the post of Deputy Under Secretary of State for Education, the first woman in the history of the civil service to be promoted to such a high position.

Dr Khunying Amphon Meesuk.

• **July 1.** HM the King presides over the opening ceremonies at the National Stadium marking the sixtieth anniversary of the Boy Scout Movement in Thailand.
• **Nov 14.** Withdrawal of American troops from Thailand is suspended due to the civil wars in Laos and Cambodia. • **Dec 19.** A highway collision kills the Supreme Patriarch Ariyawongsakhatayan; the kingdom mourns for fifteen days.

1972

• **Feb 9.** Her Majesty Queen Elizabeth II and His Royal Highness Prince Philip, Duke of Edinburgh, arrive in Bangkok for a six-day visit.
• **Mar 27.** The president of India Shri Varahagiri Venkata Giri and Shrimati Sarasvathi Giri arrive for a four-day visit. • **Aug 11.** Police apprehend thirty alleged senior members of the Communist Party of Thailand. • **Aug 18.** HM the King grants amnesty to former commander Anand Punturikapa, alleged to have been the organizer of the 1951 "Manhattan Coup".
• **Sept 30.** Venice Bawkawsaw wins the WBC Flyweight World Boxing Championship—the kingdom's fourth world champion but the first southpaw.
• **Oct 12.** New hundred-baht notes are issued by the bank of Thailand. • **Oct 13.** Thailand sends a seventeen-member trade mission to the Canton Trade Fair in China. • **Nov 26.** Thousands of students burn effigies of Japanese goods outside Silapakorn University and outside the NEC headquarters protesting against Japanese business in Thailand.
• **Dec 15.** HM the King signs a new Constitution and appoints PM Thanom interim head of government.
• **Dec 19.** A new Bangkok city administration plan is proposed: a governor and deputy governor will replace the lord mayor and the city will be renamed Krungthep Mahanakorn. • **Dec 28.** While His Royal Highness Prince Vajiralongkorn is undergoing his investiture ceremony, six Palestinian terrorists break into the Israeli Embassy at gun point. Informed by Air Chief Marshal Dawee Chullasapya that they are violating a sacred

occasion, the Palestinians apologize and agree to leave peacefully on a plane to Cairo.

1973

• **Jan 31.** A massive blaze destroys the center of the northeastern provincial capital of Surin. • **Feb 1.** Their Majesties the Yang di-Pertuan Agong and the Raja Permaisuri Agong of Malaysia arrive for an eight-day visit.
• **Feb 4.** The government announces plans to offer amnesty and land to communist insurgents who surrender.
• **Mar 16.** A new Alien Occupation Bill goes into effect regulating foreigners who work in Thailand. • **Apr 1.** HM the King opens the Phra Buddhalertah Napalai Bridge, the longest in the kingdom. • **Apr 22.** The world's biggest drug haul, estimated at US$750 million, is found on a Thai trawler off the coast of South Vietnam.
• **Apr 24.** A cholera epidemic hits ten provinces.
• **Apr 28.** Oil is discovered 160 miles off Songkhla province in southern Thailand.
• **June 13.** A domestic rice shortage prompts the government to ban rice exports.
• **June 15.** Striking steelworkers take their complaints to the ILO in Geneva. • **June 18.** The table tennis team from China makes an historic first visit to Thailand. • **June 21.** A massive demonstration at Ramkhamhaeng University over the recent expulsion of nine students prompts the government to go on full alert. • **July 6.** Labor unrest continues as rail workers strike. • **Aug 14.** A major fire guts the first floor of the world-famous Oriental Hotel.
• **Aug 18.** The government asks the US to begin withdrawing the forty-to-fifty-thousand servicemen stationed in Thailand. • **Sept 27.** Eighty people are lost in a mining disaster in Chiang Rai.
• **Oct 10.** The government and students are set to clash as the former announces its decision to invoke Article XVII of the Constitution to detain twelve political activists.

HM King Bhumibol welcomes Indian President Shri Varahagiri Venkata Giri to Thailand.

A "REVOLUTIONARY PARTY"

1971

• **Nov 17.** A "revolutionary party" led by PM Thanom Kittikachorn seizes control of the nation in a coup at 7:00 pm, abrogates the Constitution, dissolves Parliament, disbands the Cabinet and declares martial law. Around 11:00 pm, HM the King gives his blessing to the "revolutionary party".

INVESTITURE OF HRH THE CROWN PRINCE

1972

• **Dec 28.** The Investiture of His Royal Highness Prince Vajiralongkorn marks the second such investiture in the Chakri Dynasty, the first having occurred in 1886 when Prince Vajirunhis became the Crown Prince. Having attended a preliminary Brahmin ceremony the previous day, His Royal Highness kneels before HM the King at the Ananta Samakom Throne Hall to accept his new title of Crown Prince Maha Vajiralongkorn, receiving his name, title seal, gold name plate, gold sword, decorations and rank emblems—a total of sixteen pieces.

HIS MAJESTY MEDIATES FOR PEACE

1973

• **Oct 13.** HM the King intervenes to diffuse a confrontation between students and the government, meeting first with PM Thanom and his delegation, who had earlier freed the twelve activists, and afterwards with a delegation from the National Students' Center of Thailand. The following day, however, violence breaks out in Bangkok.

BLOODY SUNDAY

1973

• **Oct 14.** Despite appeals by HM the King for all sides to keep the peace, riots erupt in Bangkok following the use in the morning of tear gas and live ammunition by police and military forces against students. To be remembered as "Bloody Sunday," the day of violence results in more than four hundred deaths, and ends with the resignation of PM Thanom and his Cabinet. As Thanom and his deputy Prapass flee the country, HM the King announces the Prime Minister's resignation and appoints Sanya Dharmasakti interim Prime Minister.

PM Sanya Dharmasakti.

A DANCE LEGEND ARRIVES

1974

• **Jan 10.** HM the King greets the "Queen of Modern Dance", Martha Graham.

PRINCE DHANI DIES

1974

• **September 8.** His Highness Prince Dhani Nivat, a noted scholar who acted as Regent during the reigns of both King Rama VIII and King Rama IX, dies in Bangkok.

• **Oct 11.** An estimated twenty thousand students gather at Thammasat University; similar meetings are held in Chiang Mai. • **Oct 28.** HM the King, in a speech to students at Amporn Gardens, urges all to work together to end corruption. • **Oct 31.** All of the assets of former Prime Minister Thanom, his son Colonel Narong Kittikachorn and former deputy Prime Minister Prapass are frozen over allegations of corruption.

• **Nov 29.** Strikes erupt across the country in many industrial sectors.

• **Dec 8.** Supreme Patriarch Somdej Phra Mahawirawongse dies at the age of seventy-seven; Patriarch Somdej Phra Ariyawongsa Khatayan is named Acting Supreme Patriarch.

• **Dec 17.** HM the King issues a Royal Decree dissolving the National Legislative Assembly to enable a new one to be appointed. • **Dec 27.** Rising world oil prices prompt the authorities to cut power and dim street lights in the capital. • Chinese-Thai relations resume with Deputy Foreign Minister Chatichai Chunhavan's visit to Beijing.

1974

• **Jan 10.** The arrival of Japanese Prime Minister Kakuei Tanaka sparks student protests and an anti-Japanese goods demonstration.

• **Jan 18.** Police launch a nationwide campaign against profiteers and hoarders. • **Apr 15.** Shooting of the new James Bond movie *The Man with the Golden Gun* begins in Thailand.

• **May 22.** The entire Cabinet resigns.

• **May 29.** HM the King reappoints Sanya Dharmasakti Prime Minister. • **June 4.** Air America formally announces that it is ceasing its operations and turning all of its equipment over to Thai Airways.

• **June 13.** Thirty-four workers' associations jointly submit a list of labor demands to the government.

• **July 19.** The National Assembly votes to use Article XVII to seize all property of the three former military strongmen—Thanom, Narong and Prapass.

• **Aug 24.** Strikes hit the kingdom's hotel industry.

• **Oct 6.** The National Assembly passes a Draft Constitution; it is promulgated two days later.

• **Oct 9.** The Interior Ministry announces that half a million hilltribe people will be granted Thai nationality.

• **Oct 14.** HM the King leads the nation in symbolic

cremation ceremonies for the victims of the bloody uprising of October 1973.

• **Nov 30.** Farmers end a seventeen-day demonstration in front of government house with a rally of twenty thousand demanding land claims.

• **Dec 28.** Former Prime Minister Thanom is arrested after secretly entering the kingdom; two days later he returns to exile in Singapore. • **Dec 31.** HM the King, in his New Year's address to the nation, urges unity among all Thais, especially in such difficult times.

1975

• **Feb 13.** HM the King dissolves Parliament.

• **Feb 14.** The House of Representatives elects Democrat Party Chief Mom Rajawongse Seni Pramoj Thailand's fourteenth Prime Minister.

• **Mar 4.** The new coalition government announces plans to expel the remaining 25,000 American servicemen in Thailand.

• **Mar 7.** After just two weeks in office, the government is defeated in a no-confidence motion.

• **Apr 17.** The communist Khmer Rouge take power in Cambodia sweeping into capital Phnom Penh and emptying it of its residents.

PM Seni Pramoj.

• **Apr 28.** Their Majesties the King and Queen celebrate their Silver Wedding Anniversary.

• **May 1.** The Vietnam War is over as Saigon falls to the North Vietnamese Army and the communist government in Hanoi. • **May 18.** A demonstration at the American Embassy symbolizes rising anti-American sentiment. • **June 20.** The Stock Exchange of Thailand opens. • **July 1.** PM Kukrit and Chinese Premier Chou En Lai sign a communique normalizing Sino-Thai relations.

PM Kukrit and Chinese Premier Chou En Lai.

• **July 16.** Saensak Muangsurin becomes junior welterweight world boxing champion.

• **Aug 13.** Buddhists nationwide mourn the collapse of the That Phanom Chedi in Nakorn Phanom.

• **Aug 19.** Protesting police hold a rally in Bangkok and ransack PM Kukrit's residence.

• **Aug 20.** Vocational students violently attack Thammasat University. • **Aug 23.** The communist Pathet Lao sweep into Vientiane and take control of the government of Laos. • **Sept 20.** Buses in Bangkok stop as transport workers strike. • **Oct 20.** Thailand appeals to the UN for help with its more than seventy thousand Indochinese refugees. • **Dec 5.** His Majesty the King celebrates his forty-eighth birthday, entering his fifth twelve-year Buddhist cycle.

• **Dec 15.** During an address at the annual Trooping of the Colors at the Royal Plaza, HM the King warns that Thailand is now the target of an enemy that wants to take over the country.

1976

• **Mar 1.** Socialist Party for Thailand leader Dr Boonsanong Punyodyana is assassinated amid growing social tension. • **Apr 3.** The Democrat Party wins the general election by a landslide.

• **Apr 20.** HM the King appoints MR Seni Pramoj Prime Minister leading a four-party coalition.

• **Aug 1.** Foreign Minister Bhichai Rattakul starts a process of rapprochement with Laos and Vietnam during visits to Vientiane and Hanoi.

• **Aug 21.** PM Seni is granted an audience with HM the King to report on the controversial and clandestine return of former deputy Prime Minister Prapass.

• **Aug 22.** Violence erupts during an anti-Prapass rally at Thammasat University. • **Aug 23.** After being grant-

General Prapass.

ed an audience with HM the King, Prapass retreats back into exile.

• **Oct 3.** Students launch nationwide protests following the government's failure to force into

exile former Prime Minister Thanom, who recently returned in secrecy and entered the monkhood.

• **Oct 5.** Anti-Thanom student protesters occupy Thammasat University, which closes. An army radio station calls for public violence against the students.

• **Oct 6.** Thammasat University students are beaten, shot, and lynched in an orgy of violence against them propagated by the police, army and others. The military moves in, the Constitution is suspended, and high court justice Thanin Kraivichien is named Prime Minister.

• **Oct. 18.** Sweeping powers of arrest are granted to new Prime Minister Thanin Kraivichien.

Prime Minister Thanin Kraivichien (middle).

• **Oct 20.** The tenth Constitution is promulgated.
• **Dec 7.** All charges against former Prime Minister Thanom, his son Narong and former deputy Prime Minister Prapass are dropped.

1977

• **Jan 26.** PM Thanin announces plans to offer an "eight-year tax holiday" and other incentives to foreign investors. • **Jan 30.** Khmer Rouge troops attack three villages on the Thai-Cambodian border, killing thirty.

• **Feb 3.** During a visit to Thailand by Singapore Prime Minister Lee Kwan Yew, the two countries announce across-the-board preferential tariff reductions of 10 percent on all products traded.

• **Feb 5.** The Thai-Malay "Hot Pursuit" border pact is signed. • **Feb 17.** The Private Secretary to HM the Queen, Mom Chao Vibhavadi Rangsit, is killed in a helicopter crash while distributing Royal Gifts to Border Patrol police in the south.

• **Mar 4.** 229 detainees from the October 6, 1976 riots are released. • **Mar 10.** Sixteen foreign ambassadors meet and pledge support for the government's Fourth Economic Development Plan.

• **Mar 25.** Fifty Thai villagers die at Bang Wan Kha as Burmese forces shell the border area.

• **Mar 26.** An attempted coup by a small group of Army officers is put down.

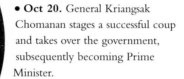
Prime Minister Kriangsak Chomanan.

• **Apr 30.** PM Thanin invokes Article XXI of the constitution to dissolve the Bangkok Metropolitan Authority and the Bangkok Metropolitan Assembly.

• **May 31.** A two-hundred-ton oil spill severely pollutes parts of the Chao Phraya River.

• **Oct 20.** General Kriangsak Chomanan stages a successful coup and takes over the government, subsequently becoming Prime Minister.

• **Dec 5.** His Majesty the King bestows upon Her Royal Highness Princess Sirindhorn the title of "Maha Chakri", meaning "The Great Chakri".

PM KUKRIT PRAMOJ

1975

• **March 14.** HM the King appoints Mom Rajawongse Kukrit Pramoj, brother of PM Seni Pramoj, Thailand's fifteenth Prime Minister.

DEATH OF A SCHOLAR PRINCE

1976

• **Sept 6.** The kingdom's greatest scholar and pioneering statesman, His Royal Highness Prince Wan Waithayakorn, dies at the age of 85. Following his early education in Bangkok, Prince Wan received a scholarship to study at Marlborough College in Britain where he won no fewer than seventeen awards for academic excellence, after which he earned a bachelors degree with honors in history from Balliol College, Oxford. He then embarked on a highly successful diplomatic career representing Thailand at the League of Nations prior to being elected president of the General Assembly of the United Nations. Despite his considerable diplomatic successes, however, Prince Wan will be remembered as the person who introduced so many new terms into the Thai language, including the Thai words for the United States of America, revolution, mass media, television and development.

1978
• **Nov 5.** HRH the Crown Prince is ordained as a monk.

1981
• **Apr 1.** Their Majesties and PM Prem flee together to Khorat in the wake of a coup attempt by the "Young Turks" group of military officers. After a nationally broadcast radio announcement by HM the Queen that PM Prem is staying with the Royal Couple as their guest, the capital is retaken, with only two casualties, by troops loyal to PM Prem as opposition crumbles—the coup's leader, General Sant Chitpatina, is forced into exile in Burma.

1978

• **Jan 11.** The first economic, technical and aviation agreements are signed with Vietnam.
• **Feb 10.** Import of a range of luxury goods is banned in an attempt to tackle the trade deficit.
• **Feb 16.** The government orders forces to move against opium warlord Khun Sa and his troops in his Chiang Rai stronghold. • **May 16.** The government orders that a plan for a rapid transit system be drafted and implemented within five years.
• **Aug 29.** The minimum wage is raised to thirty-five baht a day. • **Sept 15.** The National Legislative Assembly passes an Amnesty Bill freeing the "Thammasat 18" after almost two years in prison; the accused had pleaded not guilty to charges of communist activities, treason, murder, attempted murder and illegal possession of war weapons.
• **Sept 29.** General Prem Tinsulanonda replaces General Serm na Nakorn as Army Commander in Chief. • **Oct 2.** Floods cut major road and rail links in the north and northeast; when they eventually subside, thirty-seven people will have lost their lives and nearly 2.5 million rai of farmland been inundated across twenty-eight provinces.
• **Oct 16.** The Chao Phraya River rises to 1.93 meters above sea level at Memorial Bridge, flooding much of Bangkok and Thonburi. • **Oct 18.** Eighteen-year-old Siriporn Savanglam is crowned Miss Asia.
• **Dec 8.** Thailand hosts the Eighth Asian Games at which more than five thousand athletes compete for seven hundred medals; the kingdom finishes with eleven gold, ranking fifth behind Japan, China, North Korea and South Korea.

1979

• **Jan 4.** On a mission of peace to Vientiane, PM Kriangsak appeals to Lao leaders to, "forget the misunderstandings of the past and begin a new era of mutual understanding and good relations".
• **Jan 8.** Thailand closes its borders to refugees from embattled Cambodia. • **Feb 27.** Air conditioners in all government offices are switched off indefinitely as one of a series of measures to reduce energy consumption.
• **Mar 4.** President Ne Win of the Socialist Republic of the Union of Burma arrives for a three-day visit.
• **Apr 8.** The president of the People's Republic of Bangladesh and Begum Ziaur Rahman arrive for a three-day visit.• **Apr 21.** The Social Action party led by former Prime Minister MR Kukrit wins eighty-three of the 301 seats in the general election but declines to start a government.
• **May 11.** At a joint session of the House and Senate, Prime Minister Kriangsak receives approval to form the forty-second government since the 1932 coup; says Kriangsak, "I am glad that the Parliament has confidence in me". • **June 2.** Fifty people are burned alive in Phang-nga province when a bus collides with an oil truck. • **June 3.** The Navy is ordered to repel all boats arriving with refugees from Vietnam. • **Aug 21.** Fifty-one people die

when an out-of-control freight train plows into a city-bound passenger train. • **Oct 15.** The number of Cambodian refugees in the kingdom swells to 91,000.

1980

• **Jan 17.** Eight thousand striking workers are fired by the Thailand Tobacco Monopoly when they defy a back-to-work order issued by the Prime Minister; they are reinstated on January 23—without the cost of living adjustment they have sought.
• **Feb 4.** PM Kriangsak calls for a halt to the buying and selling of votes in Parliament.
• **Feb 10.** Oil prices are raised 24 to 72 percent depending on grade. • **Feb 19.** Chalard Vorachat calls off a hunger strike after thirty-four hours without achieving his goal of lower oil prices.
• **Feb 28.** PM Kriangsak resigns at a parliamentary session convened to hear the government defend its recent oil price hikes.
• **Mar 3.** HM the King appoints General Prem Tinsulanonda Prime Minister. • **Mar 19.** The new government announces oil price reductions.
• The director of TV Channel 7, Chaicharn Thienprapass, is assassinated.
• **Apr 11.** Their Majesties the King and Queen preside over a mass cremation for national heroes killed in communist suppression operations.

Prime Minister Prem Tinsulanonda. • **Apr 28.** Their Majesties the King and Queen celebrate their thirtieth wedding anniversary.
• **July 5.** The government declares the entire twelve-hundred-kilometer border with Laos closed.
• **July 22.** The Cabinet slaps a 15 percent surcharge on excessive electricity consumption.
• **Aug 26.** The government passes a new anti-corruption bill. • **Oct 1.** Bangkok schools are ordered closed due to heavy flooding.

1981

• **Jan 8.** Power rates are raised for the third time in twelve months, this time by 15 percent.
• **Jan 14.** Figures show that droughts, floods and rising oil prices caused the consumer price index to rise 19.7 percent the previous year. • **Feb 24.** Former student leader Thirayuth Boonmee emerges from exile in the jungle and surrenders to military authorities.
• **Mar 25.** Indonesian President Suharto arrives for a two-day visit. • **Apr 15.** The Eastern Seaboard Industrial Deep-Sea Port Development Committee chaired by PM Prem decides to put a multi-million-dollar heavy industrial zone in Rayong province.
• **May 5.** On the occasion of the thirty-first anniversary of his coronation, HM the King grants amnesty to fifty-two suspected coup-plotters. Although General Sant and seven other plotters are not mentioned in the Royal Pardon, the House of Representatives passes a bill granting amnesty to them all on May 22. • **May 24.** One of the heaviest rainfalls ever recorded—221.6 mm in two days or about one-seventh of the annual

Thirayuth Boonmee

total—submerges most of the streets in the capital.

• **June 6.** Time bombs attributed to Muslim extremists from the south rock three crowded shopping centers in Bangkok injuring forty people.

• **June 10.** Interior Minister Prathuang Kiratibutr resigns over increasing public concern about rising crime. • **June 22.** Fugitive coup leader General Sant returns from self-imposed exile in Burma.

• **July 3.** The president of the Republic of Korea and Madame Chun Doo Hwan arrive for a four-day visit.

• **July 30.** The Army uncovers a huge Communist Party arsenal in Bangkok. • **Sept 9.** A new daily minimum wage of sixty-one baht is announced for Bangkok and its five neighboring provinces.

• **Dec 9.** Domestic and international postal and telecommunications services are cut for nine hours as Communications Authority of Thailand workers strike.

1982

• **Feb 8.** Fifteen people are injured when a homemade bomb explodes in a Bangkok cinema.

• **Feb 25.** Their Majesties the King and Queen preside over the opening of Naresuan Dam in Phitsanuloke.

• **Feb 26.** In a bid to bridge the gap between rich and poor, the government announces that it will lower personal income taxes, raise the business tax on banks and introduce a property sales tax.

• **Mar 16.** The American Embassy in Bangkok announces a 25 percent increase in economic and military aid to Thailand. • **June 4.** All twenty-four cabinet members targeted in a no-confidence debate survive following a secret ballot. • **June 25.** Parliament throws the Prem administration into its most serious political crisis to date when it rejects the final reading of a government-sponsored bill calling for major amendments to the Constitution.

• **July 3.** Thailand formally recognizes the coalition government of Democratic Kampuchea, hosting a grand banquet at the Ministry of Foreign Affairs for the president, HRH Prince Norodom Sihanouk.

• **Sept. 9.** A powerful bomb explodes beside the Ministry of Defense injuring seven. • **Dec 2.** A powerful bomb explosion at the former Iraqi Consulate in Bangkok kills the Police Department's top bomb disposal expert, Lieutenant Colonel Surat Sumanat. • **Dec 13.** The rector of Khon Kaen University is ousted by student protesters.

Tawee Ampornmaha.

1983

• **Jan 7.** Thailand officially launches a massive petrochemicals complex to be built on the Eastern Seaboard. • **Feb 3.** HM the King issues a Royal Command to reopen Parliament for an extraordinary session to hear a constitutional amendment bill.

• **Mar 13.** Democrat MP Chalard Vorachat vows a hunger strike to the death if the constitutional amendment draft passes its final reading.

• **Mar 16.** Parliament rejects by a ten-vote margin an Army-backed attempt to amend the Constitution; Parliament is subsequently dissolved and elections called for April 18. • **Mar 26.** A bomb explodes in

front of Democrat Party headquarters. • **Apr 18.** The Prem government receives a new mandate in the general election.

• **Apr 30.** HM the King signs a Royal Command reappointing PM Prem. • Former underground leader and Prime Minister Pridi Banomyong dies in Paris of a heart attack at the age of eighty-three.

• **Sept 25.** Their Majesties King Hussein Bin Talaland and Queen Noor Al-Hussein of the Hashemite Kingdom of Jordan arrive for a three-day visit. • **Sept 28.** A record downpour of 97.6 cm in a single day creates havoc on Bangkok roads.

1984

• **Jan 11.** The Narcotics Control Board announces a program to reduce opium cultivation by 37 percent within ten years. • **Feb 3.** A radical one-way system introduced on seventeen Bangkok roads creates havoc.

• **Feb 29.** The president of the Federal Republic of Germany and Madame Karl Carstens arrive for a three-day visit. • **Apr 16.** More than eighty thousand Khmer civilians flee to refugee camps along Thailand's eastern border as Vietnam's dry season initiative against Kampuchean nationalists gains momentum.

• **May 22.** HM Queen Rambhai Barni dies at age eighty. • **July 2.** HM the King is presented with an honorary Doctor of Law degree from Tufts University; the presentation states that HM the King's, "lifelong commitment to the health, education and well-being of the Thai people is an example to leaders of all nations". • **July 3.** In an initiative to alleviate worsening traffic conditions, HM the King instructs police to stop blocking roads for unofficial Royal Motorcades.

• **Jul 30.** A charitable event turns to tragedy when nineteen of the nation's poor, mostly children, are trampled to death in a frenzied stampede for free rice.

• **Aug 14.** Boxer Tawee Ampornmaha returns home to a hero's welcome as Thailand's first Olympic silver medalist.

• **Sept 14.** PM Prem flies to the US for treatment of a heart condition.

• **Oct 4.** Doctors confirm the kingdom's first AIDS case. • **Oct 8.** Twenty-two-year-old Sot Chitalada becomes Thailand's eighth world boxing champion when he wins the flyweight crown from Mexico's Gabriel Bernal. • **Oct 16.** Sir Jeffrey Slaney, president of Britain's Royal College of Surgeons, presents an Honorary Membership to HM the King.

• **Nov 13.** Railmen go on strike across the country leaving thousands of passengers stranded for three days.

• Khaosai Galaxy knocks out Eusebio Espinal to win the World Boxing Association's junior bantamweight crown at Rajdamnern Stadium.

• **Dec 12.** Their Majesties King Birendra Bir Bikam Shah Dev and Queen Aishwarya Rajya Laxmi Devi Shah of Nepal arrive for a four-day visit.

THE ROYAL BARGES

1982

• **Apr 7.** For the first time in fifteen years, Their Majesties the King and Queen and Members of the Royal Family lead a flotilla of fifty-one Royal Barges down the Chao Phraya River as part of the Bicentennial celebrations of the Chakri Dynasty.

A PAPAL VISITATION

1984

• **May 10.** His Holiness Pope John Paul II arrives in Bangkok for a two-day visit that includes blessing 45,000 of the faithful at the National Stadium.

THE "YOUNG TURKS" TRY AGAIN

1985

• **Sept 9.** Led by former colonel Manoon Roopkachorn, the "Young Turks" attempt once again to overthrow the Prem government; although the coup lasts only a day and fails, lives are lost, including those of two foreign journalists.

VISIT THAILAND YEAR

1987

• **Jan 3.** Thailand Tourism Year gets underway with a grand parade attended by the Prime Minister.

His Majesty King Bhumibol attends the funeral of Her Majesty Queen Rambhai Barni.

1985

• **Jan 2.** PM Prem gets tough with striking state enterprise workers, announcing that in the future they will return to work or face losing their jobs.
• **Mar 11.** The president of the People's Republic of China, Li Xiannian, and Madame Lin Jiamei arrive for a five-day visit. • **Mar 17.** HM the Queen sees The King and I on Broadway.

HM King Bhumibol with Chinese President Li Xiannian.

Actor Yul Brynner with Her Majesty Queen Sirikit.

• **Apr 9.** A magnificent state funeral is held for HM Queen Rambhai Barni. • **May 2.** Amid much public protest the House of Representatives passes a controversial executive decree outlawing pyramid scheme chit funds. • **Aug 4.** About three thousand inmates at Bang Kwang maximum security prison stage a violent sit-in demanding that the government commute their sentences; ten prisoners are killed as police quell the protest. • **Nov 14.** Independent Major General Chamlong Srimuang wins a landslide victory in the Bangkok gubernatorial elections.
• **Dec 8.** Thailand celebrates the first day of the Bangkok Asian Games with a gold medal in gymnastics; as the games close on December 17, the kingdom leads the medals tally with ninety-three gold to runner-up Indonesia's sixty-two.

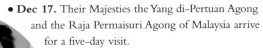

• **Dec 17.** Their Majesties the Yang di-Pertuan Agong and the Raja Permaisuri Agong of Malaysia arrive for a five-day visit.
• **Dec 31.** Thirteen convicts armed with grenades take the governor of Sakhon Nakhon Prison hostage.

1986

• **Jan 9.** HM the King presides over the opening of Khai Laem Dam in Kanchanaburi.
• **Jan 22.** China contracts to buy a massive 1,137 million baht worth of Thai rice.
• **Mar 19.** The Bangkok Metropolitan Administration announces tough penalties for litterbugs with maximum fines of 2,500 baht.
• **Apr 8.** A bomb explodes at the Erawan Hotel an hour before US Secretary of Defense Caspar Weinburger is due to arrive for a dinner hosted by PM Prem. • **May 9.** Bangkok's highest rainfall in five hundred years causes widespread flooding while flash floods throughout the kingdom claim forty lives. • **May 30.** Newly appointed Army Commander in Chief General Chavalit Yongchaiyudh says that he will declare his assets to prove his integrity. • **June 26.** The two hundredth anniversary of the birth of Sunthorn Phu, the kingdom's most famous poet. • **Jul 17.** Klong Toey Port is paralyzed for two days as hundreds of dockers go on strike in protest over a cabinet decision to allow the Express Transport Organization to operate mobile cranes.
• **Aug 5.** PM Prem is reappointed Prime Minister, Thailand's sixteenth. • **Aug 29.** The Army reinstates twenty-eight "Young Turk" officers discharged in the wake of the abortive 1981 coup.
• **Dec 17.** Their Majesties the Yang di Pertuan Agong and the Raja Permaisuri Agong of Malaysia arrive for a five-day visit.

A Statue of Poet Sunthorn Phu (top left).

1987

• **Feb 16.** Army Commander in Chief General Chavalit Yongchaiyudh declares that he will not stand by and let the country collapse as a result of political squabbling. • **Apr 11.** Twenty-one passengers drown when a ferry capsizes off Surat Thani.
• **May 5.** Following a nationwide poll, the honorific title "The Great" is bestowed on HM the King at a party hosted by PM Prem in celebration of the forty-second anniversary of the coronation.
• **Jul 6.** The Interior Ministry proposes a Condominium Act to the Cabinet that for the first time will allow foreigners to own units.
• **Aug 15.** Pathet Lao soldiers seize Ban Rom Klao, a hill in Phitsanuloke, in a disputed border territory held by Thailand, setting off a bloody war that will lasts for months.

Thai troops ready for combat in border war with Laos.

• **Aug 29.** Thai secret agents arrest a Briton and a Czech believed to be members of a Soviet spy ring using Thailand as its base of operations.

• **Aug 31.** More than eighty people are killed when a Thai Airways Boeing 737 crashes into the sea and explodes off the island of Phuket.

• **Oct 13.** The Cabinet approves a decree that prisoners with AIDS will not be included in amnesties.

• **Oct 21.** President Mohammad Zia-ul-Haq of the Islamic Republic of Pakistan arrives for a four-day visit.

• **Nov 18.** Their Majesties King Juan Carlos I and Queen Sophia of Spain arrive for a five-day visit.

• **Nov 27.** Having spent more than two years in jail, thirty-three of the forty "Young Turks" involved in the September 9 coup are freed.

• **Dec 5.** HM the King celebrates his sixtieth birthday, thus completing the auspicious fifth cycle of Buddhism, and the last lot of sixty-baht bank notes are issued to commemorate the occasion as a year of celebrations ensues.

1988

• **Jan 7.** Their Imperial Highnesses Prince Hitachi and Princess Hanako of Japan arrive for an eight-day visit as the private guests of Their Majesties the King and Queen. • **Jan 23.** PM Prem lays the foundation stones for five multibillion-baht petrochemical projects, a banner day for the Eastern Seaboard Industrial Deep-Sea Port Development Committee.

• **Feb 4.** Britain's Prince Charles and his wife Princess Diana arrive in Bangkok as part of the celebrations for HM the King's sixtieth birthday.

Their Royal Highnesses Prince Charles and Princess Diana of Wales visit.

• **Feb 12.** In the world's biggest drug bust since April 22, 1973, 1,280 kilograms of heroin are seized at Klong Toey Port. • **Feb 18.** Thai and Lao military officials sign a ceasefire pact to end months of bloody fighting over some seventy square kilometers of mountainous terrain in Phitsanuloke, a conflict that has cost Thailand 402 lives and 2 million baht.

• **Mar 2.** Their Majesties the King and Queen preside over a ceremony to mark the ninetieth birthday of Supreme Patriarch Somdej Phra Ariyawongsa Khatayan at Wat Rat Borpit Sathitmaha Srimaram.

• **Mar 5.** Forty thousand Lao youth attend a concert for peace in Vientiane performed by Thai rock groups.

• **Mar 28.** President Muhammad Ershad of the People's Republic of Bangladesh and Begum Raushan Ershad arrive for a four-day visit.

• **Apr 29.** Following the mass resignation of sixteen Democrat ministers led by Deputy PM Bhichai Rattakul, HM the King issues a Royal Decree proclaiming the dissolution of Parliament and announcing a general election on July 24.

• **May 9.** Khaokor Galaxy joins his twin brother Khaosai as a world boxing champion when he takes the WBA bantamweight title.

PM Prem (center) opens petrochemical complexes.

• **May 21.** More than three hundred Thais living in the US rally in front of the Art Institute of Chicago demand the return of the Taplang Narai Bantomsin lintel to Thailand. • **Aug 5.** HM the King's Royal Project to promote the cultivation of cash crops other than opium wins the prestigious Magsaysay Award for international understanding. • **Aug 27.** Supreme Patriarch Somdej Phra Ariyawongsa Khatayan dies.

• **Sept 9.** More than seventy people die when a Vietnamese airliner crashes as it approaches Bangkok's Don Muang Airport.

• **Nov 1.** Their Majesties Sultan Haji Hassanal Bolkiah and Raja Isteri Pengiran Anak Saleha of Brunei Darussalam arrive for a four-day visit. • **Nov 10.** The Taplang Narai Bantomsin lintel is returned to Thailand.

1988

• **May 23.** Miss Thailand, nineteen year old Porntip Narkhirunkanok—better known as "Pui"—is crowned Miss Universe.

A GRATEFUL CITIZENRY CELEBRATE THE LONGEST REIGN

1988

• **July 2.** HM the King becomes the longest reigning monarch in Thai history, having been on the throne for forty-two years and twenty-three days; the longest previous reign was that of HM King Chulalongkorn (1868-1910).

PM CHATICHAI CHUNHAVAN

1988

• **Aug 2.** Chart Thai leader Major General Chatichai Chunhavan becomes Thailand's first elected Prime Minister in twelve years.

TRADE AS THE ENGINE FOR PEACE

1989

• **Apr 28.** Prime Minister Chatichai and Vietnamese Foreign Minister Nguyen Co Thuch meet in Bangkok at a symposium on Trade in Indochina.

PRIME MINISTER
ANAND PANYARACHUN

1991

• **Mar 2.** Federation of Thai Industries chairman, and chairman of Saha Union Company, diplomat and businessman Anand Panyarachun heads the administration as Prime Minister.

• **Nov 24.** The death toll rises to 230 in the worst flooding to hit the south in decades.
• **Nov 30.** The Cabinet agrees not to award any more logging concessions and considers revoking all such concessions nationwide.

1989

• **Jan 4.** A Saudi Arabian diplomat is shot dead in Bangkok. • **Jan 10.** The cabinet approves two executive decrees terminating 301 logging concessions around the country. • **Feb 19.** Their Majesties King Karl Gustaf and Queen Silvia of Sweden arrive for a five-day visit as the private guests of Their Majesties the King and Queen. • **May 6.** PM Chatichai meets Cambodian Prime Minister Hun Sen for talks in Bangkok. • **Sept 8.** The Army says that Thai soldiers are contracting AIDS at the rate of a case a day.
• **Sept 14.** Members of the influential Chulachomklao Military Academy Class V are promoted en masse to key Army positions. • **Oct 18.** His Royal Highness Prince Philip of Britain arrives for a four-day visit in the capacity of president of the World Wildlife Fund and is received by Their Majesties the King and Queen. • **Oct 29.** The kingdom's first petrochemical complex at Mabtaphud comes onstream.
• **Nov 4.** Typhoon Gay slams into Chumpon and Prachuab Khiri Khan provinces leaving a fifty-kilometer swath of flattened villages and forests and 450 dead.

The devastation of Typhoon Gay.

• **Nov 13.** HM the King becomes the longest reigning monarch in the world following the death of His Serene Highness Prince Franz Joseph II of Liechtenstein.

1990

• **Feb 1.** Three Saudi Arabian embassy officials are killed in two separate shootings.
• **Feb 3.** The Kingdom of Saudi Arabia bans the recruitment of Thai workers. • **Feb 20.** Saudi Arabia bans its citizens from traveling to Thailand.
• **March 15.** HRH Maha Chakri Sirindhorn makes an historic Royal Visit to Laos, marking the healing of relations between the two countries.

HRH Princess Sirindorn on her state visit to Laos.

• **March 27.** Acting Supreme Commander and Army Commander in Chief General Chavalit Yongchaiyudh resigns two years ahead of retirement, and joins the Cabinet as Deputy Prime Minister and Defense Minister.
• **June 12.** General Chavalit resigns from the Cabinet amid resistance to his appointment from other ministers; analysts predict an imminent coup.
• **Aug 12.** PM Chatichai orders a mass evacuation of Thai workers from Kuwait following the Iraqi invasion.
• **Sept 23.** Thirty-eight students drown when their sightseeing boat capsizes in the reservoir of Ubolrat Dam north of Khon Kaen.
• **Sept 24.** A gas truck explosion on Bangkok's New Petchaburi Road claims fifty-five lives and permanently maims numerous others.
Sept. 30. GATT rules that a Thai ban on imported cigarettes is illegal.

A gas truck explodes at city-center.

• **Oct 14.** Ramkhamhaeng University student Thanavuth Klinchua immolates himself in protest against the government and dies in the hospital. • **Nov 14.** The Bangkok Metropolitan Administration announces a plan to build an overhead mass transit system in Bangkok's central business district. • **Nov 21.** Thirty-eight people are killed when a Bangkok Airways turboprop crashes on Samui island.
• **Dec 17.** Their Majesties the Yang di-Pertuan Agong and the Raja Permaisuri Agong of Malaysia arrive for a four-day visit.

1991

• **Jan 1.** In his annual New Year's message, HM the King calls for honesty and resolve, adding, "please do not get bored with democratic rule. Don't feel annoyed by differences, which do not mean division."

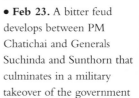

General Suchinda Kraprayoon.

• **Feb 23.** A bitter feud develops between PM Chatichai and Generals Suchinda and Sunthorn that culminates in a military takeover of the government

General Sunthorn Kongsonpong.

under the "National Peace Keeping Council", the arrest of the Prime Minister, and the appointment of a new Cabinet. • **Mar 9.** Former Prime Minister Chatichai is freed from custody and promptly flies to Britain. • **Mar 14.** The military National Peace Keeping Council disbands unions in state enterprises.
• **May 27.** In the kingdom's worst air disaster, a Lauda Air jetliner en route to Vienna from Hong Kong via Bangkok crashes in Suphan Buri killing 223 passengers. • **June 4.** PM Anand Panyarachun says his government will not sign a monopolistic multibillion-baht telephone expansion project with the Charoen Pokphand group in the original form approved by the Chatichai government.

• **June 10.** People's Republic of China President Yang Shangkun arrives for a six-day visit.

• **July 2.** The Cabinet cuts import duties on cars from 180-300 percent to 20-100 percent—placing imported cars on a vastly more competitive footing with locally produced models. • **July 13.** PM Anand visits Japan, "to put Thailand back on the map".

• **Aug 3.** Former Prime Minister Chatichai returns from London to defend his honor against allegations that he amassed unusual wealth as leader of what has become known as the "Buffet Cabinet".

Sept 26. His Imperial Majesty Emperor Akihito of Japan arrives for a four-day visit, his first since his enthronement. • **Oct 14.** Thailand hosts the World Bank-IMF meeting; the government declares a two-day

PM Anand addresses the World Bank-IMF meeting.

holiday to ensure a smooth flow of traffic in Bangkok.

• **Dec 22.** Boxer Khaosai Galaxy retires undefeated.

Retiring champion Khaosai Galaxy.

1992

• **Jan 1.** A 7 percent value added tax is launched amid much confusion, resentment and profiteering.

• **Jan 6.** Lao People's Democratic Republic President Kaysone Phomvihane and Thongvin Phomvihane arrive for a ten-day visit.

• **Mar 10.** HM the King pardons eleven senior judges facing dismissal for their alleged instigation of an uprising against Justice Minister Prapasna Uaychai.

• **Apr 7.** Supreme Commander Suchinda Kraprayun becomes Prime Minister. • **Apr 16.** Dressed in black, opposition parties protest PM Suchinda's rise to the premiership since he has never been elected as an MP. • **Apr 20.** More than fifty-thousand people join the opposition parties in a show of defiance against PM Suchinda.

• **May 4.** Palang Dharma Party leader Major General Chamlong Srimuang announces a fast to the death for democracy at a huge anti-Suchinda rally at Sanam Luang. • **May 16.** More large-scale anti-Suchinda demonstrations take place at Sanam Luang.

• **May 17.** Military forces raid the rally and take away Major General Chamlong.

• **May 23.** PM Suchinda resigns.

• **June 4.** Opposition parties pick Chuan Leekpai to set up a government. • **June 30.** PM Anand dissolves the House of Representatives and calls for a new elec-

tion on September 13. • **July 12.** Top military commanders testify to a government appointed investigation committee that former PM Suchinda ordered the use of force to crush the May 17-20 pro-democracy protests. • **July 20.** Major General Chamlong receives the Ramon Magsaysay Award for government service.

• **Aug 1.** PM Anand orders the transfer to lower posts of three top military officers involved in the May bloodshed. • **Aug 12.** The nation celebrates Her Majesty the Queen's sixtieth birthday as she enters her sixth twelve-year Buddhist cycle.

• **Sept 13.** The Democrat Party emerges with the most seats in the general election and proceeds to form a new government under party leader Chuan Leekpai.

PM Chuan Leekpai.

1993

• **Feb 2.** An invention by HM the King—a floating low-speed air jet which adds oxygen to water to improve its quality—receives a patent, #3127, from the Intellectual Property Department.

• **Feb 15.** Hungarian President Arpad Goncz and Zsuzsanna Maria Goncz arrive for a four-day visit. • **Feb 16.** The Dalai Lama arrives as part of a group of Nobel Prize Winning laureates

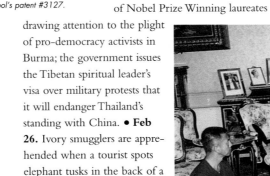

HM King Bhumibol's patent #3127.

drawing attention to the plight of pro-democracy activists in Burma; the government issues the Tibetan spiritual leader's visa over military protests that it will endanger Thailand's standing with China. • **Feb 26.** Ivory smugglers are apprehended when a tourist spots elephant tusks in the back of a pickup truck on Silom Road in downtown Bangkok.

• **Apr 6.** HM the King grants an audience to UN Secretary General Boutros Boutros-Ghali. • **May 10.** A fire at the Kader doll factory claims 187

MAJOR GENERAL CHAMLONG

1992

• **May 8.** Major General Chamlong ends his fast and resigns as PDP leader in order to take command of the pro-democracy demonstrations.

A TRAGEDY STRIKES

1992

• **May 18.** Military forces suppress demonstrators massed in front of the Public Relations Department. Riots ensue, shots are fired, scores of people are killed, thousands more arrested and several government buildings torched.

A ROYAL INTERVENTION

1992

• **May 20.** HM the King grants an audience to PM Suchinda and prodemocracy leader General Chamlong and in a televised audience, seen throughout the nation, instructs them to reconcile; the government lifts the curfew and releases the protesters who had been arrested.

A GAMBLER LOSES

● **Nov 15.** Speculator Vivat Srismmascheep, heavily in debt for shares that have gone down in value, holds a gun to his throat at the Stock exchange of Thailand while demanding a relaxation of loan repayment terms and an infusion of cash into the market by the government to raise share prices. He shoots himself but miraculously survives virtually unscathed.

CUTTING THROUGH THE RED TAPE

1995

● **Oct 14.** Offering concrete proposals to deal with the worst national flood crisis in 200 years, HM King Bhumibol personally directs Thai government officials to put aside departmental differences and get to work on flood prevention measures and disaster relief.

Klongtoey's poor neighborhoods burn.

lives as workers are burned alive behind locked fire exits.

● **May 27.** HM the Queen is voted "Woman of the Year" by Stanford University.

● **June 20.** Thailand wins the SEA Games soccer tournament, beating Burma 4–3 in the final.

● **July 8.** Former Central Investigation Bureau deputy commissioner Police Lieutenant General Chalor Kerdthes and seven others are formally charged with misappropriating tens of millions of baht worth of jewelry stolen from a Saudi Arabian prince.

● **Aug 2.** Arsonists suspected of separatist links torch thirty-three rural schools and offices in the south.

● **Aug 13.** The Royal Plaza hotel in Khorat collapses, claiming a hundred lives.

● **Sept 17.** The Forestry Department announces the start of a three-year reforestation project to honor HM the King's Golden Jubilee.

● **Nov 4.** The Palace announces the forthcoming publication of HM the King's translation of William Stevenson's novel *A Man Called Intrepid*.

● **Dec 16.** HM the King personally donates three million baht to help ease the capital's traffic crisis.

● **Dec 18.** Thailand's first communications satellite—Thaicom I—is launched from French Guiana.

1994

● **Feb 11.** Czech Republic President Vaclav Havel and Madam Olga Havlova arrive for a six-day visit.

● **Mar 17.** Police accidentally uncover what appears to be an international plot to blow up the Israeli Embassy, in the form of a huge truckbomb found on the back of a vehicle seized following a minor road accident.

● **Apr 23.** An anti-personnel bomb explodes at a crowded Nakhon Si Thammarat railway station killing three. ● **June 16.** Activist Chalard Vorachat, on a hunger strike for democratic amendments to the Constitution for twenty-three days, is taken into police custody and charged with *lèse-majesté*; he was to be found innocent.

● **Aug 29.** A devastating fire rages through the Klong Toey Port slum community.

● **Sept 20.** Flash floods at a Nakhon Nayok recreational park, Wang Takrai, claim twenty lives.

● **Oct 30.** PM Chuan rejects US President Bill Clinton's request to station ships with military equipment in the Gulf of Thailand. ● **Nov 5.** Their Royal Highnesses Crown Prince Naruhito and Crown Princess Masako of Japan arrive in Bangkok on a stopover en route to Saudi Arabia and a banquet is held in their honor.

● **Dec 12.** Residents of

Kampheng Phet claim to have sewn the world's longest flag, the Thai national flag, measuring 3m x 90 cm, for the nationwide celebrations of HM the King's Golden Jubilee.

1995

● **Jan 15.** Twenty-five people including eighteen teachers from Bangkok's Santa Cruz school are killed on a field-trip when their bus hurtles over a cliff.

● **Feb 14.** Lao People's Democratic Republic President Nouhak Phoumsavanh and Madame Bounma Phoumsavanh arrive for a six-day visit.

● **Apr 3.** Fifteen people are killed when an express train en route from Bangkok to Trang collides with a ten-wheel truck. ● **Apr 9.** Oil spills smear a 30 km stretch of shoreline between Ban Chang and Muang districts. ● **Mar 19.** Thousands gather at Sanam Luang to pray for HM the King's full and speedy recovery from a heart problem. ● **Apr 14.** After more than a month under the close scrutiny of his physicians, HM the King assures the nation of his recovery.

● **June 14.** Twenty-four people drown when an express boat landing on the Chao Phraya River collapses

PM Banharn Silpa-archa.

during the morning rush hour.

● **July 2.** A general election is held amid allegations of widespread vote-buying; 17 billion baht is estimated to have been spent.

● **July 13.** Banharn Silpa-archa becomes Thailand's twenty-first Prime Minister and forms a new government. ● **July 18.** Her Royal Highness the Princess Mother dies peacefully at Siriraj Hospital at the age of ninety-four; adored by all Thais, a one-hundred day mourning period is ordered by HM the King.

● **Sept 16.** Their Royal Highnesses Prince Akishino and Princess Kiko of Japan arrive in Bangkok to lay a wreath at the Dusit Maha Prasart Throne Hall in homage to HRH the Princess Mother.

● **Sept 19.** HM the King calls for steps to be taken to avert economic havoc from what has been the worst flooding in two hundred years; meanwhile, hundreds of crocodiles float out of captivity and into the wild in Ayutthaya. ● **Oct 14.** The financial cost of the floods since July is estimated at 3 billion baht.

● **Oct 20.** Fire rages through The Mall—a giant shopping complex in Bangkok.

● **Nov 21.** The Finance Ministry announces a 30 billion baht rescue fund to shore up share prices fol-

1996 • **March 10.** His Majesty King Bhumibol and the nation witness the cremation ceremonies of his much loved mother, Her Royal Highness the Princess Mother S Mahidol, including the procession of the Funeral Chariot carrying her body (right) and the final procession of the Royal Urn containing her ashes (left). Greatly admired by the Thai people, the Princess Mother, bore two kings—Ananda Mahidol and Bhumibol Adulyadej—and dedicated much of her life to charitable works. A trained nurse, she took great concern for the health of the Thai people and founded the Volunteer Flying Doctor's Service to provide free medical services to village people who would not otherwise have had access to professional medical treatment.

---

lowing the recent stock market plunge.
• **Nov 22.** A huge fire destroys the popular Central

The SEA Games.

department store on Chidlom Road in downtown Bangkok. • **Dec 9.** The Eighteenth Southeast Asian Games hosted by Thailand opens in Chiang Mai.

1996

• **Jan 11.** Thailand's fourth oil refinery, a 2-billion-dollar project on the Eastern Seaboard, comes onstream. • **Jan 16.** The Olympic Council of Asia grants Thailand approval to host the 1998 Asian Games.
• **Jan 18.** Former MP Thanong is extradited to the US to face drug-running charges.
• **Jan 20.** Thailand and the US announce an agreement on bilateral aviation rights. • **Jan 21.** A five-point plan to counter election fraud is drawn up by the Local Administration Department.
• **March 1.** PM Barnharn opens a two-day ASEM (Europe-Asia) meeting at which twenty-five national leaders—ten from Asia—and the president of the European Commission meet to discuss trade, investment and joint ventures between the regions.
• **Mar 16.** A national seminar considers the Eighth Five-Year National Economic & Social Development Plan that will go into effect in 1997 and will focus on human resource development.

• **Mar 17.** PM Banharn leaves on an official visit to Burma, the first by a Thai Prime Minister in sixteen years. • **Apr 19.** The government launches a campaign to curb water and air pollution.
• **Apr 11.** Saengchai Sunthornwat, director of the Mass Communications Organization of Thailand, is gunned down in his car.
• **Apr 21.** Highlighting an ongoing protest against the government and its policies, farmers and other disaffected groups set up a "Village of the Poor" outside Government House.
• **May 9.** His Majesty King Bhumibol's new translation of the Buddhist story Mahajanaka, and the book's accompanying gold, silver and alloy medals, are formally consecrated by His Majesty and blessed by His Holiness Somdej Phra Nyanasamvara, the Supreme Patriarch.
• **May 10.** In a controversial move, the Banharn government survives a no-confidence vote by ending the debate early. • **June 2.** Independent candidate Bhichit Rattakul is elected governor of Bangkok by a landslide on an anti-pollution and traffic-solution platform.
• **June 5.** HM the King becomes the world's first recipient of the International Rice Award in recognition of his efforts to improve agriculture and the quality of life of farmers; the gold medal is presented by the International Rice Institute based in the Philippines.
• **June 9.** A year of festivities culminates in joyful celebration on this Golden Jubilee of His Majesty King Bhumibol Adulyadej's Accession to the Throne.

— *John Clewley and Simon Kind.*

1996 • **August 4.** To the delight of the entire kingdom, Featherweight boxer Somluck Kamsing created sporting history this evening, beating his Bulgarian opponent to win Thailand's first-ever Olympic gold medal. A vociferous crowd of Thai supporters shouted their support as Somluck, a sailor with the Royal Thai Navy, outpointed his opponent 8 to 5. "I've done it," Somluck said after the fight. "This is a victory to rejoice His Majesty's Golden Jubilee. He inspired me to win today."

1996 • **June 9.** The entire kingdom celebrates the Fiftieth Anniversary of His Majesty King Bhumibol Adulyadej's Accession to the Throne —the Golden Jubilee. Thousands enjoy the day of festivities at Sanam Luang and Rajdamnern Avenue, which is decorated with seven arches and brilliant lighting. Religious ceremonies, sporting events and entertainment activities are held across the kingdom, culminating in the lighting of candles at 19.19 hours.

The Achievements of Thailand
1946-96

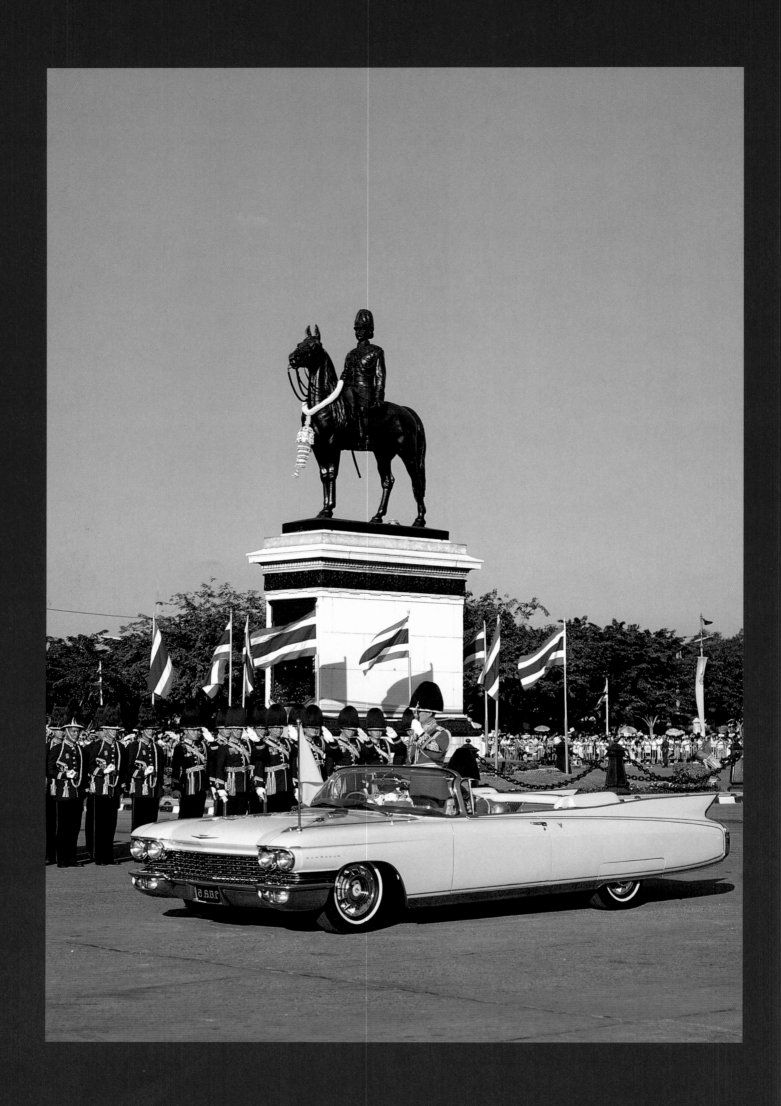

1

THE MONARCHY

M L Thawisan Ladawan

OVER A PERIOD OF MORE THAN SEVEN HUNDRED YEARS, THE THAI MONARCHY HAS EVOLVED INTO AN INSTITUTION THAT IS IN MANY WAYS UNIQUE, NOT ALWAYS FULLY COMPREHENDED BY OUTSIDERS.

Its absolute form ended with the Revolution of 1932, when King Prajadhipok (Rama VII) agreed to serve under constitutional restraints, yet it continues to be one of the most powerful elements in Thai society, a focal point that serves to unify people of all backgrounds and shades of political thought and gives them an intense awareness of what it means to be Thai. This has been dramatically shown on a number of occasions during the present reign of His Majesty King Bhumibol Adulyadej—on the 1982 celebration of the bicentennial of the Chakri Dynasty, on his sixtieth birthday in 1987, and, most spectacularly of all, on the Golden Jubilee of his reign in the present year.

The intensity of the respect felt by Thai people for their King arises in large part from the distinctive form the modern monarchy has taken under his leadership over the past fifty years. At the same time, it also goes back to the earliest days of Thai history and to some of the past rulers who continue to serve as models of kingship and dedication.

Facing page: King Bhumibol in a ceremonial procession with the statue of Rama VI in the background; Right: Their Majesties the King and Queen of Thailand.

Background

Thai concepts of monarchy have their origins in Sukhothai, founded in the early part of the thirteenth century and generally regarded as the first truly independent Thai capital. Here, particularly during the reign of King Ramkhamhaeng the Great (1279-1317), was born the ideal of a paternalistic ruler alert to the needs of his people and aware that his duty was to guide them, a markedly different view from the divine kingship practiced by the Khmers who had previously ruled.

This system was memorably reflected in a famous historical inscription found among the ruins of Sukhothai. Dating from AD 1292, it describes life in the first capital and contains the following passage, still well-known to all Thai schoolchildren:

"[The King] has hung a bell in the opening of the gate over there; if any commoner in the land has a grievance... which he wants to make known to his lord and ruler, it is easy; he goes and strikes the bell which the King has hung there; King Ramkhamhaeng, ruler of the kingdom, hears the call; he goes and questions the man, examines the case, and decides it justly for him."

For nearly seven centuries, this concept of a benevolent, accessible monarch has remained a Thai ideal. It has not always been fully realized, particularly during the Ayutthaya period when Khmer ideas of divine kingship came back and the ruler virtually lost contact with most of his subjects. It never entirely disappeared from the national consciousness, however, and it was still there, ready to be resurrected, when the rulers of the Chakri Dynasty ushered in a new era in 1782.

King Rama I, founder of the dynasty, attempted to re-create the lost Ayutthaya when he built his new capital at Bangkok—splendid in many ways, especially the still-dazzling Grand Palace and Temple of the Emerald Buddha, but essentially medieval in outward aspects. The king was still known as Chao Jivit, the Lord of Life, surrounded by complex ritual and holding absolute power over every aspect of his kingdom, from social matters to national defense. To a foreign observer, mindful of the revolutionary ideas then at work in the West, it might seem that little had changed.

Yet behind this traditional façade, something new was stirring—or, perhaps more accurately, something as old as the relationship between King Ramkhamhaeng and his people in legendary Sukhothai. The Brahmanic and animistic elements of royal ceremony, which had been so strong in Ayutthaya, remained intact; but, at the same time, deeply-rooted Buddhist beliefs returned to play a prominent part, and in occasionally subtle ways the King once more became a recognizably human figure. One example can

be seen in the numerous laws, decrees, and proclamations that issued from the palace. In theory, of course, the King, or the Lord of Life, was under no obligation to explain what he did, however controversial, and few Ayutthaya kings would have dreamed of doing so.

Nearly always, though, Rama I sought to justify his decisions, placing them in historical context and clarifying them with rational argument. This revealed, in the words of historian David K. Wyatt, "an active, creative intelligence...not merely content to transmit the past but wanting to shape the past and in doing so shape the future."

By the time of Rama I's death in 1809, the kingdom had been consolidated and the threat of invasion by traditional enemies had receded. Other external events were less favorable, however, and his successors responded by further redefining the role of monarchy in Thai life, shrewdly adapting it to a world that was changing with bewildering speed as neighbor after neighbor fell under European colonial rule.

One of the most notable was His Majesty King Mongkut, or Rama IV. Before coming to the throne in 1851, he had spent twenty-seven years in the Buddhist priesthood, an experience unique in the history of the Thai monarchy which, in turn, gave him unique insights into the life of ordinary people. Nor did he forget what he had learned when he became the Lord of Life. In the words of A.B. Griswold, one of his biographers, "He did not regard his subjects as chattels. He had known them as real people, lived on friendly terms with their brothers and their sons in the monasteries, received their arms and hospitality when making his long pilgrimages. He had known the villagers and country folk as well as the townspeople. He had seen how some officials are just and kindly, others corrupt and grasping. He had talked much with humble men—coolies and slaves, peasants and

Top: Buddha statue in Sukhothai; Left: Portrait of Rama I; Above: Statue of King Ramkhamhaeng.

elephant hunters, fishermen and pearl divers...
These were all his people, his world was not
confined by the walls of palace and monastery,
his responsibility not limited to guarding the
welfare of grandees and monks."

It was King Mongkut who, in 1833, redis-
covered the famous inscription in Sukhothai. He
brought it to Bangkok, along with a stone seat
believed to have been used by King

Top: A painting showing
King Mongkut receiving
foreign ambassadors;
Above: King
Chulalongkorn.

Ramkhamhaeng as a throne, and later
the words of the inscription were to
serve as a kind of guide to his conduct
as a ruler. He concerned himself with
almost every aspect of Thai life, from
wide-ranging reforms of the Buddhist
priesthood to improvements of
provincial administration. Moreover, he
established warm relations with a
number of foreign powers and negotiated trade treaties that contributed greatly
to the country's future prosperity.

His Majesty King Chulalongkorn
(Rama V) was a more than worthy
successor to this remarkable man. Over
the course of a reign that lasted forty-two years,
he brought about dramatic social and political
changes and, through skilled personal diplomacy
on travels abroad, helped preserve Thailand's
independence. Like King Mongkut, he made a
point of traveling extensively within his own
country, often incognito, to get to know ordinary

people and their problems. Prince Chula
Chakrabongse, in his history of the Chakri
Dynasty, writes, "With the scarcity of photographs and newspapers, he was usually for a
long time unrecognized. On these occasions he
accepted simple hospitality, sometimes himself
helping to cook a meal, attended village wed-
dings, but much more important, he saw and
heard at close quarters the results of his benevolent rule and increasing reforms."

King Chulalongkorn passed away in 1910.
Soon afterward, the winds of change grew
fiercer and more unpredictable, and monarchies
all over the world began to fall, some to violent
revolutions. Even where they survived, their luster was often greatly dimmed, their real power
almost non-existent. Thanks to its paternalistic
nature, Thailand's absolute system survived
longer than most; but it, too, ultimately suc-
cumbed to the demand for popular government.

In a sense, it may be said that the Lords of
Life themselves engineered the end of their total
power. The broad reforms initiated by King
Chulalongkorn and continued by his successor,
King Vajiravudh, laid the foundations for self-
government; moreover, their policy of sending
bright young Thais, from all levels of society, to
further their education abroad made the introduction of new political ideas almost inevitable.
King Prajadhipok (Rama VII), the last absolute
monarch, was personally committed to the idea

Overview of the Chakri Dynasty

The Chakri Dynasty was established in 1782 by the ruler generally known as King Rama I, who also moved the country's capital across the Chao Phraya River from Thonburi to Bangkok in the same year.

Nine Chakri kings, known as Lords of Life, have occupied the throne, contributing significantly to the development of Thailand during periods of external threat as well as prosperity. King Rama I (1782–1809) restored economic and political stability following the disastrous defeat of Ayutthaya by the Burmese and also strengthened the social order through the introduction of new laws. By the next reign, the country was enjoying peace and security, and King Rama II (1809–24) was able to turn his attention to a variety of cultural projects, including literary works of his own composition and support of the arts in general.

King Rama III (1824–51) devoted much effort to the founding and upkeep of Buddhist monasteries, especially in Bangkok. His tolerance and open-mindedness also paved the way for the establishment of the first Protestant missionaries, who introduced Western medicine to Thailand, as well as the start of limited trade with Western powers to avert possible foreign invasion.

The tactful diplomacy of King Rama IV (1851–68) enabled Thailand to remain independent while neighboring countries fell to colonial rule. Openly receptive to foreign influences and ideas, he was the first Thai king to master Western languages and was a keen student of modern science; he concluded important commercial treaties with Western powers which led to greatly increased trade.

His son Rama V (1868–1910) reigned for an eventful forty-two years and was responsible for a broad range of reforms that transformed almost every aspect of Thai life. He abolished slavery, expanded the country's communications system and reorganized provincial administration. The first Thai king to travel abroad, he also initiated a policy of sending Thai students to foreign countries for their education.

King Rama VI (1910–25), educated abroad, continued the process of modernization and established Thailand's first university; in addition, he was an accomplished writer and poet whose works are still studied in Thai schools. The absolute monarchy came to an end during the reign of King Rama VII (1925–35) when a group of civil servants and military officers staged a bloodless coup on June 24, 1932 and demanded constitutional government. The King remained on the throne until 1935 when, unhappy over certain changes, he abdicated while in England for medical treatment.

His nephew, ten-year-old Prince Ananda, succeeded him but continued his studies in Switzerland while a Council of Regency reigned. In 1946, the young King tragically died while on a visit to Bangkok and his brother, the present King Bhumibol Adulyadej, became the ninth ruler of the Chakri Dynasty.

— WILLIAM WARREN

KING BUDDHA YODFA ● QUEEN AMARINDRA
(RAMA I)   1738–1826
b.1737 r.1782 d.1809

QUEEN SRI SURALAYA ● KING BUDDHA LOETLA (RAMA II) ● QUEEN SRI SURIYENDRA
1770–1837   b.1768 r.1809 d.1824   1770–1836

KING NANGKLAO (RAMA III)   KING MONGKUT (RAMA IV) ● QUEEN DEBSIRINDRA
b.1788 r.1824 d.1851   b.1804 r.1851 d.1868   1834–61

QUEEN SUNANDA ● KING CHULALONGKORN (RAMA V) ● QUEEN SUKHUMALA
1860–80   b.1853 R.1868 D.1910   1861–1927

QUEEN SAOVABHA ●   ● QUEEN SAVANG VADHANA
1864–1919   1862–1955

PRINCE MAHIDOL ● PRINCESS SRI
OF SONGKHLA   NAGARINDRA,
1892–1929   THE PRINCESS MOTHER
                 1900–95

QUEEN INDRASAKDI ● KING VAJIRAVUDH   KING PRAJADHIPOK
1902–75   (RAMA VI)   (RAMA VII)
PHRA NANG CHAO ● B.1881 R.1910 D.1925   B.1893 R.1925–35(ABD.) D.1941
SUVADHANA
1905–85   PRINCESS GALYANI
                   VADHANA
PRINCESS BEJRARATANA   1923–
1925–

KING ANANDA MAHIDOL   KING BHUMIBOL ADULYADEJ ● QUEEN SIRIKIT
(RAMA VIII)   (RAMA IX) B.1927 R.1946   1932–
B.1925 R.1935 D.1946

PRINCESS UBOL   CROWN PRINCE MAHA   PRINCESS MAHA CHAKRI   PRINCESS
RATANA   VAJIRALONGKORN   SIRINDHORN   CHULABHORN
1951–   1952–   1955–   1957–

Top: King Prajadhipok (Rama VII), the last absolute monarch, on the throne; Above: Prince Ananda Mahidol; Right: Coronation of King Bhumibol Adulyadej in 1950.

of a constitution and, given more time, would undoubtedly have granted one without external pressure.

As it was, on June 24, 1932, a small group of officials, most of them foreign-educated, staged a coup d'état in Bangkok. The King was in Hua Hin on the Gulf of Thailand when he received the news, along with a demand for him to agree to a constitution. He did so in a simply-worded document as historic as any composed by his distinguished forebears, and thus ended 150 years of absolute rule by Chakri Kings.

The change, however, was felt principally in Bangkok, and even there within a relatively narrow segment of the population. The vast majority of Thais still retained their ancient reverence for the monarchy as an institution and also for the man who embodied it, whatever limitations might be placed on his powers.

It was to be a long time before the new system could be truly tested. In 1934, His Majesty King Prajadhipok went abroad for medical treatment and, a year later, disillusioned by the undemocratic nature of the regime, he abdicated. His successor was ten-year-old Prince Ananda Mahidol, a grandson of King Chulalongkorn, but as he was then at school in Switzerland he was represented in Bangkok by a regency. Except for a brief visit in 1938, he did not return to his homeland until after the war, and tragedy ensued

shortly afterward when on June 9, 1946, he was found dead in his quarters at the Grand Palace.

His younger brother then came to the throne as King Bhumibol Adulyadej, but he, too, was a largely symbolic presence until he completed his studies and returned to be officially crowned in May of 1950. At last Thailand had a ruler in residence, together with a beautiful young Queen, Her Majesty Queen Sirikit, whom he had married a week before his coronation.

A Modern Monarchy

Born in 1927 in Cambridge, Massachusetts, where his father, Prince Mahidol, was studying medicine, the new King had lived mostly in Switzerland with his mother, sister, and elder brother. The family had moved there after Prince

Mahidol's early death and except for the 1938 visit had been cut off from their homeland by the Second World War. He had a relatively normal youth, displaying notable talents in both music and engineering, and becoming fluent in

THAILAND King Bhumibol Adulyadej – The Golden Jubilee 1946-1996

three European languages as well as feeling at ease in a variety of cultures. When he suddenly found himself the ninth Chakri ruler, he returned to complete his education, changing from science to political science and law in recognition of his new role.

In his Oath of Accession to the Throne, as his ancestors had done, King Bhumibol Adulyadej pledged to "reign with righteousness for the benefit and happiness of the Siamese people." But what sort of reign would it be? After fifteen years of tumultuous change, during most of which the ruler had been merely a name to most Thais, was there still a place for monarchy? If so, what form would it take?

Any doubts about acceptance of the monarchy were quickly dispelled. Vast crowds in Bangkok had already shown their enthusiasm during the ceremonies that accompanied the royal wedding and the coronation, which members of the younger generation were seeing for the first time. In 1955, the King and Queen made a pioneering trip to the impoverished northeast, then a remote region that had not only never seen a ruling monarch in person but that also, with some reason, felt itself to be neglected by the central government. For twenty-two arduous days, the Royal Couple toured the region, visiting villages as well as cities, talking to ordinary people as well as monks and local officials. The response was overwhelming. Hundreds of thousands of people, some of whom walked days from isolated hamlets, turned out for even a fleeting glimpse of their King. The warmth of their greeting was unmistakable; so, too, was the extent of their

needs as revealed in the conversations His Majesty had with those he met.

This decision to bring the monarchy into direct contact with the provincial population was perhaps the most important of all those taken by His Majesty. Today he and members of the Royal Family spend almost seven months of the year in one or other of the royal residences that have been built outside of Bangkok—at Chiang Mai in the far north, Sakon Nakhon in the northeast, Hua Hin on the Gulf of Thailand, and Narathiwat in the south. From these, defying discomforts and inconveniences, His Majesty has visited every province in the country, going to even the most remote villages by helicopter, jeep, train, boat, or, on occasion, on foot, to ascertain for himself local conditions. In the process, he has become the most traveled monarch in Thai history, as well as the best informed about a wide range of rural difficulties.

Often assisted by other members of the Royal Family—Her Majesty the Queen, His Royal Highness Crown Prince Maha Vajiralongkorn and Their Royal Highnesses Princess Maha Chakri Sirindhorn and Princess Chulabhorn—the King takes careful notes on these trips and later initiates steps to provide assistance, always working through the appropriate government agencies but sometimes using his own funds in the early stages. He has established the Chai Pattana Foundation to provide initial or emergency financial support for subsequent development projects. A directive is never simply issued; the impetus comes from the local population, who must agree with the proposal and cooperate to see that it is successfully imple-

HRH The Princess Mother with her children, Prince Bhumibol Adulyadej and Princess Galyani Vadhana.

1982 Bangkok's bicentennial also celebrated two hundred years of rule by the Chakri dynasty with various ceremonies that included a rare Royal Barge procession along the Chao Phraya river.

Three Momentous Occasions

1987 A crowd celebrates His Majesty the King's sixtieth birthday, marking His Majesty's completion of the fifth cycle, with his royal portrait looming overhead; Inset: A lavishly decorated float at the celebrations.

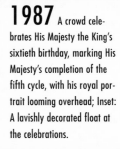

1988 Celebrations marking the King's breaking of the record of the longest reign of forty-two years and twenty-three days.

passing lowland areas as well. Migratory tribal peoples living in the mountainous region that forms Thailand's borders with Laos and Myanmar had become an increasing problem to the government, partly due to their destructive slash-and-burn technique of clearing land, partly due to the traditional cultivation of the opium poppy. Under His Majesty's project, a wide variety of new crops have been introduced to replace opium, and educational and medical facilities have been brought to permanent settlements. International recognition of the Royal Project's effectiveness has come in many forms, including financial grants and expert assistance by several foreign governments. In 1988, it was selected for the Ramon Magsaysay Award in the area of international understanding. In short, it may be said that through the Hilltribe Development Project, His Majesty has given the tribal people a "sense of belonging" to Thai society and, in effect, prevented them from falling prey to the Communists, which would have cost the government vast sums of money in security expenses and may have entailed the loss of many lives. As it was, scarce resources could then be channeled for the development of the country's economic infrastructure.

mented. Over 2,000 "royally-suggested" projects have been started in this way. Some are basic, such as irrigation and water-conservation schemes in the arid northeast or drainage and land-reclamation in the south, which faces the problem of floods. In others, imaginative solutions have been applied. His Majesty was the guiding force behind an artificial rain-making project which started in the late 1950's and took over ten years to experiment and develop so that the first field operations began in 1969 at Khao Yai National Forest in Nakhon Rachasima province. Thereafter, the successful methods were repeated countless times throughout the years all over the kingdom whenever conditions were suitable. Neighboring countries have also called on Thai teams to give assistance in times of drought.

Another early endeavor was His Majesty's Hilltribe Development Project in the north, now known as the Royal Project and encom-

Besides bringing obvious benefits to the country, such activities have had other results, less tangible but no less important. They have made the monarchy a potent moral force in Thai society and given His Majesty a paternal image that inspires both respect and deep affection.

During a student-led uprising in 1973, both sides turned to the King for advice that eased tensions and prevented serious bloodshed. He

This page: Members of the Royal Family reaching out to the people in various community projects.

THAILAND King Bhumibol Adulyadej – The Golden Jubilee 1946-1996

HRH The Princess Mother (1900-1995)

One of the most beloved members of the Royal Family was Her Royal Highness the Princess Mother, whose death on July 18, 1995, plunged the entire country into mourning. In many respects, her life was like a fairy tale, a rise from obscurity to lofty renown; in others, more revealing of her character, it was a study in selfless dedication, first to her family and then to public service.

Born a commoner, she was orphaned at an early age and spent part of her childhood under the care of a lady-in-waiting to a royal princess. She became interested in public health and studied at Siriraj Hospital, graduating at the top of her class in nursing and midwifery in 1917. Three years later, she won a royal scholarship to continue her studies in the United States.

It was in Boston, Massachusetts, that she met His Royal Highness Prince Mahidol, who was then at Harvard University. The chance meeting led to romance, and after permission was granted by King Vajiravudh (Rama VI) they were married at Srapatum Palace in Bangkok on September 10, 1920.

The Princess Mother's desire for higher education was shared by Prince Mahidol and both were also eager to help modernize Thai medicine. Accordingly, they returned to the United States where the Prince continued at Harvard and the Princess Mother studied sanitation and preventive techniques at Simmons College. They pursued their studies in other countries as well. Their first child, Princess Galyani Vadhana, was born in London in 1923, and their second, Prince Ananda Mahidol, in Heidelburg in 1925. They were back in the United States when Prince Bhumibol Adulyadej was born on December 5, 1927, in Cambridge, Massachusetts.

Prince Mahidol died at an early age, shortly after their return to Thailand. In 1933, following the end of the absolute monarchy, the Princess Mother took her three children to Switzerland, where they grew up and completed their formal education.

On the abdication of King Prajadhipok in 1935, Prince Ananda Mahidol was proclaimed king, with his duties handled by a Council of Regency until he reached maturity. He died during a visit to Bangkok on June 9, 1946, and Prince Bhumibol Adulyadej suc-

ceeded to the throne.

The Princess Mother now embarked on a career of public service that spanned nearly half a century and involved an extraordinary amount of work in rural Thailand. Inspired by Prince Mahidol's devotion to medicine, she founded the Volunteer Flying Doctors Foundation under the auspices of which doctors, nurses, and other specialists flew to remote provinces, usually accompanied by the Princess Mother. More than twenty organizations came under her patronage, ranging from the Leprosy Foundation to the Nursing Association. She took a particular interest in the Border Patrol Police, who live in often dangerous conditions, as well as the hill tribe people of the far north, who called her Mae Fah Luang, "the Royal Mother Descending from the Sky," because of her frequent visits to their far-off villages by helicopter.

To the Thai public in general she was affectionately known as Somdej Ya, the Royal Grandmother, at once warm and caring and a model of selfless dedication to helping others.

– W. W.

Above, left: The Princess Mother with her son, King Bhumibol; Above, right: As a member of the team of flying doctors, she attends to a patient; Left: In memorial of the Princess Mother; Below: Her cremation ceremony on March 10, 1996.

provided equally wise counsel during Thailand's struggle against a communist insurgency, suggesting solutions aimed at relieving rural poverty and inspiring confidence in the government's sincerity. Following the end of the conflict in Indochina in the mid-70's, it can be said that because of His Majesty's leadership and wisdom, Thailand did not become the next "domino" to

fall to Communism, as had been expected by some quarters in the Western world.

In May of 1992, violence once again broke out between pro-democracy civilians and military troops; television audiences around the world viewed the scene when leaders of both factions were granted an audience by the King, whose advice ended the confrontation. More recently, he has advised on ways to solve Bangkok's seemingly endemic problems of traffic congestion and flooding, often going out personally to inspect the most serious areas.

Ceremonial Role

In addition, His Majesty presides over a large number of other functions, many of them deeply rooted in Thai tradition. Three times a year, at the beginning of each season, he ritually changes the robes of the sacred Emerald Buddha, and, as a devout Buddhist, also participates in numerous merit-making ceremonies at temples all over the country. He is regarded, however, as the Upholder of All Religions, and as such has actively promoted better understanding between the majority of Thais and minority groups like the Muslims of the far southern provinces. All new ambassadors present their credentials to His Majesty and he grants audiences to foreign heads

Top: The King at the Trooping of the Colors in the Royal Plaza;
Left: The King and the Crown Prince receiving donations from members of the public at the Temple of the Emerald Buddha.

The Garuda as a Royal Symbol

Right: Garuda symbol at the entrance of Bangkok Bank; Far right: A cushion with the Garuda emblem in the Royal Palace.

The Garuda, a fierce-looking bird often depicted with a human torso and hands, is one of numerous figures from Indian mythology that have been incorporated into Thai art, usually by way of Khmer influence. In Hindu legend, it served as the mount for the god Vishnu and represented the aerial world; its enemy is the *naga*, or divine serpent, which it is often shown fighting or eating.

Since in early Thai capitals the King was traditionally compared to Vishnu, the Garuda became closely associated with royalty. In the Bangkok period, it was adopted as the emblem of the King of Thailand and also of the Thai nation. As such, it appears on the royal scepter and royal standard, as well as on government stationery and as badges on the caps of civil service officials. It is also found among the decorations on many buildings in the Grand Palace enclosure such as the Dusit Maha Prasat Throne Hall, dating from the reign of King Rama I, on thrones such as the Phra Thinang Busbok Mala where

early Chakri Kings gave royal audiences, as the figurehead on some of the royal barges, and on countless items made for royal use.

Certain commercial companies are granted permission to display the Garuda over the entrance to their headquarters. This should not be confused with the British concept of "By Royal Appointment," suggesting that firms so honored supply goods or services to the Royal Household. Rather, the symbol is awarded at His Majesty's personal discretion as a sign of royal approval to companies that have rendered outstanding economic and charitable services to the nation. Such an award is rarely bestowed and is considered a great honor by recipients; it can also be withdrawn from any who are later found unworthy.

– W. W.

of state, diplomats, and officials of the Thai government. As Head of State, he convenes Parliament at the beginning of each new session, and every draft law is submitted to him for his signature before promulgation.

Early in his reign he began attending graduation ceremonies, personally handing out degrees to the graduates of every Thai university as well as to those of military academies. The recent growth in the number of such institutions has made it necessary to delegate this responsibility to other members of the Royal Family in some cases, but His Majesty still presides over the ceremonies at the older ones like Chulalongkorn and Thammasat Universities, even though they extend over several days.

For over two decades, His Majesty has devoted himself almost entirely to his developmental projects and the performance of his ritual duties. In earlier years, however, he traveled extensively to more than thirty countries and met nearly all the leaders of the contemporary world. He also entertains visiting monarchs and heads of state when they come to Thailand and thus maintains a broad knowledge of current affairs.

In June of 1988, King Bhumibol Adulyadej became the longest-ruling monarch in Thai history, surpassing in that month the forty-two year reign of his grandfather King Chulalongkorn. This year he celebrates his Golden Jubilee, an even more notable landmark that makes him the longest-reigning of any ruler in today's world. For the past half century, because of His Majesty's benevolent reign, foresight and vision, Thailand has achieved much in terms of economic growth, general prosperity of the people and security for the nation.

The countless events planned throughout 1996 and the outpouring of affection from all Thais pay tribute both to the ancient institution of monarchy and to the singular man who has transformed it into a vital modern force.

Above, right: The King handing out degree scrolls during a graduation ceremony; Below: A royal white elephant;

Right: King Bhumibol presiding over the Golden Jubilee celebrations on June 9, 1996; Overleaf: The spectacular Wat Phra Keo, or Temple of the Emerald Buddha.

2

DEMOCRACY IN THAILAND

Dr Likhit Dhiravegin

THE PRESENT *THAI POLITICAL SYSTEM WAS BORN OUT OF ITS HISTORICAL DEVELOPMENT AND PECULIAR ENVIRONMENT. PUT AGAINST AN IDEAL POLITICAL SYSTEM, SUCH AS A DEMOCRATIC FORM OF GOVERNMENT IN THE WEST, THE EXISTING THAI POLITICAL SYSTEM APPEARS TO BE DEVIANT.*

However, it can be argued that in whatever form the present political system has evolved, stemming from its unique developmental process and environmental components, it is probably not likely to be repeated elsewhere. As a result, any discussion as such will have to take into account these peculiar characteristics which, in the final analysis, are uniquely Thai. These characteristics have gone through the process of incremental change and thus the system can, to a certain degree, be considered "development" in its own right.

Broadly defined, a "good" political system is one which is somehow "functional" in its environmental context. Tautological as this definition may sound, it is undeniable that the present Thai political system, dubbed Thai democracy, or sometimes referred to as a halfway democracy, is more or less functioning. Despite its imperfections, Thai democracy is likely to continue well into the future.

The Thai democratic system has evolved over the decades through a series of political turbulences. The painful process of democratic development has seen both ups and downs—mostly downs—but the people persist in fighting for their political freedom. This has resulted in three political bloodsheds. The first was the October 14, 1973 student-led uprising which resulted in the downfall of the military regime of Field Marshal Thanom Kittikachorn. This was followed by a three-year interlude of a democratic system. The embryonic democracy was again killed in a bloody coup d'état on October 6, 1976. Subsequently, the Thai political system was turned into a halfway democracy, which was an attempt to bring about a fusion between the old and the new elements. This halfway democracy, dubbed a demi-democracy in this essay, can be argued to epitomize the evolution of the Thai political system up until the May 17-20, 1992 bloody political event known as the Black May Event, the third bloody event in the modern history of Thai politics.

In order to grasp the

Facing page: King Bhumibol opening Parliament; Inset: Interior dome of Parliament House; Right: Democracy Monument.

development of this halfway democracy, one must understand its genesis.

Demi-democracy, or a halfway democracy, is by definition a blending of two elements—the old order and the new. It is thus half traditional, that is, authoritarian, and half modern, that is, democratic. To be sure, one can argue that such a "neither fish nor fowl" system is at best window-dressing, a dictatorial regime under the cloak of democracy. However, when an investigation of the evolutionary process of the present system is undertaken, it would appear that such a system has inevitably emerged from a process that is natural and probably desirable. Given the record of political trouble and, at times, turmoil of the decades since 1932, a balanced system under what has been dubbed a halfway democracy may be the only choice, at least for the initial period.

Demi-democracy: Its Genesis

If one is to describe the traditional Thai political system of Ayutthaya and its offshoot, early Bangkok, one would have to say that it was nothing more than an authoritarian political system, what sociologists would term a patrimonial system. It was characterized by a centralized administrative system under a handful of ruling elite in a traditional bureaucratic structure. The three main functions expected of the political system were the keeping of law and order, defense against external invasion and the performance of religious rites which were to bring blessings to the populace and the kingdom. In return, the political system was bent on three extractive functions: taxation in cash or in kind, mostly in kind; use of labor for the construction of palaces and

temples, and in public projects; and the requirement to fight against enemies in times of war, or blood taxation. Social equilibrium and harmony were elicited by a social order sanctioned by religious beliefs and social values. The emphasis was on the maintenance of the status quo. The system characterized by the attributes mentioned above continued until the advent of Western imperialism.

Starting with King Rama IV, a reform program along Western lines, such as the introduction of Western knowledge and the abolition of outdated customs and beliefs, was gradually undertaken. This modernization (Westernization) program was intensified by King Chulalongkorn the Great (1868–1910), who pushed full speed ahead with the reform program, known as the Chakri Reformation, in 1892. In the process, a number of changes took place in such areas as administration, fiscal policy, the legal system, military organization and the abolition of the corvée and slavery systems. In essence, the monarch successfully transformed the traditional Thai kingdom into a more or less modern nation-state with a modernized bureaucratic system. But the growth of the new bureaucratic system also gave rise to a new group of elites, notably those who were educated abroad. Amidst the winds of political change which swept through Europe and Asia—especially the revolution of 1911 in China, in which the Manchu Dynasty was overthrown—a wave of political demand for change also started to take shape during Rama VI's reign in 1911. It was known as the R.S. 130 Rebellion.

In fact, an appeal for political change was submitted to the monarch even during King Rama V's reign in 1885. A group of royal family and noble family members submitted an appeal to King Chulalongkorn to introduce a legislative assembly along the lines of Western democracy to which the King did not comply, citing the absence of readiness on the part of the general populace. Given the lack of educated masses at

Left, top to bottom: Demonstrators hold up portraits of the King and Queen during anti-government protests in central Bangkok in May 1992; Above: Various newspaper reports of civil unrest and the military crackdown.

the time, and given the precarious international situation in which the Western powers were waiting to exploit the Asian countries' weaknesses, it was understandable why the proposal was rejected. In fact, events after the 1932 revolution staged by the People's Party only attested to the analysis made by King Chulalongkorn. Despite the fact that the 1932 revolution occurred forty-seven years after the 1885 incident, the general populace had not changed. The revolution took place with very little involvement or understanding by the man on the street. In essence, it was a coup d'état of the military bureaucrats against the monarchy. In fact, what happened was an offshoot of the modernization process started by King Chulalongkorn which had

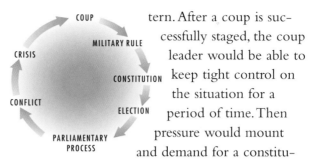

boomeranged. The growth of the bureaucratic institution had given birth to a bureaucratic elite, notably military officers, who sought to bring about political changes, a phenomenon which King Chulalongkorn himself must have anticipated.

The period from 1932 to 1957 (the year that Field Marshal Sarit Thanarat took over power) can be dubbed a struggle between bureaucracy and democracy. The most salient features are the numerous political troubles characterized by coups and rebellions and the dominant figure of Field Marshal P. Phibun Songkhram, who was Premier for almost fifteen years out of the twenty-five-year period. The period was noted for military dominance in politics and conflicts in various areas, notably conflicts over power and policy, conflicts between the old elite and the new, conflicts among the military factions in the army, conflicts between the army and navy, and conflicts between the military and police. These political conflicts resulted in ten coups and rebellions in this period, including the one in 1957 staged by Field Marshal Sarit Thanarat. The process can be summarized as a vicious circle.

The vicious circle proceeds along this pat-

Above: Field Marshal Phibun Songkhram, Prime Minister from 1938 to 1944 and 1948 to 1957; Right: Sarit Thanarat, who was Prime Minister from 1959 to 1963.

tern. After a coup is successfully staged, the coup leader would be able to keep tight control on the situation for a period of time. Then pressure would mount and demand for a constitution would be voiced. This would lead to the promulgation of a Constitution, to be followed by a general election and the forming of a government in a parliamentary process. Then conflicts would start and turn the whole process into confusion and eventually a crisis. At this particular juncture, the military would seek an opportunity to stage a coup, thus completing the circle.

The Pho Khun Political System of Sarit; National Development Policy and Social Change

To break the vicious circle, Field Marshal Sarit Thanarat staged a coup in 1957 and, after a one-year interlude, staged another coup in 1958, to be followed by a consolidation of political power. He then assumed absolute power. With the positions of Supreme Commander and Commander-in-Chief of the Army and later Director-General of the Police Department, Sarit assumed the premiership. His was a rule of absolutism. Article 17 of the Interim Constitution allowed him as Premier—and, in theory, with the consent of the Cabinet—to take any necessary drastic measures against acts which

were viewed as harmful to national security and stability, to law and order, and to moral principles. As a result, summary executions were carried out against such criminals as heroin traffickers, arsonists and communist suspects. Many people were detained as hooligans, violating the principle of habeas corpus. For a while, Sarit was hailed as a strong leader who commanded respect and awe among the other military leaders. Sarit then launched a commendable project, a national economic development policy. This came out in the form of economic planning starting with a six-year plan. Sarit sought to engage numerous technocrats in the development process. Universities were created in the provinces in the north, northeast, and south. Meanwhile, foreign investment was encouraged by incentives—such as tax-holidays and the build-up of infrastructure including dams and roads—to facilitate the process of industrialization. Sarit's political system was characterized as the *pho khun,* or patriarchal rule, a fatherly, benevolent dictatorship with a three-tiered governmental structure—the government, the bureaucracy, and the people. Such democratic institutions as political parties, elections and constitutions were at best window-dressing for Sarit and an annoying impediment to swift and decisive action.

True to his belief, Sarit appointed a Constituent Assembly, acting also as a Legislative Assembly, to draft a Constitution, but the tacit agreement was that the drafting process would drag on as long as possible to give him enough time to continue with his national development program. Sarit never even paid lip service to democracy. What he had in mind was to be a kind of benevolent patriarchal ruler who would

Below, left: The Ministry of Defense; Below, right: Government House, where the Prime Minister's office is located; Inset: Sculpture inside Government House.

The Structure of the Government

The lowest-ranking official in Thailand's government hierarchy is the *phu-yai-ban,* or village headman, who is popularly elected. Neighboring villages are organized into groups known as *tambon,* which, depending on topography and population density, may consist of anywhere from two to twenty-eight villages, and the *phu-yai-ban* of each *tambon* elects one of their group to be the *kamnan,* a sort of super headman. The *kamnan* serves as the link between the villagers and the *nai amphoe,* or district officer, the next highest official who in turn is directly responsible to the provincial governor.

Ministries are the next step up the pyramid of power. There are fourteen of these, including the Office of the Prime Minister, which was established in 1933 and has steadily grown in power since, particularly over the past three decades. Directly under the Prime Minister's Office come such divisions as the Budget Bureau, the Board of Investment, the National Statistical Office and the National Intelligence Agency.

The largest ministry is the Ministry of Interior, whose departments include Local Administration, Rural Development, Public Welfare, Labor, Public Works and the Police (divided into Metropolitan, Provincial, and Border Patrol services). The Ministry of Commerce regulates external and internal trade; the Ministry of Agriculture and Cooperatives covers fisheries and forestry as well as farming; while the Communications Ministry controls aviation, harbors, highways, land transport, and post, telegraph and telecommunications. The Education Ministry is in charge of elementary and secondary schools as well as fine arts and religious affairs. The Ministries of Defense, Industry, Finance, Foreign Affairs, Justice, Public Health, University Affairs, and Science, Technology, and Energy oversee their relevant areas of authority.

The Cabinet, with the Prime Minister as its Chairman, fashions national policy, which in turn is subject to approval by a Parliament composed of both elected and appointed members. All legislation passed requires the King's approval and signature, after which it is published in the Royal Gazette and becomes law.

Judicial power is exercised by three

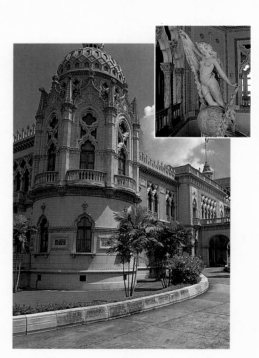

types of law courts. At the lowest level is the Court of First Instance, which in the Bangkok metropolitan area includes civil, criminal, central juvenile and magistrates' courts and outside the capital only a provincial court and juvenile and magistrates' courts of provincial status. The second level is the Bangkok-based Court of Appeal which hears appeals from all parts of the country. The third and highest level is the Supreme Court, also in Bangkok, which hears appeals only on points of law.

–W. W.

do anything for the welfare and well-being of the people and that in itself would be sufficient to legitimize his rule or grip on political power. In essence, what Sarit wanted to achieve was to freeze the process of political development, especially democratic development, which he saw as a useless, troublesome, and disruptive process; instead he concentrated on economic development and social improvement. One is reminded of the modernization program of King Chulalongkorn. In fact, it might not be incorrect to surmise that Sarit tried to emulate what the Great Monarch had achieved.

But then, as in the case of the Chakri Reformation, whose outcome boomeranged, Sarit's national development program started to produce results which were expected by the planners but also started to undermine the very political system which had brought them about. Sarit was lucky to pass away before he could see the boomerang-effect of his national development program. The drama unfolded during his successors' rule, that of Field Marshal Thanom Kittikachorn and Field Marshal Prapass Charusathien, in a dramatic event known sometimes as the October Revolution. This was the October 14, 1973 political upheaval in which the military regime was overthrown by a mass uprising of half a million people. This was an event which merits careful analysis for its waves of impact could be felt far and wide and, indeed, it shook the political system to its core, providing significant political implications for later periods and for the future of Thai politics.

The October 14, 1973 Uprising and the October 6, 1976 Coup

The October 14, 1973 uprising—in which the military government of Field Marshal Thanom Kittikachorn and Field Marshal Prapass Charusathien was overthrown by student-led mass demonstrations which culminated in shoot-outs with almost a hundred people killed and a

number wounded—was the first major bloody political event after 1957. It signaled the end of a military regime which had been in power since 1958, when Sarit took over power in his second coup. Factors leading to the October 14 upheaval were many, including the essential factors of factional struggles and conflicts among the military as a result of the demise of Sarit. However, what is important for an understanding of the event is the socio-economic changes which took place as a result of Sarit and company's national development policy.

It should be remembered that basic to Sarit's political system was the freezing of the political structure, while the development of the economy and the education of the people were given due attention. But as the national development policy started to bear fruit, it inevitably led to changes in the environment which made the political system of Sarit unfit for the new situation. Most notable was the emergence of new social groups as a result of socio-economic changes which had taken place. The changes in the economic and social environment included a shift in the economic structure from a mainly agricultural base, with rice as the main crop for export, to a base with more manufacturing industries and cash crops; the development of a greater degree of urbanization; an increase in the number of middle-class people, especially import-export businessmen, bankers, financiers, and industrialists; and an increase in college graduates resulting from university expansion. These new social forces soon started to make demands upon the closed political system. Against this backdrop, other factors served as a catalyst for a mass demonstration against the

Top, right: Field Marshal Thanom Kittikachorn succeeded Sarit Thanarat as Prime Minister in 1963 and was in power until 1973; Right: Field Marshal Prapass Charusathien, his Deputy Prime Minister.

government. The details and analysis of the event have already been given elsewhere. The above-mentioned socio-economic changes rendered the Sarit *pho khun* political system irrelevant and provided an environment which nurtured the downfall of the military regime created by Sarit and continued by Thanom and Prapass.

If October 14 indicated the end of a military regime of the Sarit type, it also served as the beginning of the end of a fully democratic form of government. During the three-year inter-lude—in which there were four elected governments and one semi-democratic form of government headed by Prof Sanya Dharmasakti right after the October 14 event—Thai society witnessed the most discouraging political phe-nomena in modern Thai political history. Violence embraced such methods as political assassination, grenade throwing at political demonstrations and rallies, an attack on the Prime Minister's house, and an attack on and the burning of Thammasat University. Given this sit-uation, even the most optimistic observers would conclude that the days of open politics were numbered. What was most worrisome was the polarization of political ideology between the left and the right. For a while it seemed as if the

Thai political fabric was being ripped at the seams. One is reminded of Samuel Huntington's argument of "political development and political decay" characterized by a high degree of politi-cal participation as a result of the growth of political consciousness, while the degree of political development in the form of a political institution and a process to regulate the partici-pation of the new social forces born out of socio-economic changes lagged behind; this imbalance between political modernization (political consciousness and hence the demand for participation) and political development (institution building) led to turmoil, termed decay by Samuel Huntington.

The October 6, 1976 bloody coup—which took place at Thammasat University and includ-ed political violence and atrocities unprecedent-ed in modern Thai political history—was in fact a backlash of the political turmoil preceding it. It brought the military back into Thai politics. Despite the fact that after the coup the new government was headed by a civilian, a former judge of the Dika Court (the Supreme Court), it was in essence a civilian dictatorship backed by the military. The "Oyster Government", as it was known (the military served as the shell of the

Left, top to bottom: Students carried pho-tographs of the King and Queen during the October 1973 uprising; Demonstrators taking a jubilant bus ride after setting fire to the police headquarters on October 15, 1973, fol-lowing a decade of mili-tary rule; Top, right: Student demonstrators at the Democracy Monument during the 1976 military coup.

oyster to protect the flesh, i.e., the government), lasted only about a year. Another military coup took place on October 20, 1977, bringing an end to the one-year nightmare under a civilian dictatorship which in many regards was more horrifying than the military government under Sarit. The anti-communist, ultra-rightist policy turned Thai society into a state of suspended political tension. But what was significant politically was that, if anything, it proved that the military was still a factor to be reckoned with in Thai politics, and the military was an element which the political system in Thailand, regardless of form, would have to accommodate. In the final analysis, the October 6, 1976 coup signified a military comeback to politics to claim its right, whether it was justifiable or not. Since then the military has played an increasing role in the Thai political process, albeit in a modified fashion. The military and its role in the political process, and the demands pressed upon Thai society by the new social forces, led to a political system in which the two elements could share a halfway democracy.

Thai Politics Under the Halfway Democracy

Halfway democracy can be interpreted in several ways.

General Kriangsak
Chomanan, Prime
Minister from 1977
to 1980.

First, it was a ploy by the government in power at the time of the promulgation of the Constitution of 1978 to make sure that it could continue to stay in power for as long as possible. This allegation was constantly made against General Kriangsak Chomanan, who was Prime Minister at the time the Constitution was put into practice. There were two important provisions. First, the Prime Minister did not have to run for election. Anyone with support from the Parliament, an elected House of Representatives and an appointed Senate could become the Prime Minister. Second, permanent civil servants and military officers could concurrently hold career positions and political posts. These provisions would

last for four years, after which the Constitution would come closer to a complete democracy with a number of changes. One was that permanent civil servants and military officers would not be allowed to hold bureaucratic positions and political posts at the same time. If they chose to be appointed to political positions, they would have to resign from their bureaucratic positions. The power of the Senate, which was still open for permanent civil servants and military officers, would be greatly reduced. This situation led to attempts by some military officers to amend the Constitution, asserting that the existing Constitution with this provisional clause was not suitable for Thailand because it prevented permanent civil servants and military officers, who were knowledgeable people, from rendering service to the country. Although attempts to have the Constitution amended failed a number of times, it was to become a hot political issue which will plague Thai politics for some time.

Second, halfway democracy can be said to be reflective of a realistic approach toward Thai institution building. It is in essence a fusion of the old and new elements or the old and new social forces. It is apparent to observers of Thai politics that, despite all the changes taking place in Thai society, the power structure and societal institutions have remained more or less intact. This is especially true of the military and civil bureaucrats. These elite groups will continue to play a dominant role in Thai politics for some time and conceivably well into the future.

There are four reasons for this. First, Thailand has never been colonized. The absence of a colonial rule has allowed the powerful elite to keep their position of power and status intact. This is different from those societies in which the colonial powers undermined the power of the traditional elite by uprooting them in one way or another. Second, Thailand has never experienced a social revolution as in Russia in 1917 and China in 1949, which, needless to say, uprooted the social systems by turning everything 180 degrees and thereby eliminated the traditional elite. Third, Thailand has never been forced to undergo drastic changes by an outside power as were Germany and Japan after the Second World War, although there was a suggestion to such effect. Lastly, Thailand was not greatly affected by the Second World War. Neither the physical damage nor the institutional or systemic damage was substantial enough to warrant any concern. Indeed, with a few exceptions, Thailand emerged from the war pretty much intact. Because of the above reasons, the Thai power structure and the elite have remained in a position of power and status continuously. They are a group of people which the political system has to accommodate; otherwise, they will find ways to express themselves and press their demands for a place in the power structure. They represent the old elements which have been discussed.

But on the other side of the coin, there is a new group of people emerging due to socio-economic changes that have taken place as a result of the national development policy of Sarit and his successors. This group includes import-export businessmen, bankers and financiers, industrialists and the middle-class intelligentsia. In addition, there have emerged unionized industrial workers and state-owned enterprise workers who have become increasingly vocal about their demands. These new social forces also have to be accommodated by the political system. As a result, something which can accommodate both the old and new elements has to be worked out.

The most realistic political system which has been devised is what has been dubbed halfway democracy, which has been in operation in some form or another since 1978. It allows for the selection of a Prime Minister who does not have to subject himself to political competition or humiliation in political campaigns in a general election. Former Prime

Ministers—General Kriangsak Chomanan, General Prem Tinsulanonda—were both military men. This fits with the Thai traditional political culture and values by having strong men in power, men who assume a position of power by invitation.

At the same time, the majority of the Senators are military officers who are appointed, first as a means to divide the pie, satisfying the various factions vying for power and prestige in Thai society, and second, as a form of political reward to buy off those elements who might cause problems for those in power. It is thus a neat arrangement which should satisfy both the traditional elements—the civil servants and military officers—and the new elements consisting of the groups from the newly emerged social forces discussed above.

The system had been working for more than a decade under General Kriangsak and General Prem until General Chatichai Chunhavan became Premier and was toppled in the coup of February 23, 1991 led by General Sunthorn Kongsompong and military officers who called themselves the National Peace-keeping Council.

What followed was a one-year military-supported government headed by Anand Panyarachun, a former civil servant in the Ministry of Foreign Affairs who left officialdom to join the business sector. A new Constitution was drawn up with the essential elements of the halfway democracy remaining intact or even more congenial to military dominance. After the general election of March 22, 1992, General Suchinda Krapayun, the Supreme Commander and the Commander-in-Chief of the Army, left

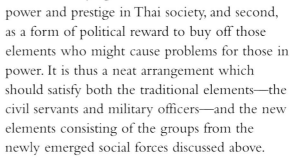

Bottom: Prem Tinsulanonda, Thailand's longest serving Prime Minister, who was in office from 1980 to 1988; Above, top to bottom: General Suchinda Kraprayun at a press conference after his successful February 1991 coup d'état; General Sunthorn Kongsompong, chairman of the National Peace-keeping Council.

THAILAND King Bhumibol Adulyadej – The Golden Jubilee 1946-1996

his posts to take up the premiership with the support of five political parties. It was a situation which fitted aptly into the pattern of a halfway democracy. But then the new government was met with public protest demanding a premier chosen from among the elected members of the House of Representatives. It ended in a bloody massacre known as the Black May Event which took place between May 17 and 20. The situation was similar to the October 14, 1973 event, but different in magnitude. For one thing, the participants in the demonstration consisted of people of all walks of life. Unlike the mass uprising of 1973, which consisted mostly of students, the May event consisted of the middle-class, many of whom were in the high income bracket. The media and information technology played a significant role in turning the tide against the government. It indicated beyond any doubt that the socio-economic changes witnessed in the 1970's had now reached another dimension. The political awareness of the people had also developed to another level. A discussion of the changes which have taken place should give the reader a clearer picture.

Meeting at a headman's house in a village.

If the 1973 uprising was caused partly by a change in the social and economic aspects of Thai society, the changes which have taken place over a period of almost two decades since are naturally much greater in magnitude and nature.

In the first place, in the past two decades, Thailand, or more precisely Bangkok, has undergone tremendous changes in its physical structure. Anyone who had been away from Thailand for some years would go into a state of shock at the sight of the high-rise buildings which form the Bangkok skyline these days. It has become a mini-Tokyo. A concomitant effect is certainly the traffic problem and a population density accompanied by the worst imaginable consequences. This situation has naturally made the people more concerned about how the city and the country should be run. The election of the Governor of Bangkok has become a serious business because the efficiency of the office-holder now has an impact upon the life of the city dwellers. Gone are the days when the people could afford to be apathetic about what is going on. With the rise of urbanization and its magnitude of problems, it has also aroused polit-

Democracy at the Village Level

The key person responsible for village organization and administration is the *phu-yai-ban*, or village head. This elected village leader, performing at the most basic level of the bureaucracy, is responsible for many important tasks in the community.

Although usually men, since 1983 many women have been elected village heads. The *phu-yai-ban* must be a householder, resident for at least six months in the village, be at least twenty-five years old and literate, and have no political party affiliations. Retirement is mandatory at sixty years of age.

The tasks the *phu-yai-ban* must attend to include recording all births and deaths, arranging for ID cards and house registration, as well as representing villagers in their dealings with the government, especially the local district office. Clearly, the *phu-yai-ban* is a person with considerable influence and this can be seen from his mediating role in village

disputes and arguments. Moreover, he or she must oversee all communal projects which might range from a local temple fair or religious celebration to the repair of bridges or construction of the village school. The *phu-yai-ban* does not work alone; usually two deputies will be designated, and advice will be available from the local temple abbot, senior monks and the local head teacher. Senior members of the community are always consulted on serious matters.

The *phu-yai-ban* is linked to the administration of villages in the area via *tambon* councils, which are controlled by an elected *kamnan*, or *tambon* head. District officers from the local government administration will also assist the *tambon* councils. Until the promulgation of the Tambon Council and Tambon Administration Organization Act in March, 1995, district officers were the main controllers of the *tambon* councils, but following the law change, more power has been given to elected officials (especially the *kamnan* and the *phu-yai-*

ban) to suggest and then organize development projects for their district which are appropriate to the local community. This act was introduced as a measure to devolve some power from central administration to that at the local level. And instead of imposing authority via the district officer, these officers must now offer advice and then let the local people decide for themselves what development is needed.

– *JOHN CLEWLEY*

ical consciousness. The Thai people, or more accurately the Bangkokians, now have a new political outlook. Indeed, one can argue that Bangkok has now given birth to the features of a democracy. For example, in the March 22, 1992 and September 13, 1992 general elections, two political parties contended in Bangkok, in contrast to a single party election. The people also voted for the party rather than the individuals, generally speaking.

Second, over the past two decades, Thailand's economy has undergone substantial changes. It has departed from the import-substitution industrial model into an export-promotion pattern. More than half of the exports of Thailand are manufactured products, indicating a qualitative change in the production pattern. Thai merchandise is now in competition with that of other countries in the world market. Investment from abroad in industries, real estate, and the stock market have turned the country into an investors' paradise leading to a double digit growth rate for some years. This structural change picked up where the 1970's left off. The country has almost reached the stage of being classified as a newly-industrialized country.

Third, closely related to the above, is the development of an economic infrastructure and telecommunications system. In this age of information technology, the development, once begun, went at a very fast speed. Today, one can send a fax from one's car to another person's car in a different country. The cellular telephone

makes it possible for a businessman on the golf course in a suburb of Bangkok to discuss a business deal with his counterpart in the United States, Tokyo, or Taiwan. Information technology and the need to keep abreast of the world situation have also led to the availability of satellite discs, cable television and the Internet. The world has become increasingly smaller. But it has also led to a greater knowledge of the global situation and how Thailand needs to adapt to the changing world. Any gross deviation from the correct trajectory would be frowned upon by well-informed businessmen, academicians, and technocrats. This only adds to the degree of political consciousness and, hence, democratic sentiments.

Fourth, over the past two decades, there has emerged a considerable number of young business professionals and entrepreneurs. The yuppies who have used business opportunities to make their fortunes have taken on the world trend of an open political system. Many of these young businessmen were among those who participated in the October 14, 1973 uprising. They see very clearly the linkage between political stability and business prosperity. They are also influenced by the notion that a democracy is the only guarantee of a viable political system. They are much more democratically-minded than their counterparts in the military bureaucracy. As a result, the demonstrators who took part in the protest against the government headed by General Suchinda consisted of a sizable number of so-called "mobile telephone" or "motorcar driving" protestors. From a survey conducted by the Association of Social Sciences of Thailand on May 17, 1992, it was discovered that a large number of the pro-democracy protestors were from the middle class with high incomes and high educational attainment (see table).

Fifth, added to the above is the world trend toward democratization and an emphasis on economic development. The collapse of the Soviet Union and the changes that have taken place in

Top, left: A reminder to members of the public to vote; Top, right: Residents in Bangkok checking their names before voting outside a polling station on March 22, 1992, in the general election following an army coup a year ago; Left: A temple polling booth; Above: Election poster of recently elected Governor of Bangkok, Bhichit Rattakul.

AGE, OCCUPATION AND INCOME DISTRIBUTION OF PROTESTORS							
Age	**%**	**OCCUPATION**	**%**	**INCOME**	**%**		
-20	2.0	Gov't Official	14.8	-5,0000	14.1		
20-29	39.4	State-owned Ent.	6.2	5,000-9,999	28.5		
30-39	36.5	Private Employee	45.7	10,000-19,999	30.0		
40-49	14.2	Propriator	13.7	20,000-50,000	15.5		
50+	6.7	Student	8.4	50,000+	6.2		
No Ans	1.0	Others	10.2	No Ans.	5.7		

Eastern Europe have sent a shock wave to other socialist states. These new trends are marked by an outcry for an open political system and economic development so that the fruits of success can be distributed among the people. These two trends cannot escape the notice of the Thai people who have access to news and development beyond the country's borders.

With that as a backdrop, it should not be surprising that the military, employing an archaic method of distorting information and imposing a government against the will of the people, ended up as a complete failure. The new political parameters simply rendered the old system irrelevant.

Given that this is something to be happy about, one must also admit that in terms of democratic development, there is still much left to be desired. The quality of politicians, ideological commitment, organization of political parties or even the supreme law of the land, the Constitution, still need great improvement. But to grasp a total picture of the problems embedded in the system, a macroscopic view is imperative.

A Macroscopic Perspective

The political system in Thailand, as already discussed, changed from an absolute monarchy to a constitutional monarchy in June 24, 1932. But the democratic system adopted at that time has met with ups and downs. The development process has also been intermittently interrupted by coups d'état, both bloodless and bloody. The most dramatic events, as already discussed, were those of October 14, 1973, October 6, 1976 and May 17–20, 1992. The first event was a mass uprising which overthrew the military regime of Field Marshal Thanom Kittikachorn and Field Marshal Prapass Charusathien. The second event involved a massacre at Thammasat University followed by a military coup. The third event was a violent suppression of pro-democracy protestors, an event similar to the October 14, 1973 uprising which also brought down the government.

Since 1932, the country has been plagued by political turbulence characterized by the vicious cycle discussed earlier. It is a common practice to attribute the failure of democracy to military intervention in politics as can be seen from the number of coups and rebellions, totaling eighteen, since 1932. There have also been two mass uprisings. However, there is also the other side of the coin. A weak civilian government and the lack of a system

Center: King Bhumibol urging the reconciliation of Prime Minister Suchinda Kraprayun and pro-democracy leader Chamlong Srimuang in a televised broadcast on May 20, 1992.

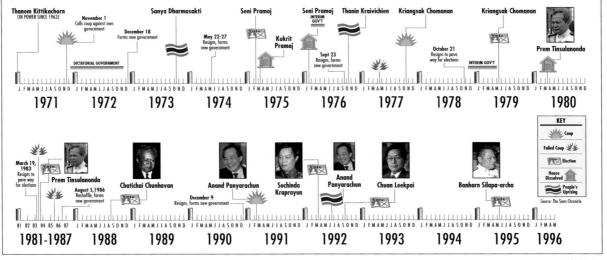

source: The Nation

which can successfully manage conflicts are also very important factors which need to be analyzed. Most analysts of the problems of democratic development in Thailand have focused on a few factors which are very useful in understanding the causes of the system's failure. But if one is to pin down the various factors which need to be identified in order to rectify the problems, a macro-view is imperative. Moreover, one has also to take into account the milieu, domestic as well as international, under which the political system functions.

The macroscopic framework which can be used for analyzing the problem of democratic development in Thailand includes three structures. On the top is what can be called the superstructure. It consists of the Constitution, the political parties, the electoral system,

Parliament, the government, and the bureaucracy. At the bottom lies the substructure which involves the local government. This part is very important because it involves the majority of the people. It will serve as the foundation upon which the superstructure is to grow and, as will be pointed out later, the emphasis given to the superstructure in the past, while neglecting the substructure, has brought about the negative political consequences affecting the development of a democracy today. The structure which serves to link the superstructure with the substructure is the intermediate structure. It comprises pressure or interest

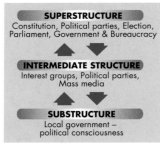

groups, political parties, and the mass media. It should be noted that political parties serve on two levels, in both the superstructure and the intermediate structure.

The diagram on the left provides a holistic picture showing the linkage of the various elements in the three structures. If one is to identify the most important variables in the democratic development in Thailand, it can be strongly argued that in the superstructure, the political

party is the most important element. Indeed, political parties as a major political mechanism of a democracy can be developed to such an extent that they can filter the bad elements from the good ones when it comes to the recruitment of members and candidates to stand in an election. We would then have what would be a good group of people to run and serve the people. If the parties are decent with a strong ideology as a foundation, the electoral process should be a fair one. Hence the House of Representatives could consist of good politicians, and as a result, provide good government. Viewed in this context, political parties can be viewed as a principal factor, whereas the remaining elements are just derivatives. It is to be noted with gratification that this realization has led to a number of proposals to help nurture the development of political parties such as to provide financial subsidies for parties of meager means.

On the substructure, it is imperative that a decentralization of power takes place. This is to guarantee that political and administrative powers would not be over-centralized and turn the situation into Bangkok-centrism which has been the case. More importantly, hand in hand with decentralization of political and administrative powers, attempts must be made to extend economic development and business vibrancy into the provinces. This will work positively for rural and provincial development. It will also allow greater revenue through a new system of local taxes to finance local government. The two key factors, political parties and the decentralization of power or local government, are imperative for democratic development.

Top: An anti-government rally in May 1992; Left: A speaker at a political rally.

Conclusion

Thai democracy has come a long way. If there is any event that epitomizes the struggle for democracy to be installed in Thai society, one can argue that the government formed after the September 13, 1992 election, symbolically as well as substantively was a democratic government in the true sense of the word. It was a government led by Chuan Leekpai, a man of common family background. His father was a school teacher and his mother a vendor of food and fruits in a market. Chuan represented an idealized country boy who had made it. He was trained as a lawyer and was a self-made man. But instead of attending to his legal career, he turned to politics and after more than twenty years of experience, climbed to the top post as the country's twentieth Prime Minister. His government lasted two years and eight months before, subjected to political pressure, he declared the House of Representatives dissolved. In the July 2, 1995 election, the Chart Thai Party won the majority of seats in the House and its leader, Banharn Silpa-archa was named the country's twenty-first Prime Minister. Like Chuan, Banharn is a commoner who has made his fortune in business. Both men have striking similarities. Neither was from a bureaucratic, military, or civil background. The stories of the two men tell a great deal about the Thai social system. In a sense, they are indicative of the great potential of the society to move ahead with democratic development.

Chuan Leekpai can be said to have performed reasonably well during his two years and eight months in office. How Banharn will per-

form remains to be judged by history.

Indeed, of the potential candidates for premiership in the last election, there were altogether six men with high profiles. Chuan and Banharn could be said to represent the common people. General Chavalit Yongchaiyudh and General Chatichai Chunhavan, both from the army, were also potential contenders for the posts but did not make it. They represent the military bureaucrats or the old guard. The last two were Dr Amnuay Viravan and Dr Thaksin Shinawatra, both of whom have earned their doctorates from the United States. They represent the modern generation, suited for the age of information and globalization. What is interesting is that the sons of common people are running the show. They are populists who know how to capture the people's hearts. But in the long run, there is a likelihood that the modern generation such as Amnuay and Thaksin will replace them. The top military, it can be surmised, is likely to find themselves having to adjust politically or they might find themselves out of place and out of time.

On the positive side, one can argue that Thai democracy is here to stay. But one has to be braced for disappointment since it is certain that the process will not be a smooth one. There will be political conflicts of various types. But as long as the system can be sustained, it will have a future. There are simply no other systems left to choose from. The socialist system is now dying a natural death while a military regime can at best keep law and order only for a short time. The only choice left for the Thais is to nurture their fledgling democracy.

Top: Chuan Leekpai at the Democrat Party headquarters being confirmed as Prime Minister;
Below:
Banharn Silpa-archa;

Right: Parliament in session; Overleaf: The people honoring the slain pro-democracy demonstrators in May 1992.

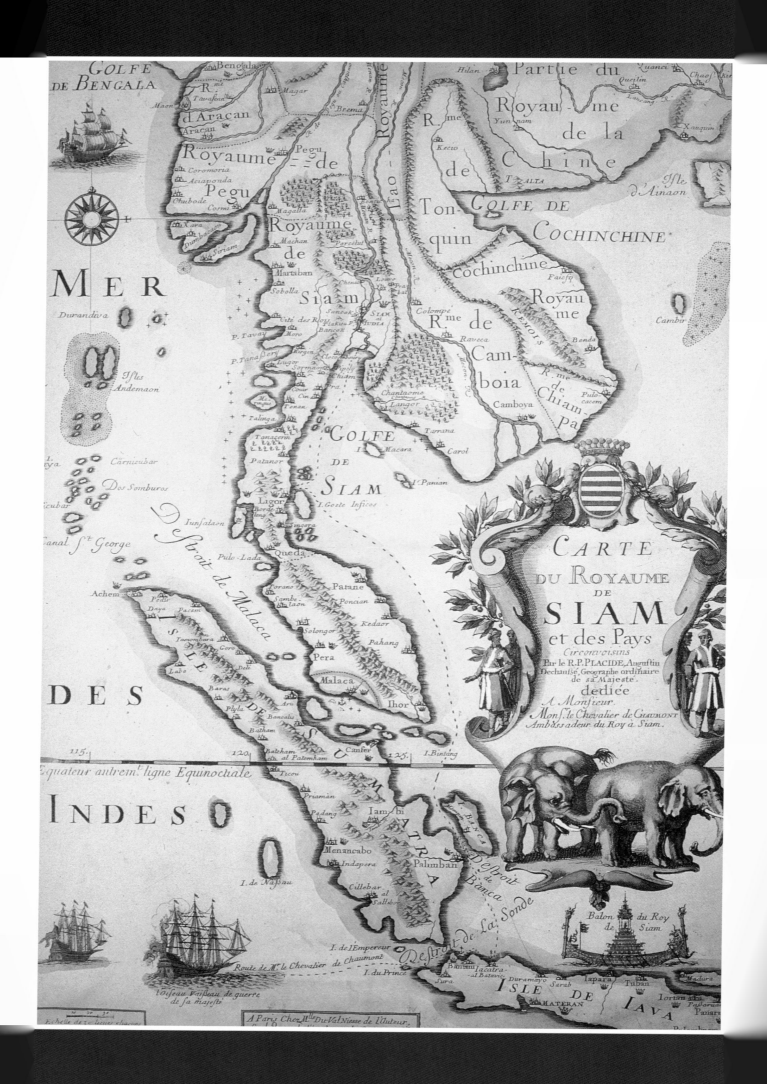

GOLFE DE BENGALA

Partie du Royau-me de la Chine

MER

INDES

INDES

D'Stroit de Malaca

GOLFE DE SIAM

Royaume d'Aracan

Royaume de Pegu

Royaume de Siam

Tonquin

Cochinchine

Royaume de Camboia

R.me de Chiampa

GOLFE DE COCHINCHINE

Isle d'Ainaon

Isles Andemaon

Canal S.t George

ISLE DE SUMATRA

Equateur autrem.t ligne Equinoctiale

Route de M.r le Chevalier de Chaumont

ISLE DE JAVA

Destroit de la Sonde

Destroit de Banca

CARTE DU ROYAUME DE SIAM et des Pays Circonvoisins
Par le R.P. PLACIDE, Augustin Dechaussé, Geographe ordinaire de sa Majesté.
dediée
A Monsieur
Mons.r le Chevalier de CHAUMONT
Ambassadeur du Roy à Siam.

Balon du Roy de Siam

A Paris Chez M.rs Du-Val Niesse de l'Auteur.

3

THAILAND'S FOREIGN POLICY

Anand Panyarachun

O N JUNE 9, 1996, ABOUT SIXTY MILLION THAI PEOPLE ACROSS THE REALM JOINED TOGETHER TO CELEBRATE THE FIFTIETH ANNIVERSARY (GOLDEN JUBILEE) OF HIS MAJESTY KING BHUMIBOL ADULYADEJ'S ACCESSION TO THE THRONE OF THE KINGDOM OF THAILAND.

As we look across the decades, we can only marvel at the momentous transformations that have taken place in this Southeast Asian kingdom where His Majesty has reigned for half a century. At present, Thailand has achieved remarkable political stability. It is on its way to becoming a newly industrialized economy with a strong focus on international trade. With a stronger economy comes greater capabilities and responsibilities to facilitate Thailand's neighbors in their efforts at human resources and infrastructure development. All these developments are taking place within a relatively peaceful regional environment. Nearly fifty years ago on his official coronation, when His Majesty uttered the Oath of Succession to "reign with righteousness for the benefit and happiness of the Siamese people," Thailand was struggling to rebuild its war-torn economy; it was engaged in difficult negotiations with the Allies to be admitted to the United Nations; its political system was in a state of

flux, and anti-colonial wars were breaking out along all four points of the compass.

That Thailand was able to weather the storm unleashed by fifty years of political turmoil and conflict in Southeast Asia and transform itself from an economically underdeveloped, politically unstable and threatened nation into a stable, cohesive and prosperous modern state is, in part, a testament to the success of Thailand's foreign policy. It was able to protect its sovereignty and territorial integrity, maintain political stability, build economic prosperity and promote its political and economic interests abroad.

Thailand's success in achieving these goals can be attributed to its unique approach in conducting its foreign relations and the wise leadership and statecraft of Thai leaders. But what is unique about Thai foreign policy?

Thailand's foreign policy is first and foremost deeply rooted in pragmatism. It seeks to achieve what is possible and in the best interests of the Thai people under the prevailing circumstances, even if it entails sacrifices. For example, when the independence of the Thai nation was threatened by British and French colonialism in the nineteenth century, King Chulalongkorn (Rama V) was able to preserve the independence of the Thai nation and the freedom of its people but at the cost of giving territorial concessions to France and Great Britain. Thus, even though the size of the Thai kingdom was reduced by almost half by 1907, King Chulalongkorn was able to steer Thailand through the stormy seas of the colonial age into the twentieth century as a sovereign country, thus enabling Thailand to remain true to its name—"the land of the free."

Secondly, Thai foreign policy attempts to provide as many options as possible on how to face a particular threat. During the Second World War, when the Thai government was forced out of necessity to side with Japan, channels of communication were maintained with Great Britain and the United States through the Seri Thai (Free Thai) Movement. Thai foreign policy is thus highly adaptive and flexible. When faced with an unavoidable and insurmountable danger, Thailand is able to pursue the course of mutual accommodation. But while Thailand may make compromises, its vital interests such as its sovereignty and the safety and well-being of the Thai people remain supreme. To foreign observers, thus, Thai foreign policy is like a bamboo reed: it bends with the wind but, unlike the mighty oak, never breaks.

Thailand has indeed been fortunate to have had wise statesmen guide the country's foreign policy as well as skilled practitioners to implement it. Throughout the centuries, Thai monarchs have played a leading role in managing the country's foreign relations with its neighbors and outside powers. From the first Thai city-states in the thirteenth century to present-day Thailand, Thai kings have played the roles of policy-maker, advisor and diplomat. Whether through the cultiva-

tion of close working relationships with foreign leaders or the exercise of personal initiative in times of crisis, the kings of Thailand have helped the Thai Kingdom and people to remain essentially free from foreign rule for over seven centuries.

Even today, his Majesty the King has an important role to play in foreign policy. As a constitutional monarch, His Majesty is above politics. But while the King may not rule, he reigns over the Thai people. As His Majesty holds a special place in the hearts of the Thai people and commands universal respect, his advice on affairs of state, including foreign policy, is sought and given. The story of Thailand's foreign policy over the past fifty years is very much a part of the story of His Majesty's reign. Hence, it is only apt that we begin the story of Thailand's foreign policy at around 1946, the year His Majesty acceded to the throne of the Kingdom of Thailand.

Thailand's Foreign Policy in the Aftermath of the Second World War

Following the conclusion of the Second World War in the Pacific in 1945, Thailand faced an uncertain future. There was accusation that Thailand had sided wholeheartedly with Japan in the war against the Allied Powers and deserved harsh treatment as a loser of the war. One must recall, however, that there were over 100,000 Japanese troops in occupation of Thailand since 1941. The Thai government was under duress and had no choice but to render its

Below: The King and Queen receiving heads of state of foreign countries in Thailand: (left to right) with President Lyndon Johnson of the USA (1966); with Queen Elizabeth II of the United Kingdom (1972); with President Suharto of Indonesia (1970); with President Li Xiannian of China (1985); and with Emperor Akihito of Japan (1991).

cooperation to the Japanese occupation forces in order to preserve what remained of Thai independence, to maintain the dignity of the Thai nation and, most importantly, to spare the Thai people the horrors of war. Thai foreign policy after the Second World War aimed at gaining international understanding of Thailand's unique situation and securing its acceptance by the Allies as an equal partner in the emerging postwar order. To achieve this, Thailand's paramount tasks were to normalize its relations with the Allies and gain admission to the United Nations.

Between 1945 and 1946, Thailand entered into separate negotiations with Great Britain and France with the aim of normalizing relations. Excessive demands, particularly those involving territorial concessions and reparations, were initially made by these two countries as preconditions for normalization. The Soviet Union made the establishment of relations a precondition for Thailand's admission to the United Nations. The only assets that Thailand had then were its diplomacy and the friendship offered by the United States which had never recognized a state of war between the two countries. Led by Prince Wan Waithayakorn, Thai diplomats were able to soften British, French and Soviet demands through a combination of skill, determination, courtesy and humility.

On New Year's Day in 1946, Thai efforts bore fruit when the state of war ended between

Thailand and the United Kingdom. In the case of France, Thailand had always maintained good relations with it and with French Indochina as represented by the Vichy government throughout the war. For France, now represented by the Free French, to claim that a state of war had nevertheless existed, and that agreements previously made with Vichy had to be re-negotiated, was simply victor's justice. In the end, the Thai government accepted many of the French demands in November 1946 including the return of territory regained in 1941. In exchange, France agreed not to veto Thailand's admission to the United Nations. The remaining obstacle was the Soviet Union. Following last minute negotiations, the Soviet Union agreed not to object to Thailand's admission to the United Nations once it learnt that Thailand was willing to establish relations with it. Finally, in December 1946, Thailand achieved its goal and became the fifty-fifth member of the United Nations.

Thailand's admission to the United Nations in December 1946 was indeed the culmination of Thailand's post-war diplomacy and a triumph for Thai foreign policy. The event closed the chapter on Thailand's difficult role during the Second World War. More importantly, UN membership signified Thailand's return to active engagement with international organizations—a tradition which Thailand had maintained ever since it became a founding member of the League of Nations in 1920. Moreover, the

United Nations was seen as one of the best institutions available to advance and protect the interests of small states such as Thailand and to contribute toward maintaining international peace and security. Thus a strong commitment to the principles embodied in the UN Charter and consistent support for UN activities became a cornerstone of Thailand's foreign policy after the Second World War.

Thailand also aspired to become a center for UN development activities. This goal was initially realized in 1949 with the opening of the regional office of the Food and Agricultural Organization (FAO) in Bangkok and the UN Economic Commission for Asia and the Far East (which later became known as the UN Economic and Social Commission for Asia and the Pacific—ESCAP). As the decade drew to a close, Thailand had established itself as a responsible and active member of the United Nations.

One of the causes which Thailand actively promoted as a UN member was decolonization. With its own history of resisting colonialism, Thailand identified with the aspirations of Southeast Asians to free themselves from colonial rule. Therefore, despite economic problems at home, Thailand provided moral support and, on various occasions, material assistance to the nationalist groups fighting for independence in French Indochina and elsewhere in the region. It was also at this time, however, that ideological conflict and the interests of external powers began to impinge on Southeast Asia. The issue of decolonization, and Thailand's role in support of it, were subsequently subsumed by the emerging global ideological conflict.

The Cold War in Southeast Asia
A breakdown in the consensus between the wartime Allies shattered the dream of a new

Below, left: Princess Maha Chakri Sirindhorn; Below, right: The King's visit to a rural community as part of the Royal Project.

Thai Winners of the Magsaysay Awards

Since its inception in 1958, the Ramon Magsaysay Award has achieved the status of a Nobel Prize for outstanding individuals and groups in Asian countries. Thai winners of the coveted award reflect accomplishments in a variety of fields.

Public Service
1961: Ms Nilawan Pintong—for her voluntary participation and leadership in developing constructive civic enterprises that have given women a new and creative role in Thailand.
1967: MC Sithiporn Kridakara—for nearly half a century of pioneering experimentation and education devoted to the advancement of Thai agriculture.
1975: Phra Chamroon Parnchand—for curing thousands of drug addicts with unorthodox yet efficacious herbal and spiritual treatment in his monastery.
1978: Ms Prateep Ungsontham—for bringing learning, better health and hope to children in the slum of Klong Toey in Bangkok.
1983: Mr Fua Hariphitak—for preserving and teaching a younger generation art forms that distinguish Thailand's unique graphic and architectural heritage.
1984: Mr Thongbai Thongpao—for effective and fair use of his legal skills and pen to defend those who have less in life and thus need more in law.

1991: HRH Princess Maha Chakri Sirindhorn—for using her royal office as an instrument of enlightened endeavor for Thailand and her sparkling embodiment of the best that is Thai.
1994: Mr Meechai Viravaidya—in recognition of mounting creative public campaigns in Thailand to promote family planning, rural development and AIDS prevention.
Government Service
1965: Dr Puey Ungphakorn—for dedication, unquestioned integrity and a high order of professional skill brought to the management of Thailand's public finance.
1966: Dr Phon Sangsingkeo—for his farsighted design in creating and staffing superior mental health services for his country.
1981: Dr Prawase Wasi—for research contributions to medical science and promoting modern health care for the poor.
1992: Mr Chamlong Srimuang—for his exemplary governorship of Bangkok and his fervent insistence that elections are the sole legitimate path to political power in Thailand.

Community Leadership
1973: Dr Krasae Chanawongse—for demonstrating that a doctor dedicated to service can overcome the most stubborn of obstacles in bringing effective health services to neglected and impoverished rural people.
1987: Dr Aree Valyasevi—for his contribution in improving the diets and promoting the good health of millions of Thai children.
Journalism, Literature and Creative Communication, Arts
1971: Mr Prayoon Chanyavongse—for his use of pictorial satire and humor for over three decades in unswerving defense of the public interest.
International Understanding
1988: The Royal Project—for its concerted national and international efforts to curtail opium growing by bringing worthy livelihoods to Thailand's hill tribes.

– W. W.

post-war order governed by the principles enshrined in the UN Charter. Instead, a half-century of intense global, ideological and political confrontation began. By the early 1950's, the Cold War, as it came to be called, had spread to Asia and Southeast Asia. Small countries such as Thailand were swept by the winds of change, and consequently became engulfed in the Cold War.

Thailand viewed communist ideology as a threat not only to its political system but, more importantly, to the Thai way of life. The quandary faced by Thailand was that while it supported decolonization in Southeast Asia, it felt uneasy with the possibility of communist states emerging on its doorsteps. Unfolding events in the 1950's further added to Thailand's security concerns. The victory of the Chinese communist forces in China in 1949 and the outbreak of the Korean War in 1950 were seen as warning signals of the rising tide of communist influence.

The signing of the Geneva Agreements in 1954 marked a key turning point in Southeast Asian history. Thailand was satisfied with the agreement in that it laid the basis for the attainment of full independence by northern Vietnam, Laos and Cambodia. Yet, the celebration was bitter-sweet as the agreement represented a fork in the roads at which fellow Southeast Asian countries parted to go their separate ways. Fearful of communist expansion and in need of assistance to pursue development, Thailand chose to ally itself with the West. Other countries, such as North Vietnam, whose leaders during the wars for independence often receive Thai help, aligned themselves with the communist countries. Southeast Asia became divided, as it was during the colonial years, and the destiny of Southeast Asians came to be increasingly dictated by events controlled by foreign powers.

Alignment with the West

Thailand's foreign policy during the period of the Cold War in Southeast Asia, particularly from 1954 to 1975, was aimed primarily at defending itself against the perceived expansion of communist influence to its borders. The United States at that time was likewise concerned with the rise of communist influence in Asia. There was thus a meeting of minds on the security threat between Thailand and the United States and the Western nations. This convergence of interest led to a period of close coordination of foreign and security policy amongst the parties. Such coordination was formalized through Thailand's accession to the Manila Pact in 1954 which led to the creation of the Southeast Asia Treaty Organization (SEATO), with headquarters in Bangkok. SEATO, which grouped Thailand, the Philippines and Pakistan with the United States, France, the United Kingdom, Australia and New Zealand, pledged all members to close consultations in the event of threat and aggression against any one of its members. The multilateral arrangement was reinforced through the bilateral security arrangement between Thailand and the United States as embodied in the *Thanat-Rusk Communiqué* of 1962. This document, in effect, pledged the United States to come to the assistance of Thailand in the event of an armed attack against the latter. Throughout this period, Thailand participated in a network of security arrangements

Above, right: The King and Queen visiting Washington, D.C.; Below: ESCAP building in Bangkok and flags of members of the United Nations.

to protect itself from external threats, particularly following the outbreak of the Second Indochina War in 1961.

Another key aspect of Thailand's foreign policy was supporting the efforts of the Laotian and South Vietnamese governments, and later, the Khmer Republic government, in their struggle against their respective indigenous communist movements. Facilities were provided for the US military in its campaigns in support of the non-communist government in Indochina. For a short period of time, Thai military forces were part of the Allied forces operating in South Vietnam. In return, Thailand received extensive military assistance and training which helped modernize the Royal Thai Armed Forces and strengthened their capabilities in dealing with Thailand's own insurgency movement which began in the 1960's.

Economic Development and Foreign Assistance

Thailand was well aware that domestic stability and economic prosperity were the key long-term defenses against foreign ideological and political challenges. The most important contribution of Thailand's foreign policy during the years of the Cold War was that it helped provide a breathing space and a relatively secure environment for development and nation-building to take place. With foreign policy serving as a shield against external intervention, Thailand redoubled its efforts to accelerate economic development and extend government authority and basic services to the rural areas.

It is in this area that His Majesty the King played a pivotal role. Through royal visits to every corner of the kingdom, His Majesty was able to gain a deep insight into the problems of rural development and to initiate royal projects to solve these problems. Modern irrigation systems, new agricultural techniques and better public health facilities were the outgrowth of these royal development projects. With the establishment of Royal Development Study Centers throughout the kingdom, the benefits of research were made available to the rural population.

These efforts have won praise from the international community. In this connection, various international awards, including the following, were presented to Their Majesties the King and Queen. In recognition of His Majesty's efforts to ease the plight of the hill tribes and eradicate opium plantations in the so-called "golden triangle" area which borders Thailand, Laos and

Myanmar, His Majesty was to become the first recipient ever of the UN International Drug Control Program (UNDCP) Award for his Royal Crop Substation Projects in 1994. Likewise, Her Majesty Queen Sirikit would receive the FAO's Ceres Medal in 1979 for her efforts in uplifting the status of Thai women, particularly in the rural areas. Indeed, these efforts on the part of His Majesty and other Members of the Royal Family were the central pillar of the national endeavor to alleviate the hardship of the rural population and more importantly, strengthen national unity.

Thai foreign policy supported these development efforts by channeling foreign economic assistance, from both multilateral and bilateral sources, to the country' economic development drive. Funds flowed in from financial institutions such as the International Bank for Reconstruction and Development and the Asian Development Bank. With the UN Economic Commission for Asia and the Far East or ECAFE (now called the UN Economic and Social

Below: King Bhumibol addresses a joint session of Congress in the House Chamber on June 29, 1960. Seated behind him are Vice-President Richard Nixon and the Speaker of the House, Sam Rayburn.

Commission for Asia and the Pacific—ESCAP) in Bangkok, assistance from UN agencies was forthcoming. Through its close foreign coordination with the West, bilateral programs with Western states became an important source of economic and technical assistance. Despite the importance of foreign assistance, however, Thailand never lost sight of the fact that successful development could only be achieved through its own efforts. In his speech on security and development to the US Congress in 1960, His Majesty underlined the importance of self-reliance in pursuing development by quoting Lord Buddha's precept, "Thou art thy own refuge."

Royal Personal Diplomacy

During these years of regional conflict, His Majesty the King played a significant role in helping to maintain good relations with foreign countries and projecting a positive image of Thailand to the international public. One of the instruments used by His Majesty to forge good working relationships with foreign governments was the state visit. Between 1959 and 1967, His Majesty the King, accompanied by Her Majesty Queen Sirikit, paid state visits to twenty-three countries, most of which were in Europe and Asia. There were also two Royal Visits and five official visits during that time. Countries which received the royal couple at that time included the Federation of Malaya, Burma, the Philippines, Japan, the United States, the United Kingdom, Germany and France.

Through these exchanges of visits, His Majesty was able to develop close bonds of friendship with foreign leaders. Subsequently, this friendship was reaffirmed and strengthened through reciprocal visits by foreign heads of state, including those from Laos, Belgium, Denmark, the Netherlands, Norway, Greece, Germany, Iran, the United States, Indonesia and the United Kingdom. These close ties at the Head of State level certainly facilitated the Royal Thai Government in promoting its interests as well as increasing public awareness of

The King and Queen during their visits to various foreign countries (clockwise from top left): with President Dwight Eisenhower of the USA (1960); at a tickertape parade, New York; with President Lyndon Johnson of the USA (1967); with King Baudouin of Belgium (1960); with President U Win Muang of Burma (1960); with President Sukarno of Indonesia (1960); with Queen Juliana of The Netherlands (1960).

Thailand's position on various global issues. Most importantly, this exercise in royal personal diplomacy helped build an image of Thailand amongst the international public as a peace-loving nation committed to economic and social development through cooperation with the international community. Amidst war and destruction in the region, Thailand was seen as an island of stability. There is no doubt that these efforts by Their Majesties helped uplift the stature and prestige of the Thai nation and strengthened the morale of the Thai people during a time of great conflict within the region.

Thailand and the United Nations

Throughout the period of the Cold War, Thailand continued to support fully the activities and efforts of the United Nations in the political, economic and social fields. Cooperation in the maintenance of international peace and security was a particularly salient feature of Thai foreign policy. When the Korean War broke out in June 1950, Thailand not only voted in favor of the so-called "Uniting for Peace" resolution which empowered the UN General Assembly to authorize military response to international threats, but was also one of sixteen countries which committed troops to serve under the UN unified command in Korea. As a result, 4,000 troops from Thailand participated in the international effort, of which 348 lives were lost. In 1953, Thailand was instrumental in facilitating the UN-organized evacuation program for the return of nearly 7,000 Chinese Nationalist troops from the Burmese border. In 1956, Thailand voted in favor of the creation of the

UN Emergency Force in the Middle East (UNEF). And in 1960, Thailand was one of the supporters of the establishment of the UN peacekeeping force in the Congo (ONUC) and assumed the heavy financial responsibilities incurred by the largest peacekeeping operation of its time.

Thailand's contributions in the economic and social fields have been no less notable. Having been a member of the International Labor Organization (ILO) and the International Institute of Agriculture (the precursor to the Food and Agricultural Organization or FAO), Thailand was well aware of the benefits of functional cooperation at the international level. Therefore, Thailand actively supported the United Nation's efforts in promoting economic and social development by playing an active role in such forums as the UN Economic and Social Council (ECOSOC), the World Health Organization (WHO), the UN High Commission for Refugees (UNHCR), the UN Children's Fund (UNICEF), the UN Industrial Development Organization (UNIDO) and the UN Conference on Trade and Development (UNCTAD). Thailand's active participation was evident through its membership of these organizations' executive organs and the election of Thai representatives to serve in the bureaux of

the conference of these organizations.

The contribution of Thailand's most gifted and skilled diplomatic practitioners and technical experts in the work of the United Nations, through their services within the organization, helped nurture the United Nation's development. Between 1950 and 1957, Thai representatives served, without interruption, as chairmen of all but one of the main committee of the UN General Assembly. In 1956, Prince Wan Waithayakorn (later accorded the Royal Title of Krom Muen Naradhip Bongsprabandh), was elected President of the eleventh Session of the UN General Assembly and went on to become Chairman of the First UN Conference on the Law of the Sea in 1958. The participation of prominent Thai nationals in the United Nations has continued to the present day and this reflects also Thailand's deep commitment to the principles of the UN Charter.

On the home front, Thailand continued to transform itself into the center of the UN developmental activities in Asia and the Pacific. In 1955 six major specialized agencies and international bodies under the UN umbrella joined the FAO and ECAFE/ESCAP in establishing their regional headquarters and regional offices in Bangkok. By 1968 the number of such offices had increased to ten. At present, a total of fifteen UN-related organizations and agencies operate from their headquarters or regional offices in Bangkok. The UN presence has helped promote closer cooperation and understanding between Thailand and UN agencies.

Thailand and the Developing States

Owing to the exigencies of the Cold War, the basic orientation of Thailand's foreign policy from the 1950's to the 1970's was pro-West. Nevertheless, Thailand did not cease its efforts to cultivate ties with other countries or develop other foreign initiatives beyond the East-West axis. As early as 1955, Thailand engaged with the newly independent countries by participating in the Bandung Conference involving Afro-Asian countries which laid the foundation for the

Left: Anand Panyarachun with his wife at a ceremony marking his appointment as UNICEF's goodwill ambassador in Thailand; Below: Prince Wan Waithayakorn.

Top: King Bhumibol at the opening of the ESCAP building in Bangkok. Being greeted is UN Secretary-General Boutros Boutros-Ghali (left).

Non-Aligned Movement (NAM). In fact, Prince Wan Waithayakorn, Thailand's representative, was Rapporteur at the meeting. Although Thailand did not become part of the NAM then, it continued to maintain good relations with the NAM's principal architects, such as Indonesia and Egypt. In addition, Thailand, as a developing country, took up cause with the developing world, through its active participation in the G77 and at other forums, to ensure that their common development agendas were met.

Southeast Asian Regionalism

It was in the promotion of regionalism that Thailand would undertake the initiative. Thailand and other countries in Southeast Asia had traditionally looked to outside the region rather than to one another. This division within Southeast Asia was a legacy of colonialism and one perpetuated by the Cold War. The idea was thus conceived that perhaps it was time for Southeast Asians to turn to one another and to find their own solutions to their common problems.

Through the efforts of Thanat Khoman, Thailand's foreign minister at that time, the idea of regionalism was promoted. The Association of Southeast Asia (ASA), composed of Thailand, Malaysia and the Philippines, was created in 1962 to foster intra-Southeast Asia economic and cultural cooperation. Similarly, Maphilindo, an acronym composed from the names of its members, namely Malaysia, the Philippines and

Indonesia, was established. These two initiatives laid the intellectual groundwork for the creation of a regional grouping which would later become a key player within Southeast Asia and the Asia-Pacific.

In 1967 in Bangkok, foreign ministers from five Southeast Asian countries—Indonesia, Malaysia, the Philippines, Singapore and Thailand—signed a declaration which gave birth to the Association of Southeast Asian Nations or ASEAN. ASEAN was a truly regional initiative. It was created by Southeast Asians, for Southeast Asians. Its aims were indeed modest: to foster economic, social and cultural cooperation amongst its members. The implications, however, were immense. It was an attempt by Southeast Asian countries to regain command of their own destiny. ASEAN offered a base for the development of a regional order to govern relations within Southeast Asia which transcended the divisions of the Cold War. It was conceived that, ultimately, all Southeast Asian countries, including Burma and the Indochinese states, would be part of ASEAN.

ASEAN promoted the use of regional solutions to solve regional problems because it saw external interference as a principal cause of instability in the region. This idea was clearly enunciated in the Kuala Lumpur Declaration of 1971 where the idea of promoting Southeast Asia as a Zone of Peace, Freedom and Neutrality, or ZOPFAN, was presented. The ZOPFAN principle suggested that ASEAN should, in the long-run, pursue a policy of equidistance vis-à-vis the external powers.

In sum, ASEAN provided a new vision for the future—one that looked beyond the ongoing conflict in Indochina and the existing division of Southeast Asia into non-communist and communist states.

The winds of change began to blow in the early 1970's. Following the enunciation of the Nixon Doctrine, the United States began the gradual withdrawal of its forces from Vietnam—a process which was essentially completed by

1973. North Vietnam and the indigenous communist movements were gaining the upper hand in the war. In 1975, Phnom Penh, Saigon (now Ho Chi Minh City) and Vientiane fell within several weeks of one another. Thailand now faced neighbors governed by communist-dominated movements along its entire eastern borders and was widely tipped as the next domino to fall.

Readjustments and Rapprochement at the End of the Second Indochina War

The years 1975 to 1977 witness one of the most dramatic readjustments of Thailand's foreign policy in its modern history. With the emergence of communist governments in Cambodia, Laos and Vietnam and the US strategic withdrawal from the region, Thailand had to rely on its own resources and remain flexible in its approach to foreign relations in order to meet the challenges of the changed geopolitical situation.

Pursuing an Even-Handed Policy

One of the key policy adjustments undertaken by Thailand was to adopt a more balanced posture in its relations with external powers. The first targets of this change in Thai foreign policy was the People's Republic of China. Under the instructions and guidelines provided initially by Foreign Minister Thanat Khoman and subsequently by Foreign Minister Chatichai Chunhavan, career diplomats were tasked with making discreet probes to the PRC to explore the possibility of normalizing relations. Initial secret contacts subsequently took place at the United Nations between representatives of the two countries as early as 1971.

While the substantive groundwork was being laid for the eventual establishment of ties between the two countries, several political and military leaders began to pay unofficial visits to the PRC. Several of these visits were undertaken within the framework of sports programs. Officials would accompany sports teams and engage in Thailand's version of "ping-pong diplomacy." These exchanges of visits to promote contacts in non-political areas helped improve

the general atmosphere between the two countries. More importantly, they facilitated the primary effort undertaken by the Foreign Ministry to normalize relations with the PRC. These negotiations led to the historic meeting between Prime Minister Kukrit Pramoj and Premier Zhou Enlai on July 1, 1975, when diplomatic relations between Thailand and the PRC were established. China further pledged not to interfere in the domestic affairs of Thailand.

As part of Thailand's policy of adopting a

more even-handed approach in its relations with external powers, Thailand initiated a process to readjust its relations with the United States. Thailand, however, continued to maintain good relations with the United States through political consultations and economic cooperation. The Joint United States Military Advisory Group (JUSMAG), whose mission was to train the Thai military, would still remain in Thailand. However, given the changed geopolitical conditions in the region and the lack of a clear US policy toward Southeast Asia, Thailand began to distance itself from US policies in the region. With the end of the Second Indochina War, the presence of thirty to forty thousand US military personnel in Thailand, whose original mandate was to assist in the US military efforts in South Vietnam, was no longer necessary. Furthermore, this presence would have complicated the emerging rapprochement between Thailand and China. Both the United States and Thailand therefore agreed to negotiate the with-

Above, top to bottom: Prime Minister Kukrit Pramoj and China's Prime Minister Chou Enlai signing a joint communiqué to establish diplomatic relations between the two countries on July 1, 1975; Prime Minister Chatichai Chunhavan with the Chinese Foreign Minister Qian Qichen at Peking airport in October 1989.

THAILAND King Bhumibol Adulyadej – The Golden Jubilee 1946-1996

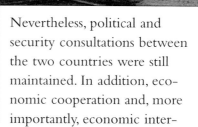

drawal of US forces from Thailand.

As negotiations continued for the rest of 1975, complications arose over the status of the small number of remaining US military personnel in Thailand in the absence of a formal Status of Forces Agreement (SOFA). Another contentious issue was whether US ammunitions depots and stockpiles in Thailand would be withdrawn or transferred for use by Thai forces in the future. One of the most sensitive issues involved the status of supposedly top-secret intelligence gathering stations such as the Ramasoon facilities. Who would exercise sovereignty over these facilities? Could the benefit from the intelligence so gathered from the facilities outweigh the political cost of their continued presence on Thai territory which would foment distrust between Thailand and the very neighbors with which it wanted to normalize relations? With the US Executive Branch weakened by the Watergate Crisis, Secretary of State Henry Kissinger and US diplomats were unable to commit the United States to a definite course of action. There were also differences within the Thai side, particularly between the civilian government and the military, on how to best approach the readjustment of relations with the United States. Nevertheless, when it appeared that no clear US position was forthcoming, Thailand acted on a last resort by setting a deadline in March 1976 for a definite US decision on how to proceed with the negotiations.

The deadline came and went. With no other feasible alternative in sight, Thailand requested the United States to withdraw its military forces as well as the intelligence-gathering facilities. The United States readily complied and withdrew its ammunitions stockpiles in the country. The contingents of US military forces departed by 20 July 1976. Only around 270 JUSMAG personnel remained in Thailand after that date. The level of military cooperation between the two countries reached its lowest levels in years.

Nevertheless, political and security consultations between the two countries were still maintained. In addition, economic cooperation and, more importantly, economic interaction through trade and investment began to gain momentum, thus laying a new foundation for relations between the two countries.

It was also during this period that Thailand began to build strong economic ties with Japan which had actually begun to invest significantly in Thailand since the beginning of the decade. As Thailand did not suffer harshly from its occupation by Japanese forces during the Second World War, the country was receptive to the inflow of Japanese capital and technology.

Rapprochement with Indochina

The stage was now set for Thailand to normalize relations with its Indochinese neighbors. Thailand did not expect the three Indochinese countries to immediately accept Thailand's offer of friendship. Nevertheless, under the guidance of Foreign Minister Bhichai Rattakul, Thailand pursued a relationship of coexistence in which states on different sides of the ideological divide could still pursue the normal intercourse of relations without interfering in one another's internal affairs.

Thailand was able to readjust its relations with Laos more quickly than with the other two Indochinese states. As relations between Thailand and Laos were never interrupted during the Second Indochina conflict, Thailand merely recognized the new Laotian government when it came to power in 1975. Regarding Democratic Kampuchea (Cambodia), Thailand and the other ASEAN members were able to agree on a collective approach in according recognition to the new government. Thai rela-

Top: Thai-US air base (1974); Inset: The last active US serviceman to leave Thailand.

tions with Cambodia were subsequently normalized in November 1975. Normalization of relations with Vietnam was more problematical. ASEAN was unable to agree on a collective approach in recognizing the new government in Hanoi. There were many residual problems to be overcome, including the question of personnel and military equipment of the South Vietnamese army left in Thailand as well as the status of Vietnamese refugees who had fled to Thailand throughout the past three decades. Nevertheless, following intense negotiations between the two sides, relations between Thailand and Vietnam were finally normalized in August 1976.

Strengthening of ASEAN Political Cooperation

It was during this period that Thailand and its ASEAN partners began to intensify their political cooperation. This amounted to an expansion of ASEAN's original mandate which limited cooperation to the economic, social and cultural fields. The shared view was that close consultations in foreign policy would strengthen ASEAN's collective political strength in con-

ducting its external relations, particularly vis-à-vis the Indochinese states. This collective political defense was necessary to promote regional resilience against attempts by outside powers to interfere in ASEAN's internal affairs. ASEAN's solidarity was consolidated by the Declaration of ASEAN Concord and the Treaty of Amity and Cooperation

in Southeast Asia which were signed at the first ASEAN Summit in Bali in 1976. The Treaty was open to accession by other states in Southeast Asia.

It thus appears that Thailand's change in foreign policy, from political alignment with the West to a more equidistant posture in its foreign relations, from confrontation to coexistence with its communist neighbors, played a part in blocking the feared westward expansion of communist influence and aggression against Thailand. At the same time, Thailand benefited from the break-up of solidarity within the Asian communist bloc. Conflict in the late 1970's between Vietnam and Cambodia, on the one hand, and between Vietnam and China on the other, dispelled the myth of an Asian communist monolith. These tensions within Indochina and between Indochina and China were to erupt in the Third Indochina War which began in 1978.

The Third Indochina Conflict and Thailand's Foreign Policy in the 1980's

On 25 December 1978, full-scale war broke out between Vietnam and Cambodia. As a result, the Khmer Rouge was expelled to the Thai-Cambodian border and a Cambodian government friendly to Hanoi was set up in Phnom Penh supported by an army of occupation. In early 1979, China launched a limited punitive invasion of northern Vietnam before withdrawing its forces. For the next thirteen years, Southeast Asia would be preoccupied with the Third Indochina conflict (or the Cambodia conflict).

At that time, Thailand perceived that it was facing a major security problem along the Thai-Cambodian border. The war in neighboring Cambodia brought border instability, destruction to Thai villages in the border areas and the influx of hundreds of thousands of refugees. These were burdens which Thailand had to bear for the next thirteen years. The presence of large numbers of foreign military forces just across the Thai border whose intentions were unclear cannot but be seen as a threat to Thailand's security.

Left, top: The first ASEAN summit in Bali in February 1976; Left, bottom: ASEAN foreign ministers meeting with Prem Tinsulanonda at Government House in February 1985.

The most important effect of the Vietnamese occupation of Cambodia, however, was that it effectively killed the rapprochement between ASEAN and Vietnam which was taking shape in the late 1970's. The chance to bridge differences between the two sides in Southeast Asia, and therefore to curtail external influence in the region, was lost. Despite several years of hope, Southeast Asia became polarized once again. To end the conflict in Cambodia, Thailand and ASEAN sought and received the support of the United Nations and most of the international community, particularly the United States, China, Japan and Western Europe. Vietnam, on the other hand, strengthened its ties to the Soviet Union and Eastern Europe and received their support for its policies in Cambodia.

For much of the 1980's, Thailand, under the leadership of Prime Minister Prem Tinsulanonda and Foreign Minister Siddhi Savetsila, and ASEAN expended much effort to try to convince Vietnam that it was in Vietnam's best interest to terminate its costly military occupation of Cambodia and allow the latter to develop as a stable and neutral country at peace with all of its neighbors. Vietnam could

Above, top to bottom: A Cambodian refugee camp along the Thai border; Cambodian refugees;
Below: Prem Tinsulanonda with
Prince Norodom Sihanouk of Cambodia.

then divert its resources to pursue economic development while a stable Cambodia would not pose a threat to any country.

Another key concern of Vietnam, as well as of ASEAN, was the possible return to power of the Khmer Rouge. In part to allay these concerns, ASEAN supported the creation of the Coalition Government of Democratic Kampuchea (CGDK), under the leadership of the universally respected Prince Sihanouk, which consisted of Sihanouk's royalist, nationalist supporters of former Cambodian Prime Minister Son Sann, and "untainted" remnants of the Khmer Rouge elite. It was ASEAN's hope that the coalition government would provide an alternative to Khmer Rouge rule and foreign occupation for Cambodians.

These arguments served as foundation for ASEAN's proposal for a comprehensive settlement of the Cambodia problem—which ASEAN and the United Nations regarded as the only viable, long-term solution to the conflict in Cambodia. The key points of this proposal included the complete withdrawal of foreign forces from Vietnam, the exercise of Cambodian self-determination through elections, the return of all Cambodian displaced persons to their homeland, the recognition of the legitimate security interests of all states in the region and the upholding of basic international principles, particularly human rights.

Partly as a result of cooperation in resolving the Cambodia problem, Thailand strengthened its ties with the major powers, particularly China, the United States and Japan. A key consequence of this development was the cessation of Chinese support for the Communist Party of Thailand, which contributed to its eventual demise in the mid-1980's. Close political cooperation between Thailand and the United States was revived. In the 1980's, Japan began to increase its profile in Southeast Asian affairs. In addition to the Cambodia problem, Thailand and Japan began to increase their consultations on other issues related to the region.

Although the Cambodia problem remained a stalemate during most of the 1980's, changes in international politics toward the end of the decade made the situation in Cambodia more fluid. Soviet leader Mikhael S. Gorbatchev's announcement in Vladivostok in 1986 of a new approach toward the Asia-Pacific, which complemented his efforts at "glasnost" and "perestroika," signaled the Soviet Union's willingness to be more supportive of a peaceful resolution to the Cambodia problem. This was followed by the easing of tensions between the Soviet Union and China, followed by discussions between China and Vietnam to improve ties. With the general trend in favor of a peaceful solution to the Cambodia problem, the path was open for Vietnam and the various Cambodian groups to come to terms. This positive trend received a strong boost with the holding of informal talks among the Cambodian parties in Pattaya in 1990 which were facilitated by Prime Minister Anand Panyarachun and Foreign Minister Arsa Sarasin. These talks paved the way for the signing of the Paris Peace Agreements in 1991 which brought an end to the Third Indochina Conflict.

The Paris Peace Agreements achieved ASEAN's fundamental goal of providing a comprehensive political settlement to the Cambodia problem. It mandated the establishment of the UN Advance Mission in Cambodia (UNAMIC) and its successor, the UN Transitional Authority in Cambodia (UNTAC), the largest UN peacekeeping mission operation since ONUC, to implement the agreement. On its part, Thailand contributed both civilian and military personnel, including an engineering battalion, to this historic UN effort. One of the main responsibilities of the Thai contingent included the clearance of a large number of land mines in certain parts of Cambodia. In addition, Thailand provided staging facilities for all UNAMIC- and UNTAC-related operations throughout their combined three-year operations.

The agreements also laid the basis for the withdrawal of all foreign forces from Cambodia. Thereafter, UN-supervised national elections were held in 1993 resulting in the establishment of the Royal Cambodian Government under the leadership of King Sihanouk. Cambodia pledged to follow a policy of non-alignment which in part took care of the security concerns of its neighboring states. The new government was bound by its Constitution and international agreements to respect human rights. A multilateral economic assistance package was created for Cambodia to assist it in its rehabilitation and reconstruction—a prerequisite for long-term stability. The Khmer Rouge has been declared as outlaws and no longer poses a credible threat to Cambodia. After thirteen years of conflict, a new alternative has been realized for Cambodians. Along with it came the opportunity to bring about the rebirth of the Cambodian nation.

A New Foreign Policy in All Directions

The decade of the 1980's witnessed the emergence of a more confident Thailand pursuing a higher profile role in foreign affairs. The growth in Thailand's self-confidence was a result of several factors. The conflict within Cambodia was regarded as a manageable threat; the domestic insurgency was defeated; and the Thai economy was geared for take-off. Accompanying this growth in self-confidence was the drive to expand the scope of Thailand's foreign policy. Hitherto, Thai foreign policy focused on security issues and, despite efforts to develop ties with the developing world, gave priority to relationships with neighboring countries, the major powers and the industrial democracies. Under the new circumstances, Thailand was now in a position to explore new avenues of cooperation with the rest of the international community.

Thai foreign policy began to expand in all directions, both regionally and functionally. One aspect of this policy was to strengthen ties with

Top, left: Lieutenant-General John Sanderson, commander of UNTAC, and Yashoshi Akashi, head of UNTAC, releasing a dove symbolizing peace; Below: Foreign Minister Arsa Sarasin.

Thai soldiers donating blankets to a Cambodian monk (1993).

the developing countries and expand links with such regions as Africa, Latin America and certain parts of Asia. The 1980's thus saw the phenomenal increase by sixty in the number of countries with which Thailand established diplomatic relations. In addition, Thailand strove to enhance the political and economic cohesion of the developing world by encouraging North-South development cooperation, promoting joint efforts to establish a new international economic order and regularizing a system of contacts and political consultations in areas of common interest.

This new phase of Thai foreign policy was also characterized by the strengthening of foreign relations along all fronts, including economic and social cooperation. At the governmental level, Thailand played an active role within the Uruguay Round of Multilateral Trade Negotiations to ensure free and fair trade. Thailand was likewise active in the push for a meaningful North-South Dialogue to resolve the major economic inequities facing humankind. The key role in Thailand's expansion of its economic ties was played by the Thai private sector. Emerging Thai multinationals were active in the search for new trade and investment opportunities, as well as new sources of raw materials.

It was also during this period that Thailand made a strong contribution in the maintenance of international peace and security. Between 1985 and 1986, Thailand served as a non-permanent member of the UN Security Council. During the tenure, Thailand served as President of the Council on two separate occasions and played a part in solving various security issues faced by the international community. A notable achievement of the UN Security Council during the period was the passage of resolution 582 (1986) which later became the foundation for UN Security Council resolution 598 (1987)—the basis for ending the nine-year-old war between Iran and Iraq. This high-profile role at the UN Security Council as well as the expansion of Thailand's economic ties with both the industrialized West and the developing countries marked the first step in Thailand's emergence as an important player in the region.

Opportunities and Challenges in the Post-Cold War Era

The decade of the 1990's gave rise to epoch-making events which transformed the world and Southeast Asia. The disintegration of the Soviet Union in December 1990 and, with it, the collapse of Communism in Eastern Europe, brought an end to the Cold War which had dictated international and Southeast Asian politics for over forty years. An era of new opportunities as well as new challenges was born.

The end of the global ideological conflict reduced the threat of a worldwide military conflict and has rekindled hopes that the resulting peace dividend would be spent in alleviating the common economic and social problems facing humankind. Instead of world conflict, there would be genuine international cooperation sustained by an effective United Nations.

But the new era has also spawned new challenges. The diminution of ideology as a factor in international relations unfroze conflicts which have as their root cause sectarian and ethnic differences. Political conflict gave way to intense economic competition which the fledgling World Trade Organization has barely kept under control. Furthermore, lines are being drawn between those countries which advocate the application of so-called universal standards on important issues, ranging from human rights and democracy to environmental protection, and those states which advocate full respect of sovereignty and non-interference in international affairs regarding these issues.

Southeast Asia has indeed been fortunate to have been spared the turmoil of the post-Cold War era. For the first time since the end of the Second World War, Southeast Asia is witnessing relative peace and stability. ASEAN has emerged as a mature organization whose members are

economic success stories in their own right. Laos and Cambodia are actively engaged in their transition toward a free-market economy, while Myanmar is engaged in national reconciliation and consolidation.

Thailand's primary foreign policy at this opportune juncture in Southeast Asian history is to promote a sense of community within the region, leading to the eventual inclusion of all ten Southeast Asian countries within ASEAN. To realize this dream of ASEAN's founding fathers, Thailand seeks to build mutual confidence and trust within the region, and between the region and the external powers. The primary mechanism to attain this objective has been the ASEAN Regional Forum or ARF which was inaugurated in Bangkok in July 1994. The ARF is the only forum which engages most of the Asia-Pacific countries and the European Union in a security dialogue. Thus far, the ARF has been successful in allowing participants to air their differences on important regional security issues, such as the nuclear problem on the Korean Peninsula and the problem of overlapping claims in the South China Sea.

The accession of Vietnam to the Treaty of Amity and Cooperation in Southeast Asia in 1993 paved the way for its admission to ASEAN in July 1995. This was indeed an historic occasion as it signified the end of the polarization of Southeast Asia into two camps. Laos has announced its intention to become a member of ASEAN by 1997. Cambodia, on the other hand, has been admitted as an observer to ASEAN, and there is every expectation that Myanmar will follow suit by 1996. All these events were a prelude to successful hosting of the historic summit of the leaders of the ten Southeast Asian countries in Bangkok in December 1995. The summit laid the foundation for the realization of a Southeast Asian community through an ASEAN encompassing all ten Southeast Asian countries.

For Thailand, economic prosperity within the region remains the initial ingredient to building a stable Southeast Asian community. In addition,

regional economic strength is seen as a prerequisite for Thailand's ability to compete effectively in the global economic environment. At the third ASEAN Summit held in Singapore in 1991, Prime Minister Anand Panyarachun proposed the establishment of the ASEAN Free Trade Area or AFTA. This proposal was endorsed by the ASEAN leaders and became one of the key driving forces for greater economic cooperation within the region. The AFTA plan to eliminate barriers to trade and investment by the year 2003 is expected to promote greater intra-ASEAN economic activities as well as to attract increasingly scarce foreign capital to fuel the regional development drive.

Outside the ASEAN framework, Thailand has actively promoted sub-regional economic cooperation with neighboring countries. The Indonesia-Malaysia-Thailand Economic Growth Triangle and the Quadrangle Economic Cooperation involving Thailand, Myanmar, Laos and Yunnan province of China are examples of efforts to facilitate cross-border trade and investment through improved sub-regional infrastructure. The signing of the Mekong Agreement by Thailand, Laos, Cambodia and Vietnam in 1995 marked the first step toward the creation of a new framework for economic and technical cooperation involving all riparian states of the Mekong River.

These efforts were reinforced at the bilateral

Top: King Bhumibol with President Nouhak Phoumsavanh of Laos at the opening ceremony of the Mitraphab (Friendship) Bridge between Thailand and Laos (1994); Inset: The Friendship Bridge.

level through extensive economic and technical assistance programs that Thailand conducts with Myanmar, Laos, Cambodia and Vietnam. Closer economic ties with Laos have been achieved following the completion of the Friendship Bridge from Nongkhai province to Vientiane in 1994, the only bridge spanning the Mekong River. His Majesty the King has been instrumental in cementing the kinship ties between the Laotian and Thai peoples throughout the decades. They reflect the larger picture of His Majesty's special interest and continuous efforts since the beginning of his reign in developing closer relations with all of Thailand's neighbors. His Majesty's efforts with regard to Laos culminated in His Majesty's official visit to the country, following the ceremony inaugurating the Friendship Bridge and through royally-sponsored development projects in Laos itself.

At the Asia-Pacific level, Thailand has played an active role in setting the agenda for the Asia-Pacific Economic Cooperation, or APEC, which groups eighteen Asia-Pacific economies. Thailand promotes the adoption of trade liberal-

ization and facilitation measures which are consistent with the General Agreement on Tariffs and Trade (GATT), and at a pace commensurate with individual countries' development plans. In this connection, Thailand targets the year 2020 for achieving free trade in the region. The Action Agenda adopted at the Osaka APEC Economic Leaders Meeting has given an impetus to freer trade and investment in this region. At the same time, Thailand continues to push APEC to give more attention to development cooperation, particularly in the area of human resources development.

Among the three current regional centers of high economic growth, namely Asia, Europe and North America, formal links have been established for quite some time between Europe and North America through a network of trans-Atlantic institutions, and between Asia and North America through APEC, the Pacific Economic Cooperation Council (PECC) and other arrangements. The weakest link in the triad has been between Asia and Europe. Concerted efforts were thus undertaken in 1994

Below, left: Prime Minister Chatichai Chunhavan meeting with Vietnamese Foreign Minister at a trade symposium on Indochina in 1989; Below, right: Thai trucks crossing the Mekong at a major trading point between Mukdahan, Thailand, and Savannakhet, Laos.

Thailand and Indochina

Thailand is geographically located right at the heart of Southeast Asia, a strategic position that is likely to increase in importance in the future. Already, Bangkok is quickly becoming a regional hub for transportation, media businesses, manufacturing, trading and, to an extent, finance. Clearly, with economic growth continuing strongly, the capital is poised to further enhance its position as one of the key business centers for the entire region.

The end of the so-called Cold War and the

improvement of relations between Thailand and its neighbors has led to rapid economic booms in the emergent economies of Indochina—especially in the Lao PDR and Vietnam. For many businesses, Bangkok is the perfect place to

organize new Indochinese operations. Since Hong Kong, Thailand's major competitor as a gateway to Indochina, is due to return to Chinese rule in 1997, Thailand is the preferred alternative. For example, Japanese trading companies such as Mitsui and car manufacturers such as Honda are using Thailand as the springboard for expansion into the Indochina region; the same is true for major US corporations such as Kodak and 3M; global advertising agencies are not only using their Bangkok bases as regional headquarters but also using their Thai staff to set up new offices and train overseas employees in Indochina.

Linked to the Indochina countries are Myanmar, and the south-western province of Yunnan, both of which are experiencing strong economic growth. These two nations are forming part of what experts call the "Growth Quadrangle"—between Laos, Myanmar, China and Thailand. This region has tremendous potential and Thai investors are highly active, while the Thai government is supporting infrastructure development.

Tourism is also developing rapidly in the Indochina region. Bangkok is the preferred point of entry for many tourists, who will then move on from Thailand to Indochina. New

roads and bridges are underway to facilitate transport within the region. And the historic opening of the Mitraphab (Friendship) Bridge between Thailand and Laos in 1994 certainly marks a turning point in the region. More bridges are planned on the Mekong River downstream and when these are built it will be possible to travel through Thailand to the Vietnamese coast—these developments will certainly increase the importance of Thailand's Isan (northeast) region as a gateway to Indochina. Furthermore, Thailand's northern region is now being linked with Myanmar, Laos and China and new roads are now being constructed in the area.

– J. C.

to explore means to strengthen this link. They culminated in Thailand's hosting the inaugural Asia-Europe Meeting (ASEM) in March 1996, the first ever meeting between the leaders of Asia and Europe. The Asian participants included the seven ASEAN countries, China, Japan and South Korea while Europe was represented by the fifteen members of the European Union and the European Commission. The meeting announced a vision for a *New Comprehensive Asia-Europe Partnership for Greater Growth.* This partnership envisions increased political dialogue between the two continents; greater economic cooperation, particularly in the areas of trade, investment and transfer of technology; increased participation of the private sector; and intensified cooperation in functional areas. Many concrete follow-up actions were agreed upon in order to maintain the momentum for forging closer links between Asia and Europe. Such links should contribute toward strengthening global political stability, open regionalism and the multilateral regime of an open global, rules-based trade under the World Trade Organization.

Thailand's foreign policy continues to emphasize active cooperation within the United Nations, not only to realize the goals and objectives of the UN Charter but also to strengthen the efficiency and effective functioning of the United Nations in all aspects in order to help prepare it for the challenges of the next millennium. At the heart of Thailand's current contributions are its vice-chairmanship of the UN General Assembly's working group on Security Council reform and its active participation in the negotiations and implementation of an Agenda for Peace and an Agenda for Development initiatives. Thailand continues to support the UN's effort in maintaining international peace and security by contributing a small contingent of military observers to the UN Iran-Iraq Observer Mission (UNIKOM) and by

assisting the UN's efforts in alleviating the plight of the peoples of Somalia and Rwanda. There is every expectation that, in the years ahead, Thailand will continue to be one of the United Nation's strongest supporters, not out of altruism but rather out of the realization that, in this increasingly complex and interdependent world, its own national interests are unavoidably intertwined with those of humanity at large and that it is only through the United Nations that these intertwining interests can be safeguarded.

As one of the staunchest supporters of the concepts of sustainable economic and social development, human rights, humanitarian assistance, the rights of women and children, environmental protection and other relevant initiatives and principles, Thailand has been actively engaged in international negotiations in realizing the objectives of these concepts. At the Vienna Conference on Human Rights in 1993, Thailand advocated the universal promotion of human rights while taking into account the differing social contexts of individual countries' development. At the World Summit for Social Development in Copenhagen in March 1995, Thailand clearly enunciated its support for the integration of social issues, particularly the rights of socially disadvantaged groups, such as women and children, in economic development at both national and global levels. These concerns about the rights of women were repeated at the UN fourth World Conference on Women in Beijing in August 1995.

The prospects for Thailand's foreign policy in this new era of opportunities and challenges are bright. With strong domestic economic fundamentals and internal stability, Thailand has emerged as a key player in the process of building peace, stability and prosperity in the Southeast Asian region. The anchor of the region remains ASEAN—which hopes to expand its membership to include all ten states in Southeast Asia. With promising economic and political trends in Southeast Asia and the wider Asia-Pacific region, the goal of a Southeast Asian community, within the framework of the Asia-

Top, left: The inaugural Asia-Europe meeting (ASEM) in Bangkok (1996); Above: Thai and United Nations flags.

Pacific Economic Cooperation (APEC) and reinforced by the emerging ASEM process, remains the best guarantee for maintaining Thailand's security, prosperity and sustained competitiveness into the twenty-first century.

Conclusion

From 1946 to 1996, Thailand has seen immense changes in the region and the world. Through times of turbulence and times of peace, Thailand has adjusted its foreign policy to protect the country's sovereignty and preserve the welfare of the Thai people. As one reflects on the past fifty years, one cannot but pay respect to the efforts and determination of Thai leaders of all eras to ensure that Thailand is where it is today. The present decade sees Thailand poised to play a leading role in fulfilling the aspiration which has been in the hearts of Thai leaders since the time when it was the only independent country in Southeast Asia, namely, the creation of a peaceful region free from external interference. This aspi-

Right: The King, in a photograph taken with other heads of state during the first Asia-Europe Meeting; Below: Students at the Asian Institute of Technology.

ration has recently been deepened with the common desire within the region to create a peaceful and prosperous community of Southeast Asian nations. This is, indeed, a time for optimism.

During the past half-century, the one constant in Thai foreign policy has been the commitment of His Majesty King Bhumibol Adulyadej to ensuring the security, stability and prosperity of this kingdom. This commitment has been a pillar of strength during years of difficulty and a source of encouragement and hope as Thailand takes the next few steps toward the twenty-first century. As we celebrate fifty years of the reign of His Majesty King Bhumibol Adulyadej of Thailand, the longest reign in Thai history, we pay homage to the wise counsel that His Majesty has given to the conduct of Thai foreign policy in the modern history of the Thai nation.

Information for this article was provided by ML Bhirabongse Kasemsri (former Thai Ambassador to Washington, D.C.), Deputy Permanent Secretary Saroj Chavanaviraj, Ambassador Nitya Pibulsongkram and Ambassador Tej Bunnag. The preparation of this article was done by Dr Suriya Chindawongse from the Ministry of Foreign Affairs of Thailand.

Asian Institute of Technology

A highly visible symbol of Thailand's prominence as a regional center is the Asian Institute of Technology (AIT), which, in the course of more than thirty-five years, has achieved an international reputation as both a center of higher learning and an instrument of development.

The concept of the Institute originated during a meeting of the Southeast Asia Treaty Organization Council of Ministers held in Manila in 1958, when it was decided to

establish a SEATO Graduate School of Engineering in Bangkok. King Bhumibol Adulyadej issued a Royal Decree on July 30, 1959 announcing that the school would be established at Chulalongkorn University, and the facility opened in September of that year.

At the time, almost no graduate programs were being offered by the tertiary educational institutions of South and East Asia, despite the growing need for technically qualified personnel in the region, and this is cited as one of the reasons for AIT's success. Another is the diversity of the faculty, drawn from many countries and committed to the highest standards, while a third is the fact that from its inception the Institute's academic programs have been closely related to the needs of Asia. Also from the beginning, the student body was not restricted to nationals of SEATO members but came from other countries in the region as well.

Toward the end of 1967, the SEATO ties were shed and the Institute became fully independent under its present title, with a charter from the Royal Thai Government granting it the status of an autonomous, international institution empowered to award degrees and

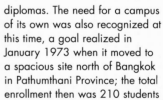

diplomas. The need for a campus of its own was also recognized at this time, a goal realized in January 1973 when it moved to a spacious site north of Bangkok in Pathumthani Province; the total enrollment then was 210 students from twenty-four countries, and the full-time faculty numbered thirty-six members with eight associated specialist lecturers.

Over the years, the facilities have steadily expanded, made possible by donations from both Asian and Western governments. Besides the academic programs, in fields ranging from Environmental Engineering to Water Resources Engineering, the Institute has continued to conduct a broad variety of research projects into specific Asian problems, among them public sanitation, waste water treatment, urban planning, low-cost housing, and the development of new tools for agriculture. Many AIT graduates have become high-ranking officials in their home countries, and there are active alumni associations throughout Asia.

– W. W.

4

THE THAI ECONOMY–
FIFTY YEARS OF EXPANSION

Dr Ammar Siamwalla

T HE FIFTY YEARS OF HIS MAJESTY'S REIGN HAS SEEN MORE CHANGE THAN ANY OTHER HALF-CENTURY IN THAILAND'S ENTIRE HISTORY. THE MAIN ENGINE OF CHANGE HAS BEEN THE ECONOMY, AND ITS POWER HAS REWROUGHT THE ENTIRE FABRIC OF THAI SOCIETY, IN THE PROCESS TRANS-FORMING THE LIVES OF HIS MAJESTY'S SUBJECTS.

For better or for worse, the way of life that the Thais led until the eve of the Second World War is now forever gone.

It has also been a half-century of contrasts. The almost unilineal economic expansion contrasted with the few-steps-forward-and-few-steps-back character of Thai political evolution. Periods of ideological confrontation punctuated long spells of cold and sometimes even cynical pragmatism. Economic nationalists vied for power and influence with those who advocated an open economy. Whole new classes of people rose, while local communities were fast disappearing as distinct groups in society. Relationships between Thais and Chinese veered from animosity to tolerance, and eventually to assimilation. But, in the long run, the unrelenting economic expansion bore down on the social and political eddies and gave them a direction which they would

otherwise have lacked. What prevents the history recounted below from being a story of "one-damn-thing-after another" is this uninterrupted economic expansion.

Thailand in 1946

His Majesty the King ascended the throne under deeply tragic circumstances. If we survey the conditions of his subjects, the scene was also quite depressing. A child born in 1946 had a one in eight chance of dying before it reached its first birthday (the current figure is less than one in thirty). If it was born in the countryside— and at that time more than four-fifths of all Thais were living in rural areas—its chances would be even poorer. The mother had a good chance of dying during childbirth, and since the average woman goes through childbirth about five times during her lifetime (to make up for the high probability of

Facing page: Cargo at Klong Toey port;
Right: Barges on Chao Phraya river.

her losing some of those children), her life expectancy would be shorter than her husband's.

An adult was still prey to various infectious diseases. True, he would have at his disposal ample natural resources culled from the forests that were seldom far away from his home, making his life that much easier. At that time more than half of the country's land area was covered with forests. It is also true, however, that much of the area was not accessible or accessible only at the risk of contracting malaria, which was rampant. The countryside was far from uniformly tranquil places of nostalgia. The demobilization of the troops at the end of the Second World War without adequate pay had led to widespread banditry and insecurity. Little in the way of public services reached the countryside. It was a rare village that had access to roads (the central plains' villagers, however, had access to water transport), and even rarer to have access to electricity.

Then, as today, agriculture was the main livelihood of the rural population. But people were more dependent on it than now. As only one crop was grown a year, it occupied only half a year of a farm family's available working time. As at present, many from the northeast would migrate to the central plains to obtain work as harvesters. On the other hand, non-farm work was not easily available, and therefore many perforce remained at home. In many areas, people would barter goods and services, more because of the lack of locally available cash and the expense of transport than because of an innate disdain for the use of money.

The commerce of the country was dominated by the Chinese—then a distinct and separate community from the Thais. Rice typically provided well over half of the country's export earnings and consequently, the great rice exporting houses were the apex of the local business community. Teak, tin and rubber provided the rest of Thailand's exports. What little industry existed was there to process these export commodities, with rice-milling and saw-milling taking up the lion's share.

The financial prospects for Thailand at the end of the Second World War looked equally unpromising. As a result of its involvement with the Japanese during the war, Thailand was required to pay reparations of 2 million tons of rice to the victorious Allies. True, eventually, heroic negotiations pared the amount of reparations to insignificance, but the uncertainty created by the negotiations and the monopolization of the rice trade caused a great deal of turmoil in the rice market.

The monetary system was in chaos. During the war the Japanese had asked the Thai authorities to issue large amounts of baht to finance their military expenditures in Thailand. The baht was supposedly backed by the issuance of yen credit balances in the Yokohama Specie Bank. These reserves of course became worthless with the defeat of Japan and the baht went into a tailspin. The inflation of the time, which saw the real value of the currency depreciate sevenfold toward the end of the war and then another 20 percent in the first two years after the war, was the worst ever experienced in Thailand's eco-

Above, left: A floating house built on a *klong* of Bangkok during the early years; Left: New Road in the late 1940's.

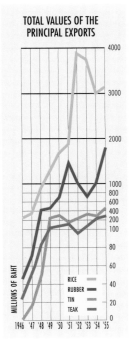

TOTAL VALUES OF THE PRINCIPAL EXPORTS

MILLIONS OF BAHT

RICE
RUBBER
TIN
TEAK

1946 '47 '48 '49 '50 '51 '52 '53 '54 '55

1947	1,383,772,267
	968,398,209
1948	1,747,022,613
	2,076,211,309
1949	2,273,741,444
	2,776,762,208
1950	2,625,032,083
	3,472,829,945
1951	3,704,893,121
	4,412,908,933
1952	5,524,467,900
	4,618,739,730
1953	6,471,534,385
	5,771,832,345
1954	7,021,527,551
	6,177,014,221
1955	7,502,648,580
	7,120,548,285
1956	7,655,127,171
	6,923,196,576

IMPORTS
EXPORTS (Baht)

Source: International Trade, Customs Department

Far right: A Chinese immigrant.

nomic history. The inflation did not just erode the real incomes of the civil servants but almost wiped them out so that the incomes of the top echelon among the civil servants were less than 3 percent of the level before the war.

The Financial Advisor at the time wrote: "In May 1946 Siam was starting from scratch; the till was completely empty and the only asset she possessed was her potential power to acquire stocks of foreign exchange."[1]

The resilience of the Thai economy, that "power to acquire stocks of foreign exchange," showed through quickly. By 1947 inflation had almost disappeared, helped by the recovery of her exports, soon to be followed by the commodity boom arising out of the Korean War. The main reason for this turnaround was the recovery in rice production from the low levels that prevailed in the highly insecure conditions in the countryside during the war.

Economic Nationalism and Corruption— Laying the Foundation (1947-58)

The stabilization achieved by 1947 was based on a system of multiple exchange rates which generated considerable foreign exchange profits for the government. The reverse side of the same coin is that this was an implicit tax on exports of primary commodities, particularly rice. The implicit taxation of rice through this mechanism evolved later on into an explicit tax called the premium. This taxation of rice exports had significance beyond its immediate impact on government finances because it depressed domestic rice prices. It thus became a means by which the government could subsidize the urban population among whom the most important group at that time were the civil servants. In this way, the devastation that wartime inflation had brought

upon their real incomes was mitigated, some of the burden being shifted to the rice farmers instead.

But the stability thus achieved did not last long. In 1952 there was a misguided attempt to try and revalue the free market rate of the baht, ostensibly to curb inflation. It is difficult to rationalize this action since by that time the commodity price inflation from the Korean War boom had changed into a price drop. Oral tradition has it that the government felt that a higher value of the baht would be prestigious for the country. If so, this concern for prestige was in keeping with the notions of economic nationalism that, apart from massive corruption (on which more below), were the hallmarks of that period.

Traditionally Thai economic nationalism was directed at two different sets of foreigners. The first were the Europeans and Americans. During the nineteenth century, their governments concluded a series of agreements with Thailand which considerably limited the fiscal autonomy of the Thai state, as well as giving their governments extraterritorial jurisdiction over their citizens and subjects residing in Thailand. Well before the Second World War, however, these unequal treaties had been renegotiated to everyone's satisfaction.

The second set of foreigners were of a different kind. They were the Chinese immigrants and their descendants who had over the years amassed considerable economic power. Relations between Thais and Chinese had been reasonably amicable and many of the Chinese immigrants had gradually assimilated into Thai society. Beginning from about 1910, however, these relations deteriorated, and the Thai state began to impose greater restrictions on the many freedoms which they used to enjoy. These restrictions began under the absolute monarchy and were continued, indeed intensified, when the People's Party assumed power in 1932, and reached a peak between 1949 and 1952.

The actions taken by the Thai government in some ways were a reaction to events in China. Thus the deterioration in 1910 can be associated with the rise of nationalism in China. The intensification of the anti-Chinese policies had as its backdrop the triumph of the Communist Party in mainland China in 1949. While most Chinese living in Thailand at first welcomed this event, they soon shifted their position as the Communists' land-reform program took away their lands in China—many Chinese had invested their life savings in the land. At the same time the Thai authorities took a more strident anticommunist stance, and travel between China and Thailand also became more hazardous politically. Financial remittances also became more and more restricted.

The upshot of all these events was that the Chinese in Thailand began to be weaned away from the ties that bound them to their motherland. As their children grew up, parents found it more attractive to send their children to Thai schools. At the time the pains endured by the Chinese community were not trivial and abuses of their civil rights undoubtedly occurred. It can

also not be denied that through this process the foundations were laid (almost inadvertently) for the incorporation of a foreign community containing Thailand's wealthiest businessmen into general Thai society—a task which can today be considered essentially complete.

However this assimilation could not have been predicted in the 1950's either by the Chinese themselves or by outside observers. Before that was achieved, the Chinese had to go through a period when they were "pariah entrepreneurs"[2] doing their business under the "protection" of the leading military and police leaders. Many of these men in uniform were "invit-

ed" to join the boards of leading banks and businesses, which themselves continued to be run by the original Chinese owners. Thus was born the alliance between Chinese business leaders and Thai politicians.

Such an alliance was not without its dangers for the Chinese: added to the normal uncertainties that attend business decisions, they had to back the right political horse. The penalties that attended wrong forecasts were not trivial, but provided the cards were played right, they were not fatal either (see the story of Chin Sophonphanich on page 143).

The anti-Chinese policies of the late 1940's and the 1950's had as their stated objective the need for Thais to take over the levers of economic power. One result was the peculiar form of alliance that arose as a consequence. But this was only one prong in the overall strategy of economic nationalism. It was supplemented by another consideration. Until then, the main wealth acquired by the Thais was through public service, and this wealth was sharply curtailed by the postwar inflation. Since no government chose to make good this erosion of public servants' salaries, the military-dominated government that held power between 1947 and 1957 took measures to acquire access to the country's wealth by means other than taxation.

The means they used was through the creation of public or quasi-public entities.[3] A holding company, the National Economic Development Corporation (Nedcol), was created to run some of these enterprises. Private activities in many areas were banned and monopoly rights were conferred on these state enterprises and on the War Veterans' Organization which served as a front for the leading members of the military.

Entities could be created at the stroke of a pen but running them was altogether another matter. Here is what the World Bank later had to say about the investments made by Nedcol: "The concept behind each of the projects was probably sound.... But none of the projects was properly studied at the beginning. There is little

Left, top: Opening of a new bank in Chinatown, Bangkok; Left, bottom: A Chinese lantern-maker.

doubt that each of them has cost much more than it should have, and that none will be profitable at all until put under the control of experienced managers." (IBRD 1966: 92)

Nedcol's problems were unique only in their severity—the company was eventually closed down, and its debt taken over by the government. Other enterprises started by the government suffered from similar problems. The troubles of these companies played a significant role in the fall of the Phibun Songkhram government and the rise of Field Marshal Sarit Thanarat.

It is conventional to think of the policies in this period as an aberration when set against the economic performance of the later periods. In many ways they were, particularly, when we look at the country's macroeconomic performance (the growth rate of Gross National Product was only 3.9 percent per annum between 1951 and 1958) and at the harsh climate of repression against Chinese businesses—which were almost all that Thailand had in the way of a commercial sector. But in another sense, it was a formative period during which the two elites, military/political and business, starting from a position of animosity, were forging an alliance and developing a system of payoffs which would be perfected in the following period.

Shipping vessels, from the traditional (top) to the modern (bottom); Inset: A panoramic view of a bay near Pattaya, where many vessels anchor.

The Golden Age of Growth (1958-73)

When Sarit took over full power in 1958, he instituted extensive economic reforms within the system—the most extensive in the postwar period. It was nothing less than a redirection of economic policies. From a vague and haphazard policy of economic nationalism, with doses of anti-business policies under the guise of anti-Chinese policies, the reforms clearly pointed the country in the direction of a more open economy and the promotion of private businesses including foreign-owned enterprises. The key text that guided government policies during this period was a report (IBRD 1959) from a World Bank mission. This mission stayed in the country for a full year and came up with extensive suggestions for changes in the direction, management and organization of economic policies. This was the basis of the reforms instituted by the Sarit regime.

It would be a mistake, however, to think of this episode as an example of blind subservience to foreign (in particular US) interests. The mission report itself acknowledged a close collaboration between the World Bank team and officials of the Ministry of Finance. That the reforms were extensively and successfully implemented indicated their acceptance at critical levels within the bureaucracy or, more accurately, the technocracy, for the Sarit reforms marked the birth of the technocracy as we understand it today.

The key role of macroeconomic management must be placed in the context of the overall Sarit program. In his role as a super patron, the Prime Minister had pronounced that the country needed to "develop" and to expand its educational base in order to join the ranks of progressive countries. "Development," in his view, entailed extensive government investment in basic infrastructure.

Without careful husbanding of resources, large public investments could easily lead to inflation and foreign exchange crises—a common enough pattern in other developing countries. It is Thailand's good fortune that the charismatic leader's grand vision was effectively wedded to the cold pragmatism of the country's financial officers. The leading civil servants in the Ministry of Finance at the time, particularly

Puey Ungphakorn (see next page), were steeped in the traditions of financial conservatism, but at the same time were sympathetic to the need of the country to develop. For them that meant not only accelerating economic growth but also spreading prosperity to the impoverished rural areas.

The institutions that were put in place during the five years of Sarit's premiership to manage the macroeconomy have withstood the test of time. Ever since, four agencies, the Budget Bureau, the National Economic Development Board (later known as the National

Economic and Social Development Board), the Fiscal Policy Office and the Bank of Thailand, would jointly work out the annual budget and submit it for approval by the Cabinet. All except the Bank of Thailand were created during the Sarit period. Certain rules were written into law limiting the size of the fiscal deficit and the creation of new debt. Above all, government guaranteeing of private debt was forbidden—this was the core problem of the Nedcol debacle. With these reforms, the management of the Thai macroeconomy shed the indiscipline of the Phibun regime of the early 1950's and resumed the conservative slant of the prewar royal governments.

At the same time, the anti-Chinese (and by extension, the anti-business) policies of the Phibun government were scaled down. True, the new men who came in with the Sarit coup against Phibun in 1957 kept the old traditions alive and began to take over chairmanships of key enterprises, particularly commercial banks. Also, many of the monopolies, notably for pork supplies to Bangkok that were set up under the Phibun government, continued into the Sarit era. However, no new public monopolies were set up. Indeed, in the new investment promotion law, there was the stipulation that once a particular activity has been promoted, the government would not set up its own enterprise in that activity.

The investment promotion law had been in existence since the Phibun government, but it was constrained by a formidable list of conditions. The main message was conveyed to foreign investors by the Sarit reform of the law: they were now welcome into Thailand. This message contrasted with the general attitude of ambivalence, if not antipathy, that had been prevalent since the People's Party came to power.

The new investment promotion law also set up a new agency, the Board of Investment (BOI). This agency did not just provide a welcome mat for foreign investors; it also played a

Three Men Who Made an Impact

It is difficult to describe the present Thai economic landscape without being reminded of the work of three men of vastly different backgrounds who were occasionally sharply in conflict with one another. It is natural to begin with the most powerful of them, Field Marshal Sarit Thanarat, Prime Minister from 1959 to 1963.

Born in 1908 to an army family, Sarit had an unexceptional military career until the critical year of 1947 when he happened to be commanding an infantry battalion in Bangkok in one of the landmark coups. He rapidly rose to be contender for the succession to Phibun Songkram, in rivalry to General Phao Sriyanon, whose power base was the police department. In 1957 he easily removed Phibun from power, and after a year took full dictatorial power as Prime Minister, after a coup d'état.

After taking power, the field marshal redirected the course of the government to a program of economic development and adopted a plan proposed by the World Bank. This program of development entailed the opening of the economy, major investments in public infrastructure and a gradual withdrawal of the government from industrial investments, the latter being put in the hands of the private sector. Far from putting barriers against businessmen, he began an active program of investment promotion. He also presided over a reform of the government fiscal system, whose main features are still in place today.

Sarit Thanarat

For all these positive achievements, Sarit was far from an honest politician. At his death, he was found to have amassed a fortune worth 2.8 billion baht. The paradox could perhaps be reconciled if one bears in mind that he was the first generation of army officers who were never educated abroad and were thus untainted by western ideas that afflicted those of the Phibun generation. His concept of leadership was that of being the most powerful patron in a society permeated by patron-client relationships. A less flattering but just as accurate portrayal is that of a Mafia godfather dispensing favors to those who supported him and unleashing the full force of his power on those who stood in the way. But the godfather was not a mere gangster. He appreciated the contributions of academics and scholars to the development of the country because, as a great patron, he must have his country grow to be a powerful force in the world arena.

One of these scholars was Puey Ungphakorn, who came from a very different background. Born of Thai Chinese parents of modest economic means, he graduated from a local university before obtaining a scholarship to study in England where he obtained a PhD in economics. His education was interrupted by the Second World War, during which time he served in the Seri Thai resistance movement, having been dropped by parachute onto Thai soil by British planes. When he returned with the degree after the Second World War, he joined the Ministry of Finance and had a sufficiently distinguished career to be appointed Deputy Governor of the Bank of Thailand at the age of thirty-seven. He soon resigned from that post because of a conflict with the government and rejoined the Ministry of Finance to be posted to the United Kingdom. His integrity in conducting the affairs of the government became known to Sarit (ironically it was in connection with an illegal activity of the field marshal himself). When Sarit took power, he was installed as the first director of the newly formed Budget Bureau. He later became the first director of the Fiscal Policy Office at the Ministry of Finance and then the Governor of the Bank of Thailand, all of these within the five years during which Sarit was Prime Minister.

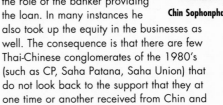

Puey Ungphakorn

During these five years, Puey was instrumental together with colleagues at the Ministry of Finance in instituting various reforms by which the macroeconomic management of the country was transformed. As Governor of the central bank, he tried to exert greater control over the commercial banks, weaning them away from a close connection with politics and politicians, even though the politicians at the time were military men who were accountable to no one, and could have sacked him.

Significantly, when he was strengthening the banks, the politicians did not touch him. It was only toward the later period in his life, when he increasingly devoted his time to promoting rural development and giving a voice to Thailand's poor that the military had their revenge. This man of reason and integrity, who probably did more than any military man to build up Thai capitalism, was accused of being a Communist and was forced to leave the country in 1976, when ideological fervor (on both sides) was at its peak.

Bangkok Bank, the most powerful commercial bank at the time Puey was Governor of the central bank, was run by Chin Sophonphanich. Born in Thailand in 1910 to a poor Chinese family, but schooled in China without any university education, Chin fitted the stereotype of the Chinese who rose from poverty to become a billionaire by sheer dint of hard work and business acumen. Before his association with the Bangkok Bank, he was successively an odd-job man, then a clerk and then assistant manager at a lumberyard in Bangkok. He then set up his own shop (later three shops) that sold general merchandise.

Toward the end of the Second World War, he joined up with a number of Thais and other Chinese businessmen to establish Bangkok Bank. He then became its "compradore," that is, an independent agent who brought business to the bank and guaranteed the loans given by the bank. In 1952 after the bank faced a liquidity crisis, he took over as the Managing Director, no doubt helped by the fact that he could negotiate an injection of capital from the Ministry of Economic Affairs. General Siri Siriyothin, a member of the Rajakru faction, which then supported the Phibun government, took over as the Chairman of the Board.

When Phibun and the Rajakru faction were overthrown by Sarit in 1957, he went into temporary exile. The bank then negotiated to have General Prapass Charusathien, Sarit's right hand man, as Chairman to replace General Siri, who had become a liability. Soon after, Chin returned to Thailand.

Because of his wide contacts among the Chinese businessmen in his capacity as the compradore, Chin was able to establish Bangkok Bank as the premier bank among exporters during the export boom of the 1970's. More than that, when these commodity traders diversified, Chin was able to continue to give support. In doing so, he did not merely play the role of the banker providing the loan. In many instances he

Chin Sophonphanich

also took up the equity in the businesses as well. The consequence is that there are few Thai-Chinese conglomerates of the 1980's (such as CP, Saha Patana, Saha Union) that do not look back to the support that they at one time or another received from Chin and his bank.

The bank's power and influence were such that it could step in and occasionally take over a regulatory function from the government. Thus in the early 1980's when the surplus capacity in the textile trade threatened its future, and after the Ministry of Industry had failed to control the trade's expansion, it fell to the bank to use its financial muscle to impose order on the industry.

The three men used their power, influence and charisma to build up different parts of the social order that came to dominate Thailand during the ninth reign. Of these, the parts that were built up by Sarit in the political arena lasted only ten years after his death. Probably that is to be expected of a system that was built on personal patronage. Puey's institution-building within the bureaucracy and of the central bank—including its remarkable ethos of absolute integrity—survived far longer. Of more significance was his insistence on making banks more professionally and less politically oriented. Chin weaved in and out of the political constraints that bound a businessman of Chinese origin, but eventually lived to reap the full benefits of Puey's success at building up a sound banking system for Thailand.

– Dr Ammar Siamwalla

more important role as a venue whereby domestic private firms could officially provide feedback to the government concerning its policies. For its time, this was a radical departure. The setting up of this bureaucratic organization, together with the chartering of the Board of Trade (by an act of Parliament), marked the final end of the policy of confrontation and the establishment of a dialogue between business and government.

Although the BOI was set up to promote investment in industries, an area in which Thailand was then quite weak, it did not meet with much success during the period. True, new industries were set up which in time would grow to be the leading sectors in the economy, such as in the textile and automotive sectors, but these results were still decades away. It is a moot point whether these industries would ever have come into existence without the protection and tax breaks, sometimes quite generous, which were liberally showered on the would-be industrialists. It is also debatable whether the costs borne by the taxpayers and consumers were

worth the distant benefits. It was, however, widely felt at that time that the promotion policy was a success, in the narrow sense that government offers were made which were taken up by businessmen, both domestic and foreign.

With the government and business elites thus coming to a *modus vivendi*, the stage was set for an era of continuous economic expansion. The economy grew at 7.2 percent per annum between 1958 and 1973. The main engine of this growth was the phenomenal expansion of the agricultural sectors and this was made possible because of a conjunction of events and policies.

Thailand, like its neighbors in mainland Southeast Asia, started the postwar period blessed by a relatively abundant land resource. Much of this land was under forest, but a large proportion could be cultivated. Most of the 17 million Thais

Above: An automobile assembly plant; Below, top: Thai employees of a Japanese factory; Below, bottom: A paper plant.

Role of the Government in Economic Development

Since the 1960's, which was the real start of Thailand's industrialization, the government has taken a proactive and highly visible role in encouraging economic development. The first long-range economic plan was introduced in 1961 (the first Six-Year Economic Development Plan; later plans were changed to five-year periods); the current plan is the seventh five-year plan. To facilitate manageable economic growth, various government agencies were established: the Budget Bureau, the National Economic and Social Development Board (NESDB), the Industrial Finance Corporation of Thailand

(IFCT), and the Board of Investment (BOI). Other key agencies such as the Industrial Estates Authority of Thailand and the Thai Factory Development company were added later in the 1970's.

Thailand's fiscal policies have long been admired for the sound economic management principles that have created the conditions for sustained growth. This has been achieved through cooperation between the Budget Bureau, the Ministry of Finance and the Bank of Thailand, along with research and advice from the NESDB.

Perhaps the best known agency is the BOI, which was set up to attract and process foreign investment. Originally the BOI encouraged foreign businesses to come to Thailand to manufacture products for export as the nation was, and still is, to a large extent, basing industrialization on export promotion. To further assist this process, the Department of

Export Promotion was established under the Ministry of Commerce. As a result, the BOI has five overseas offices (in Japan, Europe and the USA), and some forty-seven commercial counselors' offices at Thai embassies around the globe.

Under the BOI, export processing zones have been set up throughout the nation—with zones 1 and 2 being in or around Bangkok and zone 3 in the provincial areas (the latter was set up to encourage development away from Bangkok to the provinces). Working closely with the IEAT, industrial estates now dot the nation and provide complete facilities for companies manufacturing at these sites.

The BOI assists both foreign companies seeking to locate in Thailand, and Thai companies wanting to export or expand into the region. Incentives in the form of outright ownership, tax holidays and tariff reductions on imported machinery are available, as well as services which can link a foreign company with a Thai partner in the form of a joint-venture.

Indeed, the BOI has been so successful in attracting foreign investment that it is now actively involved in training its counterparts in the Lao PDR and Vietnam.

– J. C.

living in 1946 occupied strips of land near the rivers, mostly of the Chao Phraya system, in the northeast along the Mun and Chi rivers, and along the railway lines. They had gradually expanded away from the river and the rail lines.

Forested lands were cleared and converted into paddy fields. The upland areas had been left unoccupied, much of it on account of malaria.

The actions of the government quickly opened up these unoccupied uplands. The DDT program made the clearing of malaria-infested forests less hazardous. Above all, the road building program made these lands attractive to settlers because when they started producing, the output could be easily marketed. The government also unintentionally promoted the clearing of the forests by giving large logging concessions to private companies. In theory, these required the concessionaires to replant the trees that they

cut down, but enforcement was lax, with the result that the cleared forests were quickly occupied, sometimes by the people who were hired by the concessionaires to clear the land. In addition, considerable illegal logging outside these concessions also took place with the same consequences.

Thai farmers, like agriculturists the world over, had been clearing whatever land was available for centuries. However the land clearing movement of the 1960's and the 1970's proceeded at an unprecedented tempo. Population growth intensified the pressure on the land. At 3.1 percent per annum during the 1960's it was higher than ever previously recorded. Further, the modern land-clearing practice was aided by machinery—in this case, the machinery was provided by the loggers. After the land was cleared, tractors could be used to cultivate the land. Whereas before, with animal power, a farmer could cultivate at most 4 to 5 hectares, with tractor power that limit was raised and a farm size of tens or even hundreds of hectares became manageable.

Once the land was cleared and farmed, the product could be easily sold, aided by the access to the new roads that were built in a burst of expansion during the 1960's. The result was a continuous growth of agricultural exports during the 1960's. Sugarcane acreage expanded continuously. Other crops which were grown in small quantities before they became major export items, first maize, then kenaf, followed by cassava. Thai farmers adopted these crops one by one and produced them largely for the export markets. The output expansion was achieved almost entirely by means of area expansion, rather than by an intensification in the cultivation of existing lands. Yields remained low.

Aside from the construction of infrastructure, these pioneers received little help from the government (the promotion of the sugar industry was the sole exception). In one case (cassava), the government even actively discouraged the crop on the grounds that it is destructive of the soil. This abstention from intervention was not detri-

Top: Clearing land for road-building; Above: A sugar plant; Inset: Sugar.

mental to farmers. It could even be argued that it was to their benefit, given the general ineffectiveness of the government in adopting sensible sectoral policies. In one area, however, the neglect of the government was storing up problems for the future.

As the farmers were clearing and occupying new lands, they did not receive any clear titles to them. The law in this respect was completely at variance with the practice on the ground. For example, it stated that any land which was not occupied was government land. Large parcels of this supposedly unoccupied land were put under forest reserves, to be looked after by the Royal Forestry Department, which had relatively little manpower to look after all the lands that were put in its charge. Even for those lands which were not under forest reserves, the issuance of the titles was proceeding at an extremely slow pace. Consequently, many farmers (in fact the majority of the upland crop farmers) were farming on lands which in the eyes of the law did not belong to them. Owing to the absence of legal recognition, settlers in many areas had to seek protection from local strongmen, and the basis was created for a new rural elite. The availability of land had the potential of creating an egalitarian social order, but sadly, that opportunity was missed, a major policy failure of that period.

At that time, this shortcoming was not noticed. The farmers also did not seem to have been adversely affected, except perhaps in their access to credit. It was only in the 1980's as the land frontier was closed, that the problems creat-

ed by the government's negligence began to assume a larger profile in the political and social agenda.

The most dynamic part of the agricultural sector was in new upland crops and in rubber. But even in rice, the traditional crop for Thai farmers, output grew, although there was also an intensification, particularly in the central plains. In this case, the long history of irrigation investments going back to the fifth reign was at long last beginning to pay off. In the first decade of the twentieth century, the Dutch engineer van der Heide originally conceived of having a diversion dam across the main channel of the river, supplemented by one storage dam further upstream. With the construction of the Chao Phraya irrigation dam in the early 1950's, and the storage dam at Yanhee (which now bears His Majesty's name), van der Heide's conception became reality. The lower Chao Phraya system now has flood prevention capability and supplemental irrigation during the wet season, as well as the capability to provide water during the dry season to a substantial proportion of the command area. By the end of the 1960's, dry season cultivation in the central plains began to take off, helped by the new varieties of rice that were developed in the Philippines by the International Rice Research Institute.[4]

A consequence of agricultural expansion was the continual growth of the exports and the increasing strength of the baht internationally. We shall return to an assessment of whether the growth eventually benefited the men and women who labored to clear the forests and farm the lands. There was no doubt, however, that the agricultural sector ended up absorbing a considerable number of people and kept Thailand rural for the time being. This availability of land and the growth in agricultural production kept the Thai rate of urbanization low, compared to other countries at the same level of income. Also, almost uniquely among its Asian neighbors, each Thai farmer had, on average, a larger parcel of land to work with in 1980 than he had in 1960.

A rubber factory.

Agricultural growth was ultimately responsible for the overall growth of the economy. But the rapid expansion of the economy during the 1960's eventually undid the Sarit system of government. This system rested on the exercise of absolute power, first by Sarit, and on his death by his milder successor, Field Marshal Thanom Kittikachorn. But the very economic growth that this regime fostered led to the emergence of a middle class as well as a class of intellectuals that did not feel beholden to the government. This class of intellectuals was also a creation of the reforms and expansion of the universities, which saw a considerable growth in the number of full-time lecturers. They viewed the Thanom regime as increasingly anachronistic. In retrospect, the collapse of the regime in the student uprising in October 1973 looks inevitable, but at the time the surprise was in its suddenness.

The Oil Shocks—Teetering on the Brink (1973–85)

The Thanom regime was brought down in the same week as the six-day war and the Arab boycott which brought about the first oil shock. 1973 was thus also a watershed year globally. Two decades of unprecedented expansion for the rich industrialized countries had come to an end. The confidence and optimism which seemed to pervade global economic issues also died with it.

For Thailand, this marked another end. The opening up of politics created by the rising of 1973 was a permanent achievement. Since then, generals came and went as heads of governments

Development of Thai Industrial Exports

In 1946, at the beginning of His Majesty's reign, Thailand's principal exports were rice, rubber, tin and teak. The nation's exports at the time were based almost entirely on agriculture and unprocessed raw materials. According to International Trade figures from the Customs Department, exports were worth 968 million baht in 1947, with rice (approximately 300 million baht) being the most important export item. Few analysts would have predicted that by the end of 1994, Thailand would garner a 1 percent share of total world trade, with exports passing the historic 1 trillion baht mark (1994 final total: 1.25 trillion baht).

During the rapid economic growth of the 1960's, agricultural exports diversified dramatically. In the early 1960's, for example, rice accounted for 50 percent of all crop production but by 1970 had declined to 35 percent. Rice is still a vital part of agricultural production (Thailand is the world's largest exporter of rice) but it is now joined by tapioca, fruit, fisheries and other agro products.

In the 1970's the government encouraged industry via a policy of import substitution. Consumer goods and light manufacturing were given incentives and industrial production started to take off. By the end of this decade, a new wave of development started, led by export production. Foreign investors, looking for new overseas manufacturing sites, started to move to Thailand. In 1985, a dramatic change occurred: for the first time in the nation's history, industrial goods started to outpace agricultural goods in exports (see graphs below).

The rapid development of Thailand's manufacturing capacity led to another major shift in 1993 when, for the first time, high-tech, value-added exports surged past labor-intensive exports such as textiles, footwear and jewelry. While the labor-intensive products continue to grow by some 8 percent a year, the more high-tech products are growing by 25 to 40 percent a year. Clearly, the Thai economy is maturing rapidly, following the path of the advanced economies of Japan, South Korea and Taiwan.

Moreover, Thai exports are being sent to more markets than before; over 170 countries received Thai products in 1993. However, the big traditional markets—the United States, Japan and the European Union—remain the main destinations for Thai exports, accounting for 53.6 percent of all exports in 1993. Nevertheless, there is a growing trend for increased trade between Thailand and other ASEAN members, and this is likely to grow in the future as economic growth and trade expands throughout the Asia-Pacific region.

– J. C.

COMPOSITION OF THAILAND'S EXPORTS: BY GROUP OF PRODUCTS (UNIT: %)

[Source: Thailand Export Focus, Alpha Research/1994]

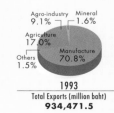

1980
Total Exports (million baht)
133,197.2

Agro-industry 8.2%
Mineral 3.8%
Manufacture 35.6%
Agriculture 48.4%
Others 4.0%

1993
Total Exports (million baht)
934,471.5

Agro-industry 9.1%
Mineral 1.6%
Agriculture 17.0%
Others 1.5%
Manufacture 70.8%

or of juntas, but they had to seek to win legitimacy by getting the approval of elected parliaments. This more competitive style of politics can only be of long-term benefit for the country, but in the immediate aftermath, particularly in the years from 1973 to about 1980, Thai politics became quite divisive.

The system of macroeconomic management that was created during the Sarit era continued without major changes. Two assumptions which underlay this system were no longer valid. Domestically, it was predicated on an authoritarian political system, not subject to populist pressures to overspend and undertax. Internationally, it was predicated on a degree of stability in the world economic and financial system, which, as we have seen, no longer held true. To navigate between the shoals of domestic political pressures and international instability required considerable skill. The Thai macroeconomic leadership—technocrats almost to a man—managed the transition rather better than most other developing countries. However, it was by no means plain sailing all the way. Thailand very nearly became a problem debtor in the 1980's.

As mentioned, the domestic political scene during the period saw a degree of polarization between left and right which was unprecedented for Thailand. The democratization between 1973 and 1976 and the sharp reaction which followed in 1976-7 exerted great demands on the budget. Even a government as authoritarian as that in power in 1976-7 felt compelled to buy off various groups within the country. In 1976, with the military triumphant, a loan of 20 billion baht to purchase arms to fight the Communists was approved by the Cabinet. This was followed by further loans which were easily enough obtained. Remember that this was a period when foreign commercial banks were awash in petro-dollars, and the famous statement made by one of their managers: "Nations do not go bankrupt." In the early stages, in fact, Thailand was from their point of view quite an attractive borrower, having previously been following a conservative borrowing policy, and whose stock of debt owed to foreigners were almost balanced by its healthy reserves.

By 1985, the combined public and private sector indebtedness to foreign lenders had ballooned to 39 percent of GDP from less than 1 percent in 1973.[5] Both public and private sectors (particularly the commercial banks) expanded their indebtedness, but the public sector's debt grew at a faster rate, so that by 1985, it stood at 60 percent of the total stock of net debt.

Foreign debt as high as 40 percent of GNP was not excessive. Had the funds borrowed during this period been used for productive investments, the increased indebtedness would have been sustainable. However, this was not the case. Arms purchases with borrowed money have already been alluded to. With the second oil shock, further loans were contracted to finance the public sector deficits—deficits which were incurred because of the government's reluctance to adjust domestic prices of energy and of many public utilities to reflect the new configuration in the world markets. Furthermore, the tying of the baht to the dollar which was rapidly appreciating between 1978 and 1985 stimulated imports, reduced export competitiveness (particularly for industrial goods) and brought in high interest rates as a consequence of the tight money policies of the Federal Reserve Bank in the United States. The high interest rate in turn discouraged investment and resulted in higher payments to service existing loans. All of this

Left, top: Bank of Asia building in central Bangkok; Left, bottom: Bangkok Bank headquarters.

played havoc with the current account of the balance of payments, the deficit on which rose to more than 6 percent of GNP in 1978–80 and in 1982.

By 1982, just before the Mexican default, the technocrats were again taking charge of macro-economic policies, and the old conservative policy stance resumed. Over the four years between 1982 and 1985, the Thai government sweated the imbalances out of the economy. Fiscal discipline was reimposed, better controls were placed on foreign borrowing by the public sector, and

Below, left: Bank of Thailand; Inset: Newly minted bank notes.

on the finances of the public enterprises. The baht had already been devalued because of a speculative attack in 1981 by 15 percent. It was again devalued in 1984 by roughly the same percentage, but this time more as an act of policy than out of necessity. In addition, the government made a decision in 1984 no longer to tie the baht solely to the dollar, but to an unannounced basket of currencies. The consequence of this policy of austere demand management was that the growth rates dipped to an average of 4.6 percent between 1980 and 1985.

Banking

There is a wide variety of institutions in the Thai financial system. It is dominated by privately-owned concerns, particularly commercial banks, which have accounted for as much as 70 percent of all financial institutions' total assets during the past two decades (see table).

Commercial banking dates back to 1888 when the first bank (foreign-owned) was opened. The first Thai commercial bank, the Siam Commercial Bank, was opened in 1906. Initially, foreign banks were the most active but their dominance was disturbed by the Second World War. Indeed, just before the end of the war, in 1944, the Bangkok Bank was founded, starting a new chapter in the nation's financial history. Other new banks followed and their emergence coincided with the start of His Majesty's reign in 1946. Meanwhile, Bangkok Bank has gone on during the past fifty years to become Southeast Asia's largest commercial bank.

During the first and second waves of economic growth (the first in the 1960's emphasized infrastructure development and agricultural diversification; the second, in the 1970's, emphasized import substitution), the banking system developed gradually under strict government supervision. The third wave of economic development, which began in the

FINANCIAL INSTITUTIONS IN THAILAND							
				(billions of baht)			
	Operations began	No	No. of branches	Household savings captured	Capital account	Credits extended	Total assets
Commercial banks	1888	30	2,581	1,552.2	170.2	2,161.9	2,528.1
Finance companies	1969	92	42	293.7	66.9	547.7	671.0
Credit foncier companies	1969	18	-	3.4	1.2	5.1	6.2
Life insurance companies	1929	12	1,016	53.0	12.5	19.7	66.9
Pawnshops	1916	1,797	-	6.9	7.3	13.8	17.8
Government Savings Bank	1946	1	525	130.4	11.1	18.5	150.9
BAAC	1966	1	266	19.0	6.1	62.0	76.9
Government Housing Bank	1953	1	18	38.3	3.5	53.5	57.1
Industrial Finance Corp. of Thailand	1959	1	7	-	7.7	35.9	57.1
SIFCT	1992	1	-	-	0.3	0.1	0.6

early 1980's, saw a radical shift to export production. And as the economy shifted toward world markets, the financial sector has had to change to meet the demands of greater competition.

Real change, however, came in the latter part of the 1980's, as the economy jumped into double-digit growth. Measures were introduced by successive governments to liberalize and deregulate the Thai financial sector. External pressure to deregulate came from the conclusion of the Uruguay Round and the setting up of the World Trade Organization (WTO); the proposals on liberalizing global trade in goods and services have meant that Thailand must open its financial sector within the next eight years. As a result, the government has introduced legislation that will open up the Thai financial markets to free trade.

Specific measures include accepting obligations under Article VIII of the International Monetary Fund's Articles of Agreement, as well as exchange control relaxation. Banks and other financial institutions have been given wider roles in all markets. The Stock Exchange

of Thailand (SET) was reorganized in 1992 to include a regulatory body, the Stock Exchange Commission.

But perhaps the boldest move, and one which puts Thailand ahead of many Asian nations, has been the introduction of off-shore banking via the Bangkok International Banking Facility (BIBF), which is designed not only to make the market open and competitive (mainly by allowing more foreign banks to set up branches), but also to allow Thailand to become a regional funding center. At the end of 1994, forty-seven banks had been granted BIBF licenses: eleven Thai commercial banks, eleven foreign banks already operating full branches, and twenty-five foreign banks yet to operate full branches. By 1997, some of the new foreign banks will be granted full branch status, while the Provincial International Banking Facility (PIBF) will encourage banks to develop provincial branch systems.

For Thai banks, the real challenge ahead will be how to deal with increased competition—both domestically and in the ever-more closely connected trading of global financial markets.

– J. C.

The instability generated first by laxness and then by austerity also took its toll on the financial sector. Beginning in 1979 and continuing on till 1984, many finance companies and one commercial bank collapsed. A few more commercial banks were brought back from the brink of collapse by government assistance. Mismanagement and sometimes outright fraud were no doubt responsible for many of these failures, but the economic slowdown also precipitated them where otherwise a strong growth of the economy would have camouflaged the poor returns on their investments.

Developments in the global economy affected not only the macroeconomy and its management, but also the various sectors as well. Dominating the scene were the two oil shocks. Their impact, however, differed significantly. The first shock, in 1973, was accompanied by a substantial rise in food and commodity prices worldwide as well. Thailand's major exports at that time happened to be commodities, mostly food. The adverse effect of the increase in the prices of imported oil was therefore mitigated to some extent by the increased food prices.

The sharp increases in the price of food dur-

ing 1972 to 1974 eventually petered out, but even then, the prices of most agricultural commodities remained somewhat above trend through the rest of the 1970's. The expansion of land areas observed during the 1960's therefore continued through most of the 1970's—if anything, there was an acceleration of that trend. The northeast in particular experienced a cassava boom. Between 1968 and 1980, cassava production doubled every

four years. Dry-season cultivation of rice in the central plains continued to expand to the point where the water stored in the Bhumibol and Sirikit dams during the rainy season was insufficient to meet dry season demand.

The agricultural boom of the 1970's proved to be an Indian summer, however. By 1980, forest lands available for clearance became increasingly difficult to find. The worldwide expansion in agricultural production capacity (particularly through investments in irrigation) as a result of the food scare of the early 1970's led to continual surpluses and a depression of agricultural prices throughout much of the 1980's. The removal of various export taxes proved insufficient to insulate the farmers from the effects of this depression. For the first time since the statistics on poverty were collected, its incidence increased during the first half of the 1980's. Until the early 1980's, outmigration from the rural areas was mostly seasonal, with most migrants returning to farm their lands during the rainy season. With shrinking agricultural opportunity, migrants stayed longer in more permanent factory jobs.

With these market conditions, the comparative advantage which Thailand used to enjoy in agricultural production (and which it still does) had suddenly become a liability. It was a liability because it dictated that Thailand continued to export products whose international prices were declining. At the same time, however, it was acquiring a new comparative advantage in products of light labor-intensive manufacturing, notably garments, gems and jewelry, canned tuna fish and assembly of electronic products. Rapid expansion in these new areas was, however, hampered between 1980 and 1984 by the high value of the baht. Once the exchange rates were realigned, the boom in exports of manufactured goods began.

Above: Bhumibol dam; Left: Some of the products of the manufacturing sector are canned fish (left, top), garments (left, bottom) and gemstones (facing page, top, inset).

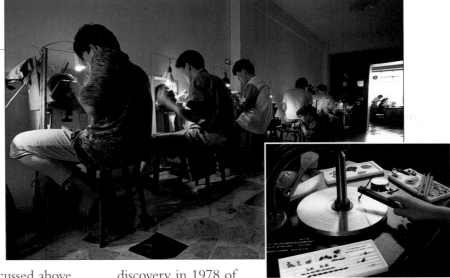

A great deal of the economic travails of this period arose from the reluctance of the government to adjust the domestic price structure fully to the increase in energy prices, particularly after the second oil shock in 1979. This failure to adjust prices was part and parcel of the macroeconomic policy failure discussed above. Against this policy failure must be set the formation of a new institutional framework for the energy sector. A new Petroleum Authority of Thailand was formed and put under professional management. It became the keystone of different public enterprises dealing with energy. Similarly, two refineries which were granted as concessions to private firms Sri Racha and Bangchak were taken over by the government on the expiry of their contracts and also put under professional management.

The country experienced a windfall in the discovery in 1978 of large natural gas deposits in the Gulf of Thailand, which helped to reduce the dependence of this sector on imports. In the eyes of the technocrats, the gas reserves were also to be the foundation of Thailand's heavy industry on the Eastern Seaboard. A petrochemical project was launched. There was also to be a fertilizer plant, but that was shelved amid great controversy.

From the vantage point of the present, with our knowledge of the boom of the late l980's, the dozen years covered in this section appear as a period of transition between the agriculture-

Right: Processing gemstones; Below: The Stock Exchange of Thailand.

The Thai Stock Market

When the then-Prime Minister HE MR Kukrit Pramoj presided over the opening of the first office of the Thai Stock Exchange on June 20, 1975, the Thai capital market truly came into being. Prior to this historic occasion, the capital needs of Thai companies were met largely by the private banking sector.

Attempts at creating a brokerage business had been made before; in 1953, for example, the Bird Co. Ltd. became the first company in Thailand to operate a brokerage business. In 1962, a group of business people set up the Bangkok Stock Exchange Co. Ltd but the government and the general public did not really get behind the idea and the securities business remained static for over a decade.

In 1976, after the first twelve months in operation, only twenty-one companies were listed on the Stock Exchange of Thailand

(SET); total turnover was 23.70 million baht, with a daily average of just 3.4 million baht. The SET index closed at 84.08. For the first decade of SET's existence, the index rose steadily, until the boom years of 1986 to 1990, which coincided with the nation's astonishing double-digit economic growth. It was during this period that SET became firmly established as one of the major regional bourses. Moreover, as companies rushed to list on the exchange, it became clear that SET was playing an increasingly important role in raising funds for business expansion.

In order to join the global trading system and meet exacting international standards, the government computerized the system on May 31, 1991 and enacted the Securities and Exchange Act on May 16, 1992. The new legislation introduced a regulatory body, the Securities and Exchange Commission (SEC), which supervises the securities capital market. SET now has a clearly defined structure, globally-linked computerized information systems and legal safeguards to protect all investors. Above all, SET is now in a position to promote savings and mobilize funds for industrial expansion.

SET has come a long way since those first twenty-one companies were listed on the bourse twenty years ago. At the end of the first quarter of 1995, some 403 companies were listed with a market capitalization of 3.16 trillion baht. The total value of corporate securities was 2,113 billion baht with daily average turnover of 8,628 million baht. SET is fast becoming one of the key bourses in the region. In 1997, the exchange will move to a custom-built facility, which will house all operations, at the Queen Sirikit Convention Center site.

– J. C.

the dollar in that basket from about a half to 90 percent. The baht consequently went down in value with the dollar.

The consequence was a boom of unprecedented proportions. Thailand experienced double-digit growth rates in three consecutive years beginning in 1987. This spurt was fueled initially by an export boom in which manufactured goods now played an overwhelming role, shunting aside agricultural exports altogether as the main engine of growth that they had been until 1980. The expansion of industrial production and exports was sustained by increasing investment, particularly from Japan, Taiwan and Hong Kong, largely because these economies were faced with the need to realign their production in the wake of rapid appreciation of their currencies during these years. Thailand was the "flavor of the month" among stockbrokers worldwide, and a great deal of portfolio investment also flowed in, fueling in turn a huge stock market boom. Beginning in 1988, the speculative fever spilled over into the real estate market and led to a construction boom, and large increases in land prices.

Despite the heady atmosphere that these various booms generated, Thailand in these years provided a good object lesson of the adverse consequences of excessively rapid growth. The enormous expansion in the stock and property markets diverted a great deal of entrepreneurial talents into activities which, by their very nature, could not be sustained. This diversion of human resources was particularly burdensome because it was becoming clear that while Thailand had a comparative advantage in producing labor-intensive manufactures that it was exporting during this period, it could not hope to continue in these sorts of activity for much longer. Domestic wages were going up, gradually at first, but sharply by the end of the 1980's, and as other

driven growth of the golden age of 1958-73 and the industry-driven boom of the last ten years. Many of the painful episodes were adjustments toward what would become a better future.

Those who lived through the period, however, could not have the foresight to be so sanguine. Politically, the situation was one of foreboding, even alarm, as the Communists took over power in Vietnam, Laos and Cambodia. The domestic political polarization was fierce enough to preclude sound management of the economy. The problems plaguing the financial sector, particularly in the latter half of this period, also dampened investments considerably. The public sector, in its push for austerity beginning in 1982, also had to postpone many infrastructural investments, with consequences that were to be felt in the 1990's.

The Industrial Boom (1985–95)

By 1985, the worst of the adjustment pains were over. In addition, Thailand received two unexpected bonuses from the rest of the world. The first was the sharp drop in petroleum prices in the beginning of 1986. The second was the reversal of the trend in exchange rates with the dollar beginning to depreciate. The government then made a critical decision, setting the stage for the boom that followed: it decided to tamper with the basket of currencies that determined the value of the baht, and increased the share of

A canned pineapple factory.

developing countries were adopting an export-based development strategy, it was a matter of time before other countries with lower wages than Thailand could out-compete Thai suppliers. Thailand's industrial future depended upon the ability to upgrade continually the technology and skills possessed by its firms and its workers. A system which awarded speculative skills was unlikely to generate that ability.

Thailand was and is fortunate in attracting foreign investors. They play a strategic role in expanding Thailand's technological skills and particularly in training its workers, but a near

Below, clockwise from top left: Hualampong railway station; A road in Bangkok with the expressway overhead; Klong Toey port; Don Muang Airport.

total reliance on what these firms provide is clearly not in Thailand's long-term interests.

While the first few years of expansion rested on the spare capacity that was available because of the growth recession in the early 1980's, very soon that spare capacity was used up. Severe strains were building up on Thailand's infrastructure, particularly in transport and telecommunications. At this point the government made a fateful decision to begin privatizing the provision of these basic services. It did not do so by selling off the state enterprises that were in charge, and letting them face competition.

Infrastructure

For centuries, the traditional means of transportation in the nation was either by water, making use of the many rivers, or by rough track. The four major regions were, by and large, cut off from the rest of the country. When His Majesty acceded to the throne in 1946, communication and transportation were both in a primitive state, even though there were rail links between regions and single-lane highways. Air transport between the regions was unheard of at the time.

In the 1960's, the government placed more emphasis on infrastructure development; highways, rail tracks and ports were all developed in tandem with the growing economy. Successive five-year plans have placed greater emphasis on mobilizing resources for much needed infrastructure development. Today, the land transportation system consists of a road network of 170,000 km and a rail network of over 4,000 km (to all regions except Phuket); air transport is covered by six international and twenty-nine domestic airports; and water transport is served by eight international deep sea ports.

Telecommunications is rapidly expanding: in 1983, just 463,231 telephone lines were in use, but by 1993 this had risen to 2,184, 892 lines, and by the end of 1996,

this figure is expected to increase to 6 million lines [all above figures from "Investment Opportunities Study: Infrastructure in Thailand," BOI, 1995]. Other infrastructure areas, such as electrical power production and transmission, are also rapidly developing.

With economic growth rates averaging more than 8 percent since the early 1980's, bottlenecks have emerged in some key areas. As a result, successive governments have designated extra resources to infrastructure development. By the year 2000, we can expect a complete double-track rail network, four-lane highways and ring roads between and around major provincial cities. A second major international airport will be operational and linked with the growing Eastern Seaboard region. Indeed, several futuristic projects are currently assessed; these include a high speed rail track and the Global

Transpark (an integrated, high-tech manufacturing and transportation facility linked to similar facilities in Germany and the United States), both to be located on the Eastern Seaboard.

Infrastructure problems in Bangkok, especially horrendous traffic jams, have long been a major headache for Bangkok residents and business people. To ease pressure, various mass transit projects (rapid rail and road systems, expressways and so on) are being developed and are due to come on stream by the end of this decade. By this time, the capital will have much more complete and efficient transportation, telecommunications and freighting networks, enabling it to become one of the major business hubs (and a center for transportation, telecommunications, finance and tourism) in the entire Asia-Pacific region.

– J. C.

Rather, their monopoly was kept intact, but they were made to give "concessions" to private companies to undertake major new investment projects. This was the route followed for the expansion of the telephone network and the urban transport system.

If truth is the first casualty of war, public interest was the first casualty of the system of concessions that were granted during this period. While the system of piecemeal privatization of the public services has a great deal to recommend it, the contractual arrangements that underlay these concessions required considerable sophistication and integrity among the negotiators. The negotiation process in turn had to be fair and the results transparent to the public. None of these conditions was met. The implementation of these concessions seems to have

combined the delays, inefficiencies and political interference of the public enterprises with the greed of the private sector. The consequence can be seen in the notoriously chaotic traffic of Bangkok, for which no solution appears to be in sight.

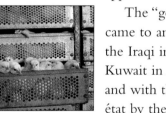

The "good times" came to an end with the Iraqi invasion of Kuwait in August 1990, and with the coup d' état by the army against the elected Prime Minister, General Chatichai Chunhavan in February 1991. The speculative bubble burst but, fortunately, the rest of the economy had a soft landing, and growth in production continued albeit at the more moderate pace of 7 to 8 percent, again with the industrial sector leading the way.

Industry in Thailand has traditionally been concentrated in Bangkok and its environs. The government has made many attempts to reduce the concentration of economic activities in

Bangkok, the two main instruments deployed being the spread of infrastructural services to the countryside and differential tax treatment through the BOI privileges.

The spread of the physical infrastructure has been a long process. The road network was built up in the 1960's and the early 1970's. During the 1980's, electricity was made available to nearly all villages in Thailand. What still needs to be done is to make the telephone system also available in the rural areas, but then Bangkok itself still suffers from a shortage of lines.

The BOI's generous tax privileges to investors who located their plants in the outer provinces have been of long standing. In their way, they have been effective particularly during the last few years. Unfortunately, BOI has had a habit of defining Bangkok and its environs (the area to be discriminated against) quite narrowly, and then gradually widening it. Firms would locate their plants just over the border. With each widening of the definition of Bangkok, the urban sprawl would expand some more, but there was little effect on the more distant parts of the country.

The failure of industry to move to the countryside was particularly unfortunate when set against the crisis that was hitting the countryside. Farmers were facing low prices (the years 1985-7 were particularly bad), and their productivity was not rising. The main explanation for the stagnation in productivity seemed to be the decline in public investments, particularly in irrigation. Large-scale irrigation projects were no longer pursued, and the impact of small-scale projects was at best doubtful. Under these circumstances, with industrial jobs beckoning them, it is hardly surprising that farmers' sons and especially daughters were streaming to the new factories. This led in turn to a shortage of agricultural labor and worsened that sector's crisis. Rural population is being hollowed out by this process, with its most vigorous members away in the factories. The full social consequences of this have yet to be addressed by policy-makers.

Left: A chicken farm.

The Long View—An Assessment of Economic Changes

Between 1950 and 1995, the total output of goods and services grew by more than seventeen times. The best guess for the previous fifty years (1900-50) was that output grew by less than three times, barely more than the growth in population.

Two questions arise from this simple fact. How was this growth possible? And, what are the consequences? Simple questions tend to have complicated answers. Take the question of causation first. It is wrong to assign a single cause to a very complex process. What would be more in the realm of possibility is to stress the preconditions which generated this process and allowed them to continue.

Recall that the high economic growth of the postwar years really began with the Sarit reforms of the late 1950's. The single most important achievement of those reforms was the establishment of economic stability. Without this achievement, Thai entrepreneurs would be easily diverted to speculative activities which, from a long-term point of view, are unproductive, to themselves and certainly to the national economy.

But, let it be emphasized, economic stability by itself, while necessary, was insufficient to generate growth. Before the Second World War, Thailand had enjoyed economic stability, but not much growth. Indeed, some argue that the quest for stability was then so obsessive as to be detrimental to growth.

Economic stability after the Sarit reforms was, however, allied with another process, that of capital formation, and it is here that some real changes have taken place. Key to this change was the incorporation of the Chinese entrepreneurs as a class into Thai society. It is true that in the past descendants of Chinese immigrants had gradually assimilated and become Thais, but they did so as individuals. More to the point, they did so after accumulating wealth as tax farmers or

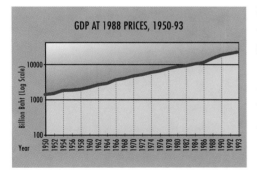

Top, right: A rice mill in Chiang Rai.

monopoly traders on behalf of the monarchs, and when their children assimilated, they became part of the officialdom. The expansion of rice production for exports and the heavy immigration of Chinese in the first half of this century, as well as more aggressive Chinese and Thai nationalism, had made the process of assimilation somewhat more difficult. But Chinese entrepreneurs continued to accumulate wealth, primarily from rice processing and trade. Although no reliable estimates exist, it was widely assumed that the bulk of this wealth flowed back to China.

The closing off of mainland China after 1949 and the *modus vivendi* achieved with the Thai political leadership set the stage for Chinese entrepreneurs to redirect their energies to the Thai economy. In the process, they set up commercial banks which helped focus those energies much more profitably, certainly to themselves, and, as a byproduct, to the national economy as well.

We have thus far focused on developments in Thailand and to some extent in China, but of course the rest of the world was not standing still during this period. It is alleged that the Thai economy has only recently been caught up by the "globalization" of the world economy, and that is the explanation for the recent rapid expansion. But surely, Thailand had joined the world economy since it signed the Bowring Treaty in 1855, which limited the import duty on general merchandise to 3 percent *ad valorem*, later 5 percent. This remained in force until 1935, when fiscal autonomy was returned to Thailand. How much more open could an economy be? Yet, at one time, it was argued that it was precisely the inability to protect its industry which kept the Thai economy from industrializing and from growing.

This is not to say that the rest of the world has had no impact on the economy. The impact came largely through the technology that became accessible. Being backward in this area, Thai entrepreneurs could draw on considerable technology almost available "off the shelf." Almost, but not quite. To acquire such technology itself requires skill on the part of Thai factory workers and managers—and, lest it be forgotten, of Thai farmers using the tractors and threshers as well. Without investments made in schools and universities over this period, the acquisition of such technology would have been much more difficult. Despite the large investments made, they are proving insufficient for Thais to keep up with the pace of technology worldwide, and our ability to acquire and master new technology is a matter of serious concern.

What then are the consequences of this enormous economic expansion? Two divergent answers are given, reminiscent of the dispute between those who see half a glass of water as half-full and those who see it as half-empty.

Thais are *on average* five times richer than they were fifty years ago. Of course, this increase in the average hides a great deal of disparity in the gains to economic expansion, but it is mere sloganeering to say that, as a result of the growth, "the rich have gotten richer, and the poor poorer." Economic growth has indeed trickled down to the poor. If we define the poor

as those receiving less income than is needed to maintain adequate nutrition, then the poor have been reduced from 57 percent of the population, or 15 million persons, in 1963 to 25 percent of the population, or 13.8 million persons, in 1988. The fall in the number of people who are poor would have been more dramatic had the trend not been interrupted and indeed reversed in the first half of the 1980's—the number of poor in fact stood at 10 million in 1980. Since 1985, the downward trend in the number of poor has continued. It is difficult to imagine how the decline in poverty would have taken place without economic growth.

It is not only in terms of incomes that people have become better off. The physical quality of life has also improved. Not only has infant mortality declined but the picture holds true of health care generally. Without the scourge of AIDS, the picture would be even more triumphant. True, the wonders of Western medicine sometimes come at a heavy price, but the rural poor at least have the option of paying that price to buy good health. Their situation is of course not a pretty one, but compare this to the situation a hundred years ago, when even princes and princesses could not be prevented from dying from cholera. Measured against this, the sheer availability of that option, however expensive, should not be underestimated.

The AIDS problem, of course, is a standing indictment of the type of economic system that we have developed. It is hard to imagine its spread without the rampant prostitution that we now have, and there are grounds to believe that the prostitution is

NUMBER AND PERCENT OF PEOPLE WITH INCOMES BELOW POVERTY LINE 1962–88

(chart: millions on left axis 10.00–16.00; percent poor people on right axis 0–60; years 1962, 1968, 1975, 1980, 1985, 1988)
— Percent Poor
— Number of Poor People

Below, top: Vaccination of primary school students; Below, bottom: Pregnant women in front of a bus promoting population control.

itself a consequence partly of the unequal distribution of income that has accompanied our growth. But before we go on to attribute all the blame to economic growth, let us remind ourselves that Central Africa is also experiencing rampant AIDS (also propagated through the sex industry) without experiencing much in the way of economic growth.

Other than health care, the provision of public services to the rural population has continued apace. The 1960's and the 1970's saw the extension of the road network, the 1980's of electricity and the 1990's of household water supply. The formal agricultural credit system was greatly expanded in 1975, and now makes up the bulk of the credit supplied to farmers, compared to their dependence on informal lenders at exorbitant interest rates in earlier times.

Each of these gains has introduced much convenience and reduced the isolation of rural life, but each of these gains comes with question marks hanging over it. Road-building has facilitated migration, and according to some, the break-up of families. Those who see this as a new phenomenon overlook the history of northeastern villages which is replete with accounts of migration of whole villages to escape war, pestilence and starvation. Electricity has encouraged a consumerist society, it is alleged, usually by Bangkokians speaking in the comforts of an air-conditioned room. The availability of credit is also alleged to have encouraged indebtedness, overlooking the peculiar needs of agricultural production.

It would be absurd to deny that in too many areas and to too many people, economic growth has introduced real pain and hardship. There is no excuse for two hundred factory workers dying in a fire—and this is merely the most dramatic episode that threw into relief daily occurrences in unsafe factories. There is no excuse for many Bangkok families having to have breakfast in their cars to "beat the traffic." There is no

excuse for the air quality over Bangkok. There is no excuse for so many Thais living in poverty while the country continues to increase its fleet of Mercedes cars. There is no excuse in all these cases because Thailand can afford to solve, or at least ameliorate, many of these problems with the wealth that economic growth has generated. The failure is a failure of collective will. Surely the most telling criticism against economic growth is that it has dissolved traditional social bonds and communities, without forging new bonds and new organizations to understand and tackle the problems that it has created.

Measured against the reality of the past, much has been accomplished and Thais can be proud of these achievements. Measured against what is possible to achieve with the wealth generated by five decades of growth, much is wanting. Critics of economic growth are wont to paint the past in rosy colors in order to put in relief the shortcomings of the present. Such a tactic may be effective propaganda but it is bad history. It denigrates the achievements of the past five decades, but far more importantly, it detracts from the task of finding real solutions to the real problems of today.

Top, right: The Bangkok skyline; Inset: A modern shopping center; Overleaf: An aerial view of an expressway in Bangkok.

5

AGRICULTURE AND FISHERIES

Chulanope Snidvongs Na Ayutthaya

ONE OF THE FEATURES WHICH DISTINGUISHES THAILAND FROM ITS NEIGHBORING COUNTRIES IS THE LONG TRADITION OF THE MONARCHICAL INSTITUTION, THE HISTORY OF WHICH DATES BACK AS LONG AS THE HISTORY OF THE KINGDOM OF THAILAND ITSELF.

Not only does the monarchy lie at the essence of Thai society, a feature of this institution that has been passed on from kingdom to kingdom, from dynasty to dynasty, is that the monarch rules over subjects as would a father over his children. Even with the change from absolute to constitutional monarchy, the respect and the love the people uphold for the monarch continue to provide a strong foundation holding Thailand as a nation and as a society together. King Bhumibol Adulyadej, the present King Rama IX, has continued this kingly tradition. Since his coronation, he has made it his mandate and prime concern as a king to reach out to his people, to understand their conditions of living, their problems and their needs. Through his travels to the provinces, he has crossed traditional barriers and established a new concept of the modern monarch as caring, understanding and willing to act.

Thailand has a predominantly agro-based economy with the majority of the people still living in the rural areas. In 1990, 73 percent of the 54.55 million people[1] were farmers living in the rural areas.[2] His Majesty devotes much of his time traveling to these areas, taking photographs, maps and careful notes from his consultation with the people, government officials and experts. The sight of the King talking and listening to his people during his travels has become familiar among the Thai people, adding to the esteem and gratitude they feel.

This essay aims to highlight key aspects of His Majesty's involvement in agricultural activities and provides some insight into some of the social, economic and technological developments of agricultural production. A brief profile of the agricultural sector will be given, including the basic economic indicators, the employment and income situation, the impact of the green revolution on production and the export performance in the light of changes in the market situation. The next section then moves on to provide an account of His Majesty's concerns and the development programs initiated or executed

Facing page: Working in a ricefield. Right: His Majesty the King talks with farmers during one of his many rural visits.

under His Majesty's royal patronage. These range from basic research activities, human resource development, land resource development in its technical, social and economic aspects, forestry resources and water resource development to the fishery sector.

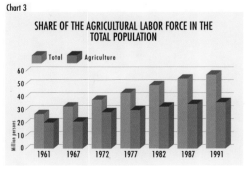

Overview of the Agricultural Sector

Basic Economic Indicators:
Within the last twenty years, Thailand's economy has been transformed from an agrarian-based one to one that can be classified as "semi-industrialized". The percentage share of the agricultural sector in the Gross Domestic Product (GDP) has been steadily declining, from 47.1 percent in 1950 to 27 percent in 1971 to 20 percent in 1985 to 17 percent in 1987.[3] In 1990, the sectoral share was further reduced to 12.6 percent. Preliminary figures for 1991 anticipated only a slightly lower share of 12.4 percent.[4] Chart 1 shows the average annual growth rate of the agricultural sector during each successive Five-Year Plan period. An observable trend is the persistent lower growth rate of this sector compared to the Gross Domestic Product (GDP). Note also the regressive growth rate of the agricultural sector itself.

Up to the Fourth Plan period when diversification was considered urgent, the agricultural economy had been dependent on the export earnings of a few traditional crops, such as rice, rubber and cassava. Within the agricultural sector, the crop sub-sector continues to be the largest in terms of value generation (see Chart 2). Value added generated by this sub-sector is still as high as 57.79 percent while those of the livestock and fishery sub-sectors were 12.5 percent and 9.44 percent of the total value generated by the agricultural sector respectively.

The Employment Situation in the Agricultural Sector:
Over the past twenty-five year period, from the First Plan to the current Seventh Plan, the agricultural sector has been the largest employment sector. However, similar to the structural shift in the composition of the GDP, there had been a decline in the labor share of this sector. The labor share of the agricultural sector in 1991 was still hovering around 60 percent, meaning, in effect, that this sector is still the largest employment sector despite its declining role in other respects (see Chart 3).

The Income Profile:
According to figures from the National Statistical Office, the top 20 percent of the population earned the equivalent of 56 percent of the total income in 1988-9, compared to 49.5 percent in 1962. In contrast, the income share of the lowest 20 percent was reduced from the already low 8 percent to 4.5 percent during the same period. The gini-coefficient increased from 0.414 to 0.478.[5]

There are two other significant developments within the agricultural sector. One is the regional disparity of income with a pattern of concentration of poverty in rural areas; the other is the change in the composition of household income with an increasing share of off-

Chart 1

COMPARISON OF GROWTH RATE OF THE AGRICULTURAL SECTOR AND THE GDP

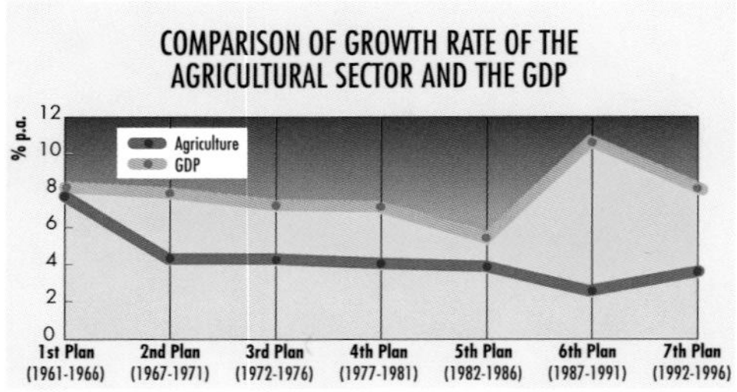

Source: NESDB
Note: 1. Growth rate of the agricultural sector during the Sixth Plan Period was estimated by the Office of Agricultural Economies.
2. The GDP growth rates for the Sixth and Seventh Plan Period was estimated by the NESDB.

Chart 2

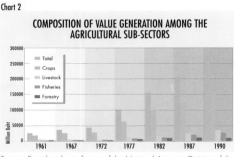

COMPOSITION OF VALUE GENERATION AMONG THE AGRICULTURAL SUB-SECTORS

Source: Based on basic figures of the National Accounts Division of the NESDB.

Chart 3

SHARE OF THE AGRICULTURAL LABOR FORCE IN THE TOTAL POPULATION

Above, left: A worker employed in the agricultural sector.

farm income which seems to indicate that income from farm produce is no longer sufficient to sustain household needs.

The Green Revolution: The green revolution has not taken off to reach any significant scale in Thailand when measured against conventional yardsticks such as the level of mechanization, the rate of adoption of new production technology and labor productivity compared to that in the industrial and service sectors. Most of the production units in the agricultural sector are small holders, characterized by a generally low level of capital input and limited application of new technology, due both to insufficient knowledge and to capital with only a small risk margin. A combination of causally related factors thus contributed to the low adoption rate of new technology amongst this group of producers, chief among them being the poor prospects caused by the long-term decline in farm-gate prices. Other reasons include price fluctuations, market distortions and, to a certain extent, the lack of security of tenure for a high percentage of small producers cultivating in recently opened up forest areas of disputable legal status.

A direct consequence of the low rate of technological breakthrough is the low productivity, a feature which is persistent for all the major cash crops such as rice, maize, cassava, soybeans and oil crops. With the exception of kenaf, the annual rate of increase in yields for all crops is consistently below 2 percent. Moreover, compared with nine other countries, yield per rai for Thailand for many crops is shown to be particularly low. The Thai rice yield is the lowest, about three times lower than the United States which

is the country with the highest yield. Thai rice yields are also shown to be lower than those of Myanmar, Vietnam, India and Pakistan. Although Thailand's maize yield is the third highest in the world, it is still only less than one-third of the highest yield achieved by the United States. Thailand's average yields for cassava and soybeans rank third in the world and for sugarcane, fifth.

Profile of the Agricultural Export Sector

Export Performance: Rice, maize, rubber, cassava and sugar remain the first five commodities which generated the most export values. Maize retains a steady second position in terms of export value whereas other crops take turns as the commodity generating the highest export value. Between 1982 and 1991, these five commodities remained important export earners, although fishery products may have increased in importance in contrast with the declining performance of sugarcane and maize.

The export values of the five traditional export commodities, however, show a declining trend, with the ratio of the aggregate export value dropping from 67 percent in 1982 to 45 percent in 1991. This signifies that there has been

Above, right: An orchid laboratory; Below, left: Cassava; Below, right: Sugarcane.

an increase in the value of exports generated by other agricultural commodities, which is a positive change since it is likely to lead to the reduction of the effects of price fluctuations of world prices for any one commodity. Other than fishery products, the livestock sub-sector has also significantly increased its importance as a supplier of both the domestic and export markets. Between 1982 and 1991, with the exception of buffaloes, there have been increases in all other livestock production. The highest growth was in the production of poultry and duck with growth rates of 3.81 percent per annum and 3.44 percent per annum. Cattle production during this period increased at a rate of 2.07 percent per annum. Between 1972 and 1981, the export value of agricultural exports increased by 20 percent per annum. The growth rates of export values, however, slowed down to only 12 percent per annum between 1982 and 1991, a significantly lower rate than that of the non-agricultural sector which was 31 percent per annum. As a result, the sector's share of the total value of export earnings decreased from 73.5 percent in 1977 to 51.5 percent in 1987 to 35.4 percent in 1991. The trade balance of the sector has nevertheless been positive throughout, in contrast to the trade deficit situation of the economy as a whole.[6] The net gain for the sector in 1991 was 113,167 million baht.

This page: A rice field in northern Mae Sarieng; Left: A duck farm.

The Impact of the Changing World Market Situation on the Thai Agricultural Sector:

In an age of globalization, it has become increasingly less meaningful to see the performance of the agricultural sector operating within the confines of the country, particularly in the case of Thailand where a large proportion of the GDP is generated by foreign exchange earnings from the export of agricultural commodities. To a large extent, the performance of the export sector hinges on world trade conditions, on price changes that result from adjustments of the demand and supply situation of the export markets, on changes in policies of importing countries and corresponding adjustments in terms of trade. While the concept of free trade is endorsed in principle, protectionist policies are still widely practiced, creating barriers of entry into certain export markets and effectively violating the principle of comparative advantage, the effects of which more often than not fall upon Less Developed Countries more than Industrialized Countries.

Comparing Thailand with other exporting countries of major agricultural commodities such as the European Community, the United States and Japan, the subsidies which these governments provide are, respectively, 164, 950 and 3,508 billion baht, which are equivalent to 39 percent, 21.3 percent and 32 percent of the income from sales of agricultural commodities of these countries, whereas in the case of Thailand, the ratio of subsidies only amounts to 2 percent of the value of agricultural commodities. This is an indicator that if all distortions were to be lifted, Thailand can become a very competitive exporting country.

Areas of His Majesty's Prime Concerns

Throughout the fifty years of his reign, His Majesty King Bhumibol Adulyadej has made concerted efforts in addressing many of the fundamental problems of the agricultural sector ranging from the technical to the socio-economic aspects of production. His Majesty's intention is to address the plight of the poor

farmers who constitute a large number of the rural population. Because they have been unable to catch up with and benefit from the streams of change, their economic circumstances have been deteriorating, as reflected in the widening income distribution gap and the increase in the absolute number of people living in a state of poverty. This is clearly illustrated by the increasing disparity of the per capita income between the agricultural and non-agricultural sectors from a ratio of 1:6.19 at the beginning of the First Plan Period to 1:11.96 in 1990.[7]

The King's efforts to reach out to the poor reflect a profound understanding of the root causes of poverty, which are a combination of the technical, social and economic conditions which control access to various factors of production. His Majesty has a profound interest in developing resource and technical bases for agricultural development that will continue to ensure an adequate income for the farm households. Moreover, all of his efforts in these areas have been based on scientific studies, years of research and experiment. His interest and enthusiasm has inspired many scientists, government officials and various private sector groups to become involved. These combined efforts have resulted in a number of technological breakthroughs in pure and applied research and many

development projects have been launched in land resources, forestry resources, soil conservation, irrigation, fisheries and the livestock sector. In the following sections, some of these activities are described.

Development Programs Initiated and Executed under the Royal Patronage of His Majesty the King

Basic Research: His Majesty's emphasis has been on initiating research and experiments on plant varieties including cash crops such as mulberry, rubber trees, rattan and medicinal herbs. Other than varietal research, His Majesty has also commissioned research on animal husbandry and breeding of high quality livestock as well as fish breeds. All this basic research is conducted with emphasis being placed on a few basic principles, namely (i) suitability and adaptability to the local physical environment; (ii) effective diversification of on-farm production to reduce the dependency of the farm households on the market performance of a single cash crop; and (iii) introduction of supplementary income sources such as cottage industries, weaving and handicraft products.

His Majesty's philosophy is that, insofar as it is possible, the production costs of farmers must be reduced, hence the attention devoted to the understanding of farm ecosystems, crop rotation systems, the

Left: His Majesty the King visits an experimental rice field; Inset: Testing rice strains at Chitralada Palace.

use of leguminous plants as nitrogen fixing agents to minimize the cost of chemical fertilizers and biological control of pests and weeds.

A guiding principle is that technology should be suitable to the geographical and social conditions in which they are applied. To this end, His Majesty has established six Royal Development Study Centers—the Khao Hin Sorn Center in Chachoengsao province and Chantaburi province in the eastern region, the Huey Sai Center in the central region, the Phuparn Center in the northeastern region, the Hong Krai Center in the northern region and the Phikulthong Center in the southern region. The mandate given to these centers is to conduct research and experiments on production methods and technologies that will be suitable to the localities. The centers provide services and demonstrations of farming techniques as well as occupational training. Thus far, the centers have concentrated on (i) occupational development;

(ii) reforestation and afforestation programs; (iii) appropriate development and conservation measures in the watershed areas; (iv) appropriate and effective land use development, particularly for land of low productivity, and land reclamation measures; and (v) reclamation of natural resources and environmental conservation in coastal areas. The operation of these centers also has come to depict a model situation of effective coordination among the concerned agencies, avoiding a critical shortcoming of insufficient inter-agency coordination in the normal context of development administration.

His Majesty's strong belief in the effective management of natural resources came to be the working philosophy of the Hill Tribe Development Center in Chiang Mai, one of the provinces in the northern region with a large concentration of hill tribe groups. The emphasis here is given to research of suitable crops which have value that can be substituted for poppy, including research on more than fifty types of

Top, right: Strawberry cultivation in Chiang Mai; Above: Silk weaving in the north-east.

plants and edible crops and varietal improvement. Other areas of emphasis are organic pest control, grazing land in the highlands and management of watersheds and the ecosystems of the highlands. Nowadays, temperate crops grown by hilltribe groups are highly marketable and have generated satisfactory returns to the producers. Apart from production methods, there has been research on storage and packaging, improvement of transportation methods for perishable crops as well as promotion of downstream processing. Assistance to the hilltribe communities extends from the economic aspects to the provision of the basic physical as well as social infrastructures.

The King also uses the palace grounds as an agricultural research center. He has personally commissioned much of the basic research into the technical aspects of agricultural, livestock and fisheries production. His interest also extends to the design of agricultural machinery and equipment, with emphasis on simple labor-saving devices such as rice threshing and milling machines, water pumps, windmills and small electric generators, all of which stress the concept of appropriate technology assisting mainly human labor.

Human Resource Development: His Majesty's contribution to the development of human resources falls into three categories.

Firstly, he emphasizes the transfer of knowledge in various aspects of production technology. His Majesty's interest in basic research is related to his desire to promote and upgrade the quality of manpower within the agricultural sec-

tor. His contribution to human resource development in the agricultural sector stems from his efforts in initiating basic research and in building mechanisms for the dissemination of knowledge to the people.

Secondly, he provides farmers with a working philosophy. This is mainly done through his encouragement and support for organizing farmers into collective groups either as cooperatives or production groups so as to create greater bargaining power in the procurement of reasonably priced inputs and for marketing, in order to overcome one of the major constraints faced by the farmers, namely the lack of capital for investment in production inputs. Hup Krapong was the first scheme for the promotion of agricultural cooperatives. This was subsequently followed by the establishment of thirteen additional Agricultural Cooperatives, seven Land Settlement Cooperatives and two rice mills in two of the Education Centers which are managed on the principle of a cooperative. A very successful dairy farm cooperative has also been set up under the royal patronage of His Majesty the King.

Lastly, an aspect that is of equal importance, yet unquantifiable, is the moral encouragement to farmers, the comfort in the knowledge of a caring monarch whose willingness to offer assistance has inspired and influenced many effective outreach programs.

Land Resources

Technical Aspects: Of the total 320.7 million rai of land, areas that are not suitable for crop production amount to 160 million rai. It is estimated that 43.7 million rai of land already brought under cultivation is in fact unsuitable. This includes, for example, 13.5 million rai under rice cultivation, equivalent to approximately 22 percent of total rice acreage, 14.6 million rai under upland crop cultivation and 1.7 million rai under tree crop cultivation. In principle, the land use pattern of a total area of 43.7 million rai could be changed toward a more suitable cropping pattern which may result in better production performance.

To increase the utility value of land for agricultural production, His Majesty initiated research projects which involved the expertise of professionally trained scientists, in a concerted effort to solve saline and acidic soils in the central and northeastern region as well as peat soils in the south. A significant contribution in solving problems of soil erosion is His Majesty's initiatives on research on appropriate varieties of Vetiver grass which could be grown as cover crops to protect the top soils of areas prone to soil erosion. As a result of such research, many suitable varieties have been identified and introduced, and, as in many other soil conservation projects, have proved to be effective in the reclamation of some of the land for agricultural production.

Distribution and Utilization of Land Resources: Some Socio-Economic Aspects: One undesirable feature of the Thai agricultural sector is the insecurity of tenure of a larger number of settlers who are, by legal definition of the national forest boundaries, living in the protected areas.

Forest coverage in 1990 was 84.7 million rai, approximately 26.6 percent of the total area of the country, while agricultural land holding now

Top: Threshing rice;
Left: A worker using a tractor in the field.

amounts to 147.8 million rai. It has been argued that the perceived abundance of land has influenced an extensive rather than an intensive cropping pattern, a situation in which increase in output can be achieved through bringing more land under cultivation, thus postponing the necessity of rationalizing land use to ensure greater land productivity.

To a certain extent deforestation constituted the social cost which accompanied public investment programs to expand road networks, particularly in the north and northeastern regions. Clearance of forest lands was also induced by market opportunities for cash crops, especially upland crop cultivation. This, combined with a lack of a unified and comprehensive land policy

and an apparent laissez faire attitude toward land clearance and occupation, resulted in a vast clearance of forest for cultivation.

Throughout the 1970's, the expansion of agricultural land paralleled the decline in forest coverage. Net reduction of forest land between 1961 and 1981 was, alarmingly, 81.2 million rai. The increasing frequency of natural hazards combined with public pressure led to the withdrawal of all logging concessions in 1989. The effect has been to slow down marginally the rate of deforestation from 3 million rai per year to 2.5 million rai per year. Still, if this rate of deforestation continues, in thirty-one years time, there will be no more forests left in Thailand. Chart 4 illustrates the reduction in forest coverage in the

Rice Cultivation

Below: A ricefield; Inset: Rice harvest; Right: King Bhumibol sowing rice in the experimental plots at Chitralada Palace in 1961.

Rice cultivation is at the heart of Thai culture, as it has been for centuries. Rice forms the main part of people's everyday diet—apart from being eaten boiled, it is used to manufacture noodles and sweets and to make the traditional fiery liqueur, *lao khao*. When Thais talk of going to eat, they say *ghin khao*, or "eat rice." A full 60 percent of the working population is involved in rice production in some capacity and the nation's rice exports (Thailand is the world's leading rice exporter) have helped popularize sweet-smelling "Jasmine" or fragrant long-grained rice around the world.

The rice planting season begins after the Thai New Year in April or May, when His Majesty the King presides over the annual Royal Plowing Ceremony in Bangkok. This ceremony is held to give an auspicious start to the new rice planting season. When the rains start to arrive, farmers prepare their fields by turning over the soil using water buffaloes or small mechanical ploughing machines. Rice nurseries are created. Banks and canals will be repaired and the entire farming community joins together to cooperate on repairing communal facilities such as bridges, canals and small dams. Through these kinds of activities the Thais have built up their unique communal style of living.

By the start of Buddhist Lent (Asalha Puja) in July, the seedlings in the nurseries have been transplanted to the fields for the arrival of the monsoonal rains. During this period, when all Buddhist monks remain in their local temples, farmers weed their fields and try to keep pests away from the

ripening crop. This is a time of abundance and villagers join together to catch fish in the fields or hunt for frogs and land crabs.

Late November is the time for harvesting, particularly in the central plains and the north. Water is drained from the fields and many people return to their villages to help with the harvest—working together is the norm. The cut rice is left in the fields to dry and sometimes an entire family will sleep with their precious crop. The rice is then collected into sheaves and taken to the family compound to be threshed and winnowed. The hay left after the rice is milled in the village mill is used to feed livestock. For the water rich regions, particularly in the central plains, a second rice crop is planted. Each family estimates how much rice will be needed to feed everyone for the year. The rest will be sold to rice merchants. And after toiling away for many months, now will be the time for many villagers to attend to things such as house repairs which have been neglected during the rice season. There will also be time to hold temple fairs and celebrations. With the Songkran festival, the Thai New Year, just around the corner, the rice cycle will have been completed for another year.

– J. C.

beginning years of each of the Five-Year Plans up to the Seventh Plan in 1987 and to the mid-plan period, together with statistics on increase in agricultural land holding.

Deforestation and insecurity of tenure has its social and economic dimensions. The magnitude of the problem has grown such that no less than 38 million rai of land is occupied by settlers claiming de facto as opposed to legal rights and about 13,788 villages, equivalent to 24 percent of the total number of villages, do not have any ownership rights to the land.

His Majesty sees landlessness as the underlying cause of poverty and a threatening force for the remaining forest areas. A number of projects have thus been initiated combining the objectives of land allocation with that of a comprehensive agricultural extension package so as to ensure that farmers can fully utilize the land to generate income to sustain the household economy. As mentioned earlier, His Majesty is an advocate of Land Settlement Cooperatives and Farmers' Cooperatives or Groups and has been personally involved with several land allocation projects. The Hup Krapong Project under royal patronage launched this kind of project as far back as in 1968. The project allocated some 10,000 rai to 120 house-

Chart 4

CHANGES IN FOREST AREA COVERAGE

- Forest Area
- Agricultural Land Holdings

Million Rai: 180 160 140 120 100 80 60 40 20 0

1961 1967 1972 1977 1982 1987 1992

holds along with technical assistance from multi-sectoral agencies which helped turned the degraded land into fertile productive agricultural land. The Hup Krapong Royal Project was followed by four others of a similar nature in the central, northeast and the northern regions.

When the issue of the inequitable distribution of land surfaced in the early 1970's, culminating in the enactment of the Agricultural Land Reform Act of 1975, His Majesty inspired goodwill and support for the program by donating 50,000 rai of land to the Agricultural Land Reform Office for allocation to small and landless farmers. His personal contribution and formal support for the program did much to curtail the political resentment of large landowners and have ensured a degree of social and political stability which has been absent in many countries where land reform has been launched.

His Majesty is also concerned with the question of legality, with the discrepancy between customary and legal rights to land and the interconnections with the persistent encroachment into virgin forest areas. His rationalization of the situation became the underlying principle in the conceptualization of the S.T.K.[8] Program which involves the provision of rights to farmers to utilize a uniform size of forest land for cultivation; such a conditional right also dictates the way in which land is to be used and is tied to the obligation to look after the forest resources within the immediate environs. These are rights which cannot be sold and are only transferable to offspring. These ideas subsequently materialized into the Village Forestry Program. Since 1981, there have been 727,982 beneficiaries and a total area coverage of 7.4 million rai.

Land allocation was also envisaged by His Majesty as a step toward mitigating interrelated problems of deforestation, insecurity of tenure, poverty and political rights and entitlements of ethnic minority groups which inhabit the highlands in the north and western regions. With the

Top, left: Cultivated land; Bottom, left: An elephant clearing logs from the forest.

view that the hilltribe groups must be attended to for social and economic as well as environmental reasons, His Majesty initiated the first hilltribe development project in 1969.

The King intends, through his projects, to promote the well-being of the hilltribe communities so that they can grow crops that will bring in some income. His Majesty views these projects as being initiated for humanitarian objectives. The measures, which are motivated by the desire for the well-being of those living in dire conditions, aim to transfer knowledge to enable the people to help themselves and become self-reliant. The assistance given to the hilltribe groups is also seen as being instrumental in alleviating a major problem the country is facing with respect to the production and trade of marijuana, that is, through the introduction of high value crops to substitute for what has been traditionally grown. The new crops are expected to provide adequate income to help hilltribe groups to upgrade. Ultimately, the hope is that the stability of income will induce permanence of settlements thereby reducing the need to clear more virgin forests.

In short, His Majesty has transformed the control approach toward the hilltribe groups to a social and economic approach. His personal commitment to tackling the problems of the hilltribes has been instrumental in creating an awareness of the plight of these minority groups and outlined a more positive approach in dealing with the hilltribes in a manner that has helped create their sense of belonging to the Thai nation. His Majesty has drawn upon technical assistance from various public agencies, interna-

tional aid agencies and the private sector, and there are now some 126 integrated hilltribe development projects under his royal patronage.

Forestry Resources

The King's concern over the plight of the small holders and the landless is balanced by the accompanying objectives of environmental sustainability. Measures introduced therefore reflect a well thought-out approach which balances the interests of the people who inhabit the mountainous areas or the lowlands and the survivability of nature. His Majesty believes that afforestation in the high ground area above the crop and fruit trees plot on a slope should include varieties of plants which are able to provide natural fertilizers and protect the top soil for the cultivated area below the slope. In the words of the King, "Since there is abundant water in the area of the river basin, the people in the low-lying area should be encouraged to grow rice as food for the people. In the wet season, the water current will wash natural fertilizers along with the flow of the water which will accumulate in the cultivated area below. The natural fertilizers will be soaked into the soil providing sufficient fertility to cultivate rice. In the higher areas, garlic, legumes and other appropriate crops can be grown."

Efforts to replant forests should be made, according to His Majesty, to generate the supply of wood, edible fruits and forest products, as well as firewood, as a source of energy for the rural household. The King has initiated altogether 39 projects covering wide aspects of forest conservation and management, including the Village Forestry Project, forest and fauna conservation, forest fire protection and watershed conservation.

His Majesty's expressed concern has generated many positive by-products which are beneficial to the rehabilitation of the forestry

Top: King Bhumibol with Hmong hilltribe elders while inspecting a kidney bean field in 1971 planted with seeds given by the King as a substitution cash crop in place of growing opium; Above: Potatoes (top) and coffee beans (bottom) are two of the successful opium replacement crops.

resources. In honor of his Jubilee year, the Royal Forestry Department (RFD) has initiated a forest replanting project which is to cover some 5 million rai of formerly degraded forest areas all over Thailand. This project has met with active responses not only within the Royal Forestry Department but also among non-governmental organizations (NGOs), the private sector and his loyal subjects. Common to all the development projects either personally conducted by himself or initiated under his patronage is His Majesty's personal interest which works to unite the goodwill of the people to transform objectives into concrete actions that are beneficial to the common interests of the country.

Water Resource Development

For an agriculturally based economy, the water supply is one of the vital production inputs, and stability of supply is highly conditional with respect to the performance of any particular crop year. Irrigation techniques and its applications have therefore been one of the key development areas to which His Majesty has devoted much time and effort.

Of the current 147 million rai of present agricultural land, some 21 percent only is irrigated. There are slightly different ratios of irrigated

to rain-fed areas in each of the regions, the higher concentration being in the central and the northern region, as shown in Chart 5.

Small and medium-scale irrigation projects are the main themes of His Majesty's work in irrigation. A strong emphasis is placed on making the effective participation of the people and the project beneficiaries an integral part of planning and implementation from the very onset of each project.

His Majesty's concept for the hilly areas is that "a small dam should be constructed to store water for irrigation. At the same time, care must be taken not to cut down the trees along the path of water flowing from the high grounds downward in order to control and prevent soil erosion."

For watershed areas, His Majesty's concept is to construct small weirs at regular intervals, together with water pipes and water outlet systems for efficient distribution so as to provide constant moisture to replenish the soil. He says, "The construction of small-scale reservoirs along the gully at different intervals must be accelerated in order to slow down the flow of water in the forest during the rainy season and to conserve the water flowing from the high ground downward which will help raise the underground water level in the area downstream. The hemp trees can be grown on either side of the water channel. The root of the hemp tree will help absorb the water and draw up the water close to the surface which will also help provide moisture for other plants in the area."

Left, top to bottom: The King, accompanied by officials, surveys the local topographical conditions in the countryside; The King making an observation to government officials on the planting of paddy in terraces of the Chiang Rai Hill Tribes' Welfare and Development Center in 1979; Left: The King observing the floating low-speed air jet machines which add oxygen to water to improve its quality.

THAILAND King Bhumibol Adulyadej – The Golden Jubilee 1946-1996

Chart 5

IRRIGATED AREAS IN FOUR REGIONS OF THAILAND

Million Rai

14
12
10
8
6
4
2
0

North | Northeast | Central | East | South

About 40 percent of the total number of irrigation projects initiated by the King is directed toward supplying water for agricultural production, for example, for ensuring the feasibility of producing vegetable crops in the highlands and for upland rice cultivation so as to prevent deforestation, particularly around the watershed areas where shifting cultivation of the opium poppy has become a problem particularly acute in the northern region. Irrigation development schemes in the watershed areas involve constructing small weirs at different elevations. Around 25 percent of the irrigation projects provides water both for agricultural production as well as for domestic consumption, of which 7 percent is to provide clean consumption water.

A scientific breakthrough is the Royal Rain Making Scheme which was the result of years of research into chemical formulae which could be used for varying weather, topographical features and terrains. Specially equipped planes which are used to seed the clouds in areas lacking rain have produced some significant results.

Apart from developing systems of supply, His Majesty is also concerned with controlling water pollution. A solution to this problem would be advantageous for agricultural production as well as for basic needs. Here again His Majesty's emphasis is on low cost as well as natural control techniques. So far, the introduction of the water hyacinth as a biological filter of contaminated water had met with considerable success not only in terms of reducing the level of water contamination but also in terms of the by-products, namely, the supply of water hyacinth for making handicraft products.

The Fishery Sector

The fishing zones of Thailand in the Gulf of Thailand cover an approximate area of 252,000 sq km. Fishing grounds in the Andaman sea total 126,000 sq km. The aggregate freshwater fishing areas in rivers, streams and reservoirs is 6,500 sq km. Prospects for Thailand's future fishing industry and the economic survival of a large number of small-scale fishermen rest on a number of attitudinal and behavioral changes: mutual respect and strict adherence to the international fishing limits, strict enforcement of regulations regarding the use of fishing equipment, particularly by the commercial larger trawlers who employ highly destructive fishing equipment such as explosives, push nets, and so on. These destructive activities have increased the hardship of small-scale coastal fisheries and encourage the increasing risks fishermen tend to take in venturing past national fishing waters.

His Majesty's attention and efforts in the fishery sector ranges from fresh and brackish water fisheries to shrimp farming in coastal areas. His Majesty recognizes that freshwater fish provide an important source of protein for farmers. By his initiative, fisheries experts and the staff of the Department of Fisheries have concentrated their efforts in breeding research and succeeded in breeding many endangered freshwater fish species, distributing seedlings into many rivers and streams. His Majesty commissioned an inventory to be made of the fish species that can be found in swamp areas.

Responding to this initiative, the Department of Fisheries has identified a species of catfish that can survive in water with high acidic content and is a species of freshwater fish for which there is high market demand. His Majesty then commissioned further research be undertaken for commercial breeding in Narathiwat province.

As for seawater irrigation, one of the major causes for the rapid disappearance of mangrove forests, the contamination of coastal water quality and changes in the coastal ecosystems is probably the expansion and proliferation of shrimp farming and coastal aquaculture. Mangrove areas have been reduced from 2 mil-

A fishermen's village.

lion rai in 1975 to 1 million rai in 1989, and annual increases in loss are still reported. Undoubtedly, revenue from shrimp farming activities have been substantial but while investors have been able to reap sizable private profits, they leave behind some acute environmental problems that will be costly to address. It is not so much shrimp farming *per se*, however, that has been the root cause for contamination of coastal waters. Rather it is that shrimp farms have been built without proper designs for a water management system and on-farm water treatment facilities which would reduce the degree of water pollution before it is emitted into the sea. The absence of such systems is the result of the lack of technical knowledge as well as a sense of urgency for the need for such systems for the long-term sustainability of shrimp farming activities on the part of the small shrimp farmers and the willingness to trade off long-term risks for short-term economic gains. From the point of view of small entrepreneurs, it is perhaps convenient not to acknowledge that short-term private gains are at the expense of long-term social costs. There is no tradition of addressing these social costs.

His Majesty believes, nevertheless, that with proper land-use planning and installation of water treatment facilities, shrimp farming does not necessarily have to conflict with environmental concerns. Hence, he established the Kung Kraben Educational Center to conduct basic research on environmentally friendly technical aspects of shrimp farming. The center is located in Chantaburi district, one of the provinces with large shrimp farming areas. The physical environment there seems to represent the general conditions of shrimp farming, and the center's findings should be applicable.

His Majesty also established the Brackish Water Fisheries Center to function as a promotion and development center for small-scale fishermen of the border provinces in the southern region.

Recapturing the Past and Looking into the Future
In this essay, we have highlighted some of the key development areas and activities in which His Majesty has invested time and attention. While a range of activities has been indicated, they cannot fully convey the magnitude of the ensuing benefits in quantifiable terms and the depth of gratitude and sense of esteem that the people of Thailand hold for their monarch. He has provided the leadership in technological research as well as the organizational and institutional framework through which the findings can be disseminated to the intended target groups.

In him, the people, the government officials, the private sector and non-governmental organizations alike can find a common goal in helping the rural people find effective means to make a living from sustainable agricultural production.

The intense involvement of His Majesty through various royal projects has provided the inspiration and an ideal model for agricultural and fisheries development and no doubt will continue to do so for many more years to come.

Top: Fishermen in Koh Samui; Inset: A boat on a fishing trip; Left: A shrimp farm; Facing page, clockwise from top, left: Tobacco plantation; Dried goods; Orchid nursery; Fresh vegetables; A variety of fruits; Fish for sale; Overleaf: Fishing boats at sunset.

Agro-industrial Development

At the beginning of His Majesty's reign, rice, rubber and teak were the main agricultural exports. Rice has been perhaps the major agricultural product for centuries; both rice and rubber are still major exports today. While family farmers and small-scale producers still dominate agriculture—some 60 percent of the population works on the land though the figure is rapidly declining—during the past fifty years, the agro-industrial sector has expanded exponentially. A visit to any of Bangkok's fresh produce markets gives you an idea of the staggering range of vegetables, fruits, flowers, fish and fowl, crustaceans and herbs that are daily available.

A glance at the situation at the end of 1993

shows just what products are now being exported, and how far the agro-industrial sector has diversified. The top ten agro products exported in 1993 were fisheries (especially frozen shrimps and prawns, of which the nation is a leading producer), fruits (notably Thailand's famous durians and longans), rice, cassava (tapioca), various kinds of sugar, tobacco,

coffee, cut and fresh flowers (especially orchids, for which Thailand holds 70 percent of the world market), canned foods (the nation is a leader in canned tuna, sardines and pineapples) and natural rubber products. Sadly, most of the precious teak that was abundant in 1946 has gone.

Several important agro-industrial conglomerates have developed out of this sector over the past twenty years. The agro giant, the Chareon Pokphand Group (CP Group), is one of the largest animal feed producers in the world, and it initially based its growth on animal feed and livestock (poultry and fisheries). Today, it is not only a major regional producer of frozen chicken and fisheries products but also claims to be the single

largest private investor in China with business concerns in every province (including many feedmills). Interestingly, in Thailand the CP Group has diversified vertically into fast foods, as well as other areas such as telecommunications and retailing.

Thailand's varied agro-industrial products are exported worldwide to many of the 190 countries with which the nation trades. Tinned products find their way to Africa and South America, major exports such as tapioca, frozen chickens and canned pineapples go to Europe, Japan and the United States. There may well be very few dinner tables around the world that do not have a Thai agricultural product as part of today's next meal.

– J. C.

6

THAI SOCIETY IN TRANSITION

Dr Akin Rabibhadana

T HERE IS NO DOUBT THAT THAI SOCIETY HAS UNDERGONE DRASTIC CHANGES
WITHIN THE LAST FIFTY YEARS. SOME MAJOR FACTORS BEHIND THE CHANGES
MAY BE IDENTIFIED. THE FIRST WAVE OF CHANGE IS INDUSTRIALIZATION.

Industrialization has always been the hope
of all third world countries, and Thailand
is no exception. Attempts to attain this single
ambition have been persistent, and successive
governments have promoted the development
of industries at the expense of agriculture.[1] This
has eventually led to a partial transformation of
Thai society.

Another wave was the change from producing for home consumption to producing for sale
and export. Although in the central plains, this
practice, particularly for rice production, started
as early as in the late nineteenth century, it
became widespread only about forty to fifty
years ago. Later, the cultivation of upland crops
for export such as maize
and cassava started and
expanded rapidly. The
effects on social institutions should not be
underestimated.

The third wave of
change was the expan-
sion of the power and
authority of the state,
which can be said to
have seriously begun

around the end of the nineteenth century.
At that time, the aim was to create a centralized
nation state in response to the threats of
colonial powers.[2]

The state's authority was not felt in villages
and remote areas until after the Second World
War, especially after 1960. Its pervasive influence
at the village level was facilitated by better communication stemming from an improved infrastructure, in particular the network of roads. The
number of government officials posted to work
in villages and *tambon* (sub-districts) increased
considerably.[3] We shall see later how this has
affected sociopolitical institutions in rural areas.

The most subtle waves of change involve culture, education and the
mass media. The cen-
tralized education sys-
tem performed a major
role in creating a nation
state of one language,
one belief, and one tra-
dition. Thus "Nation,
Religion, and
Monarchy," as symbol-
ized in the national flag,
serve as the uniting

Facing page: The differ-
ent faces of Thais; Right:
A gathering of more
than 5,000 monks at a
Buddhist ceremony on
Makha Bhucha day.

force for the whole nation. A powerful change has occurred in the national discourse as well. Instead of contentment and self-restraint, as expressed in such counsels as *pho jai nai sing thi ton me yu* (be happy with what you have), *kin pho di yu pho di* (be moderate in your eating and living) and *lop mak, lap hai* (the greedier you are, the less you will get), we now have *ngan khu ngoen: ngoen khu ngan, bandan suk* (work is money; money is work; they will bring happiness); the traditional blessing of long life, beauty, happiness and strength (*a-yu, wanna sukkha, phala*) is now replaced by a wish for wealth (*mangkhang, ramruay*). With television now available even in the remotest areas, the poorest people are now watching, with wide open eyes, the conspicuous consumption of the city rich.

General Transformation

Within this short period of fifty years, the face of Thailand has changed so much that anyone who has been away for the last five decades would not be able to recognize it upon his return. He would find that the capital city, Bangkok, is expanding on all sides and becoming very crowded. The small, orchard-like town with sacred spires has become a congested megapolis of concrete buildings and glass towers. No traces can be found of its peaceful, tree-lined roads with crystal-clear canals along the sides. In their places are wide streets with concrete pavements, overcrowded with traffic. Gone also are the handsome brick mansions and irregular wooden houses set in a garden-like environment. Instead, gigantic condominiums, towering office buildings and departmental stores have cropped up. However, amidst these skyscrapers,

jewel-like temples and pockets of dilapidated, wooden houses and shacks, which are now called slums, can still be seen.[4] The environs of the city, which used to be fruit orchards, vegetable gardens and rice fields, have now been turned into suburban estates with clusters of colorful, similarly-designed houses for nuclear families. In the suburbs have sprouted industrial estates and ugly factories filled with troops of workers who are migrants from rural areas.

Previously isolated towns and villages have been brought into contact with the capital city. A wide network of roads which did not exist fifty years ago has been constructed. Electricity is now available in almost all areas of Thailand. On the other hand, the jungles and forests which covered most of the land area fifty years ago have almost disappeared. In their places are to be found vast stretches of land covered with cassava or maize, the major commercial crops for export. Artery highways leading to Bangkok are full of trucks carrying produce from the provinces. Trains and buses bring masses of rural youth, both women and men, to Bangkok to find jobs in the service and industrial sectors.[5] Many people have become laborers in mushrooming factories. Others are working in hotels, bars, restaurants, massage parlors and brothels. The pulse of commercial activity is accelerating, and a newly emerged class of entrepreneurs is expanding. Numerous hotels ha materialized in provincial towns, mo of which are packed with traveling salesmen.

Undoubtedly, the country has attained rapid economic growth. Gross

Left, top: Vehicles traversing an expressway in Bangkok;
Left, bottom: A truck transporting cassava.

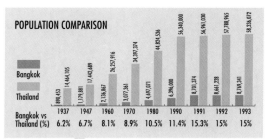

POPULATION COMPARISON

Bangkok vs Thailand (%)	1937	1947	1960	1970	1980	1990	1991	1992	1993
Bangkok	890,453	1,179,881	2,136,867	3,077,361	4,697,071	6,396,000	6,703,374	8,661,228	8,769,341
Thailand	14,464,105	17,442,689	26,257,916	34,397,374	44,824,536	56,340,000	56,961,030	57,788,965	58,336,072
Bangkok vs Thailand (%)	6.2%	6.7%	8.1%	8.9%	10.5%	11.4%	15.3%	15%	15%

THAILAND
Bangkok

Source: Viyout Chamruspant, et al., *Socio-Cultural Change and Political Development in Thailand, 1950-1990: The Northeast* (documentary research), Khon Kaen: Research and Development Institute, Khon Kaen University, 1991 (in Thai), p.282, Table 1; and Alpha Research Co. Ltd., *Thailand Figures 1992-93*, p.171; and National Statistical Office, Office of the Prime Minister, *Statistical Yearbook Thailand 1995*, p. 18.

Domestic Product (GDP) has increased from 64.4 billion baht in 1960 to 2,509.4 billion baht in 1991. The rate of growth, which has constantly been impressive, was as high as 13.4 percent in 1988.[6] The average annual income of the Thai population at current market prices increased from 4,420 baht in 1972 to 36,032 baht in 1990.[7] Thailand is no longer considered a poor country in the world community.

Major Achievements

If the aim of Thailand has been industrialization, it has almost achieved that goal in the last fifty years. There have been major changes in economic structure. The country's production structure has become increasingly based on industry and services. Conversely, the share of agriculture in the Gross Domestic Product declined from 27 percent in 1975 to only 12.4 percent in 1990.[8] In the past, agricultural exports had always been greater in value than manufactured exports. However, this trend was reversed in 1985 when the value of manufactured exports surpassed that of agricultural exports for the first time. Since then it has been growing rapidly, averaging 35.7 percent a year between 1985 and 1990. In line with the changes in the structure of production, Thailand's exports are now based mostly on industry and services.[9]

The increase in the average income of the people is significant; real GDP per capita increased by almost 5 percent a year between 1970 and 1990. It was reported that, while in 1962–3 about 57 percent of the population had income below the poverty line, in 1988–9, on the other hand, only 23.7 percent had income below the line. Although between 1962–3 and 1988–9 the population of Thailand increased by about 26 million, the absolute number of people under the poverty line went down from 16.5 million in 1962–3 to 13.1 million in 1988–9.[10]

The growth of wealth for the whole country as well as the increased income of its people has resulted in a better quality of life. Statistics show that the average life expectancy of a Thai has increased from 52.6 years in 1947 to 64.6 years in 1990. Infant mortality rates have declined from 62.4 per 1,000 live births in 1950 to 11 in 1987. In a survey covering 1979–82, about 50.8 percent of children under five suffered from some form of malnutrition. By 1986, only 25.2 percent were suffering from this condition.

Top: An aerial view of Bangkok showing a mixture of modern and traditional buildings.

During the past fifty-year period, Thailand has done very well in providing basic education for its population. The adult literacy rate increased from 68 percent in 1960 to 91 percent in 1985.[11] As a result of investment in road construction, communication has very much improved. This has the effect of reducing crime. Robbery by outlaw bands, led by renowned *ai*

sua (gang leaders), is no longer heard of in rural places. Personal property has become safer. The standard of living has risen. In the rural areas, many farmers now own motorcycles and pick-up trucks as well as television sets. The quality of drinking water has also improved, and latrines are available in most places. No longer are the people faced with such epidemics as cholera which killed hundreds and thousands during each outbreak in the past.

But although we have witnessed the general progress of Thailand, especially her spectacular economic growth, there is cause for concern about the imbalance of this growth and its impact on the society. The income share of the richest 20 percent of households increased from 49.26 percent of total household income in 1975–6 to 55.63 in 1985–6, while the income share of the poorest 20 percent declined from 6.05 percent in 1975–6 to 4.55 percent in 1985–6. How wide the income gap has become can be appreciated when we see that the richest 10 percent of households received 35.44 percent

AVERAGE PER CAPITA INCOME BY OCCUPATION					
Occupation	Average Per Capita Income (baht/year)				Annual Growth(%)
	1975-6	1980-1	1985-6	1988-9	1975-88
Professionals/Technicians	5,702.4	20,472	29,532.2	32,247.9	14.3
Executives	9,933.6	15,180	34,380	50,790.5	13.4
Clerical workers	7,752	18,840	25,152	32,069	11.5
Sales workers	7,933.2	17,280	20,268	22,598.5	8.4
Service workers	6,692.4	14,122	18,720	20,894.9	9.2
Agriculturalists	3,062.4	6,195.6	6,141.6	7,822.7	7.5
Laborers	5,481.6	10,818	12,156	14,499.7	7.8
Inactive	3,474	9,850.8	10,546.8	13,453	11.0

Source: Suganya Hutaserani and Pornchai Tapwong, *Urban Poor Upgrading: Analyses of Poverty Trend and Profile of the Urban Poor in Thailand*, Bangkok: TDRI, 1990, p. 99, Table 5.2.

of the total household income (1980–81), while the poorest 10 percent could obtain only 2.13 percent.[12] Thus economic growth has resulted in widening the income gap between the rich and the poor. Regional disparity is also increasing. The primacy of areas around Bangkok has led to serious economic differences between the Bangkok Metropolitan Region (BMR) and the rest of the country. With 15.8 percent of the total population living in Bangkok in 1988, it accounted for 50 percent of the total GDP. In that year also, per capita GDP in Bangkok was more than nine times higher than that of the poorest region, the northeast.[13]

The most serious income disparity has probably occurred between the urban and the rural areas. Income disparities between those employed in the agricultural sector and other sectors are not small and the gap is widening (see table above). And yet, the majority of the people are still engaged in agriculture.

There can be no doubt that the economic and communication tranformation must bring about changes in the way of life and the social institutions of the people. Some of these ongoing changes will be discussed, as well as the need for other types of organizations and institutions to replace those that have become obsolete. We shall begin with the situation in the rural areas where the underprivileged live.

Rural Lives and Institutions in Flux

Changes in the way of life may be clearly seen from the words of a middle-aged farmer about

Left, above: Browsing at a new stand; Left: Agricultural workers.

the differences between the past and the present. The northeastern farmer said: "It is convenient nowadays. We can go wherever we want easily, just get on the bus. But life today is so hard. We have to work all the time without rest for money. And we never have enough to spend."

In the process of development, forest areas have diminished, while the population has increased greatly. The Northeast Thailand Upland Forestry Project has investigated the extent to which rural households depend upon forest land resources for their total domestic consumption needs. On the average about one-half of the annual household consumption needs are being met from the harvesting, consumption and/or sale of forest products. Studies show that the landless and small farmers depend more on forest resources than the better-off ones.[14] With an increased population as well as denser settlements and minimal forest land, rural households can no longer depend on forest and natural products for their consumption. Money is needed to buy food as well as other everyday necessities. The development of the mass media and the availability of television have awakened the people's desire for a better standard of living. Modern inventions such as motorcycles, cars, televisions, refrigerators and western-style houses are coveted. Thus cultural and social changes have followed economic tranformation.

We will now look at what has happened to two important institutions in rural communities, namely, leadership and the family.

Below, top: A rural family who earn their income through rice farming in Supanburi; Below, bottom: A motorcycle is one of the sought-after material possessions.

Local Leadership

Respect for seniority was the basis of Thai social organization, as evident in local leadership of the old days. Thus villages in the north used to have a *kae ban* to look after the affairs of the lay population and *kae wat* to look after the affairs of the *wat* (temple and monastery). *Kae* means old, and *ban* means village. In 1897, the positions *phu-yai-ban* (village headman) and *kamnan* (sub-district headman) were set up, and elders could be elected or selected for these positions.[15] However, it was the 1943 legislation making literacy a necessary requirement that made many village elders ineligible for these positions because at that time most were unable to read and write. The headman can be dismissed from his position by the provincial governor (an official appointed from Bangkok) when he deems the headman unfit for the position because of his behavior or lack of ability.[16] The villagers regarded the *kae ban* as their man, while the *phu-yai-ban* belonged to the government.

It is said that the headman has two roles, one being the representative of the government in the village and another being the representative of the villagers. In the former role, he keeps household registrations, collects taxes and keeps the peace within his village. In the latter role, he is the spokesman of the villagers, making requests and demands of the government on their behalf. The villagers, however, felt that their headman paid most attention to the collection of taxes and to relaying government orders from the district chief (an appointed government official) to them.[17]

Up to about the 1950's, it was not too difficult to maintain a coexistence of the two conflicting roles. That was because the villages were not easily accessible, and most were left on their own. Then came insurgencies and the period of accelerated development, at which point the villagers could no longer be left on their own for security reasons.[18] Development for national security became the main policy. The National Development Council (later called the National Economic and Social Development Board, or NESDB) was set up in 1959. Road networks were constructed. Government officials trooped out to do development work in rural areas. The job of a headman became more difficult since he had to please so many different officials from

different departments, and at the same time he had to try to please his villagers. Thus these positions were unattractive to many people. Yet the job did attract certain types of people because, with all these development projects, there were benefits which an unscrupulous headman could reap with the cooperation of the officials.[19]

Rural areas of the whole country were also changing. With better communication, the commercialization of agriculture, the expansion of upland crops and numerous government projects, local merchants, middlemen, entrepreneurs and construction contractors emerged and gained wealth. These people aspired to or supported their followers to occupy the position of headman. Numerous cases of corruption by *kamnan* and *phu-yai-ban* in rural development projects can be cited. Collusion with contractors and businessmen abound. Their latest activities are in the role of middlemen selling villagers' land. In many cases, it was found that this was done not for the benefit of the villagers but for their own and those of urban businessmen.[20]

Local leadership in rural Thailand includes, besides headmen, monks, teachers, traders, health officials and town-based middlemen. Monks continue to be important leaders in secular affairs.[21] The important question is whether a village has a *wat* and whether it has any permanent monks. In 1980, about 216,099 villages in the northeast were without a *wat*. Moreover, a number of *wat* are without monks except in the Lent period. This is different from the situation in the past when a *wat* generally had forty to fifty monks since the *wat* was also an educational institution.[22] It is difficult now to view monks as providing leadership for village communities.[23]

School teachers formed another category of people who could provide leadership in rural areas. There is an elementary school in every *tambon*, and local teachers are highly respected by the villagers. Today, however, most teachers at village schools no longer live in the villages. With roads linking towns and district centers with the villages, teachers have moved to live in urban areas, riding motorcycles to and from school. Morever, their orientation is toward their national (bureaucratic) constituency rather than the villages.[24]

The majority of village entrepreneurs who have emerged during the last few decades are local people who have been able to set themselves up in business. Some of their capital is obtained through temporary employment in non-farm jobs, particularly in Bangkok.[25] In their businesses as well as in their frequent travels and associations, these entrepreneurs have links with urban-centered officials and businessmen who, in one way or another, maintain business and/or political connections with them. They may act as agents of those urban businessmen by giving loans, buying produce or selling farm inputs. Their political activities or the leadership positions they hold in the villages are often linked with their business and/or their socio-political association with outsiders. When they are successful in business, they often aspire to the position of headman. One of the major changes in the rural areas may have been the shifting of the importance in the bases of formal leadership from seniority in age, moral quality and wide kinship networks to wealth. As late as two decades ago, the number of kin in a particular locality appeared to be the strongest means to

Top: Monks collecting alms; Far left: Schoolchildren in a village; Left: Teaching in a classroom.

gain the support necessary for winning the election for formal leadership. It is different now. Wealth and business connections have become the most important assets.[26]

Family and Kinship

The Thai kinship system is bilateral. Relationships with kindred ones are traced outward from the self, and there is no corporate unit based on descent. Kinship terminology emphasizes the differences in age, implying that seniority occupies a specially important place in the behavior of kin.[27] Certainly, respect for elders has been a very important element in the Thai social structure.

The prominent features of the family system, particularly in the north and northeast, are matrilocal residence and endogamy. Most marriages in Chiangmai villages are among local people.[28] Women serve as links between men. Authority is passed from father-in-law to son-in-law.[29] It is "a system in which the people who are redistributed in affinal groups are men. The structurally significant people are female."[30] Sulaiman Potter calls it a "female-centered system in contrast to patriliny and matriliny, which...would both be male-centered systems."[31]

Thai rural women are accorded a high status. According to inheritance rules, property should be divided equally among all children, both male and female. However, the youngest daughter should inherit the house, and it is customary for men to sell out their rights to their sisters.[32] Thus women are the owners of property. They

Village Life

Right: Villagers help build the foundation for a new house; **Below:** Songkran celebration.

After a millennium of development, the village remains at the root of Thai society, despite the rapid industrialization of the past decades. And though there are regional variations in house styles and crops produced, the typical village is a cluster of wooden houses on stilts, close to water and the focal point of the village community, the *wat*, or temple. Increasingly, there will be a village school as well. Most villages contain one hundred to 150 households, with an average of three hundred to seven hundred inhabitants.

Traditional wooden houses on stilts can be found all over Thailand; the space beneath the house is used to tether livestock at night, while during the day it is a cool place for weaving cloth and making basketware. These days, fewer wooden houses are being built, due to the cost of

wood, and are being replaced by single-story concrete bungalows.

The village is a self-contained, harmonious world. There is nearly always a small village store, providing basic necessities, and a food-stall providing noodles or simple rice dishes. Children go to the village school, and young men enter the temple, usually for *khao pansa*, or Buddhist Lent (during the three-month-long rainy season). The importance of the temple to the community can be seen from the villager's commitment to giving alms to monks each morning.

Basic administration is the responsibility of the *phu-yai-ban*, or headman, assisted by two deputies, the local head-teacher and senior members of the village—disputes and confrontations are quickly defused under this system. Cooperation is the norm and the villagers will gladly give up their own time to mend communal bridges or help organize social events.

The tempo of life in the village follows the seasons and the cycle of rice cultivation, in addition to major Buddhist festivals. The yearly cycle begins with Songkran, or Thai New Year (held in April), and quickly moves to the ploughing, planting, harvesting and threshing cycle of rice production. During periods when there is little to do in the fields, many seek work in major urban centers like Bangkok, returning for the harvest.

Indeed, evidence that some things have

changed can be seen from the many motorcycles that have now replaced bicycles under the villagers' houses. Materially villagers are much better off now than fifty years ago; money sent from family members working in the cities or abroad has contributed to this, but efforts by the government to improve social services like health and education have also helped to improve the quality of life. But no matter how far away a villager may go, their dream is to return to the village one day. For most Thais, the village remains what it has always been: home.

– J. C.

own the land and are holders of the purse. Men live with their wives' relatives, particularly their wives' sisters and their father-in-law.

The most important relationship in the Thai family is between parents and children, particularly between the mother and her children. The essence of the relationship lies in the concept of *katanyu katawethi* or *bunkhun*. For one to be *katanyu* is to be constantly aware of (remembering) the benefits or favors which other persons have bestowed on him. *Katawethi* is to do something in return for the favors or benefits. *Bunkhun* is the favor or benefit bestowed, and for which one is obligated to do something in return. It is believed that the *bunkhun* of parents over their children is so great that whatever favors the children do for their parents, it will never be sufficient to repay the *bunkhun*.[33]

This emphasis on *bunkhun* gives rise to differences in the roles of sons and daughters. Daughters are expected to support their parents' families while sons are not expected to do so. While boys can repay the *bunkhun* by being ordained as monks, the daughters must repay it by working to support their parents.[34] This is the religious explanation. However, we may also look at it another way. Because women will obtain property while men join their wives' households, it is only fair that the women should work to support their parents' families.[35]

We will now try to examine the changes that have occurred. First, the belief in the matrilineal spirit cults, which used to serve as a means of social control over the behavior of family members, have now in reality dissipated.[36] Secondly, with the rapid rise in land value all over the country, sons are now claiming their right to inherit land.

Sometimes, sale of land by sons living elsewhere prevents the daughters from combining their lands and doing their agricultural work together to save costs and labor. It may indirectly force them to sell their land as well. During the last five years, much land has been sold by farmers. The proceeds of the sale are divided among those entitled to inherit the land so that no one can have a sufficiently large sum to invest in the purchase of another piece of land. The money tends to be spent on modern houses, refrigerators, cars, pick-up trucks, motorcycles, and so on.[37] Thirdly, out-migration of young men and women has greatly increased, and endogamous marriages have consequently decreased. The combination of all these factors have led to the diminished importance of women as the essential linkage of kin groups and related families in the village.

Although sons now have claims on their parents' property as well, the obligation of daughters to provide economic support to their parents has not yet been abrogated. Instead the burden has become even heavier. Traditionally, daughters were obligated to support their parents by working in the rice fields as well as growing fruit trees and vegetables. They would sell the produce in nearby markets and give the earnings to their parents.[38] In this way, daughters contributed to household expenses. Parents now place greater demands on their daughters who have migrated to work in urban areas. Far fewer demands, or none at all, are made of the sons.[39]

Migration has always been a way to relieve poverty in the indigent northeast and the upper north.[40] In the 1960's, roads linking the northeast to Bangkok were constructed. The condition of roads in the north improved later.

Influxes of migrants from both regions to Bangkok then followed. The early migrants were men and whole families. A major change in migration occurred in the late 1960's when it was found that

Top: A traditional marriage ceremony in Chiang Mai;
Far left: A girl in prayer; Left: Novice monks.

from 1965 to 1970, women exceeded men in a ratio of roughly 4:3 in the movement from the northeast to Bangkok and in the movement from the north by 5:4.[41]

Most migrants were fifteen to twenty-four years old, with women greatly outnumbering men. This change in the sex ratio must be related to the demand for female workers in Bangkok. The growth of the textile industry, for example, demanded female workers. It might also be related to the presence of foreign military personnel in Thailand for rest and recreation during the Indochinese wars and later, to the influx of tourists.[42] Undoubtedly, it must have been the expansion of the service sector that demanded the labor of women, particularly young women. Among these services was prostitution.

Many reasons have been given for their entering this profession. The most important is poverty, given the high income compared to other low-paying jobs.[43] It has been found that the remittances of daughters to their parents in the rural areas form the families' main source of income. It is interesting to note that these remittances are not used to invest in productive assets but are, most importantly, used for building modern houses and to satisfy such needs as food and clothing. A certain stigma is attached to the girls who enter this profession.[44] Nonetheless, the construction of modern houses for the parents is an act of redemption; it informs the people of what they have done, and why.[45]

Prostitution aside, the rapid growth of manufacturing exports has been possible because of female migrants. They form a large pool of young, trainable and obedient workers. The female work force has become the backbone of light export industries, which accounted for the unprecedented growth in the manufacturing sector.[46]

Earning low pay as factory workers, these women experience a conflict between the desire

Right: Women working in a factory; Below, left: Women office workers; Below, right, top to bottom: A woman working in the field; Mother and child.

The Role of Women in Thai Life

Traditionally, women have always played an important role in Thailand, particularly in village society. They are often in charge of the household finances and, in the fields, work alongside men on such seasonal chores as planting and harvesting. When, in the past, men were called away for long periods to fight as soldiers or to work as corvée laborers, women remained behind and managed the family farms or businesses.

Socially, however, their positions were accurately reflected by the Thai proverb: "Men are the front legs of the elephant, women are the

hind legs." However important their labor, they were still regarded as secondary to men, taught to accept their status and given little freedom in major decisions affecting their lives. During the reign of King Rama VI, primary education became compulsory for both women and men, and under Thailand's first Constitution in 1932 women were given equal political rights; but these apparent advances had little practical effect in everyday life. Fifty years ago, no women occupied significant positions in government, and even those who graduated with honors from a university found few careers open to them except for such traditional ones as teaching and nursing.

The situation began to change about thirty years ago, with Thailand's increasing shift from an agricultural economy to one based on industrialization. The new factories required workers, and more and more of them were women who migrated from the countryside to cities like Bangkok. A recent study found that women now account for 50 percent of the employed population, and in such key industries as export manufacture and tourism they constitute a remarkable 80 to 90 percent of the work force. Female university graduates now have a wide range of career opportunities, from banking to advertising, and salaries equivalent to or higher than those of men.

Many of the country's most successful business people, particularly entrepreneurs, are women. In cities, families in which both husband and wife hold jobs outside the home have become the rule rather than the exception.

Women are still inadequately represented in government. They held only 6.1 percent of the seats in the government that came to office in 1995 (an increase, however, over the 4.4 percent they held in the previous administration), and only one woman has been named Governor of a province (Nakhon Nayok). There is also some discrimination in the workplace, particularly at lower income levels; a study by the Asian Institute of Technology on women construction workers found that they were typically paid less than men for the same or similar work.

Nevertheless, Thai women have undeniably come a long way in the past half century, so far in fact that the old proverb may no longer apply.

– W. W.

for modernity and urban sophistication on the one hand, and the economic and emotional obligations felt toward their parents on the other. They continue to maintain and strengthen their ties to rural kin and uphold their values.[47] However, the ties appear to undergo a change when the girls become mothers. In a large number of villages in the northeast, only old people and children are left in the villages as the entire middle generation has gone to work in Bangkok and elsewhere. Daughters who have gone to work in Bangkok bring back their children to be raised by their grandparents. The grandmothers complain bitterly that the remittances sent by their daughters are insufficient for them to live on. To such complaints, the daughters respond by saying the remittances are only the fee for looking after the children, and not for the parents' living expenses.[48] We can see, therefore, that in such cases, remittances are sent not as repayment of *bunkhun*, but as a payment for the contract to look after the grandchildren.

Migration has had much impact upon vital kinship ties such as that between parent and child. Combined with the increased value of land and the closing of the land frontiers, it has also induced change in inheritance practices. This in turn affects the status of women and their role as the link between men and between households in the village. Women's obligation to support their parents' household, on the other hand, have become a heavier burden as natural resources are depleted. In some places, young women have been merchandised and enter prostitution. The status of women has gone down. Seniority has lost its power and prestige.[49] Because of modern education, new technology, and migration, parents even feel inferior to their children. Seniority has thus lost its importance as a status marker.[50]

Changes in Structure

The study of Thai society is fraught with arguments about the nature of its structure. The question of its looseness or rigidity, or persistence and change, is hotly debated. It is proposed here that the structure of Thai society contains these opposing poles in a subtle juxtaposition and may be understood in terms of the relationship between these oppositions at different times.[51]

Thai society is extremely hierarchical. Every Thai regards every other person as higher or lower than himself in the social order.[52] In old Siam, every person in the kingdom was assigned *sakdina* (dignity marks), a number of points which showed precisely his relative position as being higher or lower than other persons in the hierarchy.[53] The king stood at the pinnacle of the hierarchy, his *sakdina* being innumerable.

This hierarchy constituted not only the social order but also a moral order. Being Buddhists, the Thais believed that the attainment of a position was due to accumulated *bun* (merits or good deeds).[54] The king was the person who had infinite *bun*. Thai kingship was sacred because it represented the *dharma*, the moral order of the society.[55] Ranking was part of the moral order, hierarchy being maintained through the royal distribution of awards in the form of rank (*yot*) in accordance with the merit (*bun*) of each person.[56]

The term *bun* (merit) is frequently found together with the word *barami*. A person is said to have much *barami* when he is loved and respected by a large number of people. However, similar to the word *bun*, the word *barami* implied possession of moral quality also. In such an extremely hierarchical society, the most important relationship would be that between the senior and the junior, the *phu-yai* and *phu-noi* in Thai.[57] In our earlier analysis of the institution of leadership and the family, we noted the vital importance of the concept of "seniority" in premodern Thai society. The *phuyai-phunoi* (junior-senior) distinction pervaded the whole society. The word *phueng* (to depend on) described this

A group of youngsters exercising in Lumpini Park.

relationship. The phrase "*phueng phra borom phothi somphan*" (to depend on the merit of the king) was commonly used for those who came to live in Thai society. Thus, it was said that the Mons came to settle on both sides of the canal near Phraya Sisahathep's house to depend on his merit (*phueng bun*). (Phraya Sisahathep was a rising noble in the reign of Rama III (1809–24), and was a descendant of a Mon noble.[58]) A person who had no *thi phueng* (someone to depend on) was unfortunate indeed. The patron-client relationship is described thus by Lucien Hanks: "The coherence of Thai society rests largely on the value of becoming a client of someone who has greater resources than one alone possesses; a person is ill-advised to try to fight one's own battles independently. Security grows with affiliation, and the crowning moment of happiness lies in the knowledge of dependable benefits distributed in turn to faithful inferiors."[59]

The basic unit of Thai society was a "vertical" group, with one leader, the patron, and a number of his followers, the clients. The group was held together by the presence of the patron who linked with each member of the group individually, that is, each member separately depended upon the patron in one way or other. They might act as a group under the order of their patron, or in his defense and support, but the patron might choose to assign a specific task to or favor any one of them specially. Generally, the members of the group would be competing with each other for favors from the patron.[60] Such groups were organized into a hierarchy with the king at the apex.[61] The plan of this organization, setting up *krom* (departments) and *kong* (divisions), the *sakdina* as laid out in the law, might have been following that of an army.[62] Like an army, it was all connected by lines of command.

As manpower was a scarce resource in old Siam, this organization was a system designed for the control of manpower by the king. The number of *sakdina* correlated with the number of men. As a noble attained higher position with an increased number of *sakdina*, the larger was the

number of men under his control. By distributing *sakdina*, the king was distributing manpower, and thus, *bun* and *barami*.

This was an extremely rigid structure. The law laid down that everyone had to respect and obey his superior unquestioningly. It gave a great deal of discretionary power to the superior over the subordinates in his group. Some superiors treated their subordinates well. But most could not, owing to the demands made on them by their own superiors at a higher level of the hierarchy, such as the demand for the supply of manpower for corvée labor or war. Thus throughout Thai history people at various levels struggled to get out of one group into another to get better *nai* (superiors). Numerous commoners (*phrai*) ran away from their superiors in the departments or divisions into the forests.[63]

This widespread phenomenon was due to the fact that the *sakdina* system, with its rigid structure, was superimposed on another system, the patronage system. While the legally imposed structure forbade the changing of one's superior, the latter system permitted the selecting and changing of patrons by the clients.[64] In the old days, the quality of a leader lay in seniority and morality. The essence of good morals, in Buddhist terms, was selflessness.[65] Translated into action, he must be generous, kind and protective toward his dependents (clients). In the almost non-monetary system, the resource needed to enable anyone to be generous was manpower, whether it be a large number of kin at the vil-

lage level or followers in the towns. Anyone who could not be generous, kind and effective in giving protection to his clients would lose them. The followers would flock to others who could perform the role of a patron better.[66]

The legally imposed structure tried to stop this flow. As severe a device as the marking of the commoners (*phrai*) was resorted to.[67] And yet these measures could not control those who chose to evade the system. With vast areas of uninhabited land and the lack of communication facilities and an effective army, compromises had to be made, as could be seen in royal proclamations inviting those who had run away into the forest to return to the structure without fear of punishment. Such a pragmatic measure was called *phon-pron*, that is, giving in when it is seen to be impossible to overcome by force.

Two important consequences arose out of the situation. The first was continual attempts to avoid rules and regulations by getting out of the structure. The revolt of the oppressed against the persons in authority did not happen just because the superiors' treatment of those under them was selective and discriminating (divide and rule), but also because of the fact that each superior had different abilities in performing their roles, for example in the supply of manpower for corvée service. Such resistance to rules and regulations had become a trait of the Thai personality and had been called "Thai individualism", or more precisely "negative individualism"[68], which refers to, in the words of scholar Han ten Brummelhuis, "that particular mode of retreat, avoidance, and distrust, which colors so many forms of behavior and social relationships."[69] Together

with the pragmatic belief of *phon-pron* (to give in, to compromise with the possessor of greater force), it generated the appearance of a somewhat loose structure. The second consequence was thus the ambivalence of the traditional Thai system, with a rigid social code coexisting with an individual code of freedom.[70] In sum, the interplay of these contrasting codes led to the cyclical development from rigid structural integration (including centralization) to structural disintegration and vice versa. The old structure was on the verge of disintegration toward the end of the early Bangkok period.[71]

Threats of colonial powers provided the needed reason for the introduction of a major reform of the administration of the country. The main thrusts of the bureaucratic reformation of King Chulalongkorn beginning formally in 1882 were stated as follows: "(1) the functional organization of ministries and departments based in the capital; (2) the penetration of the provinces through the direct replacement of the local ruling aristocracy...by paid officials responsible to the capital...and (3) the buildup of the military, from an archaic and inefficient feudal levy in war...to a professionally trained force."[72]

Thus slavery, *phrai* (registered commoners), corvée labor, and the *sakdina* system were abolished. Salaried officials replaced non-salaried princes and nobles who used to be given men (*phrai*) instead of payment. Since the signing of the Bowring Treaty (1855), the Thai economy had become partially commercialized. Wealth could be acquired in other ways besides the possession of manpower.

Interestingly, the establishment of functional departments did not do away with the hierarchy of patron-client relations and even the rigidity of the old linear structure. According to William Siffin, "In the Thai system, legal-rational authority was not institutionalized in the course of the Chakkri Reformation..., and to a very substantial extent because the authoritative values upon which the reform was based were essentially tradition-

KING

ROYAL PRINCE

NOBLE

PETTY OFFICIAL

COMMONER (phrai), MARRIED

COMMONER, SINGLE, OR SLAVE

SAKDINA HIERARCHY

Top: The King occupies the pinnacle of Thai society and has the power to distribute *sakdina* (dignity marks) to those below him.

THAILAND King Bhumibol Adulyadej – The Golden Jubilee 1946-1996

al."[73] What happened was the reconstruction of the old order under the façade of a modern legal-rational system with functional departments. The characteristics of this new bureaucracy were the overwhelmingly "line" organizations with little reliance upon techniques of delegation. The organizations do not operate on the basis of continuing reference to rules and regulations. Siffin observes: "In the Thai bureaucratic system, with its particular values and pattern of authority, the legal model is likely to mislead. The source of authority is personal; the response is personal; and as for the substance of a proposal— 'the action often peters out'...The immediate source of authority is hierarchical status; and the substantive concerns of the parties to the relationship are to some degree status-centered rather than achievement-oriented."[74] Siffin wrote the above passage in 1966. It would seem that the bureaucracy was not only organized like the old structure, but also suffered the same

Below: The diverse groups in Thailand include the Chinese, the Muslims and hilltribes.

dynamics. In the reign of King Chulalongkorn (1868–1910) when its leaders were visionary, energetic and honest, the bureaucracy was efficient and could accomplish many important tasks. As time went by, however, it deteriorated and no longer served as an efficient machine. At present, the inefficiency of the Thai bureaucracy is well-known.

On the other hand, the effects of the Thai bureaucracy have become extremely widespread, permeating down to the village level all over the country. It has partly at least helped to spread "vertical" groups organized on patron-client relationship everywhere. Along with such "vertical" groups, it has sustained the opposition between "rigidity" and "looseness" (rigid structure versus anarchistic individualism).

Patron-client relations depend on the existence of hierarchy. In the old days the status markers in the rural areas were mainly based on seniority and moral quality, supported by a large

Minority Groups in Thai Life

Thailand is the land of the Thais, but it is also home to a diverse collection of minority groups, both ethnic and religious, many of whom have had a significant effect on society.

Economically, the Chinese constitute the most important of these groups. They had been a prominent presence in earlier capitals but began to come in large numbers during the early Bangkok period; indeed, according to one source, by the middle of the nineteenth century a full half the capital's population was Chinese and they controlled much of its trade. It would be

impossible today to make such an ethnic division, thanks to extensive intermarriage and social assimilation, though a recent estimate claimed that about 70 percent of Bangkok's residents are at least partly Chinese. Despite their economic power, however, there has been relatively little anti-Chinese sentiment and none of the racial violence experienced by some other countries in the region.

A much larger ethnic group is the Lao, who predominate in the northeastern part of the country and are also found in considerable numbers in the north and elsewhere. These, too, have become "Thai" in the national and political sense, but retain distinctive cultural traits in such matters as language and food; one linguist, for example, maintains that as far as spoken language is concerned the first one learned by a majority of the country's people is, in fact, Lao, or Isan ("Northeastern") as it is usually referred to in Central Thailand.

Muslims, many of them ethnically Malay, comprise Thailand's largest religious minority, concentrated for the most part in the southernmost provinces of Narathiwat, Pattani, Yala, and Satun, and are mostly of the Sunni faith. There are approximately two thousand mosques in the country (about one hundred of them in Bangkok) as well as some two hundred Muslim schools.

The number of Indians is small—less than fifty thousand—but the community exerts considerable economic power, particularly in Bangkok. They are divided almost equally into Hindus and Sikhs.

The hill tribes of the north, so popular with photographers and so often included in tourist itineraries, are in fact comparatively recent arrivals. Some like the Lahu and the Hmong began migrating into the country in the nineteenth century, but the greatest numbers came only in the 1960's and 70's, driven by the wars in neighboring Burma and Indochina. Today the northern mountains are home to an estimated half a million people belonging to a number of different tribes, the principal ones being the Hmong, Mien, Karen, Akha, Lisu and Lahu.

– W. W.

number of kin. It is doubtful whether the relationship between the leaders and the villagers was a patron-client one. Apart from this formal relationship, there were those leaders who had physical prowess. They protected their village and sometimes other villages. Some of these *nak-leng*, if well-loved and respected by the people, might have been appointed to some minor positions in the provincial bureaucracy. Rich traders, usually Chinese, might be incorporated into the bureaucracy by appointment. Their sons, at least, could enter the bureaucracy through formal education. Other Thais might do so through such formal education or the monkhood.[75]

The bureaucracy provided the only desirable career path until recently. It was the source of power and wealth. It expanded a great deal as it helped to solve the unemployment problem. Although Thailand had since 1932 a constitutional monarchy, the principle underlying the bureaucratic organization was the same as that of the old structure. The King, representing the *dharma*, distributed ranks and positions to the officials according to their *bun*. These positions, as a status marker, carry a moral quality.

One of the greatest changes during the last fifty years has been the rapid economic growth and the rise of the middle class. In fact the possession of wealth has turned out to be the most important status marker. Thirty years ago, police officers in a division in Bangkok were arguing with each other over whether they should pay respect (*wai*) to a man whom they know to be very wealthy and powerful but without moral integrity.[76] Nowadays, such a debate no longer exists. The past fifty years have seen many people becoming extremely wealthy through illegal and immoral activities such as illegal logging, drug trafficking and gambling. Some of these have

become *chao pho* (godfathers) in rural areas.[77] There are thus many people who have gathered followers through their wealth and occupy certain privileged positions, undisturbed by law enforcement officials.

Values have changed, and to be "modern" in the sense of conspicuous consumption has become extremely important. This has affected all classes and all groups of people. In the "vertical" group of patron and client, social control was largely achieved through the patron who should have moral quality (as moral quality was an important status marker). The change of the basis of status from moral quality to wealth has greatly affected social order and social control. The hierarchy is upset and social status is now separated from religion and moral quality. Anarchic individualism has grown at the expense of the hierarchical structure. We see a situation where greed in everyone and every group is almost beyond control.

In my opinion, this situation is only transitory. Thai society will be transformed in the process of industrialization. Groups are being organized on a horizontal basis, that is, people joining together because they have the same principle and/or ideal. The members of such groups would set rules and regulations to control the behavior of the people in their group as well as to protect their mutual interest. The only problem is that "vertical" groups, especially those in the bureaucracy, would try to suppress them. This is natural because these groups are threatening to the bureaucracy. Much conflict between the two types of organizations will be over scarce resources. The scarcer the resources, the more severe the conflicts may become. However, compromises may be made, thanks to the Thai capacity for *phon pron* (giving in, compromise). In such cases, the patron-client group will continue to exist, with the exception that the clients, instead of competing with each other for the favor of the patron, will join together to protect their interests and ideals.

Whatever will happen, Thai society will be transformed. Real change is imminent.

Top: Celebration of Songkran Festival in Chiang Mai; Right: An aerial view of Bangkok; Overleaf: Thais celebrating the Flower Festival in Chiang Mai.

Ever-changing Bangkok

Though many provincial capitals have grown rapidly in recent years, Bangkok is still the ultimate city to every Thai. One out of ten Thais lives in the national capital, which is forty-five times bigger than the second most populous city. The metropolitan area now covers some 1,500 square kilometers on both sides of the Chao Phraya River, and new suburbs are constantly being added.

The headquarters of almost all major domestic and foreign companies are located in Bangkok, as are all government ministries and most of the leading educational, sporting, and cultural facilities. The greater part of Thailand's imports and exports still pass through the city (although this may change as new harbors open along the Eastern seaboard), and 90 percent of the motor vehicles in the nation are registered there. It is the focus of Thailand's aviation, railway, and communications network, as well as the entry point for the majority of foreign visitors.

Given such facts, it is not surprising that

Bangkok acts as a magnet for people who come from all parts of the country to be educated, to find employment, or simply to see its famous monuments and enjoy its highly varied pleasures. Nor, perhaps, is it surprising that the ever-changing city should be confronted by a variety of problems similar to those of other large urban areas both in Asia and elsewhere.

A half century ago, Bangkok was still relatively small, with mostly low buildings of two or three stories and the network of canals that once led Westerners to call it "the Venice of the East". Government buildings were concentrated in the Dusit District, while the center of commerce was the Chinese section along Yaowarat Road. Most foreign businesses and hotels were located on or off New Road running parallel to the Chao Phraya River, still a major part of the city's life.

This began to change in the late 1950's and accelerated during the 70's and 80's. New business centers and residential areas went up far from the river, mostly on former rice fields to the east, and all but a few of the canals were filled in to create roads. Multi-story buildings rose almost everywhere, creating a new skyline within the span of a decade. Thonburi, formerly a separate community on the west

bank of the Chao Phraya, became a part of the metropolitan area. Despite some government efforts at decentralization, most of the new factories and industrial estates were built near the capital.

Urban facilities have been severely strained as a result. Bangkok now has more than a million registered motor vehicles and, because of the limited road surface, traffic congestion is heavy. Moreover, some parts of the city are sinking due to the pumping of water from artesian wells to supply suburban projects, leading to periodic flooding in the rainy season.

Experts are presently working on elaborate plans to relieve these problems, aided in such matters as traffic and flooding by wise advice from King Bhumibol Adulyadej. After many delays, a mass transit system and new expressways are being built, along with long-range flood control projects.

Whether these efforts will be successful remains to be seen. One indisputable fact, however, is that the rapid pace of Bangkok's change is unlikely to slow down in the foreseeable future.

–W. W.

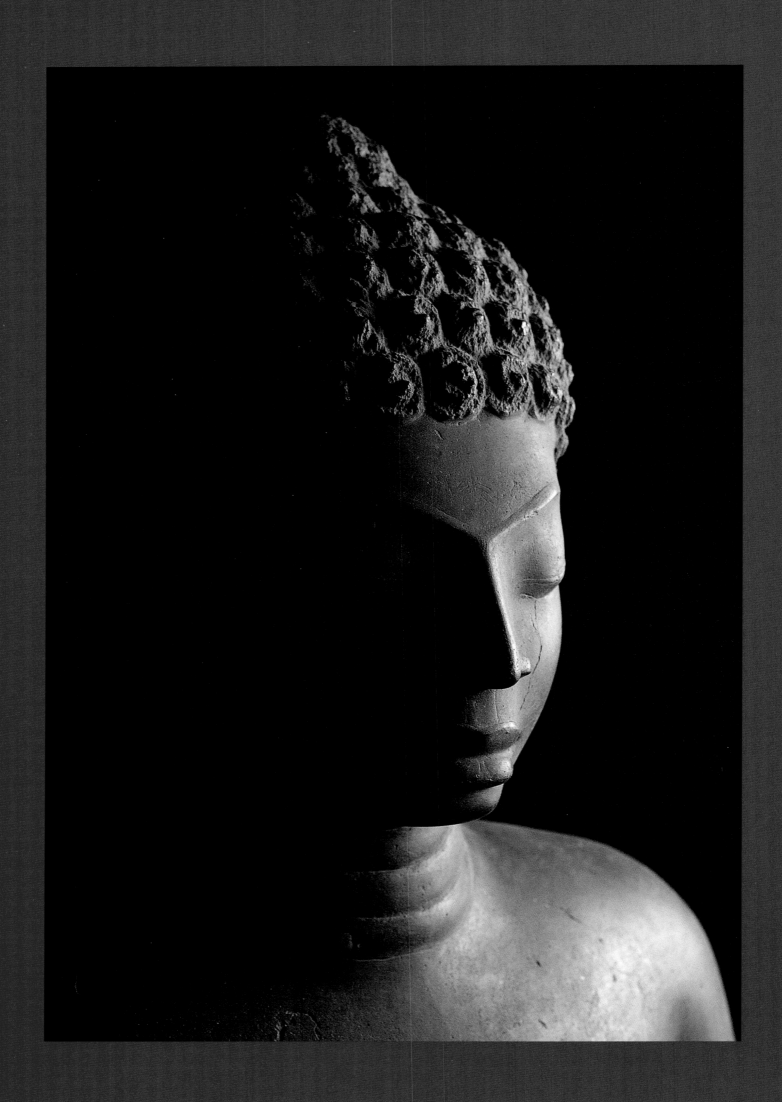

7

THAI ARTS

M C Subhadradis Diskul

T HAILAND IS A MELTING POT OF MANY CULTURES. GEOGRAPHICALLY IT IS
SITUATED IN THE MIDDLE OF SOUTHEAST ASIA WHERE THE SEA TRADE
ROUTES FROM INDIA TO CHINA OR VICE VERSA HAVE HAD TO PASS.

Therefore, the classical arts in Thailand can be divided into many periods, displaying different influences, some of them contemporary to different regions. Here we are not going to describe prehistoric art in Thailand, though many implements from the Neolithic period downward have been found, as well as rock paintings which have been discovered at many sites.

The first period of classical Thai art is called Dvaravati, after the first historical kingdom in present-day Thailand, dating from about the seventh to the eleventh century AD. Before that period there is also some evidence showing the connection between India and Thailand which might go back to the first century AD.

Dvaravati art is composed of Buddha images both in stone and bronze. They display influences from the Indian Gupta, Post-Gupta and Pala styles. The Buddha effigies can be divided into three periods. The first one shows strong Indian artistic influences and might date back to the seventh century. The second period displays indigenous character-

istics such as the style of standing erect and performing the same gesture with both hands as in the attitude of dispelling fear or preaching. This period probably extends from the eighth to the tenth centuries. It is believed that most of the inhabitants during the Dvaravati period belonged to the Mon race as a few stone inscriptions in the ancient Mon language have been discovered in central Thailand, probably the site of the Dvaravati kingdom. The last style of Dvaravati Buddha images might date back to the eleventh century and shows some Khmer influences from Cambodia.

The cradle of Dvaravati art in central Thailand spread its influence with Theravada Buddhism to the north, northeast, east and eventually down to the south of Thailand. Apart from statues, some terracotta ceramics and traces of brick architectural foundations have also been unearthed.

Buddhism and Hinduism spread at the same time from India to Southeast Asia, probably from the early Christian eras. In Thailand it has always been Buddhism

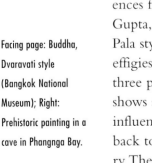
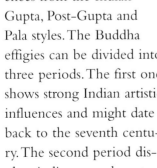

Facing page: Buddha, Dvaravati style (Bangkok National Museum); Right: Prehistoric painting in a cave in Phangnga Bay.

of the Theravada sect that predominated. Hindu statues have also been discovered in Thailand from this early period. A small stone found at Chaiya in southern Thailand is probably not only the earliest found in Thailand but also the earliest in Southeast Asia. The influence came from India and the majority of these Hindu statues date from the eighth to ninth centuries.

Some scholars have defined them as one aspect of Hinduism in Dvaravati art.

In the southern part of Thailand there developed another school of art called Srivijaya style after the name of a kingdom that is believed to have ruled over the island of Sumatra, Malaysia and the southern part of Thailand from about the eighth to the

thirteenth centuries. The people professed Mahayana Buddhism. Therefore most of the statues discovered represent the Avalokitesvara Bodhisattva, a compassionate male saint of Buddhism in that sect. The architecture displays some influences from the island of Java where Mahayana Buddhism was also practiced. Buddhist votive tablets were fabricated in clay in order to present merit to the dead instead of being produced in metal or terracotta as during the Dvaravati period. The latter were probably made to prolong the life of Buddhism after its existence for five thousand years as predicted in Theravada Buddhism.

Then came Khmer influence from Cambodia. Evidence has been discovered that tends to demonstrate that the style of art called Lopburi, displaying Khmer influence in Thailand, extended from the seventh to about the thirteenth centuries. The evidence was mostly discovered in the east, northeast and the central parts of the country. The most reliable evidence is composed of Buddhist and Hindu shrines in brick and stone, the most important of which is the temple of Phimai in northeastern Thailand. It was built of sandstone and laterite and dates back to the early Angkor Wat style, about the middle of the twelfth century. Mahayana Buddhist temples which were constructed in the first half of the thirteenth century exist mostly in the central part of the country. Stone and bronze statues have also been unearthed. Some of the stone images date back to the seventh to eighth centuries but most of the bronzes were cast in the twelfth and thirteenth centuries. During this peri-

Above: Buddha, Dvaravati period; Left: Buddha, Srivijaya period (Bangkok National Museum).

od Buddhism, both of Mahayana and Theravada as well as Hinduism, were practiced. Glazed ceramics have also been discovered. The dating of the Lopburi style objects and monuments is fairly reliable because their styles can be compared to those in Cambodia which have already been researched and fixed by French scholars.

The Thai people are believed to have originally lived in south-eastern China and to have migrated down to present-day Thailand in successive waves even before the conquest of China by Kublai Khan. The Thais were strong enough to declare their independence against the Khmer in the middle of the thirteenth century and that is the beginning of the Thai Sukhothai kingdom. However before that period there might have been some Thais who lived in small principalities in the extreme northern part of Thailand as we have found some forms of art in Thai style in those areas.

This Northern Thai style is sub-divided into two periods. The first one, the early style, probably dates from the eleventh or thirteen to the fifteenth centuries. Buddha bronze images resemble those of the Pala school in northeastern India by having a halo in the form of a lotus bud or a gem on top of the head, large hair curls, a round face with arched eyebrows, a prominent chin and a smiling expression. The body is stout, displaying a short end of the robe over the left shoulder. The Buddha is usually performing the attitude of subduing Mara (the evil spirit) with his right hand on his right knee and sits in a cross-legged posture over a seat decorated with two rows of lotus petals. Architecture of this period has rarely been discovered. That is the reason why the beginning date of this early period is still conjectural.

The second period of Northern Thai art displays Sukhothai influence and dates from the sixteenth to the eighteenth centuries. The Buddha effigies, which are mostly in bronze, are sometimes dated by inscriptions. Many temples in brick belonging to this period exist. As the extreme northern part of Thailand was ruled by the Burmese from the late sixteenth to eighteenth centuries, late Northern Thai art displays many artistic influences from Burma.

The Sukhothai style dates from the thirteenth to the fifteenth centuries. Though it was short-lived, Sukhothai art is reckoned as the most beautiful artistic expression of Thailand, especially the walking Buddha images. The Buddha of this period has a halo in the form a flame-like motif. The hair curls are small. The face is oval with arched eyebrows, a hooked nose and a gentle smiling expression. The shoulders are large compared to the thin waist. The long

THAILAND King Bhumibol Adulyadej – The Golden Jubilee 1946-1996

Left: Buddha, Sukhothai period (Bangkok National Museum).
Bottom: Buddha, U-thong style (Bangkok National Museum).

flap of cloth hangs over the left shoulder down to the navel and terminates in a zigzag design. During this period the four postures of the Buddha were popularly represented: seated, reclining, standing and walking. Bronze Hindu images were also cast and given a gentle smiling expression like that of the Buddha. Glazed ceramics were fabricated and exported far and wide. Temples in brick abound, some showing Sri Lankan influences through Theravada Buddhism which was propagated to Thailand

during this period. A Sukhothai-style stupa called the Lotus-Bud stupa became very popular during this time. Stucco was also used as decorations on many religious buildings.

From the twelfth to fifteenth centuries AD, there developed another style of art in central Thailand. This style is usually called U-thong and was probably fabricated by Thai artists. It shows influences from Dvaravati, Khmer and Sukhothai art. The Buddha images can be divided into three succes-

THAILAND King Bhumibol Adulyadej – The Golden Jubilee 1946-1996

sive periods according to their prominent components. Their constant characteristics are a flame-like motif halo, especially for the later two periods, a small band on the forehead, a long flap of cloth on the left shoulder, the attitude of subduing Mara, a folded-leg seated posture and a base that curves inside. Most of the Buddha images are in bronze. Very few examples of architecture from this period have been discovered.

As the city of Ayutthaya was the capital of

Thailand for about four hundred years, from AD 1350 to 1767, the art of Ayutthaya is divided into four successive periods. The first one continued the second and third periods of U-thong style for one hundred years. The second period lasted about two hundred years and displays Sri Lankan influence through Sukhothai art. The third period of about fifty years came around the second half of the seventeenth century, when Khmer art was revived at Ayutthaya and then western influ-

ence came through expanding trade and diplomatic relations with countries in Europe, especially France in the reign of Louis XIV. In the last period of another fifty years, in the first half of the eighteenth century, many temples were restored by King Borom Kot who reigned from 1732 to 1758. There was, however, hardly any new construction.

Ayutthaya architecture is built of brick. The earliest structure as the center of a Buddhist monastery was constructed in imitation of a Khmer tower but later on Sukhothai influence crept in and the round stupa became very popular. During the third period of Ayutthaya art the Khmer form of structure was introduced again.

Early-fifteenth-century mural paintings were discovered only in 1957 inside a crypt of the main tower of Wat Ratburana at Ayutthaya. They represent scenes of the past lives of the Buddha as well as some Chinese figures. Ceramics were ordered from China but with Thai designs. Stucco and terracotta workmanship has also been discovered.

The last period of the classical Thai arts belongs to the Bangkok or Ratanakosin style, from 1782 to the nineteenth century. This period can be termed as eclectic. During the first three reigns of Bangkok (from 1782 to 1851) every monarch tried to imitate the splendor of Ayutthaya but in the reign of King Rama IV or King Mongkut (1851–68) western art became very popular and had an influence over nearly

Left to right: Both Buddhas are from the Bangkok period; Below: Buddhist temple, Ayutthaya period.

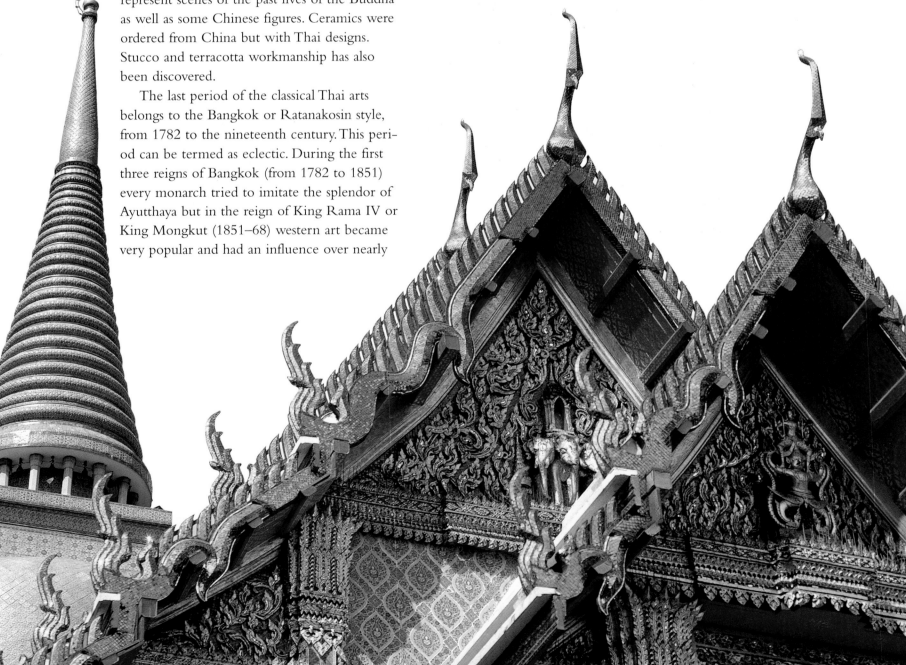

every aspect of life of the high society in Bangkok. The most noticeable can be seen in the mural paintings of the period. In the following reigns western influence spread even more because many young Thai men were sent to be educated in Europe. However, despite these foreign influences, Buddhist monasteries and most of the buildings in the Grand Palace continued to be constructed in Thai style as can

be witnessed from the Marble Temple which was built by command of King Rama V, or King Chulalongkorn, in the early twentieth century. In his reign (1868–1910), some buildings were a mixture between Thai style and that of the west such as the Chakri Mansion inside the Grand Palace but some such as the Vimanmek Pavilion, a tourist site built of teakwood, was totally western.

The S.E.A. Write Awards

Each year, for the better part of a week, Bangkok becomes a major cultural center for the surrounding region. This is due to the S.E.A. Write Awards, a unique function at which writers from a wide diversity of backgrounds have a rare opportunity to meet one another at the historic Oriental Hotel.

The awards came into being in 1979 as a means of honoring literary achievement in the five original members of the Association of South East Asian Nations (ASEAN) –

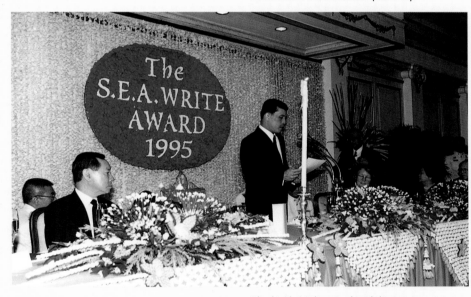

Above: HRH Crown Prince Maha Vajiralongkorn presenting his speech at 1995's award ceremony; Right: Thai winner, Paiwarin Khao-ngam, who won for poetry in 1995.

Thailand, Malaysia, the Philippines, Singapore, and Indonesia; Brunei joined the group a few years later and Vietnam in 1995. Among the objectives of the event is "to create a wider awareness of literary wealth among the ASEAN countries" and to bring the winners together for a series of events that includes sightseeing, meetings with local writers, a prize of US$1,000, and a gala dinner presided over by a member of the Thai royal family.

In each country, a committee composed of writers and leading critics considers the nominees, who must have produced an original work with some relevance to his or her nation or region within the previous five years, and makes the final selection regardless of race,

sex, or religion. Fiction in any of its forms – novels, short stories, poems, folk tales, etc. – is acceptable, and it may be written in any language used in the entrants' countries. Only a few of the past winners have used English, though this is generally the only language most share when they gather to receive their awards.

Recognition has come to a broad range of writers. Last year's Thai winner, for example, was Paiwarin Khao-ngam, whose philosophical poetry deals with rural people who immigrate to the city, while the 1987 Malaysian awardee was a playwright whose dramas are based on Islamic concepts and the Singaporean winner was an 84-year-old poet who writes in classical Chinese.

The Thai royal family has been part of the S.E.A. Write ceremony since its inception. Her Majesty the Queen has presided over several and since 1984 HRH Crown Prince Vajiralongkorn has honored the affair with his presence. Another prominent feature is an address by a guest writer; in past years these have included James Michener, William Golding, Han Suyin, Margaret Drabble, Gore Vidal and Paul Thereux.

Apart from the check, the plaque, and a free holiday, how do S.E.A. Write winners benefit from these awards? The most important way, to judge from conversations with some of them over the years, would seem to be the pleasure of recognition on a broader level than most have enjoyed during their years, plus the opportunity to meet and exchange views with fellow writers from neighboring cultures.

– W. W.

The SUPPORT Foundation

Queen Sirikit inspecting the products of the SUP-PORT Foundation.

From the day that Her Majesty the Queen was crowned at the Ceremony of Coronation on May 5, 1950 in the Baisal Taksin Hall of the Grand Palace, she has made it her duty to be at the King's side on every possible occasion, especially when His Majesty traveled to maintain close contact with the people in all corners of the kingdom. Such royal trips have been taken in order to gain first-hand knowledge about rural living conditions and with that insight a number of projects have been royally initiated to alleviate some of the hardship of the community.

While His Majesty the King launches agricultural projects to relieve the farmers' hardships, Her Majesty the Queen looks for income-generating occupations to supplement their basic earnings. The Queen has long concluded that most Thais are dexterous, industrious and meticulous, and because each region has its own indigenous raw materials and cottage industries, handicrafts could be readily promoted. Royal encouragement was thus initially given by sending expert teachers at Her Majesty's expense to train farming families in the central plains to make accessories out of

local materials such as cloth remnants, sisal or clay, while extension workers were sent to the northeast to support the raising of silkworms and the production of raw silk. Expert weavers were also sent to various villages in the north, south and northeast to promote the traditional use of natural dyes and traditional patterns for weaving cotton and silk.

More comprehensive training programs were further implemented by Her Majesty with the establishment of the Foundation for the Promotion of Supplementary Occupations and Related Techniques (SUPPORT) on July 21, 1976, initially with her private funds, in order to provide opportunities for farming families to be trained in traditional handicrafts as well as to preserve and ensure the continuity of regional Thai arts and crafts which were in danger of dying out. Trainees usually come from modest backgrounds and are inadequately educated but as the SUPPORT training emphasizes excellence, basic instruction is thorough and comprehensive. The curriculum aims at giving the future artisans skills handed down through the generations by the most able Thai craftsmen. At the same time, it prepares the trainees to go beyond the rote repetition of skills and patterns taught to them; it prepares them to give free rein to their artistic creativity.

Trainees study in a free-hand drawing course in which they are initiated into the intricacies of Thai motifs and patterns until they have the competence to accurately represent their models in full detail on paper. They are then introduced to all the technical aspects of the materials and the tools used in the crafts in which they will specialize. Subsequently they are instructed by experienced artisans in every step of the production process for their

particular craft. Trainees are constantly reminded of the Foundation's motto, "Improvement is our spirit and perfection our aim." While they are in training they are given full room and board as well as a stipend. Materials and tools needed for their training are free. The period of training depends on the complexity of each individual craft and courses are scheduled so that they do not interfere with the farming season.

Trainees can choose from among twenty-one different crafts, namely artificial flower-making, bamboo basketry, ceramics, drawing and painting, rattanware, *yan lipao* basketry, collage with *malaeng thap* beetle parts, damascene ware, gold and silver niulloware, gold- and silver-smithing, woodcarving, marble- and soapstone-carving, shadow puppet-carving in hide, cotton rug-weaving, supplementary weft-weaving, silk *mudmee* weaving, hand-embroidery, stucco sculpture, and mother of pearl inlay, sewing and dressmaking, as well as handmade packaging.

The handicrafts made by the SUP-PORT Foundation trainees at the Training Centre in Chitralada Villa of Dusit Palace or at training centers in the various regional royal residences are presented to Her Majesty for her inspection and comments throughout the various stages of production. After the final royal inspection the trainees or graduates are then able to market their products through the SUPPORT Foundation for sale both at home and abroad. All SUPPORT Foundation products are created with the best of materials and display technical proficiency and refined craftsmanship.

— MOM RAJAWONGSE PUTRIE VIRAVAIDYA

204

The Siam Society

The Siam Society, under Royal Patronage, was founded in 1904 by a number of residents, both Thai and foreign, with the stated objective of investigating and encouraging the arts, science and literature of Thailand and neighboring countries. It maintains an extensive library of books on Asia, offers frequent lectures on various subjects, publishes a regular journal and occasional books and organizes trips for members to places of cultural interest in Thailand and also to foreign countries.

Shortly after its founding, the Bangkok Natural History Society became amalgamated with the society and published bulletins dealing with natural history and other scientific matters.

Most of Thailand's leading scholars during this century have been involved with the society, either contributing articles to the journal or serving as president, often both. Among these have been Prince Damrong Rajanubhab, regarded as the father of Thai history, Prince Dhani Nivat, Prince Prem Purachatra, Prince Subhadradis Diskul, Phya Anuman Rajadhon, Dhanit Yupo and Piriya Krairiksh; King Rama VI also wrote articles on Thai literature. Noted foreign members have included Reginald le May, Alexander B Griswold, Eric Seidenfaden, and George Coedes, all of whom were responsible for pioneering studies in Thai arts and culture.

Writing in the first issue of the journal, Dr O Frankfurter, the first President of the Society, observed, "I consider that we are the workmen to collect the materials on which the master-builder may at some future day erect the edifice, in the shape of an encyclopedic work on Siam." To many scholars, especially those working abroad, the journal itself after nearly a hundred years of publication constitutes such a comprehensive work of reference.

The formation of an Ethnological Museum was included in the original plans of the society, but this did not become a reality until the 1960's when Kraisri Nimmanahaeminda, a member from Chiang Mai, donated his northern-style ancestral home for the purpose. This structure was moved to the society's compound in Bangkok and now displays a large collection of woodcarvings, textiles and household utensils. A traditional central-style Thai dwelling has also been added to the compound.

Now about to enter its second century, the Siam Society continues to be a leading center for scholarly research into all aspects of Thai culture and natural history.

– W. W.

Jim Thompson and the Thai Silk Industry

Jim Thompson arrived in Thailand a few days after the end of the Second World War in 1945, part of an American military group that also included Alexander Macdonald. The following year, Macdonald would found the *Bangkok Post*, the first post-war English-language newspaper, while Thompson would embark on the revival of one of the oldest and most beautiful Thai handicrafts.

Thai silk was probably produced in the ancient capital of Sukhothai and was certainly a well-known craft during the Ayutthaya and early Bangkok periods. Changing tastes, however, and particularly the arrival of cheaper machine-made textiles from Europe and Japan, had almost destroyed the industry. By the time Thompson appeared on the scene, it was confined to relatively few weavers, mostly in the northeast, who worked part-time and produced largely for village consumption.

Thompson's primary contributions were in two areas. First, he persuaded some of the weavers to use wider, more efficient looms and color-fast chemical dyes instead of the traditional vegetable dyes that achieved lovely, delicate colors but soon faded unless carefully protected. Second, and equally important, he drew on contacts in the United States and Europe to open foreign markets for the textile and make it, for the first time, a significant export product.

The timing was also fortuitous. Older Asian silk-weaving centers such as China and Japan were devastated by the war and could not resume production for some time. Meanwhile, there was a growing demand for luxury fabrics, particularly from the fashion and decorating industries.

Thai silk first appeared on the world stage in 1950 when the costume designer Irene Sharaff happened to see some of Thompson's material and used it in Mike Todd's *Peepshow*, actually for a number called "Blue Night", for which the music was composed by King Bhumibol Adulyadej. ("Thailand's Orchestra-Leading King Writes Songs for Broadway Show", read the headlines in the *New York Times*.) Miss Sharaff used it much more spectacularly for *The King and I* a year later, resulting in a flood of orders for Thompson's Bangkok company.

Soon the shimmering material was to be seen in fashion collections by Valentina and Pierre Balmain, the Canaletto Room of Windsor Castle, the various homes of heiress Barbara Hutton, London's Savoy Hotel, and the movie *Ben Hur*. By the end of the 1960's there were dozens of other silk companies besides the one founded by Thompson, and Thai silk had become perhaps the country's best-known export.

In March of 1967, while on a holiday in northern Malaysia, Jim Thompson mysteriously disappeared; no trace of him has ever been found. During his twenty-odd years in Thailand, however, he had created an industry that continues to thrive, and is a lasting memorial to a remarkable man.

– W. W.

Clockwise from top left: Jim Thompson; Silk-weaving; Jim Thompson overseeing a silk weaver at work; Jim Thompson's shop; Facing page, top, left: Modern sculpture by Montien Boonma; top, right, top to bottom: Paintings by Sompop Budtarad; bottom, left to right: Paintings by Kamin Lertchaiprasert.

The Contemporary Art Scene

The contemporary art of Thailand is full of paradoxes and enigmas. It has its own genesis and turning points which are often baffling and inexplicable. To trace its development during the past five decades one has to take into account that such complex processes of tradition and change are divergent and never linear.

The Thais' ability to assimilate and conglomerate art styles of other cultures with their own was apparent during the periods of Indianization, Khmerization and Sinicization. Eclecticism and coalescence are the essential characteristics which occur repeatedly in Thai art. Westernization and the cult of modernity became sources of inspiration in the visual arts through pivotal figures such as Corrado Feroci (better known as Silpa Bhirasri). It was he and several Thai scholars who instigated the founding of the School of Fine Arts which later became Silpakorn University.

When King Bhumibol Adulyadej ascended the throne in 1946 the contemporary art scene was still blossoming. The National Exhibition of Art, which began in 1949, became the main arena for Thai artists to display their concepts and virtuosity which were encouraged to reflect contemporary life by means of study from life and nature. It was a shift from the idealized perception of tradition-al Thai art to Western pedagogic standards of artistic representation. However, at times Thai artists looked back to tradition for revitalization. The search for arcadia and nostalgia caused them to explore themes related to the lost past and tranquil scenes of the countryside as the source of inspiration. Serene images of women bathing, children playing games, and wooden houses on stilts by the canals were favorite themes for tempera painting and printmaking.

During the 1960's, King Bhumibol Adulyadej's fascination with portrait and life painting became an inspirational source for numerous Thai painters. Not only did His Majesty preside over opening ceremonies of the National Exhibition of Arts, his oil paintings were also displayed. Artists who worked closely with him were the late Indonesian painter Raden Basoeki Abdullah and Piriya Krairiksh. Frequently, Thai artists were invited to Chitralada Palace to attend painting sessions with life models.

Exposure to contemporary Western art styles through the mass media and travels abroad allowed Thai artists to venture into abstract art. Abstraction became regarded as an international language which could be practiced and understood by all nationalities. Several Thai artists attempted to conglomerate the formalism of Western art with the use of spiritual symbols and indigenous colors to allow abstract art to be acceptable and easily interpreted among local viewers. In reaction to abstraction, reinterpretation of Buddhist art was encouraged by various Thai painters as a means to preserve cultural heritage and national identity.

Thus, figurative art took many forms of expression which included socially oriented and political art in the 1970's when civilians and the military clashed in bloody riots and demonstrations. The Artists' Front of Thailand and the Open Exhibition of Thailand produced important activities related to the movement for democracy.

During the 1980's and 1990's, government and corporate intervention in the arts scene resulted mainly in art that serves national identity and business enterprise. Art contests and exhibitions related to national pride, royal birthday cycles and religious celebrations were promoted by patrons to reflect patriotism and imagined nationhood. The production of art objects for a consumer society has become common due to demand from both the corporate and government sectors. Despite control of artistic expression through consensus art there are those whose concept and work thrive to reflect the entropic conditions of contemporary life resulting from pollution, ecological collapse, social malaise, violence and corruption.

– DR APINAN POSHYANANDA
Chulalongkorn University

Thai Movie Industry

Since the first movie was shown in Thailand on June 9, 1897, Thailand has produced some four thousand films. However, the modern period of Thai cinema really began after the Second World War, and coincided with the beginning of His Majesty the King's reign. Between 1945–7, only ten films were produced, but by 1948, fifty films a year were being produced. This burst of activity was dampened by political uncertainty in the 1950's. The movie industry got right back on track in the 1960's, a period many regard as the "Golden Age" of Thai movies. It was a time dominated by two stars: Mitr Chaibancha and Petchara Chaowaraj. From 1961 to 1970, these two dominated the business; nearly half of the eighty movies made a year during this period starred the dynamic duo. Sadly, Mit's tragic death in a helicopter accident while filming Insee Thong brought the period to an end. A new generation of direc-

tors and stars, and new technology (filmmakers started switching from 16 mm to 35 mm films from 1970) ushered in a new era. New talents such as Piak Poster and MC Chatri Chalermyukol and newly graduated directors such as Yutthana Mukdasanit, Apichat Photipairoj and ML Pantevanop Tevakul all brought new and exciting ideas to the screen. Epics (in the style of David Lean), social realism, documentaries and musicals made their way to the screen as new production companies cranked out a staggering two hundred movies a year (this did not decline until the 1980's), helped, no doubt, by a government tax on imported films. The 1970's produced such classics as Wai Onlawon (starring Piak Poster), Thong Poon Kok Paw, Rassadorn Tern Khan (both starring MC Chatri Chalermyukol) and Phlae Kao (starring Choet Songsee); the latter movie launched the career of evergreen action star, Sorapong Chatri. Another remarkable film was Look Isan, Wichit Kunawut's moving story of poverty in the northeast of Thailand. The 1980's was a period of crisis and reflection for those in the movie industry. Production

dropped to one hundred films a year, mainly due to competition from foreign films, the availability of nationwide television, and home video. Nevertheless, several award-winning films did get made. Mua Puen (starring MC Chatri Chalermyukol), Nam Phu and Phi Sua Le Dok Mai (both starring Yutthana Mukdasanit) are excellent examples of well-made Thai movies.

In recent years, movie production has declined further. Those films that have been made have often been of the "formula" genre (action, teen romance and so on), with little room for more artistic work. But there are still artists working in film production; the recent commercial success of MC Chatri Chalermyuokol's telling look at teenage drug addiction, Sia Die, shows that quality films can score at the box office. Perhaps one of the most heartening developments during the past years has been the formation, in 1984, of the National Film Archive. So many irreplaceable films have already been lost but the archive has managed to save over four hundred films. Given the fact that the movie business in Thailand is already nearly a hundred years old, it is heartening to know that some of that celluloid history is now being preserved for future generations.

– J. C.

Top, left to right: Nam Phu poster; Movie poster featuring star Sombat Metanee; Ploy Talay poster; Center: A movie billboard; Left, clockwise from top, left: Still from Plae Khan; Still from Luk Isan; Still of star of Nam Phu.

Popular Music

Top: His Majesty The King playing the trumpet with a band; Below, clockwise from top, left: Michael Jackson in concert, Bangkok; Maestro Acharn Ken Dalao (right) performs the traditional form of *mor lam*; Thai classical music meets jazz—the electric guitar and the *ranat*; Tewan Sapsanyakorn, Thailand's internationally known jazz musician;

Below, left: Spectacular chorus girls at a typical *luk thung* concert; Below, right: Pompuang, *luk thung* megastar; Overleaf: Mural at Wat Phra Keo.

Since the beginning of Thai society, Thais have cannily assimilated various kinds of music and produced something that is distinctly Thai. This is certainly the case with classical music, which has influences from India, China, Cambodia, Laos, Myanmar and Indonesia but is still very Thai in character. The same can be said for both folk and popular music.

Thai popular music really started during the 1930's when musicians started to experiment with Western orchestration and Thai melodies.

This led to the development of the romantic ballad style, *luk grung*, often associated with Bangkok, and *luk thung*, or Thai country music. *Luk thung* (literally, "child of the field") has developed over the past forty years as a blend of *pleng talad* ("market songs"), *lam tad* (a narrative folk style from the central region), *pleng puen bahn* (folk songs), *ram wong* (folk dances), classical music and elements from *likay*, a kind of traveling comedy show. Like many of Asia's indigenous pop styles, *luk thung* came to maturity in the 1950's and 60's led by the undisputed King of *luk thung*, Suraphon Sombatchareon. The songs are always plaintive, emotionally sung and

form part of a spectacular show that might feature eight or nine singers and a chorus of dancers.

Another local style that has risen to popularity during the past thirty years is *mor lam*. This is the traditional folk music of the Laotian people of the northeast. It is based on the rhythms of the *khaen*, or bamboo reed organ and features a male and female singer who "joust" all night. Both the traditional and a more pop-oriented form are still immensely popular throughout the nation.

At the same time as these forms were developing, Thai pop music (based on the music of Western pop but with Thai lyrics and melodies) came of age. In the 1960's this was known as *wong shadow* (*wong* means "group" and shadow comes from the 1960's British pop group of the same name) but more recently it has become known as "string". Today, string can be rock, disco, hip hop or rap, reggae, rhythm and blues or a ballad. Superstars such as Thongchai 'Bird' Macintyre can sell a million albums and are popular in neighboring countries. They may also feature in advertising campaigns for popular consumer goods. An idea of how developed the industry is can be seen from the fact that in 1994 the music market was estimated to be worth 750 million baht and is estimated to grow to 1 billion baht by the end of 1996.

Bangkok has a lively music scene that incorporates everything from concerts by international superstars such as Michael Jackson to jazz greats such as Benny Carter. His Majesty's prowess as a jazz player is well-known and has spurred local musicians to develop jazz in Thailand. Internationally known multi-instrumentalist Tewan Sapsanyakorn plays to packed houses in the capital, as well as prestigious overseas jazz festivals such as the North Sea Jazz Festival. Tewan, along with Thai classical music masters such as Fong Nam, have also experimented with fusions that mix Thai classical music with jazz and rock music.

– J. C.

8

MANAGING THE ENVIRONMENT

Phaichitr Uathavikul

O VER THE PAST THREE DECADES, THAILAND HAS SUCCEEDED IN
MAINTAINING AN AVERAGE ECONOMIC GROWTH RATE OF AROUND
7 PERCENT PER ANNUM, ONE OF THE HIGHEST SUSTAINED RATES
IN THE WORLD.

This achievement has, however, been attained at a high price in terms of the natural resource base and the environment. It has become increasingly clear that unless the present trend of sharply deteriorating natural resources and rising pollution can be arrested and reversed, long-term growth will become unsustainable. In this essay I shall single out certain problem areas for discussion as an indication of the seriousness of the present situation and its implication for the future growth and development of the country.

Diminishing Resources

Thailand has a total land area of about 513,115 square kilometers (320,696,950 rai[1]) of which approximately 167 million rai, or around 52 percent, are suitable for agriculture. As a result of population pressures and the failure to change over to a more intensive form of agricultural production, an increasing amount of land has been cleared and brought under cultivation with

catastrophic results to the forest cover. By the mid-1980's, about 167 million rai of land had been brought under agricultural use, indicating that most of the land suitable for agriculture had been used up, and further expansion could be accomplished only through the use of marginal land. Between 1986 and 1990, an additional 16 million rai were brought under agricultural cultivation, leading to lower productivity and increasing deterioration in land quality and the environment in general.[2]

Soil erosion has become a particularly serious problem affecting about 107 million rai of agricultural land. This is equivalent to about 65 percent of all land suitable for agriculture. Inappropriate agricultural practices, including improper use of chemical fertilizers, have led to a rapid increase in saline and acidic soil. It has been found, for instance, that by 1992 no less than 28 percent of all land in the northeast had been affected by salinity to some degree.[3]

In the case of water, another basic resource, the overall availability remains good[4], but this should be considered in the context of a rapid increase in the demand and the potential for shortages in certain key areas of the country. The overall demand for water in 1990 was about 33,000 million cubic meters and this is projected to rise to 45,000 million cubic meters by the year 2000.[5] Shortages are already causing concern in such areas as the Bangkok Metropolitan Region (BMR) and have become serious in the case of the Eastern Seaboard industrial complexes. The overall water quality in major rivers and waterways remains good except in the vicinity of large urban areas. For instance, the water quality in the lower reaches of the Chao Phraya and the Tha-Chine rivers has deteriorated sharply, reaching a level of pollution which renders the water unfit even for industrial purposes.[6]

The forest cover of the country has dwindled rapidly. Between 1960 and 1983, the average loss was as high as 3.3 million rai per year. The

government canceled all logging concessions in 1989, but the destruction continues at more than 1 million rai annually. The forest cover declined from 53 percent of the total land area in 1961 to only 26 percent in 1993.[7] It is self-evident that this trend, unless it is reversed soon, will lead to catastrophic results in climatic conditions, water resources and the whole ecological system. A similar fate has affected mangrove forests. In 1961 there were 2.3 million rai nationwide, but this amount declined by over 50 percent to less than 1.1 million rai in 1993.[8] The continued destruction of mangrove forests contributed to a precipitous decline in coastal marine resources. In conjunction with overfishing, it has led to a drastic reduction of catches in the Gulf of Thailand.

Environmental Pollution

The rapid deterioration in the natural resource base as outlined above is matched by the decline in the quality of the environment. Water pollution has become an endemic problem in urban areas of all sizes. Most of the

canals and waterways in urban areas have become heavily polluted as a result of the indiscriminate discharge of untreated household, commercial and industrial effluents. This has in turn led to the sharp deterioration of

water quality in all major rivers in the vicinity of cities. The Public Works Department has drawn up a plan, which was endorsed by the Cabinet, to invest 41 billion baht for the construction of treatment facilities in thirty-six provinces, while the Bangkok Metropolitan Administration has partially implemented a scheme costing 34 billion baht.[9] It should be noted, however, that even if the BMR program is fully implemented, it will only be able to handle 40 percent of the total daily effluents of approximately 3 million cubic meters.

Air pollution has also become a matter of increasing concern. In 1994, the concentration

Left, top: Water in the lower reaches of the Chao Phraya river is badly polluted; Left, bottom: Polluted shoreline in Phuket; Above: A traffic policeman wears a mask to protect himself from traffic fumes. Above: Toxic waste in Klong Toey port.

of suspended particulate matters (SPM) in the vicinity of major thoroughfares and congested streets in Bangkok was found to be almost 3.5 times the permissible level, while that of SPM below 10 microns (PM-10), which are particularly hazardous to health, was 2.6 times the maximum allowable limit. Carbon monoxide in similar areas has increased sharply and has almost reached the permissible limit.[10] Other large urban areas are also facing similar problems.

Another increasing health hazard in urban areas is the problem of garbage collection and disposal. In 1994, for the entire kingdom, the quantity of garbage generated per day increased from 30,000 tons to 33,000 tons, an increase of 10 percent. The Bangkok Metropolitan Area (BMA) accounted for 23 percent of the total amount, and of the remaining 26,000 tons, about 70 percent was left in open garbage dumps or burnt in the open air. Even in the BMA, over 13 percent of the garbage collected was still left in open garbage dumps.[11] Hazardous waste has become a major problem. In 1994, the total amount of such waste was estimated at 1.35 million tons, 990,000 tons of which were produced by the industrial sector.[12] Only about 300,000 tons could be properly treated and disposed of, leaving about 1 million tons unaccounted for. As for contaminated waste from hospitals and medical establishments, it was found that in 1993, of the 871 hospitals in Bangkok and the provinces, only 423 (49 percent) had treatment facilities for contaminated waste.[13]

Cultural Preservation

The preservation of historical, artistic and cultural sites and buildings has become another area of increasing concern. Owing to the long history of Thailand, lasting more than seven hundred years, historical sites abound in the country. On the other hand, since most of the buildings were constructed of wood, not many have survived except those from the Ratanakosin period. Even these are quickly disappearing, and if adequate preservation is not undertaken in the near future, most of these irreplaceable cultural heritage structures will be lost forever. Since the promulgation of the new Environment Act in 1992, The Department of Fine Arts, Ministry of Education and The Ministry of Science, Technology and Environment have increased considerably their activities in surveying and registering such sites and buildings in several provinces, but it should be noted that budgetary allocations for preservation work remain very limited.[14]

Management without Commitment

The rapid deterioration in the natural resource base and the environment has thus become a serious threat to the quality of life of the people and to the prospect for long-term growth of the country as a whole. This fact is well-recognized by the general public. In a nationwide opinion poll carried out in July 1995, over fifty thousand respondents were asked to rank the ten most urgent problems which should be tackled by the recently-elected government. Environmental problems were ranked fourth by Bangkok

Right, top to bottom:
Flooding in Bangkok;
Passengers in "long-tailed boats" in the *klongs* of Thonburi;
Inset: Close-up of restoration work.

residents and eighth by people in the rest of the country.[15] The difference in ranking is probably an accurate reflection of the seriousness of the problem as perceived by the urban and rural segments of the population.

This relatively high level of public awareness and concern should be viewed in the context of the capacity of the country to manage its environmental problems. In March 1992, a new Act for the conservation and promotion of the environment was enacted, giving the government unprecedented power to act decisively in this matter. The Ministry of Science, Technology and Energy was extensively reorganized as the Ministry of Science, Technology and Environment (MOSTE), with three major departments empowered to deal with environmental affairs.[16] Tackling environmental problems would also require a substantial outlay of financial resources. Although still a less developed country, almost forty years of steady economic growth have resulted in a relatively high degree of financial capacity in Thai society. The government budget of approximately US$29 billion in 1995, although small by international standards, provides a substantial financial base for effectively tackling the most urgent environmental problems. An Environment Fund of 5.5 billion baht (US$220 million) was also initiated in 1992 as a revolving fund to supplement budget allocations. As for manpower, the eight hundred officials in the three departments of MOSTE are only a small part of the large pool of relatively well-qualified staff which could be drawn on for the purpose. In sum, it would be fair to conclude that there is currently a high level of public awareness with a strong legal framework supported by a specific organization, substantial financial resources and manpower. And yet, there have been few tangible results in arresting, let alone reversing, the trend toward rapid deterioration of the natural resource base and the degradation of the environment. Why is this the case? It is essential to try and find a credible answer to this question as it is an indispensable first step toward finding an effective solution to the problem.

A facile answer would be to point to the lack of implementation of the extensive provisions of the 1992 Environment Act. It would, therefore, be necessary to begin with a brief examination of this law by reviewing its salient points. The Enhancement and Conservation of National Environmental Quality Act, B.E. 2535, was enacted on March 29, 1992 and came into force on June 4 of the same year. It differs from its predecessor, the Environment Act of 1975, in two important areas.

Firstly, it endows MOSTE and related agencies with direct enforcement power while the 1975 Act limited them largely to an advisory role. Secondly, the Act greatly broadens the areas of competence of both the National Environment Board (NEB) and MOSTE. It is by nature an enabling Act, with comprehensive provisions in five essential areas, namely: (i) protection of the environment; (ii) pollution control; (iii) establishment of an environment fund; (iv) promotional measures; and (v) implementation. The Act also establishes basic principles concerning popular participation, decentralization, the role of non-governmental organizations (NGOs) and the Polluter Pays Principle. Two special measures were also created to deal specifically with urgent and critical problem areas. These are the "environmental protection areas" and the "pollution control areas" where government agencies have been given extensive power of control and enforcement.[17] In short, the Act provides a comprehensive legal framework for the effective management of environmental problems, and the lack of action on the ground can in no way be attributed to a lack of power on the part of the

Left: A view of the forest reserve in the northeast; Right: A public sign to promote green consciousness.

systematic study. However, it is felt that even a preliminary analysis would be useful if it could point out the problem areas or significant developments which should receive special attention. Unless the problem of the lack of meaningful action is resolved, and resolved quickly, the prospect for sustainable growth might be seriously compromised.

Four Sets of Influences

In order to gain a better understanding of what has been happening in the efforts to manage environmental affairs in recent years, it is useful to divide Thai society into four sectors because they differ substantially in terms of the fundamental problems involved. These are: (i) the public sector; (ii) the private sector; (iii) academics, mass media and non-governmental organizations (NGOs); and (iv) the general public. A brief discussion of the four components is presented below as a basis for attempting to locate the causes underlying the lack of meaningful and effective action in the management of environmental affairs.

The Public Sector

The most notable feature of the government's environmental policy is its lack of initiative. This has been compounded by its apparent unwillingness, or inability, to resolve conflicts among the various ministries and agencies involved.[18] For clarity, it would be useful to divide the public sector into two parts, namely, politicians and the civil servants.

The Politicians. The most striking feature characterizing the problem discussed is the almost total lack of interest among Members of Parliament and Cabinet Ministers. In the long and extensive policy statement delivered to Parliament by the Chuan government on October 21, 1992, the problem of the environment was subsumed under various policy issues, including agriculture, energy, tourism and the rehabilitation of the Bangkok Metropolitan Region. During the two years and seven months of its tenure, the government had to face four

government. Plausible explanations for the lack of action would have to be sought elsewhere.

It is now more than four years since the 1992 Environment Act came into force, but there has been little action on the ground. The first elected government to take office after the promulgation of the Act was that of Prime Minister Chuan Leekpai (October 1992–May 1995). The action taken by the government regarding the environment can perhaps be best described as "business as usual". Unfortunately, no systematic study has been conducted on implementing the provisions of the Act. The following discussion is based on the author's personal involvement in, and close observation of, the process of environmental management. It should, therefore, be regarded only as an indicative analysis, the conclusions of which would remain by necessity tentative, pending the results of a more

Top: The Mee Klang Waterfall at Doi Inthanon park. Doi Inthanon encloses Thailand's tallest peak.

Below, clockwise from top left: Signpost to Kaengtana National Park; Doi Inthanon National Park; Wildlife at Khao Yai; Tao Ton National Park; Ramkhamhaeng National Park.

separate no-confidence debates in Parliament. The first three debates, taken together, occupied about seven days and nights when opposition Members of Parliament took turns castigating the government for all the sins of commission and omission. And yet, there was hardly any mention of environmental problems.[19] It was clear that, as far as the politicians were concerned, these problems were strictly a non-issue. Environmental affairs were simply not on the political agenda. The fourth censure debate, which brought down the government, was devoted almost entirely to the problem of land reform and the use of forest reserves, but the main thrust of the attack was concerned with

the question of corruption and malfeasance rather than the detrimental effects on the rapidly dwindling forest cover.

Why were environmental problems not on the national political agenda? Obviously, it was because the politicians did not perceive that there was any significant political pressure with regard to these problems. At first sight, this may seem surprising in view of the high level of public awareness as evidenced by the results of the opinion survey cited previously. Furthermore, a large number of NGOs have also been active in opposing many large-scale projects due to environmental concerns. A closer examination of the situation would reveal, however, that the

National Parks of Thailand

Fifty years ago, some 70 percent of Thailand was under forest cover, the population numbered only around 15 million, and few Thais were concerned about environmental and wildlife conservation. Very soon, however, this situation changed. The population expanded at a rapid pace and the demand for farmland increased accordingly; by 1991, the forest cover had diminished to between 25 and 28 percent by official estimates, though many environmental organizations believe the true figure to be around 20 percent or even less.

Concern over these developments led in 1960 to the Wild Animals Reservation Act, which set aside areas for "the conservation of wildlife habitat so that wildlife can freely breed and increase their population in the natural environment" and in 1961 to the National Parks Act, which states that land declared a national park should be "preserved in its natural state for the benefit of public education and enjoyment".

The first national park, Khao Yai, was established in 1962. Covering 2,172 square kilometers and less than three hours by car from Bangkok, it includes parts of four provinces and has recently been selected as an ASEAN Natural Heritage Site. After a relatively slow period—a decade after Khao Yai only four other parks had been gazetted—there was a major surge of activity which has not yet abated. At present there are seventy-seven national parks, thirty-five wildlife sanctuaries and forty-six non-hunting areas, along with other protected zones such as national forest reserves, botanical gardens, arboretums and biosphere reserves. Altogether these cover more than

12 percent of the country, one of the highest ratios of protected area to a total country area in the world.

There is a darker side to these impressive statistics, however. A number of the major parks have suffered from illegal encroachment by settlers and loggers, while the growth of tourism has brought not only nature-lovers but also problems of pollution and resorts being built on park land. The effects of an excess of visitors to Khao Yai forced the Tourism Authority to close a hotel and golf course it operated within the park. Constant vigilance is necessary to prevent further threats to the remaining natural heritage.

The parks vary widely in scenery and wildlife. Phu Kradung in Loei Province is centered on a mountain crowned by a 60-square-kilometer plateau, while Tarutao, the first marine national park, consists of fifty-one mountainous islands extending over 1,490 square kilometers in the Indian Ocean. Doi Inthanon, in the northern province of Chiang Mai, incorporates Thailand's highest mountain (2,565 meters).

– W. W.

politicians were probably correct in their assessment. The public might be aware and concerned, but its concern has been almost entirely passive, while NGOs are perceived as small groups of extremists with little or no grassroots support. Such an assessment may be an oversimplification, but it is apparent that unless public awareness and concern are transformed into tangible political pressure, environmental problems will continue to be largely ignored at all levels of the political process.

However, a more hopeful note was struck recently when the government of Mr Banharn Silpa-archa made its policy statement to Parliament on July 26, 1995. Environmental affairs were once again singled out as a major policy issue covering a wide range of problems from natural resources to art and culture.[20]

As a statement of intent, it is commendable, but at the time of writing it is not clear whether there has been a change in form or substance. Most of the detailed policies could be found in the policy statements of previous governments but they were scattered under different headings. Only time will tell if this development signifies a real departure in policy emphasis, or is merely a matter of presentation.

The Civil Servants. It has now become fashionable for government officials to pay lip service to the importance of sustainable development. Close observation of their actions, especially with regard to large-scale investment projects, would, however, lead to the almost inescapable conclusion that many senior officials remain antagonistic to environmental considerations and

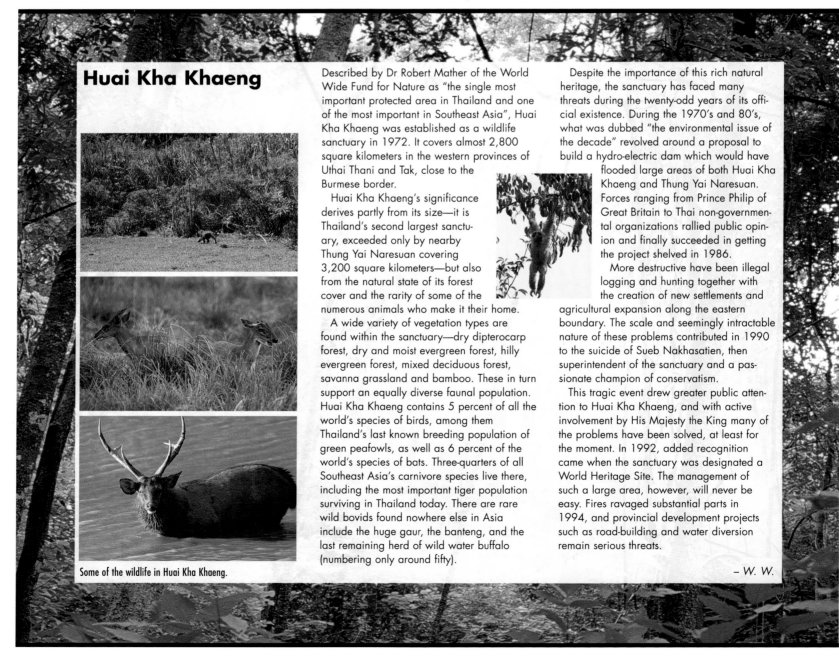

Huai Kha Khaeng

Described by Dr Robert Mather of the World Wide Fund for Nature as "the single most important protected area in Thailand and one of the most important in Southeast Asia", Huai Kha Khaeng was established as a wildlife sanctuary in 1972. It covers almost 2,800 square kilometers in the western provinces of Uthai Thani and Tak, close to the Burmese border.

Huai Kha Khaeng's significance derives partly from its size—it is Thailand's second largest sanctuary, exceeded only by nearby Thung Yai Naresuan covering 3,200 square kilometers—but also from the natural state of its forest cover and the rarity of some of the numerous animals who make it their home.

A wide variety of vegetation types are found within the sanctuary—dry dipterocarp forest, dry and moist evergreen forest, hilly evergreen forest, mixed deciduous forest, savanna grassland and bamboo. These in turn support an equally diverse faunal population. Huai Kha Khaeng contains 5 percent of all the world's species of birds, among them Thailand's last known breeding population of green peafowls, as well as 6 percent of the world's species of bats. Three-quarters of all Southeast Asia's carnivore species live there, including the most important tiger population surviving in Thailand today. There are rare wild bovids found nowhere else in Asia include the huge gaur, the banteng, and the last remaining herd of wild water buffalo (numbering only around fifty).

Despite the importance of this rich natural heritage, the sanctuary has faced many threats during the twenty-odd years of its official existence. During the 1970's and 80's, what was dubbed "the environmental issue of the decade" revolved around a proposal to build a hydro-electric dam which would have flooded large areas of both Huai Kha Khaeng and Thung Yai Naresuan. Forces ranging from Prince Philip of Great Britain to Thai non-governmental organizations rallied public opinion and finally succeeded in getting the project shelved in 1986.

More destructive have been illegal logging and hunting together with the creation of new settlements and agricultural expansion along the eastern boundary. The scale and seemingly intractable nature of these problems contributed in 1990 to the suicide of Sueb Nakhasatien, then superintendent of the sanctuary and a passionate champion of conservatism.

This tragic event drew greater public attention to Huai Kha Khaeng, and with active involvement by His Majesty the King many of the problems have been solved, at least for the moment. In 1992, added recognition came when the sanctuary was designated a World Heritage Site. The management of such a large area, however, will never be easy. Fires ravaged substantial parts in 1994, and provincial development projects such as road-building and water diversion remain serious threats.

– W. W.

Some of the wildlife in Huai Kha Khaeng.

regard them as an impediment to economic development. At the same time, those officials who are more sympathetic, nonetheless, remain rather passive. Action in support of environmental concerns would often lead to conflicts with other government agencies, powerful businessmen and influential local leaders. Under these circumstances, the safest option is for officials to protect themselves by appearing to follow the rules and regulations without actually taking meaningful action on the ground. There is evidence, however, that an increasing number of the younger senior officials and middle-level personnel are becoming genuinely committed and are prepared to take the required action as provided by the law.

The lack of interest on the part of politicians and the reluctance among government officials go a long way toward explaining why the legal power vested in the state and the considerable resources available have not been used to deal effectively with the urgent problem of environmental degradation.

The Private Sector

Three elements appear to characterize the attitude of the private sector toward environmental problems. The first is the unsurprising view that satisfying environmental requirements would only increase costs and thus reduce competitiveness. As a developing country, Thailand cannot yet afford the "luxury" of environmental niceties as is the case for Western countries. The second view, closely related to the first, holds that it is, nevertheless, necessary to give the appearance that business enterprises do care about the environment and are already attempting to do something about it. Environmental matters are, therefore, merely a matter of public relations where the basic objective is to provide the company with a good image. And if pressed further by suggestions that businesses should be doing more, there is always the third element which can serve as a useful refuge. Businesses have already fulfilled their duty by paying taxes and has actually done more than their fair share by

supporting many good causes, including those dealing with the environment. Demand for more action should thus be directed at the government rather than businesses.

However, the situation on the ground may not be quite as bleak as outlined above. There appears to be a growing number of young business leaders with a high degree of social awareness and social responsibility. It may not be too optimistic to hope that these leaders will succeed in helping to build a business culture which is more responsive to the needs of society as a whole.

Academics, Mass Media and Non-Governmental Organizations

The third group is probably the most aware and active of the four components of Thai society. Its activities can, however, be characterized as largely "negative". Academics and NGOs tend to concentrate almost exclusively on protesting against government policies and business practices deemed harmful to the environment, while the mass media is mainly focused on sensational issues. There is, of course, a number of groups and organizations engaged in "positive", that is, constructive activities, but, as a rule, these tend to be small localized bodies which are not well-known. The results of this negative emphasis are twofold. Firstly, academics and NGOs are generally regarded by the government and among

business circles as "trouble-makers" bent on impeding the progress of the country. Secondly, there is minimal continuity in the work of the NGOs. Protests are organized, necessarily, on an ad hoc basis, and once the issues are resolved, the various organizations disband and go their own way. There has thus been no opportunity for building up the sustained momentum necessary for marshaling public opinion in a more positive direction, that is, pressurizing government and business to undertake measures to conserve and rehabilitate the environment. As long as academics and NGOs remain largely negative in their approach, their effectiveness will remain rather limited.

The People
There can be little doubt that the general public is well aware of the problems posed by a rapidly deteriorating environment. The question is, if this was the case, why have the people not done anything about it. It should be recognized at the outset that there is a wide gap separating public awareness from public action.[21] The general public is, by its very nature, an amorphous entity while public action requires focus and organization. And yet, in the final analysis, the only pressure that is sufficiently potent to force both the government and businesses to take proper care of the environment can only come from the people themselves. The question thus becomes one of bridging the gap between public awareness and public action, of turning passive awareness into active participation.

When we put the characteristics of the four components of Thai society together, as briefly discussed above, the overall problem becomes clear. There has not been much action on the ground because there is a general lack of commitment in Thai society regarding efforts to

manage the environment. Commitment implies sacrifice—sacrifice on the part of all parties concerned. Unfortunately, until now, the controlling motivation has merely been one of passive concern. Few have taken the necessary step of making it their business to do something about the rapidly deteriorating situation.

Toward More Effective Management
If the above discussion is not too far from the truth, it should serve as a basis for indicating the direction of action that needs to be taken to achieve a more effective system of management. Left to themselves, it is likely that neither the government nor the business sector will have sufficient commitment to take up the challenge and provide the necessary leadership. The pressure has to come from the people, but, as pointed out, the public remains amorphous and unorganized. The only group remaining is the third one comprising academics, the mass media and NGOs. It is this group which must bear the brunt of providing the moving force for a thorough reform of the management system.

In politics, efforts should be focused on putting environmental affairs on the national political agenda. Such efforts will have to take various forms ranging from direct political action to more effective expression of public opinion. Direct action may include, for instance, the creation of a "green party" to push for social reform in general and accelerated environmental action in particular. Or it may take the form of sustained dialogue with political parties to persuade them to include environmental matters in their own political platform. Indirect action could, for example, consist of a campaign to "write to your Member of Parliament" or consciousness-raising in the mass media, workshops, seminars and public hearings. The critical element here is to convince politicians that there is a strong and direct link between public environmental concern and voting.[22]

In the case of the civil service, it would be necessary to provide a strong motivation for officials to carry out their duties properly. Part of

Top: The striking coastal rock formations of Phi Phi island.

this motivation would come automatically from the politicians if and when they are made more responsive to public opinion as discussed above. Another development which should prove helpful is an amendment to the 1992 Environment Act. The Act firmly establishes the Polluter Pays Principle and confirms the right of individuals to receive compensation from the state for damages sustained from action by government agencies or state enterprises.[23] But there is no provision for bringing damage suits to a court of law by individuals, thus rendering it extremely difficult for action to be taken against state agencies. If the Act could be amended accordingly, with clear-cut provisions for prosecution, it would be directly in the interest of officials to enforce the law in a more effective manner.

As for the private sector, it would also be

Below: Endangered species fighting for survival in Thailand— tigers and elephants.

Endangered Species

Not very many years ago, Thailand contained an extraordinarily rich variety of flora and fauna, and in many ways this is still true. One authority has estimated that 6 percent of all the world's known vascular plants are found in the country, together with 10 percent of the birds, 5 percent of the reptiles, and 3 percent of the amphibians. New species are still being discovered, among them the hog-nosed bat, the world's smallest mammal.

Much of this natural wealth, however, has either vanished within living memory or is at present seriously endangered, due to environmental destruction, hunting, or assorted human demands. The Javan rhinoceros, for example, was once plentiful in Thai jungles. Unfortunately, its horn was also much prized as an ingredient in Chinese medicine, to such an extent that during the nineteenth century some eight thousand of them were exported annually to China, with the result that none are left today. Also gone are Schomburgk's deer and, probably, the Sumatran rhino and the kouprey, a wild

bovine which was only identified in 1939. Close to extinction is the tiger, only about 250 of which are left according to one expert on big cats, as well as the leopard, the Malayan sun bear, the Asiatic black bear, Eld's deer, the Sumatran rhinoceros (smallest and most primitive of the species) and the wild buffalo.

The elephant was once a prominent symbol of Thailand; wild herds roamed the forests, and more than twenty thousand domesticated elephants were working in the northern teak industry at the end of the last century. Today, thanks to habitat loss and poaching for ivory, the number of wild elephants has declined to between two thousand and three thousand, and around five thousand are domesticated. Khao Yai, the national park with the largest elephant population, is estimated to have only about two hundred.

At least thirteen of the country's amphibians and thirty-one of its reptiles are endangered, according to Charuchin Naphitaphat, a leading authority, among them the river terrapin, the sea turtle, and the freshwater crocodile; saltwater crocodiles are probably already extinct.

The earliest official effort to deal with the problem of declining wildlife was, appropriately enough, the Wild Elephant Protection Act of 1900, which in its early form stipulated that one of every five wild elephants captured had to be given to the government. A more general law, the Wild Animals Reservations and Protection Act, was only enacted in 1960, however, when the loss was already severe; the creation of national parks a year later also signaled a growing concern.

The ultimate success of these steps will depend on broadening public awareness and support, a process in which the involvement of the Royal Family plays a significant role. King Bhumibol Adulyadej, for example, has launched numerous reforestation projects and wildlife breeding centers and frequently refers to conservation in his public addresses, while Queen Sirikit is patron of the Wildlife Fund Thailand, established in 1983 and affiliated to the World Wide Fund for Nature.

"Thailand has enjoyed a favorable habitat," the King told guests at his birthday celebration several years ago. "But it must be preserved so that it will not change from a land of gardens and rice into a desert."

–W. W.

useful to begin by enacting an amendment to the 1992 Environment Act. Article 96 stipulates that polluters will have to pay for damages caused by their action. These damages are defined as including the costs for the state to clean up the pollution; however, there is no mechanism established for individuals to take action against polluters. An amendment providing for such action would obviously go a long way toward making it a matter of self-interest for private enterprises to keep any pollution within the limits stipulated by law. Another useful course of action would be the encouragement of the non-government sector to establish an effective organization for consumer protection.[24] Such organizations would make it a matter of self-interest for businesses to become a more responsible corporate member of society. Other related matters include action such as eco-labeling, consumer intelligence and campaigns linking public opinion with consumer preference in the selection of consumer goods and services.

It has been pointed out that the third group, that is, the academics, the mass media and NGOs, will have to serve as the main mechanism for bringing about the necessary changes in Thai society for effective management of the environment. The critical factor here is to change the focus of academics and NGOs from a negative to a more positive and constructive emphasis in their activities. Concerted efforts should also be made to persuade the mass media to rely less on sensationalism and to pay more attention to constructive coverage of the news. To this end it would be necessary for academics to take a leadership role. As opinion leaders they would have to make a sustained effort to educate the public and all parties concerned regarding the need for constructive action in this field. Measures should also be

taken to strengthen the NGOs. These should include an amendment to the tax laws to increase tax allowances for contributions, to allow for more state subsidies as well as membership drives to broaden the base of NGOs and make them more directly related to grassroots developments. It would also be necessary for various funding agencies, local and international, to pay more attention to small local organizations which are quietly implementing useful and constructive projects. Too often, assistance is only provided to large urban organizations which are well-known and are expert at raising funds.

The lack of commitment on the part of the general public remains the fundamental problem. Opinion leaders will have to make a concerted and sustained effort to make it clear that it is the responsibility of every citizen to take care of natural resources and the environment, and that it is the duty of every individual to act as a custodian of the priceless heritage to be passed on to future generations. If we do not safeguard what is ours by right, we shall be robbing our children of their ability not only to enjoy a reasonable quality of life, but also to provide for their children, because we shall have failed entirely in the process of sustainable development.

Royal Leadership—An Integrated and People-Oriented Approach

The relatively high level of awareness of environmental matters among the general public can be

Left: The King in discussion with environmental officials.

THAILAND King Bhumibol Adulyadej – The Golden Jubilee 1946-1996

traced directly to the outstanding role played by His Majesty the King. Over a period of almost half a century, His Majesty has visited all parts of the country, initiating numerous projects to improve the lives of the people:

"His Majesty...has been dedicated to development work ever since 1951, having ascended the throne as a constitutional monarch....Royal visits paid to the people in the central region...during 1953-4, and to the people in the northeastern region in 1955 familiarized His Majesty with the problems which the people were facing....His Majesty has continued to visit all parts and regions of the country which include(s) each of Thailand's seventy-five provinces...and up to this present day sets aside approximately *two hundred days out of each year* visiting the rural areas, with the determination to resolve the problems facing the people and to improve their standard of living."[25] (Emphasis supplied).

The Office of the Royal Development Projects Board (RDPB) is responsible for about 1,800 royally-initiated projects covering a wide spectrum of development problems including agriculture, the environment, public health, occupational promotion, water resources development, communications and social welfare.[26] In retrospect, it can be readily seen that there are at

least three sets of very important principles behind these royal projects which could be of great value in the attempt to achieve an effective environmental management system. It is therefore necessary to examine them in some detail.

The first basic principle is that of an integrated approach, not only in terms of integrating the various sectors, but also with regard to spatial and institutional factors, as well as environmental conservation. As has been well pointed out: "His Majesty is perhaps best known to his people for his attention to water resource development....However this is an emphasis only....Its development is seen as part of a total production system including the development and management of land resources, the provision of the necessary capital inputs, agro-technical and agronomic issues and marketing. However, His Majesty's view of integrated development goes further than sectoral integration alone. He appears to see integration also in spatial and institutional terms....His Majesty emphasizes at all times in his approach the need to look after and conserve the natural resource base of an area (;) this is always in the context of making at the same time productive use of the resources to improve living standards."[27]

Long before the concept of sustainable development became widely known and accepted, it

Top to bottom: A misty view of an unspoilt piece of natural landscape; Deforestation in Tak province, Thailand.

had already been incorporated in the royal projects. This principle is obviously of critical importance to an effective environmental management system because the ecology is a complex system consisting of many components, all of which are interrelated in essential and subtle ways. It is, therefore, not likely that a narrow approach focused on a specific problem area would succeed in producing a meaningful solution to environmental problems. This fundamental lesson does not appear to have been learned and put to good use by either the public or the private sector. The problem of reforestation is a case in point. For many years now, the government has been trying to pursue a policy of reforestation without much regard for local communities, the physical environment, or the socio-economic factors involved. Needless to say, its efforts have not met with much success. More recently, the private sector has also been involved to a large degree, but it has repeated the same mistakes. It would have been a much more productive use of scarce resources if both government and business leaders had learned from the outstanding example provided by the royal projects.

The second very important principle behind the royal projects is what might be called a people-oriented approach. The key element of these projects has always been the central importance given to the people whom the projects are intended to help. The projects were developed only after extensive consultation with the local population, thus ensuring their participation. They would also seek to ensure that basic human needs were met as a pre-condition for further developments. Field demonstrations would also be emphasized to ensure diffusion and acceptance in a framework to which the local people could relate. The central role of the people in all such projects has been well recognized: "One of the significant features of the various projects has been that they are formulated after very intimate contact and consultation with the future beneficiaries of the projects. His Majesty the King spelled out the general approach in this matter in an address delivered in November 1970. His Majesty said: "In working out a program to help people, it is necessary that you know the people you intend to help... There is no short cut. One does not know a people by merely memorizing some research papers prepared by research centers. You must meet them and like them".[28] He also said, "Development must take account of the local environment in terms of the geographical environment, the sociological environment and the psychological environment. By the local sociological environment we mean certain characteristics and ways of thinking which we cannot force people to change. We can only suggest. We cannot go in to help people by trying to make them the same as us.

However, if we go in and find out what the people really want, and then fully explain how they can best achieve their aims, the principles of development can be successfully applied."[29]

In this context, we can readily identify a basic problem of government community development and environmental projects. It is in the nature of bureaucracy that these projects would normally take the form of an activity done to the people. It would be a great step forward if the basic principle is adopted of getting "to know the people you intend to help" and closely involving them in the design and implementation of environmental projects.

The third basic principle underlying the royal projects is their area-specific nature. These projects are notable for the fine degrees of differentiation in their specific provisions according not

Above, left: A tree's branches forming a lace-like effect with the sky in the background.

only to the physical but also the socio-cultural environment: "...at the center of the King's approach is the principle that agricultural and rural development policies and strategies must vary from region to region to reflect regional needs, not only in line with the physical environmental conditions, but also in relation to the socio-economic or cultural environment. It is this appreciation of the 'reality of place' that has led the King to set up the Royal Development Study Centers."[30]

Indeed, these three principles are exemplified in the six Royal Development Study Centers[31] which have been set up to date: "One of the foremost principles of His Majesty the King's approach to agricultural development is that the development of a particular area should be undertaken in ways consistent with the local environmental, geographical and social conditions. His Majesty has therefore initiated the establishment of the Royal Development Study Centers to serve as a 'successful demonstration model'....The centers conduct research and experimentation on development methods and technology which can be disseminated to the farmers and applied to each particular area or region according to the actual conditions and nature of the problems concerned."[32]

The King's Speech

The deep concern that His Majesty has about the deterioration in the environment became known, in unmistakable terms, to the general public late in 1989. On the fourth of December of every year, a day before the King's birthday, His Majesty greets thousands of well-wishers representing people from all walks of life at

Chitralada Palace. He takes the opportunity to deliver an informal speech, touching on certain problems deemed important to Thai society. On December 4, 1989, His Majesty devoted his entire speech to the problem of the environment, covering issues of global as well as national importance.

On global issues, His Majesty dwelled at length on the problem of global warming, while concentrating on the problem of water management at the national level. His Majesty was quite specific in dealing with the problem of global warming: "There are approximately 700 billion tons of carbon in the atmosphere....The burning of fuel(s) such as charcoal, coal, petroleum and other combustibles is adding 5 billion tons of carbon to the atmosphere yearly. The destruction and burning of forests gives off 1.5 billion more tons of carbon(s)...Trees all over the world can... absorb carbon at the rate of 110 billion tons per year...(but) those very trees release carbon at the yearly rate of 55 billion tons, so we are left with only half of the benefit. Furthermore, soil and other decomposing matters emit 54.5 billion more tons. So in the end, we gain only 500 million tons, and we therefore still have a 6 billion tons deficit.... The seas give off 90 billion tons of carbon dioxide to the atmosphere, while absorbing 93 billion tons... thus there is a gain of 3 billion tons. If we add all up, we get the result that carbon dioxide in the atmosphere increases every year by 3 billion tons. And this is what worries the

Top to bottom: The Mekong river in Chiang Kan, Thailand; Fishing in the Mekong.

THAILAND King Bhumibol Adulyadej – The Golden Jubilee 1946-1996

scholars. The solution is: burn less fuel and plant more trees."[33]

His Majesty concluded by pointing out the need to study the problem calmly and reasonably, while adopting an integrated approach: "If we study the problems calmly and reasonably, we will be on our way to their solution; or at least, let us try...I see in this assembly many responsible persons who are interested in the study of different branches of knowledge at different levels. The problems I mention here concern all branches of knowledge because they concern the very existence of humanity. These problems are all interdependent."[34]

Then His Majesty went on to deal with the problem of water management: "The other day we were talking about the possibility that this country will become arid in the near future, and with no water left, we will have to import water from abroad....But I don't think it will be that bad...the water cycle in this country is still adequate, it only requires proper management. If it is well managed, water is plentiful....If we use

water with caution, as well as keeping a close control on polluted water, we can survive. The topography of Thailand is still 'favorable'. I use the word 'favorable' in the sense that this country is suitable for sustaining life, indeed, Thailand is most suitable for human settlement, but we must preserve it well, lest this country of orchards and farms...become a sterile desert. It can be protected; this can be done."[35]

His Majesty ended by making it clear what was expected from the people of Thailand: "Stop to reflect first and then set yourselves to *solve the problems* as I have hinted rather strongly to you today. May you all meet with the best, prosperity and every success."[36] (Emphasis supplied).

Because of the importance of this royal speech dedicated to the cause of environmental conservation, rehabilitation and development, the government subsequently declared December the fourth as National Environment Day. And owing to the special reverence that the Thai people have for their monarch, this day became a very special day and environmental matters became a common concern for all Thai citizens.

Prognosis

As far as the environment in Thailand is concerned, the central problem is one of management. There already exists a strong legal and organizational framework for dealing with environmental problems, as well as considerable financial resources and technical manpower which could be brought to bear on the problems, but little has been accomplished on the ground. The missing link in this state of affairs is the lack of commitment among various sectors of Thai society. The immediate need is to put environmental matters on the national political agenda and to make it a matter of good business practice for the private sector to take effective measures to improve the environment. Real and effective pressure toward these ends could, in the final analysis, come only from the people themselves. However, because the general public remains amorphous and unorganized, the leadership must come from the academics, the mass media and the NGOs sector which will have to become much more positive and constructive in their approach to the problem. Various concrete measures could be employed to bring about such a desired result.

One very hopeful aspect of the environmental problems is to be found in the prominent leadership role played by His Majesty the King, through the invaluable example of the royal projects and the strong concern expressed by His Majesty on various occasions, particularly on December 4, 1989. As the embodiment of the Thai national spirit and the source of ultimate legitimacy in Thai society, His Majesty has been instrumental in making environmental affairs a common concern of the people. If a concerted effort can be made in the near future, it would perhaps not be too optimistic to hope that a meaningful and effective system of environmental management can be developed in time to ensure that sustainable development will become a reality rather than a concept for endless debate. The future of the country depends on it.

(The author wishes to thank Dr Sumet Tantivejkul for his kind advice and assistance in the preparation of this essay.)

Above: Lumpini Park, a green lung in the city of Bangkok; Overleaf: Elephants have traditionally been used in Thailand for the hauling of teak lumber and other heavy loads. They are still used to move construction materials, even in big cities.

THAILAND King Bhumibol Adulyadej – The Golden Jubilee 1946-1996

9

DESTINATION SIAM

Mechai Viravaidya

WHEN KING CHULALONGKORN BECAME THE FIRST THAI MONARCH TO VISIT EUROPE IN 1897 LITTLE DID HE REALIZE THAT, A CENTURY LATER, HIS GRANDSON KING BHUMIBOL ADULYADEJ (KING RAMA IX) WOULD PRESIDE OVER AN ERA THAT WOULD SEE THAILAND BECOME ONE OF THE WORLD'S LEADING HOLIDAY DESTINATIONS, ESPECIALLY FOR EUROPEANS.

Amidst the pomp and pageantry of late nineteenth century royalty, King Chulalongkorn's self-education in European ways stimulated "western" interest in "Siam", a name that came to symbolize mystique, elegance and classic Asian traditions. The Thai aristocrats whom he later sent to gain higher education in Europe further solidified this image, laying the first foundations of an industry that would become a major Thai economic force and the kingdom's largest foreign exchange earning sector.

In the year His Majesty King Bhumibol Adulyadej ascended the throne, and each year throughout the following decade, about sixty thousand tourists visited Thailand. Mostly Europeans, they arrived via European airlines such as Imperial Airways (now British Airways), KLM Royal Dutch Airlines and Lufthansa. King Bhumibol's reign has indeed marked the golden era of Thai tourism. Today, Thailand boasts annual visitor arrivals of 6.7 million with projections of 10 million by the year 2000. Foreign exchange earnings are forecast at 201.6 billion baht in 1996, up from 50.02 billion baht ten years earlier. There are now about a quarter million hotel rooms in Thailand and more people are working in tourism than ever before.

Visitors are attracted by many aspects of Thailand's innate character: its graceful people and their liberal ability to accept things different, its natural beauty, resplendent culture and glorious food. Add to that a lavish shopping experience and the components of a truly remarkable holiday fall into place. Thai entrepreneurs, including many of King Chulalongkorn's protégés, were quick to capitalize on the other critical Thai advantage: its unique geographical position in the heart of Asia. The airlines that started flying to Thailand on their milk-runs from Europe to Asia led to the creation of prominent travel agencies and the establishment of hotels. Marketing soon followed with the institutionalization of the Tourism Authority of Thailand and the

Facing page: Wat Arun; Right: Paraphernalia on Siam, including a guidebook and old postcards.

formation of Thai Airways International. It was this combination of Thai commercial ingenuity and strong government support for infrastructure that created this vibrant economic sector.

Thai resilience and independence have created economic stability and facilitated the growth of Thai tourism. Thailand has avoided prolonged crisis, be they political, economic or natural, thanks predominantly to the overwhelming influence of King Bhumibol. Indeed, it was this combination of stability, product appeal and entrepreneurship that led to Visit Thailand Year in 1987, an event that commemorated King Bhumibol's sixtieth birthday and later went on to boost the global tourism industry. The marketing campaign subsequently commenced by Thai Airways International, the Tourism Authority of Thailand (TAT) and the Thai corporate sector has gone into the annals of global tourism as one of the most effective of its kind. Not only did it enhance the image of Thailand overseas and expand visitor arrivals, it also inspired similar events in Malaysia, the Philippines and Indonesia, culminating in a Visit ASEAN Year in 1992 to mark the twenty-fifth anniversary of the then six-member Association of Southeast Asian Nations.

Almost overnight, tourism became a global economic force, an industry that thrives on a pristine environment, respect for cultures and cultivation of friendships. Today, nine years later, the campaign still reverberates; there is a Visit Africa Year, a Visit Vietnam Year, even a Visit

Indonesia Decade. Globally tourism has become a US$3.4 trillion industry.

While arrivals of overseas visitors have increased rapidly, the growth of domestic tourism has been even more spectacular. An estimated 32 million Thais traveled internally in 1994, outstripping international tourism by almost five to one. Indeed, tourism is now a significant contributor to rural incomes.

Perhaps the greatest example of the link between the Thai Royal Family, cultural preservation and tourism is Her Majesty the Queen's SUPPORT Foundation where hundreds of Thai artisans in everything from silverware to basket-weaving make a living. The foundation at Bang Pa-In is one of Thailand's most visited tourist spots. Important, too, is the enduring lure of Thai silk, made all the more appealing through strong and continuous promotion by Her Majesty the Queen.

Historical Traditions

Modern-day visitors are seeing and enjoying the legacies of King Bhumibol's ancestors who gave Thailand its rich history. The Chakri Dynasty, of which King Bhumibol is the ninth monarch, was born in 1782 out of the ashes of several Burmese invasions against Ayutthaya. The final, unsuccessful Burmese attack occurred in 1785, but by then the first Chakri monarch, King Rama I, had moved the Thai capital from Thonburi across the river to present-day Bangkok while he constructed two of today's most visited tourist attractions, the Grand Palace

Top: Queen Sirikit surveys baskets weaved under the auspices of the SUPPORT Foundation; Center: Old guidebooks; Left: Bang Pa-In.

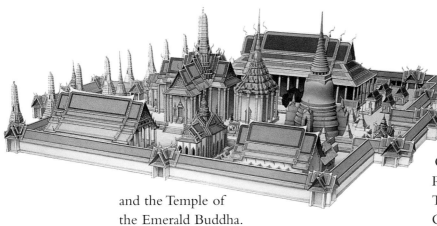

and the Temple of the Emerald Buddha.

King Rama III, grandson of King Rama I, kept European invaders at bay by limiting trade relations with them. His successor, King Rama IV (King Mongkut), achieved the same result, except that he did it by making friends with the Europeans, mastering Latin and English, and sealing a series of treaties of commerce and friendship with the United States, England, France, Prussia and several European countries. The first Thai king to correspond with world leaders, scientists and businessmen in English, he also restored another major tourist attraction, the world's tallest Buddhist Pagoda, the 127-meter Pathom Chedi, 60 kilometers west of Bangkok. It must also be quite a surprise to overseas visitors to learn that King Mongkut offered foreign assistance to the United States in the form of elephants just prior to the outbreak of the American Civil War.

King Rama IV's son, King Chulalongkorn, carried that policy several steps further, by becoming the first monarch to travel abroad, including two visits to Europe. His sons and the many young Thais he sent to study in Europe and America later returned home to start families that today are among the most prominent in Thailand. His visits to Russia and Germany so impressed their leaders that they supported Siam's independence while other European powers were rapidly colonizing its neighbors

and other nearby Asian countries. In 1876, during the reign of King Chulalongkorn, the famed Oriental Hotel opened for business. It was then that the modern chapter of Thailand's official tourism promotions began when HRH Prince Purachatra Jayakara, then Commissioner-General of the Royal State Railways of Siam, sent publicity materials on Thailand to the United States. Today, King Chulalongkorn's royal memorabilia can be seen in the Vimanmek Palace, the world's largest teakwood building and another of Bangkok's most frequently visited tourist attractions.

Those early contacts with the West were instrumental in imprinting the mystique of Siam. Authors such as W Somerset Maugham, Joseph Conrad and Noel Coward traveled through Thailand in the early 1900's, staying at

Top: An artist's impression of Wat Phra Keo; Right: Pathom Chedi.

the Oriental, recollecting their experience in celebrated travelogues and short stories. Business contacts also attracted media and public entertainment coverage. Movies, such as *The King and I*, the somewhat over-fictionalized version of an English-language tutor in the Court of Siam during the reign of King Mongkut, projected the exotic image of Siam and gave it an enduring fascination in the West.

Aviation

While media exposure was laying one of the foundations for Thailand's tourism growth, another foundation was also rising—the birth of aviation, the lifeblood of modern tourism. On January 31, 1911, a few months after King Vajiravudh (Rama VI) succeeded King Chulalongkorn, a box-like plane took off from the racetrack of the Royal Bangkok Sports Club, then located in what was suburban Bangkok, "with plenty of surrounding fields in case of emergency". That was the start of "Aviation Week" featuring demonstration flights of the European-designed flying machine by a Belgian pilot named van den Born.

Two days later, King Vajiravudh "paid an unexpected visit to the course and watched the proceedings with apparent interest," reported the *Bangkok Times Weekly*, adding, "subsequently, His

Majesty went over and inspected the aeroplane and conversed with Mr. van den Born for some minutes, after which the aviator made a short flight so that the King could see the machine start from close quarters."

In their book *Aviation in Thailand*, William Warren and veteran airlines strategist Niels Lumholdt noted that the implications of that machine were not lost on King Vajiravudh, nor on his brother, the remarkable Prince Chakrabongse, then chief of the Army General Staff. Three army officers were dispatched to France for training in March 1911 and returned to Thailand in November 1913 aboard a Brequet biplane flown on a lengthy route via Russia and Japan. They later set up an air unit in the army, the first in any Asian fighting force. This newly formed unit sent pilots to help the Allies in France toward the end of the First World War, though many of these pilots had to demonstrate their abilities under hostile conditions by driving military trucks due to the lack of aircraft at the time.

Known today as the father of Thai aviation, King Vajiravudh opened Don Muang Airport in February 1914, making it the oldest airport in the world still being used in its original location. Used initially for military, medical and mail services, it was regularly used by pioneer pilots throughout the 1920's as they flew from Europe to Asia. The first scheduled commercial airline to touch down in Thailand was KLM Royal Dutch Airlines, which landed a single-engined Fokker F-VII aircraft on October 1, 1924, on a flight from Amsterdam to Batavia (now Jakarta).

The British followed in 1933 with a flight by Imperial Airways operating flying boats, landing on the Chao Phraya river, about halfway between Don Muang and the Oriental Hotel— where the passengers were served dinner. The French, who had been involved in several airline ventures in Indochina, were also flying to

Top: Vimanmek Palace, where King Chulalongkorn's royal memorabilia is displayed; Center, left: Old postcard showing Oriental Hotel; Left, bottom: Queen Sirikit with Yul Brynner, who acted the role of King Mongkut in *The King and I*; Above: King Vajiravudh.

Bangkok by the 1930's. The German airline Lufthansa opened a Berlin-Bangkok service in July 1939.

His Majesty King Bhumibol ascended the throne in 1946 and the golden age of Thai tourism began. KLM had by then resumed flying to Thailand. By 1947, when His Majesty's reign was but a year old, Thailand had two airlines. The first, Siamese Airways Company (SAC), was set up by the Ministry of Transport and Communications, and flew from Bangkok to Chiang Mai and Chiang Rai via Phitsanulok and Lampang. In December 1947, it operated its first international service to Penang via Songkhla. Flights to Singapore were inaugurated in 1948 followed by Saigon, Phnom Penh and Hong Kong. The other airline, Pacific Overseas Airlines (Siam) Company (POAS), was a joint venture between various Thai stockholders (who owned 56 percent of the company) and the Pacific Airline Corporation of Oakland, California (which owned 44 percent). It operated four-engined Douglas DC-4s to Los Angeles via Hong Kong, Guam and Honolulu. In 1948, a third airline, Trans Asiatic Airlines (Siam) Company, an American-Filipino-Thai company that operated DC-3 aircraft to Burma, Vietnam, Macao and

Hong Kong, opened. Business was not as good as expected and the company collapsed in 1950.

SAC and POAS remained in business but began duplicating routes, leading the Thai government to decide in 1951 to buy all the shares in POAS and amalgamate the two airlines. Thus was born Thai Airways Company, Ltd (TAC), a national airline which inherited aircraft, administrative and technical staff from the two companies.

Improvements at Don Muang Airport attracted more international airlines which in turn brought increased competition for the Thai Airways Company. Thai Airways could not match the foreign airlines in aircraft type or marketing experience and lost money for each of its first nine years of operation. Various approaches to the United States for assistance failed and, in 1958, Thai Airways took the unusual step of discharging some 150 employees. At about this time the general sales manager of Scandinavian Airlines System (SAS), Hans Erik Hansen, paid a courtesy call on Lt. Commander Prasong Suchiva, the general manager of Thai Airways. They discussed cooperating to achieve economic advantage from large-scale operations through joint utilization of flight equipment, spare parts, spare engines, workshops, ground facilities as well as coordinated timetables. Thus emerged one of the world's great airline alliances.

Thai Airways had proven technical and training programs in place and had gained a high international reputation. Formed in 1946, SAS had been flying to Tokyo, Karachi, Calcutta, Rangoon, Bangkok and Hong Kong. In 1956, it lost its rights to Hong Kong and protective air policies threatened its other Asian route. A relationship with Thai Airways would strengthen its position and enable it to expand its services. On August 24, 1959, an agreement was signed to establish a new international airlines for Thailand, a joint venture between Scandinavian Airlines System (which owned 70 percent of the company) and Thai Airways (which owned 30 percent). On March 31, 1960, another agreement

was signed for SAS to provide Thai Airways with services covering administration, traffic and sales, passenger handling, planning and aircraft purchases. That year, inaugural flights were made from Bangkok to nine overseas destinations, all within the Asian region. In 1960-1, its first full year of operation, Thai International Airways carried some 83,000 passengers.

Tourism Authority of Thailand

Increased airline services nourished Thailand's tourism industry. According to official records, the 81,340 visitors in 1960 stayed an average of three days and spent a total of 196 million baht, or US$10 million, at the exchange rates of the day.

The importance of tourism had been recognized as early as 1924 when a publicity section was formed under the Royal State Railway of Siam to manage promotions as well as provide reception and facilitation services to visitors. In 1936, the Ministry of Economic Affairs proposed to the Cabinet a plan to develop and manage tourism publicity, facilitation, destinations and accommodation. The plan proposed the formation of an independent tourism body, but

it was rejected and tourism affairs were placed under the Department of Commerce. In 1949, the Publicity Department under the Prime Minister's Office proposed a tourism agency improvement project and duly had tourism affairs transferred to its control from the Ministry of Commerce and Transport. The agency was renamed the Office for the Promotion of Tourism and had its own operating budget. A year later, it was upgraded to a division called the Tourism Office.

The first independent tourism body was created during the administration of Field Marshal Sarit Thanarat. Impressed by the American tourism success which he saw during a trip to the United States, he announced in 1959 a Royal Decree on the Establishment of the National Tourist Office. Thus was born the "Tourist Organization" with its own office in a building on Sri Ayutthaya Road in Sanam Sua Pa on March 18, 1960—its official inauguration date. Three years later, its name was changed to "The Tourism Authority of Thailand (TAT)". From that moment on, national tourism promotion rapidly expanded, concentrating principally on publicity campaigns, even while recognizing the necessity to develop and conserve the country's tourism resources systematically and organize and control the travel trade.

By 1970, despite the Indochina war which ran through the 1960's and the India-Pakistan war of 1965, Thailand's annual visitor arrivals had grown to 628,671. The average length of stay had risen to 4.8 days and expenditure had risen to 2,175 million baht. Pattaya gained its

Top: Don Muang airport; Above: Shopping for antiques.

THAILAND King Bhumibol Adulyadej – The Golden Jubilee 1946-1996

first hotel, the Nipa Lodge, and became one of the first Asian resorts to win massive popularity among European tourists. The legend of the Oriental Hotel spread far and wide. In addition to the Oriental, Thailand boasted several major hotels such as Trocadero, the Royal, the Princess and the Erawan.

The TAT inaugurated events such as the elephant round-up in Surin and capitalized on the lure of the bridge over the River Kwai, the subject of a famous movie. The first annual conference of the Pacific Asia Travel Association was held in Bangkok, and Chiang Mai officially became a part of the tourist map when PATA held a marketing workshop there.

Thai International Airways

In 1964, the SAS alliance with Thai Airways was losing money despite the fact that it was the first Asian all-jet fleet operator and SAS had

intensified its sales program to fill available capacity. In 1963, a three-party pool agreement was also signed with Cathay Pacific and the then Malayan Airlines. Its 1964 advertising budget was US$100,000. Further strengthening its position as a leading Asian airline and a pioneer of new destinations, Thai International Airways began flights to Bali in 1967 and Kathmandu in 1968.

The Development of Thai Airways

Thai Airways International was born on May 1, 1960, with the departure of its first flight, a fully-loaded DC-6B, bound for Hong Kong, Taipei and Tokyo. Her Majesty Queen Sirikit presided over the inaugural ceremony at Don Muang Airport and presented special plaques to the airline's first three planes, the names of which had personally been chosen by King Bhumibol Adulyadej from the roster of famous Thai heroines.

The new national flag carrier was the result of an agreement between an older company, Thai Airways Company (TAC), and the Scandinavian Airlines System (SAS), whereby the European company would assist for a period of time in marketing, reservations and training. Its initial goal was to build up the most comprehensive coverage of Asian travel destinations of any airline; only after this had been achieved would flights outside the Asian region be considered. The first schedule thus offered services to nine Asian cities and two more were to be added before the year was out.

Almost from the beginning, the airline's "Royal Orchid Service" became the subject of

widespread comment, all of it favorable, and set a high standard that was the envy of other carriers. By 1966 THAI had the first all-jet fleet of any regional airline in Asia. During its first decade, THAI also pioneered in flying to new travel destinations. It opened Bali to jet travel in 1967 and Kathmandu in Nepal the following year. In 1967 it carried its one millionth passenger, a

remarkable achievement for a regional airline in such a short period of time.

Having achieved its regional goal, the company was now ready to move into more distant markets. Services to Sydney began in 1971, to Copenhagen in 1972, and to England, France, Germany and Italy over the next three years. The partnership with SAS ended in 1977 and the airline became wholly Thai-owned. Following the purchase of its first Boeing 747 jumbo jets, it introduced trans-Pacific service to the United States in 1980.

At present, THAI flies to seventy-two destinations in thirty-six countries. Of these, twenty-one are within Thailand and thirty-one are elsewhere in Asia, more than any other airline and one of the factors that have made Bangkok a major hub for travelers in the region. Royal Orchid Plus, its frequent-flyer program, acquired

250,000 members in its first year. At the end of 1994, THAI signed an agreement with Lufthansa which made possible smooth transfers between the two carriers, a greater variety of flights and a reduction in flying time for passengers.

– W. W.

By this time Thai Airways had competition from within Thailand. In September 1965, Prince "Nicky" Varanand, a former Thai Airways pilot, along with his sister Princess Sudasiri

Sobha, set up an airline called Air Siam. The airline gained rights to fly to the United States and several other Asian destinations. Projecting a dynamic image with imaginative advertising and cut-rate fares, it was the first to operate wide-body aircraft such as the Boeing 747 and A300B2. Air Siam suffered high leasing costs and high overheads which, together with other problems, led to financial difficulties. The intense competition with Thai Airways caused controversy. In August 1976 Thai Airways' 5,300-strong staff went on strike to protest what they perceived to be threats to the carrier's future. Government policy was changed and nationalism came to the fore. In 1977, Air Siam ceased operations, the SAS-Thai Airways alliance ended, and a totally government-owned national airline was established.

By then, the airlines had put Thailand on the global tourism map. Many more airlines were beginning to fly in from Europe and the surrounding region. Indeed, in 1970, Don Muang Airport could no longer cater to such growth. Between 1970 and 1973, it gained a

four-story passenger terminal with four sets of baggage conveyors each for the arrival and departure functions, four sets of passenger boarding bridges and four parking slots for wide-bodied aircraft. Cargo buildings, runway extension, car park expansion and a new highway flyover access to the international terminal were added. But traffic growth was so strong that it took only five years for the airport to again reach the saturation point.

That was not surprising. New routes were being pioneered to Australia, Europe and Japan. Domestic flights to Chiang Mai and Haad Yai were more frequent. Visitor arrivals to Thailand exceeded 1 million in 1973. Then, due to the Middle East war, rising oil prices and global economic turmoil, a period of single-digit growth followed. In 1976, for the first time, visitor arrivals declined by 7 percent.

The Tourism Boom

In 1980, the Tourism Authority of Thailand (TAT) announced the country's first Year of Tourism. A strong promotion campaign increased visitor arrivals by 17 percent. In 1982, TAT launched the first major promotion linked to a royal event, the Bangkok Bicentennial, which marked the two hundredth anniversary of the Chakri Dynasty. Sadly, inadequate cooperation, delays in organization and various other local and international factors, including the global recession, precluded the event from being as successful as

Top: Wat Chiang Man in historical Chiang Mai; Center: River Kwai bridge; Left: The Loy Krathong festival, a colorful Thai cultural event which usually falls in November.

originally envisaged. In 1983, Thailand suffered its second drop in visitor arrivals, down 1 percent to 2.2 million visitors.

Right: General view of the 1982 Bangkok bicentennial celebrations at the Temple of the Emerald Buddha; Below, top: A publication commemorating "Visit Thailand Year" in 1987; Bottom, left to right: Tourism Authority of Thailand's publicity posters promoting the kingdom.

The mid-1980's marked a turning point for global tourism. The Reagan Presidency in the United States saw the biggest peacetime economic growth in history and the beginning of the end of the Cold War. In Thailand, the prime ministership of General Prem Tinsulanonda averted coup attempts and the effects of four cabinet reshuffles to give the country improved economic and political stability. The economic growth led to a marked increase in business travel and as a consequence a demand for meeting and convention space. In 1984, several hotels established large meeting facilities and then spearheaded, in cooperation with the Tourism Authority of Thailand, the formation of the

Thailand Convention and Promotion Association (TCPA) with thirty-two members. In May 1988, the name was changed to Thailand Incentive and Convention Association (TICA) to reflect the equal importance of the association's role in promoting both incentives and conventions in Thailand. Perhaps the biggest event promoting conventions was held in October 1991 when

The Tourism Authority of Thailand

The Tourism Organization of Thailand, the precursor of the Tourism Authority of Thailand (TAT), was formed in the 1960's with the aim of attracting tourists to the nation's natural and cultural resources. This was largely achieved but it was not until the early 1980's that tourist arrivals really began to increase dramatically.

The TAT's basic brief is to guide the development of tourism in Thailand. Under the Sixth National Economic and Social Development Plan (1987–91), two courses of action were outlined by the government. Firstly, to focus on the importance of overseas marketing via market research, advertising and promotion and to emphasize public relations to make local destinations more widely known. Secondly, to focus on the development and conservation of tourist sites and resources. At the same time, master plans for various sites and facilities were created. The TAT launched an overseas marketing and promotion campaign called "Visit Thailand Year". This campaign was so successful that 3 million international arrivals were recorded for

the first time, generating some 50,000 million baht. Neighboring countries immediately copied this campaign.

Since this 1987 campaign international arrivals have increased steadily from the above figure to 6,166,496 arrivals during 1994, making the nation one of the most important tourist destinations in the entire region.

Under the current Seventh National Plan, the TAT is working under the following specific policy objectives: to promote international tourist arrivals in Thailand and to encourage more Thais to travel to provincial destinations; to revive, conserve and develop tourism resources; to support transportation development that will enable Thailand to be the tourism center for Southeast Asia; and to upgrade the skills of tourism personnel.

The practical application of the above

policies takes many forms—from research, marketing and promotion to conservation and restoration of ancient sites to developing tourist attractions and transport links. A few examples include eco-tourism in national parks, a Dinosaur museum in Khon Kaen, a master plan development for Pattaya and a waste water treatment system in Kanchanaburi.

In an especially important and auspicious year, the TAT planned various activities to celebrate the Golden Jubilee of His Majesty's Accession to the Throne. As part of a new three-year marketing and promotion program (beginning in 1996), the TAT is encouraging overseas Thai residents to return to Thailand to celebrate the Golden Jubilee. At the same time, the TAT is actively encouraging Thais to travel more in the kingdom, while emphasizing to potential foreign visitors the "homely" welcome of the Thais to visitors.

– J. C.

the Queen Sirikit Center opened just before the annual general assembly of the World Bank. This, the largest such facility in Thailand, plays a major role attracting trade exhibitions and congresses.

Planning for the Visit Thailand Year of 1987 began in 1985 under Prime Minister Prem Tinsulanonda. His Majesty the King celebrated his sixtieth birthday or his fifth anniversary cycle on December 5, 1987, and, seven months later on July 2, 1988, became the longest reigning monarch in Thai history, a truly auspicious occasion on which the country's loyalty and devotion to the monarch was demonstrated. It was also an opportunity to make Thailand better known throughout the world. A special committee chaired by Prime Minister Prem was established to organize and widely publicized Royal State ceremonies, both overseas and in Thailand. Seventy-two projects and activities were organized between January 7, 1986 to July 2, 1988. Though the TAT was responsible for implementing Visit Thailand Year in cooperation with other government and private agencies, the main marketing effort was carried out by Thai Airways which spent more than 4 billion baht on global advertising and promotion that year. Visitor arrivals of 3.48 million in 1987 were up 24 percent, the highest growth in fifteen years.

Beyond raising visitor arrivals, Visit Thailand

Year bolstered the local image of tourism as an economic force. Though it had replaced rice exports as the nation's top foreign exchange earner in 1982, tourism had never really been taken seriously by the local population. A survey of tourism and public opinion conducted in 1987 by TAT found, however, that 98 percent were aware of Visit Thailand Year and that 61 percent had taken part in its activities. Further, the people felt strongly that the government should give prominence to the tourist industry. Likewise, they felt that more security should be provided to tourists and the conservation of natural resources should be seriously undertaken.

Warnings—The Anand period

Sadly, 1987 produced quantitative gains but no corresponding improvement in the ability of tourism authorities to manage the growth. In 1988, following fatal crashes by some aircraft of the domestic airline Thai Airways Company, it was merged with Thai Airways International.

That led to major changes in Thai International's management structure and the resignation of many of those instrumental in the building of the company over past years. Pattaya was suffering from over-development, while Phuket seemed to be following in the same direction. Bangkok's environmental and traffic problems were becoming worse, thus reducing visitors' length of stay. A policy of giving investment incentives to any

Top, left: Festivities at the King's sixtieth birthday; Above, left: Queen Sirikit Center; Inset: Sculpture at the center.

hotel project for which such support was requested led to the rise of hundreds of hotel rooms between 1988 and 1991. Excessive competition resulted, and the situation was further worsened by the tourism downturn of 1990 to 1992. Other influencing events were the Gulf War, a military coup and a violent attempt by an unelected Thai prime minister to retain power by quelling a popular uprising in May 1992.

In June 1992, then Prime Minister Anand Panyarachun sought to put the tourism industry back on its feet after the May political upheaval by organizing the first meeting of the National Tourism Task Force. Industry representatives as a group prepared a list of their problems and proposed solutions. This was the first time the industry had acted in unison. The results were compiled into a single document and then promptly shelved by the industry. By the time the brief tenure of the second Anand government had ended, the tourism industry had recovered to some extent, and the National Tourism Task Force became only a memory.

Prime Minister Anand left behind two major legacies. The first was a proclivity to talk straight, and the second was to urge the private sector not to keep turning to the government for solutions to its problem. When Prime Minister Anand went to Pattaya, he frankly told the people there that they were the source of their own problems. He was the first to publicly discuss the impact of the AIDS pandemic on Thai tourism. His honesty has produced results. In 1995, the number of new cases of sexually transmitted

Above: Mythological statue at Wat Phra Keo; Right: Reclining Buddha at Wat Po, Bangkok.

diseases was down 77 percent since 1991. At that time, however, such frankness did not win him much popularity amongst those in the travel industry. Moreover, he made it clear that his government, indeed any government, could only be of limited help to solving the industry's problems. The bulk of the work, he maintained, had to be done by the industry itself through self-regulation and self-enforcement. Government will come and go and the tourism industry and its investors must fight for their own survival.

Challenges and Problems

Thailand as a tourist destination is known today for low prices; cut-rate charters

and organizational problems.

Those features that have attracted tourists to Thailand over the years are changing. With the rapid economic growth of the past decade, there has also been a constant dissipation of Thailand's distinctive culture and the charm and courtesy for which Thais were famous, as well as an erosion of values and change in behavior that were distinctly Thai. While mass tourism has contributed to the increased acceptance of consumerism and other ways, Thailand's own mass media, especially television, has provided a much more effective vehicle for this dissipation of Thai culture. The threat to Thailand's cultural identity does not come so much from tourism as from modern Thailand's infatuation with 'development' of which the tourism industry is a part.

We must focus our view of 'development' and actively manage the achievement of

from Europe and discounted tours from Korea, Taiwan, Hong Kong and elsewhere abound. The pursuit of numbers has been relentless. Targets have been set and much money thrown at achieving them. But the intensity of the marketing effort abroad has been out of line with the management of the industry back home. Efforts to contain the social, economic and cultural costs of uncontrolled growth in tourism have produced virtually no results. The same corps of foreign correspondents which has long made Bangkok its Southeast Asian base and which in the past reported on the benefits of tourism to this country now reports on its infrastructural

that vision. The tourism industry is no different from any other. It needs a vision and a plan consistent with our view of 'development' and sound, dedicated management of that plan. It requires appropriate government support and a sensitivity to an ever changing and discerning market. Both government and industry must look back and identify where and why mistakes were made and heed the lessons that are to be learned. Thailand has much to offer to and much to gain from a competitive and healthy tourist industry, but it must be creative and consider the good of its people in realizing these opportunities.

Left, top to bottom: Pattaya beach, a popular destination; A view of Phangnga; Above: Eastern and Orient Express, Bangkok; Overleaf: An idyllic view of the beach at Koh Phi Phi.

Provincial Destinations

Right: Koh Phi Phi;
Bottom, left: An aerial
view of the cultural
site of Sukhothai;
Bottom, right: Ban
Chiang artifact (Suan
Pakaad Palace).

At the beginning of His Majesty's reign in 1946, the tourism industry was in its infancy. The traditional tourist destinations at the time were located in historical centers such as Chiang Mai, the focal point for the northern region and the nation's second largest city, and beach resorts such as Hua Hin, which was initially a retreat for members of the Royal Family.

Most of the original provincial destinations were situated on or within close reach of the railway system; road transport was little developed at the time, so many provincial destinations were out of reach for tourists visiting the kingdom. For centuries, for example, Chiang Mai visitors had to travel via the kingdom's river system—a lengthy but certainly adventurous journey but, by the beginning of this century, with improved communications, the capital of the north could be reached in just 12 hours. Hua Hin, Thailand's first beach resort, was a favorite resting place for royalty at the turn of the century. The opening of the Bangkok-Malaysia railway line in the 1920's, however, made the resort widely popular as a train ride to the beach from Bangkok took just four hours.

It was not until the advent of mass tourism in the late 1950's that many more provincial destinations opened up. Bangkok's ideal

position as a stopover place for flights from Europe to the Far East encouraged more tourists to stay and explore the kingdom, and as a result, demand for new tourism sites and facilities grew. And, as the nation's industrialization expanded in the 1960's, so infrastructure projects—particularly road links—were developed. Roads leading into the four major regions helped develop provincial destinations. During the 1980's several new provincial airports were opened, making trips to the provinces convenient and quick. Under the eighth National Plan, the government plans to upgrade and open more airports nationwide.

External events also spurred tourism growth. At the height of the Vietnam War, some 35,000 American troops were stationed in Thailand. A sleepy fishing village called Pattaya on the Eastern Seaboard changed into a bustling center for GIs' recreation, complete with bars and nightclubs. Today Pattaya is an all-round resort that caters to a wide range of visitors. Indeed, this once small sleeping village now attracts over 2 million visitors a year (TAT figures for 1994), second only to Bangkok.

Other resorts and cultural destinations opened up during the same period. Phuket, a large island on the Andaman sea in the south, was for years a center for tin and seaborne trading. Since the 1970's tourism has been the largest revenue earner, and the presence of an international airport since the 1980's has transformed the island into one of Asia's most popular destinations.

Thailand's many cultural sites have attracted visitors for well over a hundred years. Accessibility during His Majesty's reign have made ancient cities such as Ayutthaya and Sukhothai, the Ban Chiang bronze age settlement (since 1993, a World Heritage Site) or the dramatic Khmer-style ruins at Phimai and Khao Phanom Rung very popular with visitors. National parks and sites of great natural

beauty have also been opened and are becoming increasingly sought after as more tourists become interested in eco-tourism.

As the tourism industry developed, attention in recent years has been focused on one of the great attractions of Thailand—its people. Thai people still hold traditional festivals and events, from elaborate carved candle festivals (Ubon Ratchathani) to rain making festivals via home-made rockets to vegetarian festivals to local temple fairs. Many of these unique events are now integrated with tourism promotions.

Most of the kingdom's regions are now developed for tourism, particularly the central, northern and southern regions, and all offer something quite unique. Isan, or the northeast, home to the nation's 18 million Laotian speakers, is the last region to be developed for tourism. Already it is well-known for its cultural sites such as Khao Phanom Rung and Ban Chiang, as well as its vibrant festivals and wonderful folk music. Currently, the region is the focus of a concentrated effort to develop facilities and business investment opportunities. Isan is in a strategically important position between Laos, Cambodia and Vietnam. Following the completion of the Mitaphab (Friendship) Bridge between Laos and Thailand in 1994 (which effectively links Laos to the rest of Southeast Asia for the first time), road links are now being constructed that will enable travelers to go from the northeast directly east to the Vietnamese coast. In many ways, Isan is the gateway to Indochina.

The far north of Thailand is also rapidly developing for the recent opening of Myanmar, Laos and Southwestern China (an area known by economists as the 'Quadrangle Growth Zone'). Chiang Rai is fast becoming the key focal point for this exciting new region.   – J. C.

50 Symbols, 50 Books

BENCHARONG.

Based on the Sanskrit words *panch*, meaning five, and *rang*, meaning colors, thus literally "five-colored", it is the name given to over-glazed enamel ware made in China exclusively for export to Thailand. The design motifs, along with many of the shapes, were distinctively Thai and included such mythological figures as *thepanoms* (celestial beings), *rajasing-has* (royal lions), and *kinarees* (half-bird, half-woman creatures). Production began during the late Ayutthaya period and continued until the Bangkok reign of King Rama V. At first reserved for use in the royal palace, *bencharong* later became popular in wealthy households. In the past few decades, several Thai companies have started making the ware, using traditional patterns and forms.

BUDDHIST TEMPLES can be found in every part of Thailand, their steep, multi-tiered roofs and glittering decorations adding a touch of fantasy to city streets as well as country lanes. "They are unlike anything in the world," wrote Somerset Maugham, "so that you are taken aback, and you cannot fit them into the scheme of the things you know. It makes you laugh with delight to think that anything so fantastic could exist on this sombre earth." A temple, or *wat*, actually consists of several buildings and monuments within a single compound, among them sizable, usually ornate, halls for meetings and worship, houses for resident monks, a library, a crematorium, stupas where ashes or holy relics are enshrined, and *salas*, or rest pavilions, for visitors.

THAILAND King Bhumibol Adulyadej – The Golden Jubilee 1946-1996

CHILI PEPPER. Though not native to Southeast Asia—it originated in tropical America and was brought, probably first to India, by European explorers in the early sixteenth century—the chili pepper has become such an integral part of Thai cuisine that it would be difficult to imagine its absence. There are more than 130 recognized types in Thailand alone, ranging

from large mild varieties to deceptively tiny ones that pack an atomic blast of explosive pungency, used not only in curries but also in soups, salads, condiments and almost every other dish. Contrary to some Western writers, however, Thais do not use chili peppers indiscriminately; a good cook aims at a subtle blend of flavors—sweet, salty, and sour as well as hot—to produce the creations now so popular around the world.

CHULA is the name given to the huge, star-shaped "male" kites in the traditional Thai sport of kite-fighting, often requiring teams of up to twenty men to send one of them aloft and manoeuvre it. The "female", called *pukpao*, is a more conventional, diamond-shaped kite that can be flown by a single person. Matches are held on a large field with the *chulas* on one side and the *pukpaos* on the other and begin when the cumbersome "males" cross the boundary line into "female" territory, the object being to snare one of the darting little *pukpaos* and bring her back. Considering the size of the *chulas*, this might seem a one-sided contest but in sport as in life, the agile little *pukpaos* prove an elusive prey; as often as not, they manage to loop their lines around an opponent and bring it crashing to earth on their side of the dividing line.

DURIAN is the most highly-prized of local fruits among Thais, bringing high prices during the relatively short time it appears plentifully on the market in the hot season. Among Westerners, it is also the most controversial due to its pungent smell, which reminded one writer of "exceedingly defective sanitation." About the size of a football and covered with hard, greenish-brown spikes, *Duria zibethinus* is native to Southeast Asia and is equally popular in Malaysia and Indonesia. The Thais, however, are generally credited with having developed the widest range of hybrids, bearing such imaginative names as "Golden Pillow", "Long Stem", "Frog", and "Transvestite". Durian is usually eaten at room temperature with a side dish of sweetened glutinous rice, but it is also made into ice cream and candy.

FA MUI, known botanically as *Vanda coerulea*, is the Thai name of a beautiful blue-mauve orchid native to forests of the north and one of the region's symbols. Growing at altitudes of between 10,890 and 15,180 meters and blooming during the hot season, it was once often seen in the flower markets of Chiang Mai but has now become relatively rare due to the indiscriminate collection of wild specimens. It has been crossed with other Vanda species, however, to produce many handsome hybrids, of which perhaps the most popular is *V. Rothschildiana*, displaying the same rare color but flowering more frequently at lower altitudes.

THE EMERALD BUDDHA, or Phra Keo, is the most venerated of all the countless Buddha images in Thailand. According to legend, the small figure—66 centimeters high from base to top and 44.3 centimeters wide at the lap span,

carved from a semi-precious form of jade—was found when lightning struck an ancient northern stupa. It was enshrined in several northern temples and then, for over two centuries, in Laos, from which the future King Rama I, founder of the present Chakri Dynasty, brought it back to Thailand. He made it the principal Buddha image of Bangkok, enshrined in a temple complex within the compound of the Grand Palace.

THAILAND King Bhumibol Adulyadej – The Golden Jubilee 1946-1996

FARMER'S HAT. Known in Thai as *ngob*, this appears in a number of variations, worn by both men and women. The most commonly seen resembles an inverted bowl and has been aptly described as "one of the world's best designed

products". It consists of a mesh bamboo frame which is tightly layered with palm leaves and a brim further strengthened by small wooden strips. A separate cylindrical insert, woven of split bamboo to permit expansion or contraction, ensures a proper fit and is secured in place with two crossed lengths of bamboo. The result, a hat slightly raised from the head, allows air circulation while working in the fields under a hot sun and is also singularly attractive.

FISH TRAPS, integral to most rural households, vary from region to region but mostly fall into two categories: those left in place over a period of time and inspected periodically and those designed for a quick catch in ponds or streams. An example of the latter is the *soom-pla*, a cone-shaped device open at both ends and made either of bamboo slats or woven strips; holding it by the smaller end, the farmer wades near the banks of ponds or flooded rice fields and plunges the large end into the muddy bottom

whenever fish are spotted, then removes his catch from the top opening. The *toom*, on the other hand, is an upright trap of woven bamboo in the shape of a large jar with a small opening at the bottom; soft bamboo slivers inside the opening prevent the fish from escaping.

FLOATING MARKETS have been an exotic feature of Thai life for centuries, particularly in the days when most transportation was by water. Vendors from the surrounding countryside arrive by boat at a popular *klong*, or canal, usually at daybreak, and dispense everything from fresh fruit and vegetables to cooked foods and household necessities to buyers who either live along the waterway or come in their own boats. In recent years, the floating markets of the Bangkok area have become popular tourist attractions and as a result have lost much of their traditional flavor, but many others still thrive in the countryside wherever life is centered along a waterway.

GARUDA, a fierce-looking bird sometimes depicted as part human, is one of numerous figures incorporated into Thai art from Hindu mythology, where it serves as Vishnu's mount. In Thailand, it appears on the gable boards of many Buddhist temples as well as on the letterhead of official government communications as the national symbol. It is also regarded as an emblem of royalty and is thus

prominent among the decorations on buildings in the Grand Palace compound such as the Dusit Maha Prasat which was used as a throne hall by early Bangkok kings, as well as on the King's scepter and royal standard. Certain business firms which have made substantial contributions to the public welfare are granted royal permission to display the Garuda at the entrance to their premises.

GOLD-AND-BLACK LACQUER PAINTING is a classic Thai art that reached its peak during the Ayutthaya period but that was also important in early Bangkok. The process, known in Thai as *lai rod nam,* literally "ornaments washed with water," involves the application of several coats of lacquer, after the last of which the design is drawn. Areas which are to remain black are painted with a gummy yellow substance; the entire area is then covered with a thin coat of lacquer and, when partly dry, with gold leaf. Washing with water later removes the yellow gum and leaves the gold design on a glossy black background. Doors, windows, cabinets, screens and numerous other surfaces were decorated by this technique, usually depicting religious or mythological scenes.

HANG YAO means "long tail" and is a particularly suitable name for the most popular form of water transportation in Thailand. The "tail" is a long shaft that connects the propeller with a powerful engine, sometimes from an automobile; the shaft can be raised or lowered depending on the depth of the water, thus enabling the boat to navigate in both deep canals and shallow rice paddies, often at high speed. Some degree of mystery surrounds the origin of this ingenious creation, but many maintain that it was a Thai invention and, undeniably, great numbers of them can be seen everywhere, especially on the Chao Phraya river and along the myriad canals that lead off it.

KHON, or masked drama, though now seen on relatively rare occasions, is still regarded as the theatrical form most representative of classical traditions. The story line comes from the *Ramakian,* the Thai version of the Indian *Ramayana,* an allegory of the triumph of good over evil. Staged in its entirety, the *Ramakian* has 138 episodes involving 311 different characters and requiring more than 720 hours of continuous performance; even the abbreviated versions presented in early Bangkok took more than twenty hours and were staged on two consecutive nights. The story is told largely through gestures and movements expressing both action and feeling. All the dancers once wore masks to identify their character, magnificent creations made by master craftsmen, but today masks are usually worn only by those playing demons and animal characters like the monkey-god Hanuman.

KRATHONG is a small boat in the shape of an open lotus flower, traditionally made of deftly folded banana leaves mounted on a slice of banana stalk and decorated with flowers, incense sticks and a candle. Thai legend claims the first one was made in the court of Sukhothai by a royal lady named Nang Nopamas, who wanted to impress the king on the occasion of an annual festival that honored the water spirits who played such a vital role in Thai life. Today *krathongs* by the thousands are seen at a similar event called Loy Krathong, when they are set adrift on rivers, streams and lakes throughout the country under the full moon of the eleventh lunar month.

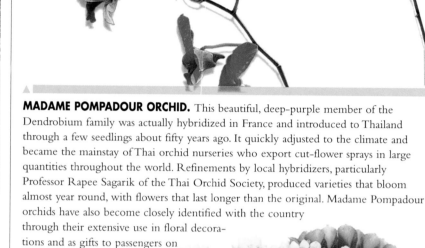

MADAME POMPADOUR ORCHID. This beautiful, deep-purple member of the Dendrobium family was actually hybridized in France and introduced to Thailand through a few seedlings about fifty years ago. It quickly adjusted to the climate and became the mainstay of Thai orchid nurseries who export cut-flower sprays in large quantities throughout the world. Refinements by local hybridizers, particularly Professor Rapee Sagarik of the Thai Orchid Society, produced varieties that bloom almost year round, with flowers that last longer than the original. Madame Pompadour orchids have also become closely identified with the country through their extensive use in floral decorations and as gifts to passengers on Thai Airways International.

LOTUS BUD FINIAL.
Architecturally, Thailand's first capital of Sukhothai displays a wide range of styles, among them Khmer, Mon and Sri Lankan. One feature regarded as uniquely Thai, however, is the lotus bud finial, possibly adapted from the rounded bud that appeared on monuments at Pagan during the Mon period but, at Sukhothai, further embellished with a gracefully tapering spire that makes it distinctive.

According to one authority, "the lotus bud tower was an original contribution of the Thai people [and] became the symbol for both the political and religious power of the Sukhothai kingdom." Many examples can be seen on the remains of Sukhothai temples, particularly Wat Mahathat, the most important religious complex in the old city.

a vast number of other flowers, such as roses, marigolds and orchids, may be included to provide accents of color), strung together into tight, almost abstract patterns with a skill that originated

extremely complex, requiring hours of labor and costing hundreds of baht.

MALAI is the name of the fragrant garlands that play such a prominent role in Thai social and religious life. The basis of most is jasmine buds (but

among women of the royal court. *Malai* ranges from reasonably simple creations like those sold on streets and outside almost every shrine to others, large and

Their uses are equally varied. Nearly everyone who visits a temple or shrine brings a *malai* as an offering, while taxi drivers hang one from the dashboard to avert accidents. One is also likely to receive a *malai* when moving into a new house, has a birthday, graduates from school, or receives a promotion at work.

MANGO AND STICKY RICE. If you ask any Thai expatriate what he misses most from his homeland, especially during the hot season, the answer is likely to be "*ma-muang khao neow*," or mango with glutinous rice. Thai hybridizers have produced numerous mango varieties, many of them very different from

MOR HOM is the traditional Thai farmer's shirt and an emblem of rural life. Collarless and usually fastened with ties at the front, it is made of cotton that is dyed a dark indigo blue and that fades and becomes softer with age. Both men and women wear such shirts when working in the fields, along with a palm-leaf hat. The *mor hom* became a political symbol in the 1980's when it was adopted by one of the candidates running for the office of Bangkok's Governor to suggest the difference between him and his affluent rivals in their proper, formal suits and uniforms; the strategy worked even with Bangkok's sophisticated electorate and he won by a landslide.

those found in other tropical countries, and one of the favorite ways of eating them is at the peak of ripeness with a side dish of sticky rice flavored with coconut milk and palm sugar and often garnished with toasted *tua thong*, the tiny yellow centers of mung beans.

NIELLOWARE, which some authorities think came to Thailand from Persia by way of India, is a craft usually associated with the far southern city of Nakhon Si Thammarat, where many of the finest examples have been produced. Silver, sometimes gold-plated, is used as the base, on which intricate designs are etched and further treated so that they stand out against the gleaming metal. Nielloware became so identified with fine Thai craftsmanship, especially in the late Ayutthaya period, that it was presented as royal gifts to foreign dignitaries, a tradition started in the reign of King Narai and still continued by the present royal family. The art has been used to adorn royal thrones and a variety of trays, bowls, vases and other containers.

NAM PLA, an amber-colored fish sauce, has been described as "the liquid essence of Thai cuisine," as basic to any Thai meal as salt and pepper are to a Western table or soy sauce to a Chinese one. It is used plain or mixed with chili peppers, garlic, and lime juice as a condiment for just about any meat, seafood or vegetable dish. The small, anchovy-like fish used for *nam pla* are salted and fermented in large jars, after which the liquid is extracted and bottled. Several brands are available, varying in color and pungency.

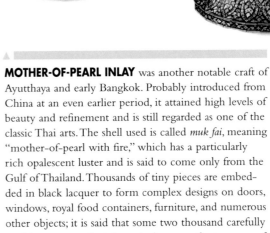

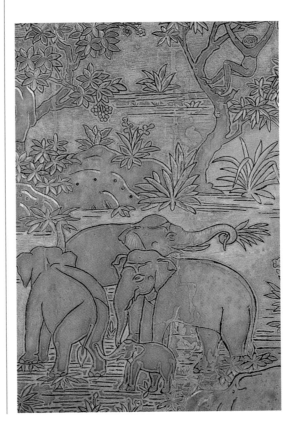

MOTHER-OF-PEARL INLAY was another notable craft of Ayutthaya and early Bangkok. Probably introduced from China at an even earlier period, it attained high levels of beauty and refinement and is still regarded as one of the classic Thai arts. The shell used is called *muk fai*, meaning "mother-of-pearl with fire," which has a particularly rich opalescent luster and is said to come only from the Gulf of Thailand. Thousands of tiny pieces are embedded in black lacquer to form complex designs on doors, windows, royal food containers, furniture, and numerous other objects; it is said that some two thousand carefully cut bits were required for a single square foot on one of the doors leading to the hall where the Emerald Buddha is enshrined.

PHA KHAW MAA is the name of the multi-purpose piece of cloth essential to every Thai male's wardrobe in rural areas. Usually made of cotton in a pattern of bold checks of contrasting colors, it can be used as a sarong while relaxing or bathing, as a shoulder cloth on cool nights, as a turban to ward off the hot sun, as a handy wrapping for goods purchased in a market, or rolled up as a pillow at night. It should not be confused with the *pha yao* and *pha sarong*, which are also worn by men but are often made of silk and regarded as ceremonial garments.

PHIPAT is the basic Thai musical ensemble, which performs on a wide variety of occasions from performances of classical dance to Thai-style boxing matches. The name derives from the *pinai*, a wind instrument which sounds somewhat like a Western oboe or clarinet; about forty centimeters long, it is made of seasoned rosewood and the tones are produced by six holes in the body, manipulated by the performer's fingers. All the other *phipat* components are percussion instruments, some with a compass of differently pitched tones.

POOM, which refers to a pyramidal shape resembling a lotus bud, is the popular name given to a traditional bowl flower arrangement more generally called *jad paan*. The core, usually 15 cm. to 20 cm. high, is made of moistened earth or clay, sometimes of sawdust, the whole of which is embedded with fresh flowers in geometric patterns. This is then set in a low, footed bowl and often placed on an altar for religious ceremonies. The most common flower used is *Gomphrena globosa*, popularly known as the Everlasting Flower or Bachelor's Button, which has the advantage of fitting together tightly like a woven cloth and also of lasting for weeks. Grander *pooms*, like those made for use by the royal family, may be fashioned of jasmine and other short-lived flowers.

RAMKHAMHAENG STONE INSCRIPTION.

Undoubtedly Thailand's most famous historical inscription, this is dated AD 1292 and eulogizes the first kingdom of Sukhothai during the reign of King Ramkhamhaeng the Great, who is also credited with inventing the Thai alphabet. It describes a caring, paternal monarchy in which every citizen had the right to petition the king for justice and also evokes an abundant, prosperous life in words every modern Thai schoolchild still learns: "This Sukhothai is good. In the water there are fish, in the fields there is rice. The king does not levy a rate on his people...Who wants to trade in elephants, trades. Who wants to trade in horses, trades. Who wants to trade in gold and silver, trades..."

RECLINING BUDDHA. This celebrated image at Bangkok's Wat Po, representing the Buddha at the moment he entered Nirvana, is 45 meters long, 15 meters high, and entirely covered with several layers of gold leaf. Apart from monumental size, its most notable features are the inlaid mother-of-pearl designs adorning the soles of its feet, showing the 108 auspicious marks by which the true Buddha can be recognized. Executed during the reign of King Rama III, who also made numerous other artistic contributions to Wat Po, these are regarded as one of the finest examples of the craft.

ROYAL REGALIA. Kept at the Grand Palace, this consists of a number of items—some dating from the first reign of the Chakri Dynasty—which each new king receives on his accession to the throne. The components of the Royal Regalia are the Great Crown of Victory (Phra Maha Pichai Mongkut); the Sword of Victory (Phra Saeng Khan Chaisi);

the Royal Staff (Than Phra Kon); the Royal Fan (Phat Walawitchani); the Royal Whisk (Phra Sae Chamari); the Royal Slippers (Chalong Phra Bat Choeng Ngon); and, most important of all, the nine-tiered Great White Umbrella of State (Phra Maha Sawetachat) under which the king sits.

RICE has been an enduring symbol of Thailand throughout its history, not only as the staple food of its people but also responsible for a major part of its economy. Village life in most parts of the country still revolves around the timeless cycle of rice cultivation in the surrounding paddy fields. The planting season usually begins in April or May with the annual Royal Plowing Ceremony held near the Grand Palace in Bangkok. Farmers then cooperate to prepare the fields, plow them with water buffaloes or

modern machinery, and, finally, flood them from surrounding streams and canals. The whole family joins to transplant the young rice seedlings, just as the monsoon rains arrive. By late November or early December rice in the north and central plains is ready to be harvested, threshed and winnowed, another communal effort that brings the cycle to a close.

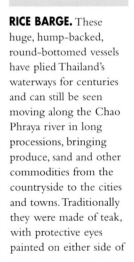

RICE BARGE. These huge, hump-backed, round-bottomed vessels have plied Thailand's waterways for centuries and can still be seen moving along the Chao Phraya river in long processions, bringing produce, sand and other commodities from the countryside to the cities and towns. Traditionally they were made of teak, with protective eyes painted on either side of

the prow to ward off evil spirits, but due to the present scarcity of wood modern ones are more often than not made of steel. Tugboats are used to pull the heavy barges which when fully loaded are almost level with the water line.

of Bangkok, and attracted equal admiration when they appeared on the Chao Phraya river, usually at the end of the rainy season when the King presented offerings to riverside monasteries. Now they are only rarely seen on special occasions such as the Bangkok Bicentennial in 1982, when fifty-one principal barges and numerous smaller craft participated. The first new barge in more than fifty years was added to the fleet in 1996 by the Royal Thai Navy, in honor of His Majesty King Bhumibol Adulyadej's Golden Jubilee.

ROYAL BARGES, ornately carved and gilded, were a feature of Ayutthaya that impressed almost every foreign visitor who saw them in grand procession, rowed by chanting oarsmen in colorful costumes. A new fleet of barges was built by King Rama I, founder

SHADOW PLAY. Probably introduced to southern Thailand from the ancient Javanese empire of Srivijaya, the shadow play is found in two forms. The older, called *nang yai*, involves large cowhide figures, usually of characters from the *Ramakian*, which are held by manipulators against or behind a lighted screen to the accompaniment of music, choral singing and narration. Another version, still seen at festivals in the south, is called *nang talung*; the beautifully-fashioned figures, also made of cowhide, are smaller than those used for *nang yai* and often have one or more moveable parts such as the chin, an arm, or a leg. Concealed from the audience, the manipulators are skilled singers and comedians whose witty contributions probably account for the form's continued popularity.

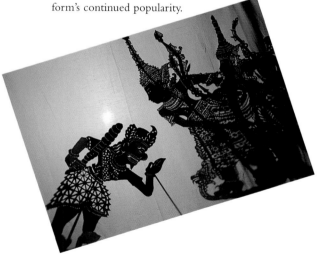

SIAMESE CATS, or at least the prized variety thus called, are not in fact commonly found in Thailand. According to one source, this blue-eyed beauty with either chocolate brown or pale grey markings got its name when a diplomat in Bangkok sent a pair to England and thus started a popular vogue; though just where he obtained them is unclear. The Thais, however, do have a distinctive cat regarded as lucky to own; it is known as a *sam si*, meaning "three colored."

SILK, Thailand's most famous luxury product, is an ancient craft that probably goes back to the first capital of Sukhothai and it was certainly used for ceremonial and royal dress in both Ayutthaya and early Bangkok. Changes in fashion and the availability of cheaper, machine-made textiles in the late nineteenth century led to a decline in silk weaving, though it recovered and became internationally known after the Second World War. The major center of silk production is the northeast, where one of the most beautiful types is *mud mii*, a process of resist patterning commonly known as *ikat*. Her Majesty Queen Sirikit has been an important influence in the revival of silk, both by setting up weaving projects in several parts of the country and also using it extensively in her own wardrobe.

SUKHOTHAI CERAMICS.
In addition to its Buddhist architecture and paternalistic monarchy, Sukhothai is remembered for its splendid ceramics. The first kilns were established in Sukhothai itself, but later the craft moved to Sawankhalok near the satellite city of Si Satchanalai. The most famous motif is a fish, usually drawn singly in profile but sometimes in pairs, head to tail, in an iron-black pigment which sometimes misfired to brown. Magnificent celadons were also produced, in glazes that ranged from sea green to cerulean blue. These wares were perhaps the first of Thailand's manufactured exports, sent in large quantities to eager buyers in the Philippines, Indonesia and Borneo.

TAKRAW is a popular Thai sport, also found in neighboring countries such as Malaysia, Cambodia and Laos. In its traditional form, a circle of players endeavors to keep a hollow ball made of woven rattan aloft for as long as possible, using all parts of their bodies except the hands and demonstrating remarkable grace and footwork. More professional forms of *takraw* have evolved in relatively recent years, with nets separating the teams or high baskets through which the ball must be sent, together with strict rules of play and scoring. Competitions of this kind are seen at such regional sports gatherings as the Asian Games.

SPIRIT HOUSE. Somewhere in almost every Thai compound, business or residential, stands an elegant little structure—traditionally a wooden replica of a classic Thai house but sometimes an ornate cement affair modelled after a temple building. This is the symbolic abode of the Phra Phum (Lord of the Land or Place), who watches over the designated area and, if properly honored, protects both the buildings and the human inhabitants. An expert like a Brahmin priest is called on to determine the precise location of this spirit dwelling, which has nothing to do with aesthetic considerations; ideally it should be close to the fence or wall surrounding the property (so as to ward off any approaching enemy), where the shadow of the house does not fall on it (for the human and spirit worlds should not overlap), and facing north or south (both auspicious directions).

THAI HOUSE. Several distinctive styles of Thai domestic architecture have evolved in different regions, of which the best known are those of the central plains and the north. The former, elevated on stout round posts, has steep roofs, panelled wooden walls that lean slightly inward, and distinctive bargeboards that curve at the ends. The components are prefabricated, which means that they can be easily dismantled, moved to a new location, and reassembled. The simplest consists of a single unit with an outside veranda, while larger ones have several units arranged around a central platform. The northern house is similar in most respects except that the walls lean outward, giving it a sturdier look, and the windows tend to be smaller; a decorative feature on many is a V-shaped carving at each end of the roof, called a *kalae*.

THAI BOXING, sometimes known abroad as "kick boxing," is a unique blend of ferocity and almost balletic grace. Any part of the body except the head can be used as an offensive weapon and any part, including the head, is a fair target. The feet are the most effective of all, usually swung in a wide arc at lightning speed. A musical ensemble accompanies the bout, stepping up its beat and intensity at exciting moments and stimulating both fighters and spectators to peaks of frenzy. Knockouts are more common in Thai-style boxing than in Western matches and when they come, it is usually the result of a well-aimed kick in the head. In the modern sport, gloves are worn instead of cloth binding.

THRONE HALL OF THE CHAKRI MAHA PRASAT.
Located in the middle part of the Grand Palace enclosure, the Chakri Maha Prasat was built in the reign of King Chulalongkorn (Rama V). The most impressive of its many rooms is the Throne Hall on the first floor, where the King receives foreign ambassadors when they present their credentials. The splendid Niello Throne (Phra Thinang Phuttan Thom), a wooden throne plated with sheets of silver and gold niello made at the command of King Rama V, stands at one end, surmounted by a nine-tiered white royal umbrella; behind it is the royal emblem of the Chakri Dynasty, consisting of a discus and a trident; on the walls hang paintings of celebrated encounters between Thais and foreigners.

WAI is the term for the well-known Thai gesture described by one authority as "a sign of greeting or mutual recognition made by raising both hands, palms joined, to a position lightly touching the body somewhere between the chest and the forehead". Exactly where they touch, and who initiates the gesture, are important for these indicate the status of each participant: the higher the hands are raised, the greater the courtesy and respect conveyed, and a junior in age or social rank is always the first to give the *wai*. It is a sign of further good manners to raise and lower the hands as slowly and gracefully as possible, keeping the upper arms and elbows close to the body and the joined palms bent slightly inward.

TOM YAM, in one of its many forms, is perhaps the most popular of all Thai soups, as admired in restaurants abroad as in its homeland. The distinctive flavors are provided by lemon grass (*takrai*), lime juice, and an often lavish addition of fresh hot chili peppers or roasted chili paste, creating a subtle blend of hot and sour with citrus overtones. A favorite version is *tom yam goong*, with shrimp, but it can also be made with other kinds of seafood.

TUK-TUK. A motorized three-wheeled vehicle seating two comfortably but many more when the occasion demands, the jaunty little *tuk-tuk* replaced the pedicab when the latter was banished from the streets of Bangkok in the late 1950's and quickly became the city's favorite form of cheap transportation. To many foreign visitors, it has also come to be a sort of symbol of Thailand's capital, thanks to the good humor with which most

tuk-tuk drivers face the daily traffic trials and the ingenuity they display in finding little-known byways to overcome it. Toy *tuk-tuks* are popular souvenirs for tourists to take back home, and a few real ones have been exported by admirers.

WAT ARUN, the towering Temple of Dawn, is one of the most prominent landmarks along the Chao Phraya river in Bangkok. In a different form, the temple was there even before Bangkok became the capital, having been first built during the Ayutthaya period; it served as King Taksin's royal chapel when he made Thonburi the seat of government. The great central *prang*, decorated with broken bits of multi-colored porcelain, was started by King Rama II but due to technical problems of building on the wet river bank it did not reach its present elevation of 81 meters until the next reign. Wat Arun was the main destination for the royal barge processions that were an annual spectacle, and the sweeping views it offers have proved irresistible to countless photographers ever since the first camera appeared in the kingdom.

THAILAND King Bhumibol Adulyadej – The Golden Jubilee 1946-1996

WALKING SUKHOTHAI BUDDHA.

Of all the numerous classic styles of depicting the Buddha in Thailand, the most celebrated is the three-dimensional walking Sukhothai Buddha, which has been called "the glory of Thai art." Cast in bronze, the image seems to float rather than walk, "a rhythmic linear abstraction of sinuous grace," in the words of one writer, at once human and infinitely spiritual, the left hand usually raised in the gesture of teaching or dispelling fear. Unlike most Buddha images, which were designed to be seen mainly from the front, this statue is a compelling work of art from any angle and was undoubtedly intended to be viewed by devotees circumambulating it in ceremonies.

WATER BUFFALO.

Strong, even-tempered, and capable of working long hours, the water buffalo is an enduring symbol of the Thai countryside. "Asia's waterproof tractor," one writer has called it, "unbeatable for getting through the sticky ooze of the rice fields." Buffaloes are seen mostly in the central region and the northeast, while oxen are preferred

in the hilly north. Some more prosperous farmers are employing modern machinery to plow their fields, but to the majority the water buffalo is still a valued member of the family, as essential today as it was a century ago.

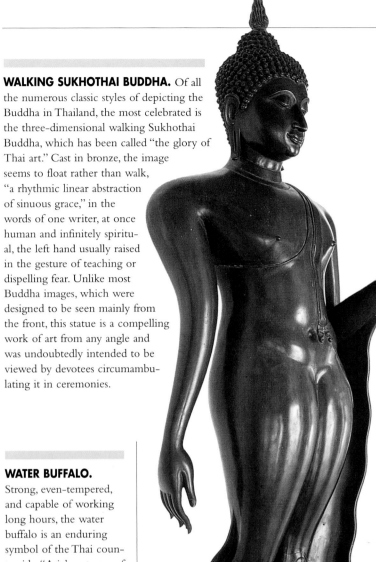

WORKING MONKEYS.

Vast coconut plantations are a familiar feature of the southern Thai landscape, and some growers, especially around Songkhla and on the island of Koh Samui have devised an ingenious solution to the problem of harvesting the nuts from the tall palms. Monkeys are trained to scamper nimbly up the trunks, select only those nuts ready for picking, and drop them to waiting workers below. A well-trained monkey can harvest several hundred coconuts an hour and save both time and effort for the plantation owner.

WHITE ELEPHANTS

have played a potent symbolic role throughout Thai history. Wars have been fought over them, statues erected to their memory, and rulers judged by the number they possessed; until 1917, the national flag of Thailand displayed a noble white elephant against a brilliant red background. The adjective is somewhat misleading. While some look conspicuously pale, others may, to the untrained eye, be scarcely discernible from ordinary elephants. To qualify, an animal must pass a complex series of tests laid down by ancient

Brahmanic belief, which covers everything from color to demeanor (its snoring, for example, should not be noisy but "should emit the pleasant sounds of classical Thai musical instruments"). By tradition all such elephants found in the country become the king's exclusive property. King Bhumibol Aduladej has had seventeen, the most any Thai king has ever owned.

WORKING ELEPHANTS.

For at least a thousand years, the Thais have domesticated and trained the wild elephants that once roamed the forests of the north and northeast in great numbers. Many were used in warfare,

especially during the Ayutthaya period, but even much later they were invaluable for carrying goods and working in the teak forests of the north; in 1900, there were an estimated 100,000 domesticated elephants in Thailand. Until a recent ban on logging, most Thai ele-

phants worked at dragging logs in the forest, a task for which they were ideally suited since being one of the powerful animals, it is able to pull about half its body weight through the forest. Elephants can be seen at work and undergoing training at the Young Elephant Training Center outside the northern city of Lampang.

BOOKS 50 on THAILAND

THAI NATIONAL IDENTITY AND ITS DEFENDERS
Edited by
CRAIG J REYNOLDS
Silkworm Books,
Chiang Mai, 1991

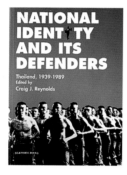

This collection of essays by Thai and foreign scholars arose out of a conference held at Monash University in 1989 to acknowledge the fiftieth anniversary of the country's change of name from Siam to Thailand. It examines the subject of Thai identity, in particular the ways the concept has been promoted by various governments since 1939.

Among the writers are Sulak Sivaraksa, an avowed critic of the name change which he views as both political and racist; Chai-anan Samudavanija, who discusses nationalism under Prime Minister Phibun Songkhram in the early 1940's and its effect on non-Thai groups like the Chinese; Anthony Diller, who treats the promotion of Central Thai as the national language despite regional dialects spoken by the majority of the population; and Charles F Keyes, who shows the nationalistic aspects of a famous case

involving a stolen lintel from a Khmer temple in the northeast.

Some of the opinions are controversial but the collection as a whole provides thought-provoking insights into the process of nation building.

MAI PEN RAI MEANS NEVER MIND
CAROL HOLLINGER
John Weatherhill, Inc.
Tokyo, 1977

Carol Hollinger was an American housewife who came to Bangkok with her husband in the 1950's. Quickly disillusioned by the isolated social life of the foreign community, she took a job as a teacher at Chulalongkorn University; and in this very personal book she describes her often hilarious experiences there and her steadily increasing love for the Thais who became her friends.

This is not merely another of the many inconsequential accounts of life in a strange culture. Carol Hollinger (who died shortly before the book's original publication in the United States in 1965) was

blessed with an unusual degree of perception as well as a beguiling sense of humor that is never condescending or saccharine. Much of what she writes about is as true today as it was nearly fifty years ago, and her observations will not only amuse but also inform any contemporary reader.

SI PHAENDIN
M R KUKRIT PRAMOJ (English version by Tulachandra)
Editions Duang Kamol,
Bangkok, 1981

M R Kukrit Pramoj, who died last year, was one of Thailand's most protean figures: novelist, journalist, actor, classical dancer, and politician (he served as Prime Minister in 1975–6). *Si Phaendin*, which originally appeared as a serial in a newspaper he founded, is the most popular of his several novels, taught in schools and adapted as a television series.

"There comes a time in a man's life," he wrote on the appearance of the two-volume English version, "when he feels the urge to set down in writing the modes and mores of a

disappearing age, of which he was a part, however small. I had this urge when I sat down to write this book in Thai over thirty years ago." The title means "Four Reigns," and it recounts life under four Chakri rulers, from Rama V (King Chulalongkorn) through Rama VIII (King Ananda), through the eyes of its heroine, Ploi, who at the beginning leaves her home to reside in the Grand Palace. The "modes and mores" of palace life are revealed through her experiences, as well as the dramatic social and political events that transformed Thai life during the period.

A PHYSICIAN AT THE COURT OF SIAM
MALCOLM SMITH
Oxford University Press,
Kuala Lumpur, 1982

Dr Malcolm Smith was attached as a physician to the Thai court during the latter days of King Chulalongkorn's reign and, after the King's death, privately to Queen Saovabha, the First Queen. This memoir, first published in 1957, offers a rare account of court life as seen through Western eyes and also of a period during which Thailand was undergoing rapid change.

Dr Smith is particularly revealing on the life of the royal women, who lived in a self-contained, all-female part of the Grand Palace known as "the Inside," with its own complex social structure, own arts and its own strict rules. In addition, he gives an affectionate

portait of the Queen, one of the most remarkable women in modern Thai history, and, in passing, provides interesting information on such topics as royal polygamy, traditional medicine, various court figures, and customs that have almost vanished.

A NEW HISTORICAL RELATION OF THE KINGDOM OF SIAM
SIMON DE LA LOUBERE
Reprint by Chalermnit,
Bangkok, n.d.

Among the many tragic results of the destruction of Ayutthaya by the Burmese in 1767 was the loss of almost all the capital's written records. Historians since in search of information about many aspects of life have been forced to turn to accounts by Western visitors, despite the obvious bias and limited viewpoints that characterize most of these.

By general agreement, the best of these early accounts is the one written by La Loubere, who headed a French embassy to the Court of King Narai in

1687. As a diplomat, La Loubere was not very effective and remained in Ayutthaya only for a few months. On the other hand, he had a sharp eye for detail and an intelligent curiosity about the strange customs he encountered; and his portrait of seventeenth-century Thai life remains a classic resource, offering information on a range of topics from food to the Buddhist faith, from architecture to popular games and family life.

BUDDHISM EXPLAINED
KHANTIPALO BHIKKU
Silkworm Books, Chiang Mai, 1994

The Venerable Khantipalo Bhikku was born in England and discovered Buddhism while serving in the British Army. He was later ordained as a monk (*bhikku*), first in India and later, in 1966, in Thailand. He lived and studied in Thailand for eleven years and subsequently established a monastery in Australia, of which he has since served as Abbott while also teaching Dhamma and meditation.

His book, in the words of the late John Blofeld, also a Buddhist scholar, "should make a powerful appeal to two kinds of person. First, those largely ignorant of Buddhism who are sincerely eager to repair that ignorance will find in it exactly what they need...Second, a good many people with a fairly extensive knowledge of Buddhism would be happy to have such a work

on their bookshelves because it provides a complete summary of all the essentials of Buddhist teaching and practice, and can be used as a handy reference book for materials that usually have to be hunted out from more than one source." Simply written and readable, this is a good introduction to the faith followed by the great majority of Thais.

LORDS OF LIFE
PRINCE CHULA CHAKRABONGSE
Alvin Redman, Ltd., London, 1960

A grandson of King Chulalongkorn, Prince Chula Chakrabongse made his home in England and wrote a number of books about his family. This one deals with the Chakri Dynasty from its founding in 1782 to the early years of the reign of the present King.

Written in a readable style, the book provides many personal details about the various rulers as well as an assessment of their major accomplishments. King Rama I, for example, united the kingdom after its disastrous defeat by the Burmese and also established Bangkok as the capital, while King Rama II's reign saw a notable artistic flowering. The most interesting chapters are perhaps those on King Rama V (Chulalongkorn) and King Rama VI (Vajiravudh), when Prince Chula and his parents were intimately involved in court life and thus had an opportunity to observe events at first hand.

SIAMESE WHITE
MAURICE COLLIS
Reprint by DD Books, Bangkok, 1986

Maurice Collis wrote a number of popular histories and biographies, several of them dealing with Burma where he worked for many years in the British Civil Service. *Siamese White* tells the absorbing story of an English adventurer named Samuel White, who came east in the seventeenth century and lived at both Mergui, on the Burmese coast, and the Thai capital of Ayutthaya while he traded and sought to make his fortune.

Of the many unusual characters White encountered, perhaps the most fascinating was Constantine Phaulkon, a Greek who rose from total obscurity to a position of power second only to that of King Narai, the tolerant Thai ruler of the time. White knew Phaulkon at the peak of his extraordinary career, just before he was overthrown by a palace revolution and executed, and Collis gives a vivid account of the momentous events that led to his downfall as well as of life in Ayutthaya, then the most cosmopolitan city in the region.

THE ENGLISH GOVERNESS AT THE SIAMESE COURT
ANNA LEONOWENS
Reprint by Chalermnit, Bangkok, n.d.

To the majority of Westerners, Anna Leonowens is undoubtedly the figure most often associated with Thailand. Her fame is not due to this memoir, first published in 1870, three years after she left the country, nor to a subsequent one entitled *The Romance of the Harem*. It comes, rather, from Margaret Landon's *Anna and the King of Siam* (1944), which takes elements of both books and which eventually became *The King and I*.

Serious historians have had little difficulty disproving Anna's exaggerated

estimate of her own importance, her falsifications of Thai history, and, most of all, her distorted picture of King Mongkut, who brought her to teach English to some of the royal children. Later research has also revealed much about Anna's own personal history which she managed to conceal during the remainder of her life and long afterward. Despite its unreliability, however, her book provides a unique glimpse of Thailand at a critical moment in its history as well as many interesting details of court life seldom seen by outsiders at the time.

JIM THOMPSON: THE LEGENDARY AMERICAN
WILLIAM WARREN
Houghton Mifflin Co., Boston, 1970

Jim Thompson came to Thailand with the American military at the end of the Pacific War and won international renown for his revival of the Thai silk industry as well as for his famous Thai-style house which is still one of Bangkok's leading tourist attractions.

This account is divided into two parts. The first describes how Thompson discovered an ancient craft then in danger of disappearing and made it perhaps Thailand's best-known luxury export through a combination of luck, talent and hard work. The second part is devoted to his mysterious disappearance while on a holiday in the Malaysian resort of Cameron Highlands in 1967; no reliable trace of him has been found in the years since but there has been no lack of bizarre theories, ranging from politics to the supernatural, most of which are examined here.

THE KINGDOM AND PEOPLE OF SIAM

SIR JOHN BOWRING
Oxford University Press,
Kuala Lumpur, 1969

Sir John Bowring, Governor of Hong Kong and Minister to China, came to Bangkok in 1855 to negotiate a trading treaty, an endeavor in which several previous British emissaries had failed. Bowring was successful, largely because the ruler with whom he dealt, King Mongkut (Rama IV), recognized the urgent need for modernizing his Kingdom but also because of his own tactful diplomacy. The result was a historic treaty that served as a model for others and that opened Thailand to lucrative trade with the West.

Bowring's two-volume work draws on many earlier sources and presents a comprehensive view of Thailand in the mid-nineteenth century, its natural resources as well as its customs. Particularly valuable is the portrait drawn of King Mongkut, the first Thai ruler to be able to communicate directly in English, who emerges as a shrewd multi-faceted man very different from the caricature offered in The King and I.

THAILAND: A SHORT HISTORY

DAVID K WYATT
Yale University Press, New Haven, 1984

Complete histories of Thailand, as opposed to studies of specific periods, are surprisingly rare, and this one by David K Wyatt is generally regarded as

the best available.

It begins with a discussion of what Professor Wyatt calls the "Tai" people and traces their migration down from southern China and their emergence as a dominant group, first in the kingdoms of La Na and Sukhothai and later during the four-hundred-year rule of Ayutthaya. Over half the book is devoted to the Bangkok period,

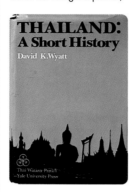

with discussions of the various Chakri kings, the early period of constitutional monarchy following the 1932 revolution, the rise of the military as a political power, and, more briefly, events between 1957 and 1982 when new forces appeared. Wyatt draws on a vast number of sources, both Thai and Western, and presents his findings in a digestible form aimed at the average reader.

MO BRADLEY AND THAILAND

DONALD C LORD
William B Eerdmans Publishing Co., Grand Rapids, 1969

The first Protestant missionaries were given permission to settle in Thailand in the early nineteenth century, during the reign of King Rama III. While they enjoyed little success in their primary objective of conversion, they nevertheless had a significant effect on the country's life in other lasting ways, as exemplified in the career of the most famous, Dr Dan Beach Bradley.

Dr Bradley arrived in Bangkok in 1835 and,

except for one brief visit back to his home in the United States, he remained there until his death in 1873. Besides being an evangelist, he was also a physician, printer, and friend to King Mongkut. He was responsible for the introduction of modern medicine, performing the first cataract operations and the first successful inoculations against smallpox. He also established Thailand's first newspaper, the Bangkok Recorder, as well as an almanac called the Bangkok Calendar, to which King Mongkut

sometimes contributed articles on Thai history and culture. "Converts or not," as the author of this book concludes, "Dr Bradley is one of Thailand's most important historical figures."

THAI STYLE

WILLIAM WARREN AND LUCA INVERNIZZI TETTONI
Times Editions, Singapore, 1989

Illustrated with over 370 color photographs, this book traces the development of domestic Thai architecture as well as various elements characteristic of Thai style in buildings and decorations.

The two outstanding traditional styles, which vary in certain structural details, are those of the central plains and of the north. In both regions the houses are made of wood in prefabricated sections and have relatively few of the purely decorative or symbolic features reserved for royal

palaces and Buddhist monasteries. The book shows numerous examples of both styles, some of them—such as the famous Jim Thompson House in Bangkok—adapted for contemporary lifestyles. It also includes sections on Western-style buildings inspired by those in neighboring colonies and on modern houses that have a distinctively Thai flavor. An architectural notebook at the end contains plans and drawings of decorative features.

MODERN THAI LITERATURE

HERBERT P PHILLIPS
University of Hawaii Press, Honolulu, 1987

Subtitled "With an Ethnographic Interpretation," this survey of contemporary Thai writing is the work of a long-time American student of Thailand's culture in association with Vinita Atmiyanandana Lawler, Amnuaycaj Patipat and Likhit Dhiravegin.

"Although the book contains literature and is about literature," Dr Phillips writes, "its primary purpose is not literary, but cultural: to show what some of the most sensitive, reflective, articulate—and sometimes theatrical and bumptious—

members of Thai society think of their own culture and experience." The writings were published during the 1960's and 1970's, and most of them reflect the political and social turmoil of that period. Among the examples included are works by the poet Angkarn Kalayaanaphong, the social critic Sulak Sivaraksa, the short story writer Khamsing Srinawk, the novelist and translator M L Boonlue Kunjara Debyasuvan, and the multitalented M R Kukrit Pramoj. The cultural significance of each selection is examined in a separate essay.

AERIAL NATIONALISM: A HISTORY OF AVIATION IN THAILAND

EDWARD M YOUNG
Smithsonian Institution Press, Washington, DC, 1995

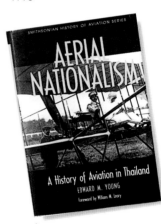

Part of a series on the history of aviation published by the Smithsonian Institute, this book will come as a revelation to those who think flying was a comparatively recent phenomenon in Southeast Asia.

The marvel of flight came to Thailand in 1911, just eight years after the Wright brothers proved that it was feasible, when a French aviator gave a demonstration on the grounds of the Royal Bangkok Sports Club. A year later, three Thai military officers were sent to France for training, which they completed in 1913. By 1916, Thailand had enough planes and pilots to participate in the annual army maneuvres, and in 1918 it sent an aviation contingent to fight on the Allied side in the Second World War. An airmail service, the first in Southeast Asia, was started within parts of the country in 1922. These exciting and little-known early events are covered by the author, as well as the later development of the Royal Thai Air Force through 1945.

CHAIYO!
WALTER F VELLA
The University Press of Hawaii, Honolulu, 1978

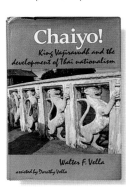

Dr Vella, who taught at the University of Hawaii, was a noted student of Thai history and wrote several books on the subject. In this one, subtitled "King Vajiravudh and the Development of Thai Nationalism," he examines the reign of King Rama VI (1910–25), a significant period that has not been widely treated by other Western historians.

King Rama VI was the first Thai ruler to be educated abroad and came to the throne after the long reign of King Chulalongkorn. Continuing the reforms of the fifth reign, he founded Thailand's first university, named after his father, and initiated the use of surnames for all Thai citizens. He also attempted to foster a spirit of nationalism to unite the Thai people, an effort that took a wide variety of forms from team sports to the establishment of a paramilitary patriotic organization called the Wild Tigers. A prolific

writer, he produced numerous plays, poems, and newspaper articles and translated the works of such Western writers as Shakespeare, Sheridan, and Molière.

LIFE AND RITUAL IN OLD SIAM
PHYA ANUMAN RAJADHON
HRAF Press, New Haven, 1961

Phya Anuman Rajadhon (1888–1969) is regarded as one of the great figures of Thai studies. During the course of a long life, he never lost his fascination for all aspects of his native culture and wrote numerous articles and books on Thai customs, language and literature, also serving at various times as Director-General of the Fine Arts Department and President of the Siam Society.

This example of his work, translated and edited by William J Gedney of the University of Michigan, is divided into three sections—The Life of the Farmer, Popular Buddhism in Thailand, and Customs Connected with Birth and the Rearing of Children—and is characteristic of his wide-ranging interests and perceptive scholarship. The chapter on the Thai farmer, for example, covers every aspect of rural life from preparing the fields to threshing the rice, with precise details about each one, while the other chapters are similarly thorough on their subjects. Some of the customs described are now rare but others can still be found in rural parts of the country.

THE ARTS OF THAILAND
STEVE VAN BEEK AND LUCA INVERNIZZI TETTONI
Travel Publishing Asia Ltd., Hong Kong, 1985

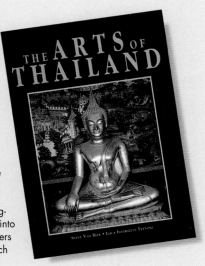

Illustrated throughout with color photographs, this is a comprehensive introduction to the full range of art in Thailand from the earliest times to the present.

The opening chapters examine the various cultures that preceded the Thai, primarily Hindu, Khmer, Srivijaya, and Mon, from whom many elements were borrowed or adapted; there is also a discussion of Thailand's less well-known prehistory, which included the extraordinary Ban Chiang culture of the northeastern region, only discovered in the 1960's. These are followed by detailed accounts of Sukhothai, the northern Lanna kingdoms, Ayutthaya and Bangkok, each divided into the various arts of that period. The final chapters are devoted to contemporary painting and such minor arts as gold work, nielloware, lacquer, mother-of-pearl inlay and theater arts.

THE ART OF SUKHOTHAI
CAROL STRATTON AND MIRIAM MCNAIR SCOTT
Oxford University Press, Kuala Lumpur, 1981

From the mid-thirteenth to the mid-fifteenth centuries, the early Thai capital of Sukhothai saw a remarkable flowering of the arts that many Thais still regard as the finest in their history. This book, written for the general reader, examines the major achievements in architecture, sculpture, painting and ceramics of Sukhothai, while also highlighting religious and political developments in other Asian countries as they relate to this period in Thai art.

It was at Sukhothai that the first distinctively Thai features emerged in

architecture and temple decoration. Some of the finest of all Buddha images were also created there, in particular the famous three-dimensional Walking Buddha cast in bronze. Potters at Sukhothai and the nearby satellite city of Si Satchanalai produced beautiful ceramic wares, including celadon, that were exported in large quantities to Indonesia, Borneo and the Philippines. The book is extensively illustrated with color and black-and-white photographs as well as drawings.

TEXTILES AND THE TAI EXPERIENCE IN SOUTHEAST ASIA
MATTIEBELLE GITTINGER and H LEEDOM LEFFERTS, JR
The Textile Museum, Washington, DC, 1992

This useful reference work by two well-known textile scholars was originally published as a catalogue

accompanying an exhibition of Thai textiles presented in honor of Her Majesty Queen Sirikit's Fifth Cycle Birthday. It is illustrated with both black and white and color photographs showing both Thai life and examples from private collections.

"Textiles," writes Dr Gittinger, "are a key to many aspects of Tai culture and even address issues of the history of the Tai people." In the various chapters, she and her co-author examine the methods of textile production, the specific uses of textiles for both clothing and symbolic purposes, weaving as an aspect of traditional village life, and the role played by textiles in Buddhism, royal ceremonies, and everyday life. Many interesting customs and beliefs are brought into the discussion so the book is useful for the general reader as well as for textile specialists.

PEOPLES OF THE GOLDEN TRIANGLE
PAUL AND ELAINE LEWIS
Thames and Hudson, London, 1984

Though representing a small part of Thailand's population—the authors estimate their total number

at a little over 400,000—the hill tribes of the far north have attracted an unusual amount of attention, partly because of their colorful costumes and cultures, partly because of the problems they have caused through forest destruction and the cultivation of opium. In this lavishly illustrated book Paul and Elaine Lewis offer a comprehensive view of the life and crafts of the major groups, based on many years of work with them.

The tribes considered are the Karen, Hmong, Mien, Lahu, Akha and Lisu. For each there are discussions of such aspects as clothing and ornaments, houses and village organization, sickness and treatment, beliefs, and customs concerning birth, death, courtship and marriage. There are also special chapters on tribal crafts, including jewelry, musical instruments, baskets and utensils, many of which have become popular collectors' items in recent years.

A KING OF SIAM SPEAKS
M R SENI PRAMOJ AND M R KUKRIT PRAMOJ
The Siam Society, Bangkok, 1987

Two scholarly brothers joined to produce this book

of letters, proclamations, and other writings by King Mongkut (Rama IV). Some are translations, while others are written in the King's own highly distinctive English; collectively they reflect his remarkable character and range of interests.

One of the proclamations, for instance, adjures his subjects on "the inelegant practice of throwing dead animals into the waterway". There are others concerning religious freedom and superstition, on false rumors, on getting drunk at the New Year's celebrations, and on the need to lay up stocks of rice during a year of shortage. Among the numerous letters are one to President Franklin Pierce of the United States, thanking him for gifts brought by the first American envoy, and another to Queen Victoria, accompanying a long list of presents sent to her. There is also a circular giving twelve ladies of the Inner Palace freedom to resign, noting that if any wanted to marry outside, "His Majesty would gladly and sincerely congratulate them."

ARTS AND CRAFTS OF THAILAND
WILLIAM WARREN AND LUCA INVERNIZZI TETTONI
Thames and Hudson, London, 1994

Besides its classic Buddhist art and architecture, Thailand also has a large number of traditional crafts that serve various needs and that are covered in this book by the same writer-photographer team who produced Thai Style.

The crafts are divided by purpose. Thus the section on "Crafts as Symbols of Status" discusses the sophisticated creations used by royalty and other high-ranking circles, while "Ceremonial Crafts" examines those that figure in certain rituals, from thrones and royal regalia to spirit houses and delicate floral

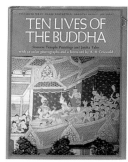

offerings. Other sections deal with the crafts of village life, often superb examples of folk art; textiles, including their uses; the woodcarvings that adorn both homes and religious buildings; theatrical crafts such as khon masks, musical instruments and shadow-play figures; and contemporary crafts that employ traditional methods of manufacture.

THAILAND IN THE 90s
NATIONAL IDENTITY BOARD
Office of the Prime Minister, Bangkok, 1991

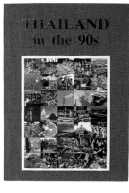

The National Identity Board, which comes under the Prime Minister's office, has published three of these comprehensive surveys of Thailand: two dealing with the country in the 1980's and this one in the early 1990's. The purpose of all of them has been to give outsiders an accurate portrait of the country's institutions and development.

Beginning with an examination of Thai history, the book contains chapters on the monarchy, the land and its people, religion,

education, the arts, the economy, government and politics, energy and natural resources, agriculture, manufacturing, science and technology, transport and communications and tourism. Each of the entries was written by an expert in the field and is accompanied by color photographs as well as relevant statistical charts.

TEN CONTEMPORARY THAI ARTISTS
BY JOHN HOSKIN AND LUCA INVERNIZZI TETTONI
Graphic Co., Ltd., Bangkok, 1984

Subtitled "The Spirit of Siam in Modern Art", this well-illustrated book examines the work of ten of Thailand's leading painters, their careers and the main themes of their paintings. An introduction traces the development of modern art in the country, particularly the contributions of Corrado Feroci, an Italian sculptor who came in 1924 during the reign of King Rama VI and remained for the rest of his life, becoming a Thai with the name of Silpa Bhirasri and powerfully influencing several generations of students.

Though contemporary in their approach, most of the artists included have been trained in the techniques of classsical Thai painting and their works blend old and new in often arresting ways. Those discussed are Tawee Nandakwang, Angkarn Kalayanapongsa, Uab Sanasen, Thawan Duchanee, Pratuang Emjaroen, Preecha

Thaothong, Worariddh Riddhagni, Watcharee Wongwathana-Anan, Chalermchai Kositpipat, and Panya Vijinthanasarn.

TEN LIVES OF THE BUDDHA
ELIZABETH WRAY, CLARE ROSENFIELD, DOROTHY BAILY, JOE WRAY
Weatherhill, Tokyo, 1972

This book explores the ancient art of Thai mural painting, particularly as applied to the moralistic Jataka tales concerning previous incarnations of the Buddha.

In all there are 550 such tales, in each of which the central character—animal, human, or semidivine—is a Bodhisattva, or Buddha-to-be, who serves either as a passive onlooker or, more often, practices one or more of the ten virtues necessary to becoming a Buddha. The final ten tales are the most popular, the culmination of the countless lives in which the virtues are brought to perfection. The authors offer summaries of these ten, illustrated by scenes from murals in a number of Thai temples, as well as informative chapters on the history and techniques of Thai mural painting.

TEMPLES AND ELEPHANTS
CARL BOCK
White Orchid Press, Bangkok, 1981

Carl Bock was a Norwegian who traveled through Southeast Asia toward the end of the nineteenth century and wrote

popular accounts of his experiences in relatively little-known places such as Borneo and upper Siam. His views are unusually free of the colonial attitudes of the period, and his natural curiosity led him to explore many aspects of culture generally overlooked by contemporary Europeans.

In Bangkok he was granted an audience with King Chulalongkorn, saw the royal white elephants, visited the leading temples and attended a National Exhibition of Thai products. The most interesting part of his account, however, is the journey he made to the far north, or what he called "the Lao states". Here he spent time in Chiang Mai, then only loosely under control of the central government, and crossed into what is today Laos; his descriptions include elephants at work in the teak forests, a tiger hunt, a leper colony, local customs and an exciting river trip.

BEHIND THE SMILE: VOICES OF THAILAND
SANITSUDA EKACHAI
Post Publishing Co., Ltd.,
Bangkok, 1990

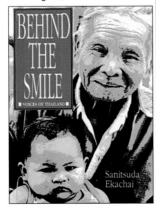

Despite Thailand's rapid industrialization in recent years, the vast majority of its people still live and work in the countryside. Even there, however, the pace of change has had enormous social and economic consequences, and this is the subject of Sanitsuda Ekachai's collection of articles, first published in the *Bangkok Post*.

Khun Sanitsuda visited three major regions and in each interviewed a variety of ordinary villagers. Everywhere she found changing lifestyles, as well as a widening gap between rich and poor. One northeastern village, for example, was populated almost entirely by the very old or the very young, the rest having been forced to leave in search of seasonal employment. In the south, a fisherman complains that modern trawlers are depriving him of his livelihood. Northerners talk of the loss of their land to rich people and the sale of children to earn desperately-needed money. The "voices" heard are nearly all sad, and they reveal often neglected truths about modern Thai society.

PALACES OF THE GODS: KHMER ART AND ARCHITECTURE IN THAILAND
SMITTHI SRIBHADRA AND
ELIZABETH MOORE
River Books, Bangkok, 1992

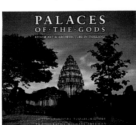

Between the ninth and thirteenth centuries, much of contemporary Thailand was part of the great Khmer empire ruled from Angkor. Visible evidence of this can be seen today in numerous architectural remains, mostly in the northeast, altogether comprising the greatest

collection of Khmer temples outside of Cambodia.

This book surveys the buildings and art of the period, with extensive photographs by Michael Freeman. Among the most impressive are Phimai, an important Khmer center near the modern city of Nakhon Ratchasime, which was linked by a direct road to Angkor, and Prasat Phanom Ruang, on a hilltop not far from the Cambodian border. Both of these temples date from the early twelfth century, during the reign of the Khmer ruler Suryavarman, and both are decorated with exceptionally beautiful stone carvings and other features of great artistic merit.

KATYA AND THE PRINCE OF SIAM
EILEEN HUNTER AND M R
NARISA CHAKRABONGSE
River Books, Bangkok, 1994

Among the many revolutionary reforms of King Chulalongkorn (Rama V) was the decision to send his sons abroad for their education. It was thus that Prince Chakrabongse, a particular favorite whose mother was recognized as the Supreme Queen, was sent to Russia to be educated as part of the court of Tsar Nicholas II. There he met and fell in love with Ekaterina Ivanova Desnitskaya, known to her family as Katya; the couple

were married without informing his father, an act that led to scandal in Thailand and the elimination of Chakrabongse as a contender for succession to the Thai throne.

This account of the romance and its aftermath was written by the Prince's granddaughter and her aunt. Through diaries, letters and other sources, it recreates the period and the ramifications—personal as well as dynastic—of the affair in fascinating detail, illustrated with numerous old photographs from the family collection.

CONSUL IN PARADISE
W A R WOOD
Souvenir Press, London,
1965

W A R Wood arrived in Thailand as a student interpreter with the British Consular Service in 1896. He remained there for the rest of his long life (he died in 1970), working in various parts of the country and, finally, in 1919, becoming Consul in Chiang Mai. Among his many books was the first history of Thailand, published in 1924 and long the standard reference work on the subject.

Consul in Paradise, originally published as *Land of Smiles* in 1935, is a collection of autobiographical sketches on a wide range of subjects, among them the Consular Courts in the

days when Thai law did not apply to foreigners, unusual cases over which he presided as a magistrate, Thai and Lao folklore, elephants and hill tribes of the north. The tone is light and amusing, the content fascinating and informative; throughout the reader is aware that the inscription chosen for his final resting place in Chiang Mai is an apt one— it reads simply, "He loved Thailand."

THE GENTLEMAN IN THE PARLOUR
SOMERSET MAUGHAM
William Heinemann Ltd.,
London, 1930

The only pure travel book ever written by Maugham, this is an account of a journey in the late 1920's to upper Burma, Thailand, and Indochina.

The Thai segment includes a visit to Lopburi, where Maugham wanted to see the house of Constantine Phaulkon, "one of the most amazing of the adventurers who have made the East the scene of

their exploits," as well as a long stay at the Oriental Hotel, where he almost died from malaria contracted upcountry. Bangkok generally failed to impress him, though he responded enthusiastically to Buddhist temple architecture ("It makes you laugh with delight to think that anything so fantastic could exist on this sombre earth") and also to life along the busy canals that were then a major feature of the city. While recovering from his illness, Maugham wrote a fairy story about the country called "Princess September," included here and also separately published later as a children's book.

THE ART OF THAI WOOD CARVING

NAENGNOI PUNJABHAN AND SOMCHAI NA NAKHONPHANOM
Rerngrom Publishing Co. Ltd., Bangkok, 1990

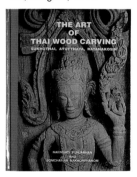

Woodcarving has been an outstanding Thai craft since the earliest days of the Kingdom, used to adorn palaces, temples and ordinary homes as well as items of furniture.

This book by two authorities on the subject treats carvings from Sukhothai, Ayutthaya and Bangkok and is illustrated with both drawings and color photographs. It includes discussions of the basic Thai decorative motifs, the tools and techniques used by traditional carvers, architectural carvings found on royal and religious buildings, and assorted other items such as Buddha images, monastic furniture, thrones and royal barges. The same authors have produced similar works on carvings from the north and from the northeast.

NATIONAL PARKS OF THAILAND

DENIS GRAY, COLLIN PIPRELL, AND MARK GRAHAM
Communications Resources (Thailand) Ltd., Bangkok, 1994

Thailand's first national park, Khao Yai, was established in 1961. Thirty-odd years later, when this guide was published, there were seventy-seven parks, thirty-five wildlife sanctuaries, and forty-six non-hunting areas along with other protected zones, covering in all an area of about 65,000 square kilometers.

The authors of this book provide a useful introduction to thirty of the main parks, presenting the history, habitat and wildlife of

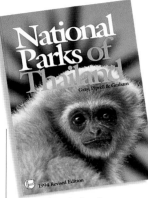

each with details on visiting facilities. The range extends from Doi Inthanon in the northern province of Chiang Mai, which incorporates Thailand's highest mountain and contains an unusually rich variety of bird life, to Tarutao, a marine park in the Indian Ocean that extends over 1,490 square kilometers and includes nearly two hundred islands. Opening chapters discuss Thailand's not always edifying history of environmental conservation, along with some of the many endangered species of flora and fauna.

DANCE, DRAMA, AND THEATRE IN THAILAND

MATTANI MOJDARA RUTNIN
Centre for East Asian Cultural Studies for Unesco, Tokyo, 1993

THAILAND: SEVEN DAYS IN THE KINGDOM

WILLIAM WARREN
Times Edition, Singapore, 1987

Published on the occasion of King Bhumibol Adulyadej's sixtieth birthday, this large-format book brought to Thailand the multi-photographer coverage used successfully in other countries.

Fifty of the world's top photographers—from Europe, America, the Pacific, and Asia—came to Bangkok in March of 1987. From there most of them fanned out to spend a week on assignment in every part of the kingdom. One, for instance, went to the remote northern mountains to explore hill tribe life, another to the opposite end among the Muslim Thais of the south; one donned scuba gear for underwater photography off Phuket, while several concentrated on the complex life of the capital. In all, they brought back more than 85,000 pictures which were then carefully culled to present a comprehensive portrait of the country. Gore Vidal, a frequent visitor to Thailand, contributed a foreword to the book.

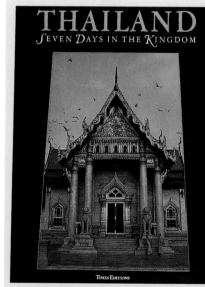

The author of this work, a well-known teacher and specialist in theater arts at Thammasat University, presents a comprehensive view of the subject that covers many centuries.

The opening section discusses traditional dance, dance-drama and dramatic literature from the first Thai capital at Sukhothai to the mid-nineteenth century, showing how the various forms developed over this long period. A revival of the classical khon dance-drama took place during the early Bangkok period;

on the other hand Western culture, introduced during the reign of King Rama IV, gained in popularity toward the end of the century, bringing many changes to old theatrical forms and the introduction of new ones. The last section of Dr Mattani's book deals with contemporary Thai theater, a field in which she herself has been very active.

SOME SPLENDID CRAFTS

PHILIPPE ANNEZ
Siam Society, Bangkok, 1994

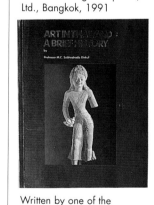

With numerous photographs by Dacho Buranabunpot, this book examines some of the Thai crafts under Her Majesty Queen Sirikit's Foundation for the Promotion of Supplementary Occupations and Related Techniques (SUPPORT), which was established in 1976.

The primary aim of SUPPORT is to train villagers in cottage industries that can be a source of supplementary income in times of crop failure or other disasters; at the same time, it has helped revive many traditional crafts that were in danger of disappearing because of cheaper, mass-produced items. Among those discussed here are yan lipao, basketry woven of a tough vine native to the far south; mud mee silk, an ikat weave that is a specialty of the northeast; nielloware, often used as royal gifts; miniature clay dolls made near the old capital of Ayutthaya; and beautiful works by silver craftsmen from the far north.

ART IN THAILAND

M C SUBHADRADIS DISKUL
Amarin Printing Group Co., Ltd., Bangkok, 1991

Written by one of the leading scholars of classical Thai art, this is a useful introduction to the country's rich heritage, particularly its Buddhist sculpture.

The survey includes pre-Thai artifacts such as those produced during the Srivijaya, Mon and Khmer periods, as well as the great works of

Lanna Thai, Sukhothai, Ayutthaya and early Bangkok. The author gives the main characteristics of each period, as well as the iconography of the examples shown in the illustrations. We see, for example, how influences from a variety of cultures—Indian, Khmer, Sri Lankan and Chinese—were absorbed and altered to create styles different from the originals and distinctive to Thailand.

THE MILITARY IN THAI POLITICS 1981-86
SUCHIT BUNBONGKARN
Institute of Southeast Studies, Singapore, 1987

The military has been a significant force in Thai politics since the end of the absolute monarchy in 1932, particularly during the long period stretching from the late 1940's through the 1980's when the Thai army played a predominant role.

Though it examines a relatively brief five-year span, this book by a Professor in Political Science at Chulalongkorn University offers a revealing look at the various factions operating within the military and of its changing priorities. As the author writes in the preface, "This period saw an interesting change in the military's perception of politics as it began to expand its role in civil affairs. This expansion included several programmes in rural development, peace-keeping duties, and mass mobilization in rural and urban areas." Chapter headings reflect the areas covered:

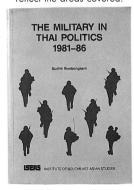

THAI COOKING
JENNIFER BRENNAN
Jill Norman and Hobhouse Ltd., London, 1981

THE TASTE OF THAILAND
VACHARIN BHUMICHITR
Pavilion Books Ltd., London, 1988

THAILAND THE BEAUTIFUL COOKBOOK
PANURAT POLADITMONTRI, JUDY LEW, WILLIAM WARREN
Weldon Owen Inc., San Francisco, 1992

During the past decade or so literally hundreds of books have been published on the preparation of Thai food, a phenomenon which reflects the worldwide interest in this subtly-flavored cuisine. The three mentioned here are generally available and have achieved more than ordinary success in various markets.

Ms Brennan's book was one of the earliest to appear and includes preliminary chapters on Thai life, the Thai kitchen, basic ingredients and sample menus, followed by a selection of recipes for dishes that range from starters to sweets. Vacharin Bhumichitr, the owner of several succcessful Thai restaurants in London, offers a number of his own favorite recipes, with illustrations of how the finished dishes should look. The last book, handsomely illustrated and in large format, is part of an international series and was published in Thailand on the occasion of Her Majesty Queen Sirikit's sixtieth birthday.

"Military Factions and Their Struggle for Power," "Politics of Compromise and Military Factionalism," "The Army and Its Increasing Commitment to Domestic Tasks," and "Legitimization of the Military's Role Expansion."

A WOMAN OF BANGKOK
JACK REYNOLDS
Editions Duang Kamol, Bangkok, 1985

This popular novel about a tough Bangkok bar girl and some of her customers was first published in England in 1956 and has gone into many editions, the precursor of countless others inspired by the same subject.

The heroine is Vilai,

known as the White Leopard, who works in the Bolero Dance Hall and who becomes an obsession to a rather innocent young Englishman. The situation is hardly original, the style often melodramatic ("You no haff house, no haff wife, no haff nussing," the White Leopard tells the besotted hero, "But I must pay for many sing. You no giff no

money, what I do?"); but the sleazy bar scene is convincingly rendered, and the novel reveals a side of Thailand that undoubtedly draws more visitors than the authorities would like to admit.

MODERN ART IN THAILAND
APINAN POSHYANANDA
Oxford University Press, Kuala Lumpur, 1992

Dr Apinan is the leading authority on contemporary Thai art and has also written *Western-style Painting and Sculpture in the Royal Thai Court* (two volumes, published in 1993). In this book, he offers a survey that covers both painting and sculpture over a span of seventy-odd years.

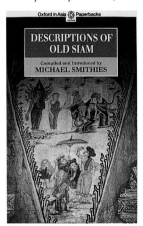

Modern art in Thailand, especially in the early years, was the product of Western influences. A pivotal figure in its development was an Italian sculptor named Corrado Feroci, who first came to the country in 1924 at the invitation of King Rama VI and, acquiring Thai citizenship and the name of Silpa Bhirasri, remained there until his death in 1962. One of the founders of what became the Fine Arts University (Silpakorn), he trained numerous artists and was also responsible for several of Bangkok's most prominent monuments. D Apinan discusses the influence of Silpa Bhirasri

and also the various phases—realism, impressionism, abstraction, etc.—through which Thai art has passed, with analyses of the leading artists.

DESCRIPTIONS OF OLD SIAM
Compiled and edited by MICHAEL SMITHIES
Oxford University Press, Kuala Lumpur, 1995

This is a collection of published impressions of Thailand, all but one of them by Westerners, who first came to the country in the sixteenth century. It offers fascinating views of the old capital of Ayutthaya and also of Bangkok during its first century before the age of mass tourism.

The earliest excerpt, a brief one, is by a Portuguese, Diogo do Couto (1542–1616), and describes the royal ceremony held at Ayutthaya to mark the end of the rainy season. Other observers include Fernao Mendez Pinto, who traveled extensively through the region in the early sixteenth century; Joost Schouten, who visited Ayutthaya in 1644 and describes the sacred white elephants; Nicholas Gervaise, a Jesuit missionary, who gives an account of men's clothes and women's ornaments; the Abbe de Choisy, who came with a French embassy sent by Louis XIV;

Francois Henri Turpin, who did not come to Thailand but obtained a rare account of the fall of Ayutthaya from a missionary who was there at the time; John Crawfurd, who came to Bangkok on a trade mission in 1821; and the famous Anna Leonowens, who describes her first meeting with King Rama IV.

REFLECTIONS ON THAI CULTURE
WILLIAM KLAUSNER
The Siam Society, Bangkok, 1993

William Klausner, an American, came to Thailand in the 1950's and has since published many articles on the country's culture and customs, a selection of which was collected for this useful book.

A number of the chapters deal with village customs in the northeast, where Klausner lived during his first few years. These explore such distinctive Thai concepts as *krengchai*, or extreme reluctance to impose on another, *khwan sanuk*, or pleasure, the role played by Buddhist beliefs in everyday behavior and other equally pervasive beliefs in the spirit world. Additional chapters examine the cultural confusions that often arise between Westerners attempting to do business in

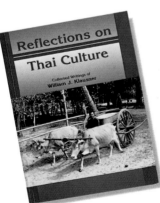

Thailand, with explanations of Thai concepts that lie behind such misunderstandings.

MENAM CHAO PHRAYA
William Warren and Jock Montgomery
Post Books, Bangkok, 1994

Though a mere 365 kilometers in length from its starting point at the northern edge of the Central Plains, the Chao Phraya River has played a dominant role in Thailand's development, both as a source of nourishment for fields and orchards and also for centuries as the principal artery of communication with the outside world.

This extensively illustrated book begins at Pak Nam (literally "river mouth"), where the Chao Phraya empties into the sea, and moves up the winding stream to its source at the confluence of two rivers at Nakhon Sawan. Past and present are explored during the journey, the first through quotations drawn from some of the many travelers who came to Ayutthaya and to Bangkok and the second through descriptions of the river as it exists today. Interspersed throughout are short essays on related subjects, such as riverine festivals, the famous royal barges, and various kinds of boats.

JOURNAL OF A VOYAGE TO SIAM 1685–1686
ABBE DE CHOISY
Oxford University Press, Kuala Lumpur, 1993

For the first time in English, translated by Michael Smithies, this is the journal kept by a Catholic priest who came to Ayutthaya with a French embassy sent by Louis XIV in 1685.

The Abbe de Choisy was possibly the most sophisticated of all the French visitors of the period, having in his youth been a noted libertine and transvestite and ending his career as Dean of the Academic Française. His account of his relatively brief stay in Ayutthaya, though less comprehensive than that of Simon de la Loubere who came two years later, is both witty and full of interesting details, especially about such customs of the Siamese

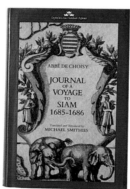

court as a royal elephant hunt and palace ceremonies. A high point is the semi-farcical scene in which Thai and French cultures clash during the presentation of Louis XIV's letter to King Narai.

THE 20 BEST NOVELS OF THAILAND
MARCEL BARANG
Thai Modern Classics, Bangkok 1994

While some may question the superlative in the title, this is a useful introduction to a subject not generally familiar to English-language

readers, by a long-time foreign resident of Thailand.

The author and translator begins with a survey of Thai literature from ancient times and then offers excerpts from novels by twenty writers of the present century, with biographical sketches of each. Among those included are M L Buppha Kunjara Nimmanhemin, a pioneer who wrote under the pen name Dorkmai Sot and whose eleven novels dealt with customs and traditions of the upper class; Boonluea Theipphayasuwan, whose work reflects the social change of this century; Chart Korpjitti, whose books sell in the tens of thousands; Nikhom Korp-wong (pen name Nikom Rayawa), winner of several literary prizes; and the multi-talented M R Kukrit Pramoj.

THAI WAYS
DENIS SEGALLER
Post Publishing Company, Bangkok, 1989

Together with a companion volume titled *More Thai Ways*, this is a collection of articles on Thai culture and customs that originally appeared in a newspaper. It is aimed at the general Western reader with relatively little knowledge of Thailand and, as such, is a useful source of information for newcomers to the country. The subjects range from ceremonies and customs to language and legends. Among the topics dealt with are such popular festivals as Loy Krathong

and Songkran; the Thai wedding ceremony; rituals that accompany ordination into the Buddhist monkhood; assorted superstitions; historical figures such as King Mongkut and King Chulalongkorn; Thai astrology; the *khon*, or masked dance-drama; popular legends; and selected "do's and don'ts" of Thai social behavior.

THAI VILLAGE LIFE
SERI PHONGPHIT AND KEVIN HEWISON
Thai Institute for Rural Development, Bangkok, 1990

Subtitled "Culture and Transition in the Northeast," this is a study of village life in a region that, despite its size and population density, is relatively little known to outsiders. The northeast, or Isan in the Central Thai language, is an area that consists of seventeen provinces, inhabited by people that are mostly of Lao ethnic and culture origin, though there are significant groups of Khmer, Chinese and Vietnamese as well as other minority groups. The Lao majority are given emphasis in this study, which covers such topics as village cultural life, traditional learning, the power of beliefs (both Buddhist and animistic), and the changes that are taking place as a result of improved communications and the recognition of the region's strategic importance.

All these books are available at all Asia Books' branches.

Appendices

NOTES

THE THAI ECONOMY—FIFTY YEARS OF EXPANSION

1. Cited in Ingram, 1971, *p. 166.*

2. The phrase is from Riggs, 1966, *p. 249.*

3. In this the military group that came to power in 1947 was not original, but continued the policies of both the left and right wings of the People's Party.

4. These new varieties are essential for dry-season cropping because they are photoperiod non-sensitive. The traditional varieties are photoperiod sensitive, which means that the rice plant will never flower during the dry season, and can be grown only during the wet season.

5. The figures are net of foreign assets held by the Bank of Thailand and financial institutions. The source is TDRI, 1986.

AGRICULTURE AND FISHERIES

1. Urban, by definition, refers to municipal areas and urban sanitary districts. The figure includes Bangkok, which had (1981) a population of 5.88 million equivalent to nearly 11 percent of Thailand's population in that year. Excluding Bangkok, the ratio of rural population will be nearly 88 percent.

2. National Statistics Office, *Population and Urbanization Report based on Population Census*, NSO, Bangkok, *p. 1.*

3. National Economic and Social Development Board (NESDB), *National Income of Thailand*, New Series, 1970–87, National Accounts Division, NESDB, Bangkok, 1998, *pp. 28–29.*

4. Estimated by the NESDB based on the Office of Agricultural Economics' figures on value added generated by this sector in that year.

5. National Statistics Office.

6. 1977 figures derived from the Bank of Thailand and the Department of Customs. The 1991 figures is derived from the Office of Agricultural Economics.

7. Based on statistics from the NESDB and the Office of Agricultural Economics.

8. S.T.K. means rights to utilize land for agricultural production to meet consumption needs.

THAI SOCIETY IN TRANSITION

1. Ammar Siamwalla and Suthad Setboonsarng, *Trade, Exchange Rate, and Agricultural Pricing Policies in Thailand.* World Bank Comparative Studies, The World Bank, Washington, D.C. 1989, *pp. 29–31, 53–61, 109, 111, 132–140, 204–8.*

2. The traditional Thai polity was a *ratcha-anacak,* a kingdom. "This term...refers to a type of polity whose model is based on Hindu-Buddhist theories of statecraft....the ruler of a *ratcha-anacak* is more than simply the lord of *muang;* he is a raja..., such a raja exercises authority...based on his personal identification with a sacred power, an identification that is manifest in the public rites the king performs. The raja occupies a throne at the center of a circle *(cak* from Skt. *cakra),* also known in Indian manuals of government as a *mandala,* which is a this-worldly reflection of the sacred cosmos. Within this circle are lesser polities whose lords recognize the overlordship of the king so long as he is able, through ritual performances or successful warfare, to demonstrate that he possesses divine authority." Keyes, Charles F., *Thailand: Buddhist Kingdom as Modern Nation-State,* Boulder, Westview Press, 1989, *p. 28., also see pp.*

27–42. See Akin Rabibhadana, *The Organization of Thai Society in the Early Bangkok Period 1782–1873,* Data Paper 74, Ithaca: Cornell University, Southeast Asia Program, 1968, *pp. 49–56,* and also Wyatt, David K., *Thailand: A Short History,* London: Yale University Press, and Thai Watana Panich Co., Ltd., 1984, *pp. 181–222.*

3. Hirsch, Philip, *Development Dilemmas in Rural Thailand,* New York: Oxford University Press, 1990, *pp. 11–12;* Hawaiian Agronomic (International) Inc., *Development Impact in the Northeast: Small Farmer Perspective on Development in Northeast Thailand,* 1987, Bangkok, *pp. 11–15.*

4. Bangkok today has a total of 1,031 slums, with a total of about 852,500 slum dwellers. According to the most recent data of the national housing authority, over 225,000 households, or 1.1 million people, live in informal settlements (or slums) in Bangkok if an average household size of 4.8 persons is assumed. This is about 14 percent of the population of Bangkok Metropolitan Region.

5. It is interesting to note that after 1974, the number of female in-migrants into Bangkok has been higher than that of males. The total number of in-migrants (women and men) is the highest in 1981, with women accounting for 60.7 percent. This share rose to 62.6 percent in 1988. However, in 1957, there were only 18 (0.9 percent) women out of 2,049 migrants from the northeast (these statistics indicate only those who contacted with the Government) (Viyout et. al. 1991:102).

6. World Bank, *World Tables 1992,* Baltimore: Johns Hopkins University Press, *pp. 22–23.*

7. NESDB, *National Income of Thailand* (1987 New Series, *pp. 26–27;* and 1990, *pp. 11, 16*).

8. Chalongphob Sussangkarn, *Towards Balanced Development: Sectorial, Spatial and Other Dimensions,* TDRI, 1992 Year-End Conference, Jomtien., *p. 4.*

9. *Ibid., p. 6.*

10. *Ibid., p. 8.*

11. *Ibid., p. 10.*

12. Chalongphob 1992 op. cit., p. 34., and Suganya Hutaserani and Somchai Jitsuchon, *Thailand's Income Distribution and Poverty Profile and Their Current Situations,* TDRI, Bangkok, December 1988, *p. 17.*

13. Chalongphob, 1992, *op. cit., pp. 30–31.*

14. Sukaesinee Subhadhira and others, *Case Studies of Human-Forest Interactions in Northeast Thailand,* Northeast Thailand Upland Social Forestry Project, KU/KKU/FORD 850-0391 Final Report 2, 1987, *p. 92.*

15. See Chirmsak Pinthong and Akin Rabibhadana Sangkhom, *Setthakkit, lae Kanmuang khong Sapphakon Channabot,* Document No.9 Thai Khadi Research Institute, Thammasat University, Bangkok, 1984, *p. 24;* Chairat Phanchareon, *Wikharoa Kan Luaktang Kamnan Phuyai Ban,* M.A. Thesis, Faculty of Political Science, Chulalongkorn University, Bangkok, 1974, *pp. 10–12.*

16. *Ibid., p.20.*

17. *Ibid., p.24.*

18. See Akin Rabibhadana, *Social Inequity: A Source of Conflict in the Future?,* TDRI, 1993 Year-End Conference, Jomtien, Thailand 1993, *pp. 9–13.*

19. Keyes, Charles F., "Local Leadership in Rural Thailand" in Neher Clark D. ed., *Modern Thai Politics.*

20. See Chirmsak Pinthong and Akin Rabibhadana, *op. cit.* and Akin Rabibhadana, *Panha kan Phattana Chonnabot, Botruan jak Korani Yokkrabat,* Research and Development Institute, Khon Kaen University, Khon Kaen 1988. See also Viyout Charmruspan et. al., *Transformations of Economic, Social and Culture of the Northeast Regions (1950–1990),* Khon Kaen, Research and Development Institute (RDI), 1993 *p. 77.*

21. Keyes, Charles F., 1979., *op. cit., p. 207.*

22. *Ibid., p. 209* and Oed Diphun ed., *Phrasong Esan Kap Kan Phattana,* NGO CORD, Bangkok, *p. 203.*

23. The education system has been separated from the wat for a long time now. Monks play many roles today, as preachers, as forest meditation specialists, as fortune tellers, and as magicians. Some have proved to be very capable local leaders. But there are so few of them. See Akin Rabibhadana, 1993, *op. cit., p.13.*

24. Akin Rabibhadana and Suchada Pattrachokchai, "Education and Social and Cultural Values: The Changing Role of Teacher", in TDRI, *Educational Options for the Future of Thailand,* The 1991 Year End Conference, December 14–15, 1991, and Keyes, Charles, *op. cit.* (1979), *p. 210.*

25. Keyes, Charles, *Ibid., p. 210–212.*

26. See Panada Phuekpan, *Esan Local Leader and Its Network: A Case Study of a Female Sub-District Head,* RDI., Khon Kaen, 1991, and Viyout Chamrempan, 1993, *op.cit.*

27. Akin Rabibhadana, *The Organization of Thai Society in the Early Bangkok Period 1782–1873,* Ithaca: Cornell University, Southeast Asia Program, Data Paper No 74, 1969.

28. Potter, Jack M., *Thai Peasant Social Structure,* Chicago, University of Chicago Press, 1976, *pp. 120, 188.*

29. Potter, Sulamith H., *Family Life in a Northern Thai Village: A Structural Significance of Women,* California: University of California Press, 1977, *pp. 19–20.*

30. *Ibid., p.20.*

31. *Ibid., p.20.*

32. *Ibid., p.19.*

33. "This great amount of *bunkhun* arises from the mere fact of having given birth to the child, reinforced by the nurturing of the child." Akin Rabibhadana, "Kinship, Marriage and the Thai Social System," in Aphichat Chamratritthirong ed., *Perspectives on the Thai Marriage,* 1984, *p. 3.*

34. "A boy can easily pay back the *bunkhun* by entering monkhood. If we ask any Thai youth the reason for entering monkhood, he would say that he is doing it for his parents. The belief is that to have an offspring ordained as a monk is a way to obtain great merit." *Ibid., p.21.*

35. Akin Rabibhadana, *Social Inequity: A Source of Conflict in the Future?,* TDRI, 1993 Year-End Conference, Jomthien, *p. 17.*

36. Gray, Jennifer, "The Road to the City: Young Women and Transition in Northern Thailand", Unpublished PhD dissertation, Macquarie University, Sydney, 1990; Mills, Mary Elizabeth, "We are Not Like Our Mothers; Migrants, Modernity and Identity in Northeast Thailand", unpublished PhD dissertation, University of California, Berkeley, 1993; and Chiralak Changsathiman, *Wikrit Thang Wattanatham,* Report for the National Cultural Committee of Thailand, 1992.

37. Akin Rabibhadana, 1993, *op. cit., p.17.*

38. See Chiralak Chongsathitham, 1992, *op. cit.*

NOTES

39. *Ibid.*

40. Pasuk Phangpaichit, *From Peasant Girls to Bangkok Masseuses*, Geneva: International Labor Office, 1982, *p. 32.*

41. *Ibid., p.35.*

42. Pasuk Pongpaichit, 1982, *op. cit., p.5.*

43. *Ibid., p.47.*

44. See Akin Rabibhadana, 1993, *op. cit., pp. 19–20.*

45. "Several people in the north stressed that they admired the girls for the loyalty which they showed toward their parents. They appreciated that the girls were not running away, but rather were showing a proper filial responsibility for looking after their parents in their old age." Pusuk Pongpaichit, 1982, *op. cit., p. 5.*

46. Mingsan Kaosac-ad, Chaiwat Roonruangsee and Jamaree Pitackwong, *Income Employment and Education of Rural Women in Northern Thailand*, Faculty of Social Sciences, Chiangmai University, 1992, Chapter 2:5. For more information on female labor, see Akin Rabibhadana 1993, *op. cit.*

47. Mills, Mary Elizabeth, "We Are Not Like Our Mothers", PhD dissertation, University of California, Berkeley, 1993.

48. From interviews with villagers in Ban Talad, Khon Kaen Provinces, 1989. Similar phenomena have been reported for many other places even in remote areas of the central region.

49. See Takashi Tomosugi, 1995, *Changing Features of a Rice Growing Village in Central Thailand, pp. 47–51.*

50. See also Muecke, Marjorie A., "Make Money Not Babies: Changing Status Markers of Northern Thai Women" in *Asian Survey*, Vol. XXIV, No. 4, April 1984 *pp. 459–470.*

51. See Cohen, Erik, 1991, *Thai Society in Comparative Perspective, pp. 36–46.*

52. Hanks, Lucien M., 1975, "The Thai Social Order as Entourage and Circle" in Skinner, G. William and Kirsch, A. Thomas, *Change and Persistence in Thai Society, p. 198.*

53. Akin Rabibhadana 1969, *The Organization of Thai Society in the Early Bangkok Period 1782–1873, pp. 97–115.*

54. Hanks, Lucien M., "Merit and Power in the Thai Social Order" in Clark D. Neher ed., *Modern Thai Politics: From Village to Nation*, 1979, *p. 96.*

55. The concept of Thai kingship relied upon three principles, the patriarchal (king as father to his people), divya avarta (king as the incarnation of the celestial gods) and dharma raja (king of righteousness, elected by the people, and abiding steadfast in the ten kingly virtues). See Akin Rabibhadana, 1969, *op. cit.*, *pp. 40–44*, and Prince Dhani, "The Old Siamese Conception of the Monarchy" *JSS XXXVI*, December 2, 1947, *pp. 91–107.* "Buddhism, in its modifications of an essentially Brahmanical cosmology, directed the moral authority of the kingship to ends in harmony with the ethical tenets of Buddhism. The brahmanical concept of Devaraja, the king as god, was modified to make the king the embodiment of the law, while the reign of Buddhist moral principles ensured that he should be measured against the law." David K. Wyatt 1966, *The Beginnings of Modern Education in Thailand 1868–1910*, PhD dissertation, Cornell University, *p. 16.*

56. Akin Rabibhadana, "Clientship and Class Structure in the Early Bangkok Period." in Skinner, G. William and Kirsch, A. Thomas, 1975, *op. cit., p.103.*

57. *Ibid., pp. 108–109*, and Akin Rabibhadana, 1969, *op. cit., p. 91–93.*

58. Satchaphirom, Phrya, 1959, *Lao hai lukfang* (Telling the Children), *p.14.* See also Akin Rabibhadana, 1975, p.109, and Suwanna Satha-anant and Nuangnoi Boonyanet, *Kham: Rongroi Khwam Khit, Khwam Chua Thai* (Words, Clues to Thai Thaughts and Beliefs), Chulalongkorn University, Bangkok, 1992.

59. Hanks, Lucien M., "Merit and Power in Thai Society", *op. cit., p.99.*

60. See Akin Rabibhadana, 1969, op. cit.

61. *Ibid.*

62. See Phra Aiyakan Tamnaeng Na Phonlaruan (Law of the Civil Hierarchy) and Phra Aiyakan Tamnaeng Na Thakan Hua Muang (Law of the Military and Provincial Hierarchy), *PK* vol. I, *pp. 182–190.*

63. See Akin Rabibhadana, 1969, *op. cit.*

64. Hanks, Lucien M., "Merit and Power in Thai Society", *op. cit., p.100.* "Among the Thai, however, the relation endures only as long as it serves the convenience of both parties. A superior may terminate benefits, or an inferior may cease rendering services at his own discretion."

65. *Ibid., p.96.*

66. See Akin Rabibhadana, 1969, *op. cit.*

67. Thai society, at that time, had no standing army. Recruitment for war was done through the sakdina system and its structure. This severe measure was introduced in the reign of King Taksin (1767–82) for wars with the Burmese after the recovery of independence.

68. Brummelhuis, Han Ten, "Abundance and Avoidance; an Interpretation of Thai Individualism", Brummelhuis, Han Ten, and Kemp, Jeremy, H., Strategies and Structures in Thai Society, Anthropological-Sociological Center, University of Amsterdam, 1984, *p. 46.*

69. *Ibid., pp. 45.*

70. Erik Cohen, 1991, *op.cit.*

71. See Akin Rabibhadana, 1969, *op. cit.*

72. Girling, John L.S., 1981, *Thailand: Society and Politics, p. 52.*

73. Siffin, William J. "The Essential Character of the Contemporary Bureaucracy" in Neher, Clark D., *Modern Thai Politics: From Village to Nation*, 1979, *p. 352.*

74. *Ibid., p. 354.*

75. See Wyatt, David K. "The Buddhist Monkhood as an Avenue of Social Mobility in Traditional Thai Society" in *Sinlapakorn 10*, 1:50–53.

76. The author was present in the room when the debate took place.

77. About Chao Pho, see also "Achraporn Kumuphismai, Nakleg nai Sangkhom Thai" in Nithi Oewsriwong ed., *Kkon Thammada, pp. 103–116.*

MANAGING THE ENVIRONMENT

1. One rai equals 0.4 acre or 0.16 hectare.

2. Office of Environmental Policy and Planning, *Report on the Quality of the Environment*, B.E. 2535–6 (in Thai), Bangkok, undated, *p. 13.*

3. *Ibid., pp. 195-6.*

4. The average quantity of surface water for the whole Kingdom has been estimated at 200,000 million cubic meters per annum: Environmental Quality Promotion Department, *Natural Resources and Environment Information of Thailand* (in Thai), Bangkok: Agricultural Cooperative Federation of Thailand Press, 1993, *pp. 51–3.*

5. Economic and Social Commission for Asia and the Pacific, *Assessment of Water Resources and Water Demand by User Sectors in Thailand*, New York, N.Y: United Nations, 1991, Table 35, *p. 68.*

6. The water quality in the lower reaches of the Chao Phrya River, from Nonthaburi to the estuary in Samut-Prakarn, was considerably worse than that in the previous year, especially in the section between Rama I Bridge and the Phra-Khanong Canal where during the dry season, from February to June, the dissolved oxygen content went down to almost 0 mg./litre, the BOD was 2.4 mg./litre and the coliform count was as high as 770,000 units. The situation in the lower reaches of the Tha-chine River was not much better: the dissolved oxygen content was 1.3 mg./litre, the BOD was 2.8 mg./litre and the coliform count was 119,000 units. See: Pollution Control Department, *Report on the State of Pollution in Thailand. B.E. 2537* (forthcoming) (in Thai), Bangkok, *pp. 1–7.*

7. Royal Forest Department, *Annual Report B.E. 2536* (in Thai), Bangkok, undated, Table 17, *p.98.*

8. Office of Environmental Policy and Planning, *Report on the Quality of the Environment, B.E. 2535–6, op. cit.*, Table 1.3, *p. 11.*

9. National Environment Board, "Budget Allocation for the Treatment of Water Pollution and the Disposal of Community Garbage, B.E. 2537" (in Thai), (mimeo.), *pp. 4–7.*

10. The highest average concentration of SPM over a 24-hour period was found to be 1.13 mg./m3 (permissible standard: 0.33 mg./m3); as for PM-10, it was 314 mg./m3 (permissible standard 120 mg./m3); the highest average concentration of carbon monoxide in a one-hour period was 45.20 mg./m3 (permissible standard: 50 mg./ m3): Pollution Control Department, *Report on the State of Pollution in Thailand. B.E. 2537, op.cit., pp. 39–42.*

11. *Ibid.*, pp. 70-1. For further discussion of the problem, see National Environment Board, "Operations Plan for Managing Community Garbage in Thailand" (mimeo.) (in Thai), 1995.

12. Pollution Control Department, *Report on the State of Pollution in Thailand, B.E. 2537, op.cit., p. 64.*

13. Pollution Control Department, *Report on the State of Pollution in Thailand. B.E. 2536* (in Thai), Bangkok, 1994, *p. 60.*

14. Over the years the budget of the Archaeology Division, Department of Fine Arts, has actually declined. From 1990 to 1995, the allocations were 234, 256, 185, 228, 232 and 215 million baht respectively: Department of Fine Arts, Ministry of Education (unpublished data) (in Thai).

15. 51,285 respondents were polled between July 10 and 17, 1995: Rajabhat Institute Suandusit. Opinion Survey, "What Urgent Action Would You Like Undertaken by the Banharn 1 Government?" (in Thai), Bangkok, 1995.

16. These are: Office of Environmental Policy and Planning (OEPP), Pollution Control Department (PCD) and Environmental Quality Promotion Department (EQPD).

17. The provisions in the case of the Environmental Protection

NOTES

Areas, for instance, include: (i) land use control; (ii) prohibition of specified activities; (iii) building control; (iv) special administrative measures and procedures; and (v) other protective measures as deemed necessary.

18. The Chuan government had not shown any degree of urgency or specific concern about environmental problems. On the positive side, it had increased budgetary allocations for wastewater treatment and garbage disposal, and the only innovation with any significant policy content was the recent Cabinet approval in principle of the establishment of a centralized agency to take care of wastewater treatment nationwide (WMA: the Wastewater Management Authority). On the negative side, there were several initiatives detrimental to the environment, such as the proposal to parcel out national forests for private tourism development, the scheme to build expressways "on" the Chao Phraya River, and an attempt to rescind a Cabinet resolution made by a previous government, which would allow for the reintroduction of "economic zones" in mangrove forests for commercial exploitation. The first two proposals were dropped after strenuous objections by the public, the mass media and NGOs, while the last was sidelined by the National Environment Board. As for conflicts among government agencies, the long drawn-out and ongoing conflicts between MOSTE and the Ministry of Interior have, for instance, caused innumerable delays in the implementation of various measures already approved by the government.

19. As far as could be ascertained, there were two such brief statements. One involved a call for the Minister of Agriculture to resign because of the failure of the Royal Forest Department to protect the forests, and another was an expression opposing the construction of a river front expressway for fear of environmental impact.

20. The government of Mr Anand Panyarachun greatly emphasized the importance of environmental matters; it also went on to implement several measures specified in the policy statement. This momentum was lost under the Chuan government. The statement by the Banharn government was quite extensive. Specific measures include community forests; strengthening of government agencies responsible for natural resources; effective land use control; amelioration of water and air pollution and hazardous waste through enforcement of the Polluter Pays Principle; drawing up of master plans for environmental investment in all provinces; international cooperation; promotion of public participation and an increased role for NGOs and local governments; and preservation of historical sites and buildings and art and culture in general.

21. There have been numerous occasions when members of the public were interviewed on television about problems of general concern, such as politics, the cost of living, or the declining quality of life. When pressed, most of them would give the standard answer that they were too busy "making a living" to do anything about the problems, and it was the responsibility of the government anyway. Reliance on the government to take care of "public" matters is deeply rooted in the Thai culture where the public concern of the individual is limited to the local community. Any larger problem is, ipso facto, the domain of the government.

22. This issue was discussed elsewhere by the author: "the first and most important element of a meaningful action plan should therefore be a concerted attempt to transform environmental issues into a key item on the national political agenda. This can be done through broad and sustained campaigns to persuade the public to make their views and concerns known to Members of Parliament, Cabinet ministers and political parties. Concerned citizens should be encouraged to write to their "congressmen", i.e., Members of Parliament in their constituency, and get across the message that their action will be critical in the next election. Once amorphous awareness and concerns are transformed into votes, politicians will vie with one another to take the necessary action." (emphasis supplied). Phaichitr Uathavikul, "Energy and the Environment: Policy Implications for Thailand", Bangkok: Thailand Environment Institute, 1993, *p. 22.*

23. Article 6 provides for the right of individuals to (i) information, (ii) compensation, and (iii) making complaints to competent officials.

24. A consumer protection body exists within the government under the Office of the Prime Minister. Its effectiveness is unknown.

25. Office of the Royal Development Projects Board, *Royal Development Projects, Bangkok,* 1995, *pp. 5–9.*

26. *Ibid., p. 19.*

27. United Nations Environment Program, *Sustainable Development of Natural Resources: A Study of the Concepts and Applications of His Majesty the King of Thailand,* Bangkok, 1988, *p. 26.*

28. United Nations Food and Agriculture Organization, *The King and Agriculture in Thailand,* Bangkok: Craftsman Press, 1987, *p. 13.*

29. Address by His Majesty as quoted in: *Office of the Royal Projects Board, His Majesty King Bhumibol Adulyadej and His Development Work,* Bangkok: Bangkok Printing Co., 1987, *p. 22.*

30. United Nations Environment Program, *Sustainable Development of Natural Resources, op. cit., p.133.*

31. The six Royal Development Study Centers are: Central Region—Khao Hin Sorn Center in Chachoengsao; Central Region, Western Sector—Huai Sai Center in Petchaburi; Central Region, Eastern Sector—Kung Krabaen Bay Center in Chanthaburi; Northeastern Region—Puparn Center in Sakon Nakhon; Northern Region—Huai Hong Khrai Center in Chiang Mai; and Southern Region—Pikun Thong Center in Narathiwat.

32. Office of the Royal Development Projects Board, *His Majesty the King's Approach towards Sustainable Agriculture,* Bangkok (undated), *pp. 21–22.*

33. Office of the National Environment Board, *Royal Speech Given to the Audience of Well-wishers on the Occasion of the Royal Birthday Anniversary on Monday. 4 December 1989,* Bangkok: Amarin Printing Group, 1990, *pp. 10–12.*

34. *Ibid., p. 15.*

35. *Ibid., pp. 15–17.*

36 *Ibid., p. 23.*

ABOUT THE AUTHORS

M L THAWISAN LADAWAN

Born in Songkhla Province, M L Thawisan was educated in Thailand at Vajiravudh College, Thammasat University, and in France at the Université de Paris. He began his government service with the Ministry of Foreign Affairs in 1944 and held a number of positions, among them Attaché of the Royal Thai Embassy in Paris (1951–56), First Secretary and Chargé d'Affaires of the Royal Thai Embassy in Brussels (1962–65), and Deputy Director of General Protocol at the Ministry of Foreign Affairs. In 1968, he became His Majesty's Deputy Principal Private Secretary and from 1969 to 1995 was His Majesty's Principal Private Secretary. He is currently a Privy Councillor. He has been awarded the Royal Cypher Medal (Second Class), the Knight Grand Cordon of the Most Noble Order of the Crown of Thailand, the Knight Grand Cordon (Special Class) of the Most Exalted Order of the White Elephant, and the Knight Grand Cross (First Class) of the Most Illustrious Order of Chula Chom Klao.

LIKHIT DHIRAVEGIN

Professor Likhit received his Bachelor of Law with Honors from Thammasat University. He then continued his education in the United States, where he received a Master of Arts (International Relations) and a Master of Arts in Law and Diplomacy from the Fletcher School of Law and Diplomacy at Tufts College, as well as a Master of Arts (Political Science) and Ph.D. (Political Science) from Brown University. Among the many positions he has held are Dean of the Faculty of Political Science at Thammasat University, Member of the Constitution Drafting Committee, and Vice President of the Thai University Research University. He is the author of numerous books and articles in Thai and English. He has been awarded the Knight Grand Cross (First Class) and the Knight Grand Cordon of the Most Noble Order of the Crown of Thailand and the Knight Grand Cross (First Class) and the Knight Grand Cordon of the Most Exalted Order of the White Elephant.

ANAND PANYARACHUN

Khun Anand was educated at Bangkok Christian College, Dulwich College in London, and Trinity College at the University of Cambridge. In 1955 he joined the Ministry of Foreign Affairs where, among other positions, he served as Ambassador to the United Nations, Ambassador to the United States and concurrently Permanent Representative of Thailand to the United Nations and Permanent Secretary for Foreign Affairs. He was twice Prime Minister of Thailand. His current positions include serving as Chairman of the Saha-Union Public Co., Ltd., Director of the Siam Commercial Bank Public Co., Ltd., Chairman of the Council of Trustees of the Thailand Environment Institute, and UNICEF Ambassador for Thailand. He has been awarded the Royal Cypher Medal (Third Class), Knight Commander (Second Class, lower grade) and Knight Grand Commander (Second Class, higher grade) of the Most Illustrious Order of Chula Chom Klao, Knight Grand Cross (First Class) and Knight Grand Cordon (Special Class) of the Most Exalted Order of the White Elephant, and Knight Grand Cordon of the Most Noble Order of the Crown of Thailand.

AMMAR SIAMWALLA

Khun Ammar received his B. Sc. in Economics with First Class Honors from the University of London and a Ph. D in Economics from Harvard University in the U.S. He has served as Assistant Professor and Research Staff Economist at Yale University, a Lecturer in the Faculty of Economics at Thammasat University, and a Research Fellow at the International Food Policy Research Institute in Washington, D.C. Among the many committees and boards on which he has served are the Economic Advisory Council to the Prime Minister, the National Research Council, the Board of Investment, the National Credit Policy Committee, and the Thai Chamber of Commerce. From 1990 until the end of 1995 he was President of the Thailand Development Research Institute.

CHULANOPE SNIDVONGS NA AYUDHYA

Khun Chulanope received degrees in Mechanical Engineering from Chulalongkorn University in Bangkok and the University of Michigan in the United States. Starting his career as an engineer with the Royal Irrigation Department, he later became Inspector General, Deputy Permanent Secretary, and Permanent Secretary of the Ministry of Agriculture and Cooperatives. He was appointed a Senator in 1987 and in 1991 became a Privy Councillor to His Majesty the King. His has been awarded the Knight Grand Cordon (Special Class) of the Most Exalted Order of the White Elephant, Knight Grand Cordon of the Most Noble Order of the Crown of Thailand, Knight Commander of the Most Illustrious Order of Chula Chom Klao, and the Victory Medal (Second World War).

M R AKIN RABIBHADANA

Dr. MR Akin received his B.A. with Honours and his M.A. in Jurisprudence from Oxford University in England, as well as an M.A. and a Ph.D. in Social Anthropology from Cornell University in the U.S.A. He began his public service as Police Public Prosecutor at the Bangkok Thonburi District Court and has since held a variety of posts, among them serving as a lecturer in Social Anthropology at Thammasat University, as Director of the Research and Development Institute at Khon Kaen University, as Consultant to the President of the Thailand Development Research Institute Foundation, and, most recently, as Chief of the Slum Development and Reconstruction Program under the Bureau of the Crown Property. He has published many papers dealing with various social matters and is a member of numerous professional associations.

ABOUT THE AUTHORS

M C SUBHADRADIS DISKUL

M C Subhadradis was born in 1923 to His Royal Highness Prince Damrong Rojanubhad, a son of King Rama IV. He received his undergraduate education at Chulalongkorn University and after working for a period at the Ministry of Education and the Fine Arts Department continued his studies abroad at the Ecole du Louvre in Paris and in England, specializing in archaeology. In addition to serving as Rector of Silpakorn University and President of the Siam Society, he has lectured on the subject of Thai art at several universities and has written a number of standard works on the subject.

PHAICHITR UATHAVIKUL

Dr Phaichitr received his Diploma in Architecture from London University and an M.A. in Regional Planning and a Ph.D. from Cornell University in the United States. He has served as Minister of Science, Technology and Environment, Minister to the Prime Minister's Office, President of the Thailand Development Research Institute, Executive Director of the World Bank, Deputy Minister of Finance, and Professor and Rector of the National Institute of Development Administration. At present he is Chairman of the Thailand Environment Foundation as well as a member of the National Environment Board, the National Economic and Social Development Board, the National Education Council, and the Board of Directors of the National Science and Technology Development Agency.

MECHAI VIRAVAIDYA

Khun Mechai was educated in Australia at the Geelong Grammar School and Melbourne University, from which he graduated in 1964. On returning to Thailand, he worked as an economist with the National Economic and Social Development Board (1965-71) and the Economic Cooperation for the Asian and Pacific Region (1971-73). In 1974, he founded the Population and Community Development Association, of which he is still Board Chairman. Among the prominent posts he has held are Governor of the Provincial Waterworks Authority of Thailand (1982-85), Cabinet Spokesman (1986-88), Senator (1987-91), Deputy Minister of Industry (1985-86) and Minister of the Prime Minister's Office (1991-82). Recipient of the Ramon Maysaysay Award for Public Service in 1994, he has also been awarded the Knight Grand Cordon (Special Class) and the Knight Grand Cross (First Class) of the Most Exalted Order of the White Elephant and the Knight Grand Cordon (Special Class) and the Knight Grand Cross (First Class) of the Most Noble Order of the Crown of Thailand.

WILLIAM WARREN

American by birth, William Warren has lived in Thailand since 1960. He lectured at Chulalongkorn University for 30 years and is the author of books dealing with Thai life and culture, among them *The Legendary American* (a biography of Jim Thompson), *The House on the Klong* (dealing with the Thompson house and art collection), *The Grand Palace* (published by the Office of His Majesty's Principal Private Secretary), *Thai Style*, *Arts and Crafts of Thailand*, and *Seven Days in the Kingdom*. His articles have also appeared in numerous publications.

JOHN CLEWLEY

Educated in England (Salford and London Universities), and a former lecturer at Chulalongkorn University, John Clewley has been in Asia, mainly Japan and Thailand, for the past fourteen years. Since leaving teaching, he has worked as a journalist, columnist, editor, writer, TV producer and photographer. His last general publication was as contributing editor/photographer to *World Music—The Rough Guide* and his last photographic exhibition, "Sounds Asia—New Perspectives on Asian Popular Music", was held at the Japan Culture Center, Bangkok, in November 1993. He is currently working as the Bangkok correspondent and photographer for *Asia, Inc* magazine and is a columnist with the *Bangkok Post*.

THAILAND King Bhumibol Adulyadej – The Golden Jubilee 1946-1996

THE SPONSORS

AMWAY (THAILAND) LIMITED was founded in May 1987 and has become one of the nation's leading direct selling companies, providing more than four hundred consumer products. With its on-going commitment to Thailand, Amway has continuously sought ways to improve the lives of the Thai people, the source of its success. Supporting many community, environmental, historical and other worthwhile projects, Amway is constantly aware of its responsibilities as a good corporate citizen in Thai society.

BANGKOK BANK PCL opened its doors for business on December 1, 1944, with a registered capital of US$160,000. Today the Bank is a public company limited with total assets of about US$41 billion. With a branch network of more than 480 domestic and twenty-six overseas outlets and staff numbering about 26,300, Bangkok Bank is one of the largest in Southeast Asia, aiming to provide quality, full service banking to all.

BOON RAWD BREWERY Since 1933 Thais have enjoyed Boon Rawd Brewery's best-loved product, Singha Beer. At the first brewery in Samsen, from selected hops, malt and pure water, Boon Rawd produced one hundred dozen Singha Soda and fifty dozen Singha Beer a day. Now, Boon Rawd has an annual brewing capacity of 1,200 million litres and supplies eighty-five percent of Thailand's beer, ninety-five percent of Thailand's soda and thirty percent of Thailand's drinking water. My Country. My Beer.

CITIBANK, N.A. has been in Thailand since 1985, and had grown to become one of the largest foreign banks in the country, ranking first in terms of deposits and third in terms of assets. With its customer-driven business strategy and wide range of financial products covering all its clients' needs, Citibank has become one of the most recognized and respected foreign companies in Thailand. Citibank, N.A., has its network of over 3500 offices and branches in ninety-eight countries and territories, spanning the developed and emerging economies of the world.

DIETHELM A wholly-owned Swiss company founded in Bangkok in 1906, Diethelm has grown to be one of the largest businesses in Thailand, representing more than one 100 Blue Chip international corporations. It employs 2,500 staff members and has a turnover in excess of US$500 million. From consumer packaged goods and food to precision instruments, pharmaceuticals, toiletries, travel and property management, Diethelm has achieved major presence and a significant market share in all the mainstream businesses it has entered.

IBM THAILAND is a world-class company at the forefront of information technology. Established since 1952, its mission is to excel in innovative IT solutions for customers through its professional staff and worldwide expertise. IBM provides a wide range of services in the area of information technology hardware, software, operational, maintenance and network services, consulting services, systems integration services and education services. IBM believes that the same information technology innovations that are revolutionizing business can provide important breakthroughs for the public and for non-profit organizations. Going beyond simple checkbook philanthropy, IBM works closely with our society to design technology solutions to comply with our commitment to better living.

JIM THOMPSON THAI SILK CO. In 1951, Jim Thompson founded the Thai Silk Company Limited which is now the largest manufacturer, retailer and exporter of Thai silk fabrics and ready-made goods in Thailand. It has more than 7,500 employees in Bangkok and Khorat Province, and is vertically integrated in silk production with sericulture farms, filature, hand and power-weaving, dyeing, printing and finishing, as well as as garment production. Jim Thompson currently has five retail outlets in Bangkok, two on Phuket and one on Samui.

LOXLEY PUBLIC COMPANY LIMITED, founded in 1939, is a leading conglomerate company in Thailand. The business activities are divided among five core businesses: information technology, industrial products, consumer products, services and infrastructure. Loxley has invested in many joint venture industries with overseas partners and is now actively investing in Indochina and neighbouring countries. Loxley's destiny is to continuously expand and transform itself in order to represent the best of what progress means to Asia and the world.

MINISTRY OF FOREIGN AFFAIRS The Ministry of Foreign Affairs of Thailand was established by His Majesty King Chulalongkorn on April 14, 1875. According to the present structure the Ministry comprises two Offices and ten Departments; while representation abroad comprises 57 Embassies, two Permanent Missions to the United Nations, 20 Consulates General and 98 Honorary Consular Representatives. The Ministry's main building is located at Suranrom Palace, Bangkok 10200, Thailand.

MITSUBISHI MMC Sittipol Co., Ltd. is a joint venture between the Lee-Issranukul family and Mitsubishi Motors Corporation of Japan. The company manufactures and distributes automobiles in Thailand and exports globally to 139 countries. Embracing 110 dealer companies and 100 vendors, the company's products include various models from passenger cars to pickups and heavy trucks. Besides producing and developing pleasant automobiles for customers, as a corporate citizen the company is also concerned with environmental problems and the sustainable development of our natural surroundings to make this world a better place to live.

THE PETROLEUM AUTHORITY OF THAILAND (PTT) is a state-owned organization, established on December 29, 1978. PTT has since been operated according to the assigned mission to create a fully integrated network of petroleum business and related industry ranging from exploration, production, transportation, storage, trading, marketing and other related ventures. PTT's vision for the years up to and beyond the year 2000 is to become a world-class self-financing integrated petroleum and related corporation operating in attractive business, primarily in Thailand and the region, balancing commercial and government objectives.

THE REGENT BANGKOK Voted one of the top "100 Hotels in the World" by the prestigious publication, *Institutional Investor*, The Regent Bangkok is a member of the Four Seasons ★ Regent International Hotels and Resorts which include thirty-seven properties in sixteen countries. The Regent Bangkok, located on Rajadamri Road, comprises 363 rooms and suites which have been newly refurbished at a cost of US$14 million to the utmost in comfort and luxury.

SIAM COMMERCIAL BANK PCL is Thailand's oldest bank. Established in 1906 at a time when the country's financial system was operated by foreign concerns, the bank was, for many years, the only local financial institution. The bank has steadily expanded during the course of this century and is now highly respected within the international financial community. Drawing on a wealth of experience, Siam Commercial Bank Pcl is today a progressive force in developing Thailand's banking services.

TCC GROUP, one of Thailand's leading conglomerates, was established by Mr Charoen Sirivadhabhakdi. It began as a trading company before eventually moving into the liquor industry and expanding into paper mills, hotels, restaurants, resorts, office buildings, financial institutions, among others. Besides owning shares in several banks and financial institutions, it operates sixteen distilleries and one winery in Thailand. It produces Carlsberg and Chang beer in Thailand. It has invested in two projects in China.

THAI AIRWAYS INTERNATIONAL PUBLIC COMPANY LIMITED was established in 1960 as Thailand's designated flag carrier of the Kingdom of Thailand. Fully owned by the Thai people since 1977, THAI currently serves seventy-two destinations in thirty-seven countries worldwide. THAI aims to expand its route net in the near future and plans to increase its fleet from seventy-three to seventy-eight aircraft by the year 2000.

THAI OIL Thai Oil Co., Ltd. was founded in 1961 to build and operate Thailand's first oil refinery. For 35 years, its mission has been to guarantee the country's energy supplies, and it continues to be the leading producer. Through continual expansion and upgrading, using technologically advanced processes and state-of-the-art equipment, the 220,000-barrels-per-day refinery is capable of producing quality products while remaining responsible to the environment. It is the country's first refinery to receive ISO 9002 Certification. In recent years, Thaioil has strengthened its core business by diversifying into related industries: namely, the production of carbon black, lube base oil, petrochemicals, and electricity.

THE TOURISM AUTHORITY OF THAILAND (TAT) With a vital and active role in the promotion of the kingdom as a major tourist destination, the Tourism Authority of Thailand is also tasked to help preserve and restore national resources in its effort to maintain the nation's quality assets. TAT is currently playing a considerable part in publicizing the Golden Jubilee celebrating the 50th anniversary of the accession to the throne by His Majesty the King, and will continue to contribute towards all national activities designed to enhance the image of Thailand.

THE NATION MULTIMEDIA GROUP PCL (NMG), founded in 1971 with *The Nation* daily newspaper as its flagship, has developed into Thailand's leading multimedia group, with numerous publications, broadcasting on television and radio, holding licenses for prestigious overseas publications such as US and Japanese comics, educational material and reference books, and having its own internet site. NMG is a publicly-listed company with a modern and progressive outlook that incorporates continual plans for expansion.

BANGKOK PUBLIC RELATIONS Bangkok PR is a full-service public relations consultancy. The consultancy offers its clients counsel and program management services based on decades of experience in the practice of public relations in the Thai context. Bangkok PR serves global leaders in wireless communications, IT and consumer electronics, health care, consumer packaged goods, and in the aerospace industry.

THAILAND King Bhumibol Adulyadej – The Golden Jubilee 1946-1996
277

INDEX

ILLUSTRATION CREDITS

The sources for the illustrations in this work are numerous. The publishers have made every effort to acknowledge the copyright holders accurately, however it was not possible to trace the publishers or heirs of certain items. An account is held open for them at our offices. The publishers apologize if any illustrations are wrongly attributed.

4–5 Photobank;
8 David Lomax/Camera Press London;
10–11 Dominic Faulder/Bureau Bangkok;
12 The Royal Palace;
13 Bureau Bangkok except *left, second from bottom* John Clewley, *left bottom* Carl de Keyser/Magnum, *right second from bottom* Dominic Faulder/Bureau Bangkok;
14 *top row, middle left* Bureau Bangkok, *middle right* Surayuth Singhanak/Bureau Bangkok, *bottom* Wiruch Thongchew/Bureau Bangkok;
15 *top left, center right, bottom* John Clewley, *center column* Dominic Faulder/Bureau Bangkok, *top right* Wiruch Thongchew/Bureau Bangkok;
16–62 Khwankeo Vajarodaya/The Royal Palace;
63 Dominic Faulder/Bureau Bangkok, except *top left* The Royal Palace;
64–65 *clockwise from left* The Royal Palace, Jim Thompson Thai Silk Company, AFP/Corbis-Bettmann, The Royal Palace, The Nation, The Nation;
66 *top left* The Royal Palace, *bottom left, top right, right middle* The National Archive of Thailand, *middle left* THAI International, *bottom right* Photobank;
67 The Royal Palace, except *top left* The National Archive of Thailand;
68 *left top, left bottom* The Royal Palace, *bottom middle and right* The National Archive of Thailand;
69 *top and second from top right* The Royal Palace, *bottom left, middle, bottom right* The National Archive of Thailand;
70 *second from top on left* THAI International, *third from top on left, bottom left* The National Archive of Thailand, *top right* Faculty of Arts, Chulalongkorn University, *middle bottom* Jim Thompson Thai Silk Company, *top left, middle center* The Royal Palace;
71 *top right* The National Archive of Thailand;
73 The Nation, except *bottom* The Royal Palace;
74 The Nation, except *center* Camera Press London, *bottom left* Bureau Bangkok;
75 The Nation, except *left, top right* Bureau Bangkok, *middle right* UPI/Corbis-Bettmann;
76 *top left* David Lomax, *center* Photobank, *right* Bureau Bangkok, *bottom* The Nation;
77 The Nation;
78 *middle left* The Nation, *bottom left* Photobank, *second middle* Reuters-Bettmann, *top left, bottom left, middle left, bottom right* The Nation, *top right* The National Archive of Thailand;
79 The Nation, except *top left* Bureau Bangkok, *bottom left* Reuters/Corbis-Bettmann, *bottom left and center* Bureau Bangkok;
80 Bureau Bangkok, except *middle, middle bottom, top right* The Nation, *middle left* Reuters/Corbis-Bettmann;
81 Bureau Bangkok, except *middle left* The Nation, *second from top right* Reuters-Bettmann;
82 *bottom left* The Nation, *right* Bureau Bangkok, *top left* AFP/Bettmann, *top right* Asia Books;
83 *top right and left* AFP/Corbis-Bettmann, *middle left* The Nation, *right* Asiaweek/Kathy Willens - AP/M Photo;
84 *clockwise from top left* Bureau Bangkok, Bureau Bangkok, Khwankeo Vajarodaya/The Royal Palace, Photobank, The Royal Palace, Photobank;
86 Photobank;
87 John Everingham;
88–91 EDM private collection, except:
88 *top*, 89 *bottom* Photobank;
92 Khwankeo Vajarodaya/The Royal Palace;
93 *top left* P J Griffith/Magnum, *top* Photobank, *second from top* P J Griffith/Magnum, *right and inset* Photobank, *bottom left, right and inset*, Dominic Faulder/Bureau Bangkok;
94 *top left* Marc Riboud/Magnum, *right, lower left* John Everingham, *lower right* Kraipit Phanvut;
95 Bureau Bangkok, except *two top right* The Royal Palace;
96 *top left, right* Photobank, *bottom left* Bureau Bangkok;
97 John Everingham, *bottom left and right* Dominic Faulder/Bureau Bangkok;
98-9 Paul Chesley;

100–101 Photobank;
102 Corbis Bettmann, *bottom* John Clewley;
103 Camera Press/London, *right* The National Archive;
104 Photobank;
105 *top* The Royal Palace, *bottom* Manit Sriwanichpoon/Bureau Bangkok;
106 *top left* Photobank, *right* The Royal Palace, *lower left* UPI/Corbis Bettmann;
107 The Royal Palace;
108 *left, top right* Dominic Faulder/Bureau Bangkok, *right below* Manit Sriwanichpoon/Bureau Bangkok;
109 Michael Freeman;
110 *top left, bottom* Dominic Faulder/Bureau Bangkok, *top right* Corbis Bettmann, *right* John Clewley;
112 *left top* Surawuth Singhanak, *right* Dominic Faulder/Bureau Bangkok;
113 *top, right* Dominic Faulder/Bureau Bangkok, *left* Wiruch Thongchew/Bureau Bangkok;
114-115 Rainer Krack/CPA;
116 Photobank;
117 David Henley;
118-119 The Royal Palace, except *far right* Dominic Faulder/Bureau Bangkok;
120 Kraipit Phanvut;
121 *top* Anand Panyarachun, *bottom left* Photobank, *bottom right* John Clewley;
122 Shari Kessler/Chiaroscuro, *bottom* The Royal Palace;
123 Khwankeo Vajarodaya/The Royal Palace;
124 *top* Wiruch Thongchew, *bottom* EDM private collection;
125 The Nation;
126 *top* The Nation, *bottom* Reuters/Corbis Bettmann;
127–128 The Nation;
129 John Everingham, *center, bottom* Dominic Faulder/Bureau Bangkok;
130 The Nation;
131 Dominic Faulder/Bureau Bangkok;
132 *top* Bureau Bangkok, *inset* Photobank;
133 *left* Reuters/Corbis Bettmann, *right* John Clewley;
134 John Clewley;
135 *top* The Royal Palace, *lower left and right* Manit Sriwanichpoon/Bureau Bangkok;
136–138 Photobank;
140 *top* P J Griffiths/Magnum, *bottom* Shari Kessler/Chiaroscuro;
141 Photobank, *inset* Paul Chesley;
142 *top* Photobank, Dominic Faulder/Bureau Bangkok, *bottom* Paul Chesley;
143 *top* Peter Ungphakorn, *left* Camera Press London, *right* Photobank;
144 Manit Sriwanichpoon/Bureau Bangkok, John Clewley, *bottom* Photobank;
145 John Everingham, *bottom and inset* Photobank;
146 Photobank;
147 *top, right* Dominic Faulder/Bureau Bangkok, *right below* Photobank;
148 *top* Photobank, *below* Bureau Bangkok;
149 Dominic Faulder/Bureau Bangkok, *inset* Paul Chesley;
150 Photobank;
151 *top* Dominic Faulder/Bureau Bangkok, *inset* Photobank, Dominic Faulder/Bureau Bangkok, *bottom (all three)* John Clewley;
152 Photobank;
153 *left* John Clewley, *right, bottom* Photobank;
154–155 Photobank;
156 *top* Paul Chesley, *bottom* Dominic Faulder/Bureau Bangkok;
157 Paul Chesley, *inset* Photobank;
158-160 Photobank;
161–162 John Everingham;
163 *top* John Clewley, *bottom left* David Henley, *bottom right* Photobank;
164–5 Photobank, *inset* Dominic Faulder/Bureau Bangkok;
166–167 Photobank;
168 *top* Photobank, *bottom* Dominic Faulder/Bureau Bangkok;
169 *left, middle* Photobank, *top right* The Royal Palace;
170 *top* John Everingham, *bottom* Photobank;
171 *top* The Royal Palace, *middle, bottom* John Everingham;
172 *top, bottom* John Everingham, *middle* The Royal Palace;
173 Photobank;
174 *top, bottom* Photobank, *middle* John Everingham;
175 *top left, bottom row* Photobank, *top right, left middle* Gilles Massot;
176–177 Photobank;
178 *top left, bottom* Photobank, *top middle, top right, middle*

center Paul Chesley, *middle left, middle right* David Henley/CPA;
179 Kraipit Phanvut/Ditto;
180 *top* Photobank, *middle* David Henley/CPA;
181 Photobank;
182 *top* John Clewley, *bottom* Photobank;
183 *top* Dominic Faulder/Bureau Bangkok, *bottom* John Everingham;
184 *top* Photobank, *bottom left* John Everingham, *bottom right* John Clewley;
185 *top* John Clewley, *bottom* Photobank;
186 *top, bottom middle* Photobank, *bottom left* Paul Chesley;
187 *top, bottom right* Photobank, *bottom left* Manit Sriwanichpoom/Bureau Bangkok;
188 Paul Chesley;
189–190 Photobank;
191 *top left* Ron Emmons, *right, bottom left* Photobank;
192–202 Photobank;
203 The Oriental Bangkok;
204–205 The Royal Palace;
206 *top left, bottom* Jim Thompson Thai Silk Company, *top right* Photobank, *middle* Graham Byfield/James HW Thompson Foundation/Hofun;
207 *top left* MR Montien Boonma, *top right, middle* Sompop Budtarad, *bottom left* Kamin Lertchaiprasert;
208 *top row, bottom* John Clewley, *middle* Paul Chesley;
209 *top* The Royal Palace, *center, bottom* John Clewley;
210–211 Photobank;
212 Paul Chesley;
213 Wiruch Thongchew/Bureau Bangkok;
214 *top* Photobank, *middle* Manit Sriwanichpoom/Bureau Bangkok, *bottom* John Clewley;
215 *top* John Everingham, *middle* Paul Chesley, *inset* Bureau Bangkok, *bottom* Manit Sriwanichpoom/Bureau Bangkok;
216 Photobank;
217 John Clewley;
218 Photobank;
219 courtesy of the National Parks, except *top left* David Henley/CPA, *right inset* Suthep Kritsanavarin;
220 Suthep Kritsanavarin, except *background* Shari Kessler/Chiaroscuro;
221 courtesy of the National Parks;
222 Photobank;
223 *top* Suthep Kritsanavarin, *bottom* Photobank;
224 John Everingham;
225 *top* Photobank, *bottom* Dominic Faulder/Bureau Bangkok;
226 Photobank;
227 *top* Photobank, *bottom* John Clewley;
228–233 Photobank;
234 EDM private collection, except *top* The Royal Palace;
235 *top* EDM private collection, *bottom* Photobank;
236 *top, bottom* Photobank, *center left, center right* EDM private collection;
237 Photobank;
238 *top* Surayuth Singhanak/Bureau Bangkok, *bottom* Photobank;
239 *top* John Everingham, *middle* Tourist Authority of Thailand, *bottom* John Clewley;
240 Photobank;
241 *top, bottom middle* Dominic Faulder/Bureau Bangkok, *bottom right* Photobank;
242 *top* Photobank, *middle, bottom* Dominic Faulder/Bureau Bangkok;
243 Photobank;
244 Wiruch Thongchew/Bureau Bangkok;
245–247 Photobank;
248–261 all EDM private collection except:
248 *top* Photobank;
250 Photobank;
251 *right* Paul Chesley;
252 *top left, bottom right* Photobank;
253 *middle left* Gilles Massot, *bottom left* Paul Chesley;
254 *middle* Photobank;
255 *top left* John Clewley, *top right, middle, bottom right* Photobank;
257 *top* Photobank, *middle right* John Everingham;
258 *bottom middle* Shari Kessler/Chiaroscuro;
259 *bottom left* Photobank, *middle* Suthep Kritsanavara;
260 Photobank;
261 Photobank, except *left* EDM private collection, *bottom right* Pisit Jiropas.